HANDBOOKS

CAPE COD
MARTHA'S VINEYARD & NANTUCKET

JEFF PERK

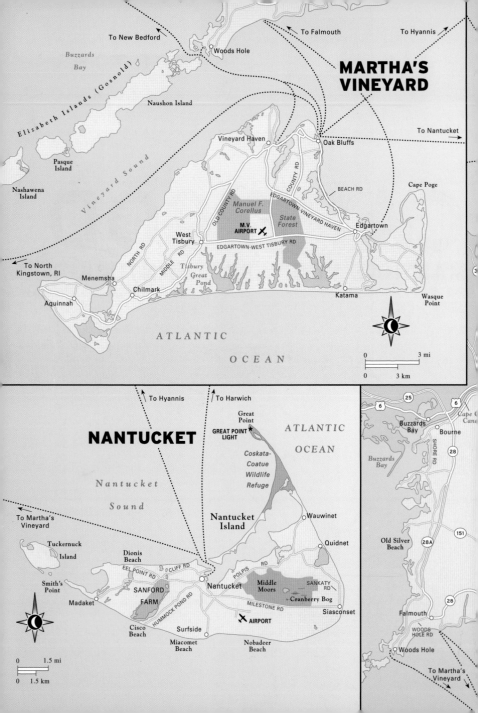

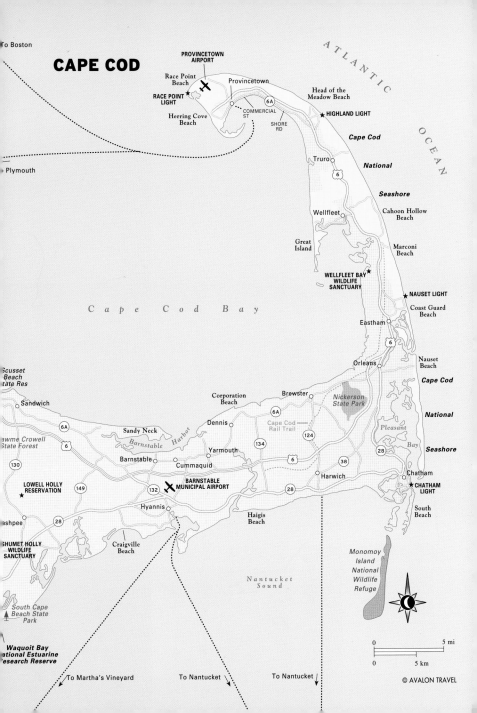

Contents

Discover Cape Cod,
Martha's Vineyard & Nantucket

It's only fitting that Cape Cod was named after the rich fisheries that lay just off its coast. After all, the creatures of the sea have shaped how the region's inhabitants have lived since the communities' earliest days. These days, the Cape and its two largest offshore islands, Martha's Vineyard and Nantucket, collectively comprise New England's leading summer resort destination. All three have historically felt the impact of many of the same forces, from glaciers to tourism, yet their personalities could hardly be more distinct.

Cape Cod is where you will find fine art galleries and fresh bait shops, side by side. Think outdoor summer-league baseball, live music on town bandstands, double-features at the drive-in, and miniature golf with a quirky maritime theme. It features beaches, hundreds of miles of them, including slack-water estuaries, freshwater ponds, rock-strewn coves, long sandy strands lapped by the rhythmic ebb and flow of the bay, and surf-hammered barrier beaches that occasionally bare the bones of old ships' hulls. Cape Cod is where you'll eat ice cream for lunch and fried clams for dinner.

Martha's Vineyard ("The Vineyard") the larger, more populous, and more readily accessible of the two offshore islands, may be best known for big-name celebrities and yacht owners, and while it's hardly inexpensive, it doesn't thumb its nose at budget travelers. Its small, easily

strollable towns brim with galleries and one-of-a-kind shops, interesting architecture, and good food.

Nantucket – a pretty little pearl of rose-draped cottages hugging narrow lanes and low, shrubby moors ringed by wide, sandy beaches – swathes itself in the mantle of history, its port town appearing to the arriving ferry passengers like a door to the 19th century. Distance and affluence have kept the populism and diversity of its neighbors firmly at bay, but it warmly welcomes day-trippers of all stripes from the mainland.

Although it's easy to assume that the small size of this region will make it possible to pack everything you want to see into a single trip, slow down and allow yourself time to explore not only what's within these pages, but also what's between the lines and beyond the margins. Given the sometimes incomprehensible layout of local roadways and the poor quality of local road signage, you're bound to lose your way anyway – and that just may be the best way to discover the real Cape and Islands.

Planning Your Trip

▶ WHERE TO GO

Cape Cod

No doubt about it, the big draws of Cape Cod are those seasonal verities of sun, sand, and surf, followed closely by golf greens and shopping. There are points of interest indoors, too—around seemingly every bend in the road is a historic landmark, local historical museum, or a uniquely themed attraction inviting exploration by inquisitive passersby. Art galleries and artisans' studios abound. Antiques stores are equally ubiquitous.

Given the vital importance of safe navigation to the regional economy, it should come as no surprise to learn that a number of 19th-century lighthouses still stand as beacons over the Cape.

Martha's Vineyard

The island of Martha's Vineyard features endless beach roads and peaceful saltwater ponds, often lit by stunning golden light that has drawn artists to the island for centuries.

Residents divide the island into down-island (east) and up-island (west). The former is home to the island's three main population centers: touristy Vineyard Haven, chic Edgartown, and charming Oak Bluffs. Up-island is more rural, with the cow pastures of West Tisbury and Chilmark sharing space with the scenic fishing village of Menemsha and the cliffs of Aquinnah.

Nantucket

Life doesn't get more idyllic (or more preppy) than it is in the cobblestoned main streets, salt-box homes, and creaking docks of this community, renowned for its past life as the whaling capital of the world. It was that status—enjoyed from about 1800 to 1840—that brought great wealth to the community, which is to this day studded with the immense captains' homes of yore. That wealth is still readily apparent today in the form of new mansions (sometimes complete with a helipad or two in the backyard), and boutique shopping throughout central Nantucket town.

► WHEN TO GO

Beach lovers and sun worshippers will have little choice but to heed the call of Cape Cod's summertime offerings; the sandy beaches, warm-weather festivals, and sea-centric and conservation land–based activities are all an outdoor enthusiasts needs to get hooked on the area in its high season. But for those who'd rather see the area than muddle through the crowds it attracts, in late September and early October the hoards thin out and give way to those who want more one-on-one time with the towns, the beaches, and the land.

Deeper into the cold winter season, from December through March, things get even calmer—if not calm altogether. Stores tend to reduce hours drastically, restaurants go dark for weeks at a time, and only die-hard visitors keep the inns and housing rental market busy. Starting as early as April, things begin to perk up again, but don't get really rolling until early June, when beach weather once again gets dependable.

IF YOU HAVE . . .

- **A WEEKEND:** Meander along the Old King's Highway, scenic Rte. 6A, from Sandwich to Orleans, overnighting at one of the lovely B&B inns along the way.
- **FIVE DAYS:** Extend your trip to the Cape Cod National Seashore and Provincetown at the Cape's very tip.
- **A WEEK:** Add Falmouth, Woods Hole, and a day trip to Martha's Vineyard.
- **TWO WEEKS:** Add Chatham and Hyannis, take a ferry to Nantucket, and spend more time on the Vineyard.

► BEFORE YOU GO

Unlike the rest of Cape Cod, the islands by definition have limited space, and are thus almost always fully booked in the high season. Heed warnings to book accommodations and make restaurant reservations well in advance. For the former, it's best to secure arrangements several weeks ahead of time, and several months in advance for holiday and festival periods.

Transportation
CAPE COD

Much of Cape Cod is accessible by bus. From Boston's South Station terminal, Plymouth & Brockton buses depart daily year-round for Hyannis and the Outer Cape from Orleans to Provincetown, while Peter Pan buses run from Logan Airport and South Station to Bourne, Falmouth, and Woods

ferry departing Nantucket

autumn's bounty on Cape Cod

Hole on the Upper Cape. Peter Pan also runs from both upstate New York and Manhattan to Hyannis via Providence, Rhode Island. In summer, Boston Harbor Cruises and Bay State Cruises offer daily fast ferries between Boston and Provincetown. Local public buses serve all the towns along the Cape's southern and eastern shores, from Woods Hole to Provincetown.

MARTHA'S VINEYARD AND NANTUCKET

Getting to and from the islands relies on ferry schedules that vary according to season. On The Vineyard, unless you are going to be spending a lot of time up-island, a car is by no means essential and can be a nuisance on the narrow, crowded roadways. The Martha's Vineyard Regional Transit Authority runs buses between all of the island's towns. On Nantucket, the Nantucket Regional Transit Authority does continuous loops between Straight Wharf in Nantucket Town and Madaket, Surfside, Siasconset, and the airport.

By far the best way to avoid the frustration of summertime traffic on either island is to avoid contributing to it by renting a bicycle.

What to Take

Packing for a visit to Cape Cod and the islands all depends on what time of year you go. In spring and fall, when temperatures can be unpredictable, sweaters and a medium-weight jacket are key to rolling with the weather's changes. In wintertime, a heavy winter coat, umbrella, and snow boots are essential. And in summer, when most visitors swarm to the area, a rain jacket is still recommended, as are a few sweaters to throw on when nights get chilly. Beach lovers should be sure to bring along the usual surfside gear (bathing suits, flip-flops, beach bags, sunscreen, a good book, and the like), though beach towels are provided at many hotels and inns. Meanwhile, in all seasons, comfortable shoes make walking the area's meandering town sidewalks a lot more pleasant.

Explore Cape Cod, Martha's Vineyard & Nantucket

▶ THE BEST OF CAPE COD, MARTHA'S VINEYARD, AND NANTUCKET

Diving into the unique attractions the coast and its islands have to offer is easy with just a little basic planning; many of the region's gems are found together in accessible clusters. While it's easy to get around the Cape and islands using public transportation, a car allows you the freedom to take leisurely drives and explore the many sights along the way at your own pace.

Wellfleet Harbor

Day 1

Begin your journey along Route 6A heading toward Brewster in the Mid-Cape, stopping at Heritage Museums and Gardens in Sandwich, the Edward Gorey House in Yarmouthport, and at whatever antique shops or art galleries strike your fancy. Watch the sun set over Cape Cod Bay from the Bass Hole Boardwalk in Dennis, or from one of the town's lovely bayside beaches. Brewster, near the east end of the Old King's Highway, has a number of historic sea captain's mansions that have been converted into B&Bs, any one of which will make a good base for these first three nights.

Day 2

Rent a bike from beside the entrance to Nickerson State Park and spend a few hours cycling the Cape Cod Rail Trail. The route is most varied to the south, with ponds, cranberry bogs, and deeply wooded stretches. This being Massachusetts, there's even a nifty little bike rotary where the main rail trail intersects with the Old

Colony spur to Chatham. In the afternoon visit Brewster's Cape Cod Museum of Natural History.

Day 3

Head north to the Cape Cod National Seashore in Eastham and Wellfleet. Spend time at Coast Guard Beach, favorite of the state's corps of wetsuited surfers, beneath the red-flashing beacon of Nauset Lighthouse. Continue to Wellfleet Bay Wildlife Sanctuary occupying the extensive salt marshes and wooded shore on the calm western side of the Outer Cape. Explore the galleries and shops of Wellfleet, perhaps the Cape's least touristy town. If you've never experienced a drive-in movie, you'll have your chance tonight after sundown at the Wellfleet Cinema.

Day 4

Bid adieu to your B&B hosts and proceed to Provincetown, the Cape's answer to Key West. Spend today visiting the galleries and shops of Commercial Street. While strolling around, don't miss stepping into the public library for excellent aerial views from the steeple reading room. In the afternoon go on a dune tour.

Day 5

P'town redux: Go on a whale watch in the morning, and then rent a bike and spend the afternoon riding the National Seashore's Province Lands trails. Time your ride so that you end up at Herring Cove Beach for the best show in town: sunset.

Day 6

Pack up the car and head south to Chatham to the Monomoy National Wildlife Refuge. Take a wildlife-watching cruise with Monomoy Island Excursions, or make a full day trip of it with a naturalist-guided walking tour, including a visit to the historic lighthouse at its tip.

Day 7

Take the morning ferry from Harwichport to Nantucket. Spend day strolling the town and visiting the Whaling Museum. Walk to tiny Brant Point Light in the late afternoon and watch the sailboats and ferries. If it's a Friday (or Monday or Wednesday in summer), go star-gazing at the Loines Observatory.

Day 8

Still on Nantucket, wake up in the downtown vicinity and take the shuttle to quiet 'Sconset, for either a beach walk or lunch at The Summer House. Alternatively, rent a bike and ride to Wauwinet for a tour at Coskata-Coatue Wildlife Refuge with the Trustees (reserve this as far in advance as you possibly can).

Day 9

Take the morning ferry back to Harwichport and drive to Falmouth, making a stop in Hyannis to check out wares in the funky stores on Main Street. From Falmouth, secure passage on one of the ferries to Martha's Vineyard, landing in either Oak

nighttime view of Vineyard Haven

TAKE ME OUT TO THE BALLGAME

One of the purest pleasures of summertime on the Cape is not on the beach by the rolling surf, but on the baseball diamonds of the **Cape Cod Baseball League** (www.capecodbaseball.org), an NCAA-sanctioned amateur league that's been around since 1885. In any given year, nearly a sixth of all the current ball players in the majors have swung a bat for one of the Cape's 10 teams, and a third of all collegiate baseball players who graduate to MLB are Cape League alumni. These stats give the league an outsized reputation as a font of that most holy of baseball grails, professional-level play without big-league attitudes or the warped influence of big-league bucks. Games are, in fact, free – a hat is passed for donations. On nearly every evening from mid-June through early August there are up to five different games from which to chose.

The league's two divisions extend between Wareham – the first off-Cape town on the shore of Buzzards Bay – in the west to Orleans in the east, playing on community and high school fields lovingly tended by a small army of dedicated volunteers. Since most of the games regularly attract 10 times as many fans as can sit in the average venue's few sets of bleachers, most attendees bring blankets or folding chairs to set out on the grass overlooking the outfields. Such casual seating arrangements and breezy outdoor settings wrap games in the distinctive easy-going ambience of a friendly community picnic.

Here's a list of the league's home fields:

Bourne Braves, Upper Cape Tech Field (Rte. 6A, Bourne, just east of the Bourne Bridge rotary)

Brewster Whitecaps, Stoney Brook School Field (384 Underpass Rd., Brewster, off Rte. 137)

Chatham Athletics, Veterans Field (Depot Station, Chatham, on north side of Rte. 28 just west of town center)

Cotuit Kettleers, Lowell Park (Lowell St., Cotuit, 1.2 miles south of Rte. 28 on Main St., then left)

Falmouth Commodores, Elmer "Guv" Fuller Field (Main St., Falmouth, 0.6 miles south of Jones Rd.)

Harwich Mariners, Whitehouse Field (Oak St., Harwich, next to Harwich High School; take Queen Anne Rd. east from Rte. 124, then turn right on Oak for 0.8 miles)

Hyannis Mets, McKeon Field (at the end of High School Rd., Hyannis)

Orleans Cardinals, Eldredge Park (Rte. 28 and Eldredge Parkway, Orleans)

Wareham Gatemen, Clem Spillane Field (55 Viking Dr., off U.S. 6, Wareham, behind the town hall parking lot)

Yarmouth-Dennis Red Sox, Red Wilson Field (Dennis-Yarmouth High School, 180 Station Ave., South Yarmouth, 1.4 miles west of Union St.)

Bluffs or Vineyard Haven. Spend the day in either town, ducking through the souvenir shops and art galleries, walking the downtown harbors of each, and making sure not to miss a stop into Mad Martha's ice cream shop.

Day 10

Take the island shuttle or rent a bike and cycle to Gay Head Cliffs and Menemsha, where the island really opens up and the crowds give way to incredible views and authentic island living. If you've still got energy left after the bike ride, hike the stunningly beautiful Menemsha Hills.

Day 11

Switch gears and spend the day in tony Edgartown, taking in the historic captains' houses and pristine waterfront homes. When you've had enough ogling, rent a bike and bring it across the ferry to Chappaquiddick island, home to the serene Mytoi Japanese-style gardens.

Day 12

Make your return to Falmouth by boat, and then be sure to visit Woods Hole Oceanographic Institute to advance your depth of knowledge of local sea life, and then further that education at the Woods Hole Science Aquarium.

► NANTUCKET WEEKEND GETAWAY

Day 1

Start the day in the center of Nantucket Town, where quaint cobblestone streets and generations-old shops sit next to posh boutiques. After strolling around and popping into a few stores, settle into a table for lunch at Straight Wharf Restaurant for fresh seafood overlooking the water. Along the way back to the hotel, check out the many art galleries, souvenir shops, and craft stores.

Day 2

Pack a beach bag, rent a bike, and ask for a map to Madaket Beach. The well-paved, beautiful bike paths along the way are lined with beach plums and wind past neighbor-hoods exhibiting the island's traditional saltbox houses. Along the way, stop and pick up first-rate sandwiches and cookies at Something Natural. Bring the lunches with you on the rest of your trip, and enjoy them during your day on the shore.

Day 3

Make it a day filled with local history. Begin after breakfast at African Meeting House, a 1827 site once used as a meeting place and schoolhouse for the island's African residents. After lunch, make your way to Nantucket's Whaling Museum, and spend the remainder of the day taking in giant whale skeletons, and more whaling lore than you can shake a harpoon at.

Nantucket's Whaling Museum

FRESH CATCH

On Cape Cod, seafood drives not only many an appetite, but many a visitor, as well. The region's reputation as a treasure trove of ultra-fresh, delicious sea creatures is well earned. Start the feast by tucking into raw oysters (some of the best in the world are served on menus around Cape Cod, hailing from the local town of Wellfleet). Local clams, too, are a favorite (medium-sized, hard-shell bivalves known as quahogs) and show up in restaurants stuffed, in fried clam cakes (a.k.a. fritters), or in the area's cream-based clam chowder.

Entrées dig even deeper into the sea: delicacies like lobster, crab, shrimp, mussels, clams, and every iteration of all of the above. Fish like cod, striper, salmon, mackerel, and bluefish are also readily available here, and you'll find them cooked every which way – fried, boiled, sautéed, marinated, braised with wild mushrooms, and baked-stuffed with bacon and stuffing.

Here's a list of some of the best places for seafood throughout Cape Cod and the Islands.

fresh oysters and lobster roll

CAPE COD
The Clam Shack, Falmouth
HannaH's Fusion Bistro, Hyannis
Abbicci, Yarmouthport
Brewster Fish House, Brewster
Abba, Orleans
Sir Cricket's Fish & Chips, Orleans
The Chatham Squire, Chatham
Finely JP's, South Wellfleet
Mac's Shack, Wellfleet
The Wicked Oyster, Wellfleet
The Lobster Pot, Provincetown
Devon's, Provincetown
The Mews, Provincetown

MARTHA'S VINEYARD
Sandy's Fish & Chips, Vineyard Haven
The Sweet Life Café, Oak Bluffs
Lola's Southern Seafood, Oak Bluffs
Alchemy, Edgartown
@ the Cornerway, Chilmark
The Menemsha Bite, Menemsha
Larsen's Fish Market, Menemsha

NANTUCKET
Black-Eyed Susan's
Centre Street Bistro
Òran Mór
Water Street
21 Federal
Straight Wharf Restaurant
SeaGrille

► MARTHA'S VINEYARD ALFRESCO

Day 1

Arrive in Vineyard Haven and charter a windjammer with Black Dog Tall Ships for a day on the water. Afterward, take a shuttle to Oak Bluffs and stroll the winding lanes of Oak Bluffs Campground. In the evening, take a 10-minute drive into downtown Edgartown and visit Edgartown Lighthouse (Edgartown Harbor), originally built in 1828.

Day 2

Pack a picnic lunch and spend the morning experiencing a unique and serene reservation area with a trip to Mytoi. The pine-forest, Japanese-style enclave has rare and exotic plants and trees and a quiet, quarter-mile trail. Follow that bit of natural splendor with a bit more: The nearby Cape Poge Wildlife Refuge includes 14 miles of walking trails and beachfront. Take a break from hiking to have lunch at one of the picnic tables. After the return hike, grab the ferry back and settle into The Newes from America for a pint and some solidly restoring pub fare. Then get back on the road leading out of Edgartown.

Day 3

Up-island, sample one of the most delicious natural resources (and namesakes) of the island at Chicama Vineyards, the first winery in Massachusetts. Take a free tour of the picturesque property, peruse the boutique's shelves filled with homemade gourmet foodstuffs and bottles of wine, and make sure to bring some back for both yourself and friends. Spend what's left of the day exploring the art galleries and cafes in nearby West Tisbury.

Day 4

You'll see the island's most magnificent corners on foot, but see more of them (equally up-close-and-personal) by bike. In Edgartown, rent bikes at Wheel Happy and turn your handlebars toward the Massachusetts Audubon Society's Felix Neck Wildlife Sanctuary. Bike riding is not allowed while within the wildlife sanctuary. Park your bike and explore the sanctuary's six miles of trails and remote beaches, surrounded by woodlands, meadows, pond, and marshes on foot.

Day 5

The paragon of Martha's Vinyard beauty glows with every evening's sunset: Aquinnah's Gay Head Cliffs, a National Natural Landmark. Spend some time perusing the stable of shops and eating some lunch, but then spend the rest of the time gawking at the striated red and amber walls of the bluffs—and catch a glimpse of the Elizabeth Islands across Vineyard Sound.

Oak Bluffs Campground

CAPE COD

Ah, Cape Cod—just take out a map and look at it. "A man may stand there and put all America behind him," wrote Henry David Thoreau, longingly summing up his several 19th-century visits. Jutting 40 miles into the Atlantic, this relatively young fishhook of sandy soil and pitch pine forest, appreciated by Thoreau for its desolation, has become one of the nation's preeminent seaside resorts; its 15 towns and hundred-odd beaches draw millions of summer residents and visitors each year. The Cape once lived off the sea, but it now depends on people who come merely to dip their toes in it.

In recent decades, new residential subdivisions, timeshare condos, summer cottages, and sprawlmarts set amid acres of asphalt have metastasized across the Cape—giving first-time visitors, with no clear sense of what it used to be like, plenty of reason to wonder what all the repeat customers from southern New England and Canada see in the place. The quaint gray-shingled and white-clapboard villages so typically associated with Ye Olde Cape do still exist, but much is of more recent vintage than you might imagine—deliberately built or renovated to fulfill the expectations of tourists who came first by rail and steamer, and later by car. The neocolonial style is now old enough to be historic in its own right, of course, but if you can't be bothered with impostors, pay close attention to your historical society walking-tour brochures. That 18th–century–style house you're admiring may actually be a product of someone's 1920s—or even 1980s—nostalgia.

Of course, the big attraction for many visitors—even those drawn by childhood

COURTESY OF THE CAPE COD CHAMBER OF COMMERCE

HIGHLIGHTS

◖ Heritage Museums and Gardens: Two centuries of Americana live on at this palatial garden estate (page 26).

◖ Woods Hole Oceanographic Institute: Deep-sea explorers reveal the mysteries of the real "final frontier" (page 32).

◖ Old King's Highway: Winding through one quaint village center after another, this route runs through the Cape Cod of yesteryear (page 47).

◖ Monomoy National Wildlife Refuge: This sandy spit off the end of the Cape's "elbow" is home to a colony of gray seals and hundreds of migratory bird species (page 54).

◖ Cape Cod National Seashore: Stroll miles of sandy beaches with nothing between you and Portugal but the waves (page 58).

◖ Highland Light: Towering 123 feet over the dunes, this is the Cape's most impressive working lighthouse, and the only one regularly open to the public (page 67).

◖ Commercial Street, Provincetown: Drag queens, local characters, and befuddled tourists all add up to a people-watcher's paradise (page 71).

◖ Whale-Watching: Seeing leviathans in their natural habitat on one of P'town's trusty vessels is anything but a fluke (page 73).

LOOK FOR ◖ TO FIND RECOMMENDED SIGHTS, ACTIVITIES, DINING, AND LODGING.

familiarity or the fact that if Grandma doesn't live in Florida, she lives on the Cape—is not so much the land as what's around it. Like sailors responding to the call of the Sirens, the sybarite hidden within every New Englander just can't resist all those beaches and all that water rolling over them. Admittedly, the call of the sizzling deep fryers is pretty seductive, too, but even Spam on stale crackers might not seem so bad if you could enjoy it while stretched out on one of the Cape's better beaches.

Even the most popular beaches can offer a soupçon of privacy if you remember that about 90 percent of the Cape's would-be sunbathers are weighed down with coolers, chairs, kids, and toys and don't walk more than 20 minutes from their cars. The big drawback for short-time visitors is that most beach parking requires either a resident sticker or a fee up to $10 or more per day, but with a few exceptions, the fees are only levied against cars—arrive by any other means, and you can enjoy the beaches for free.

Though swimming after September is out of the question for most warm-blooded mortals, the parking restrictions are lifted then and the crowds thin to a relative trickle, leaving the tide's treasures and the sumptuous sunrises and

COURTESY OF THE CAPE COD CHAMBER OF COMMERCE

Cape Cod beaches can get crowded during the summer.

sunsets to those hardy beachwalkers who put off their vacations until just this time of year. (Having a fireplace and hot bath waiting back at the B&B helps.)

Visitors who make the mistake of just taking in the view from a car window may come away with impressions of the Cape's interior as a monotonous landscape of pitch pine forest and sandy house lots. Ditch the wheels for a while and discover that any time of year, the Cape's local conservation lands and privately managed sanctuaries offer an antidote to ringing cash registers and creeping beach-bound traffic. Kayaking along a salt marsh estuary among blossoming white shadbush, sitting beside a kettle pond listening to a kingfisher's rattle, spotting redwing blackbirds among the cattail reeds of an abandoned cranberry bog, or encountering bright lady's slippers (*Cypripedium acaule*) scattered amid the moist coolness of a maturing stand of oaks—one or two such experiences and you, too, may find yourself repeating the phrase that has come so easily to generations of visitors: See you next year, back down on the Cape.

ORIENTATION

Never mind the compass. If you have a good sense of direction and an abiding faith in highway signage you'll be very discombobulated by highways marked "south" when they in fact go *north*. Instead, the operative principle on the Cape is up and down. **Up-Cape** means westward—toward the Upper Cape and that big hummock known as **off-Cape** to locals and North America to everyone else. **Down-Cape** means eastward—toward the Outer Cape, Provincetown, and Portugal. These terms make more sense if you're a sailor, or have a passing familiarity with the Greenwich Prime Meridian: Degrees of longitude descend as you head east, increase as you head west. (This also explains why New York yacht owners go "down East" to get to their Maine summer cottages.)

Further important distinctions are made between the three sides of the Cape's bent arm: **Bayside** refers to the entire rim of Cape Cod Bay, from the canal at Sandwich down to MacMillan Pier in Provincetown. The first half comprises historic and picturesque Cape villages, as venerable as Thanksgiving, along what was once the Old King's Highway (now Rte. 6A). The **south shore** faces Nantucket Sound, between Buzzards Bay and the Cape's **elbow,** at Chatham. Blatantly commercial Rte. 28, as casual as a beer belly over the barbecue and as gaudy as the Fourth of July, is the main artery of this side. And the **backside** denotes that segment that braves the open Atlantic from the Chatham elbow to the "fist" of Provincetown; most of this area is preserved for posterity as part of the Cape Cod National Seashore.

It's also worth remembering that towns on the Cape are all subdivided into distinct villages whose names, vestiges of early settlements, are maintained now only to aid postal delivery and to bamboozle out-of-towners. If you can't remember that South Dennis is north of West Dennis or that West Chatham is east of South Chatham, you clearly don't live here.

PLANNING YOUR TIME

Successfully navigating the Cape is as much a matter of timing as of geography. **High season** typically runs from Memorial Day weekend in late May through Labor Day weekend in early September. The millions who converge on the Cape during those 15 weeks spawn legendary traffic jams, long lines at restaurants, and a plethora of No Vacancy signs at local lodgings. With a gazillion vehicles trying to cross the two bridges over the Cape Cod Canal on any given summer or holiday weekend, the 70-mile journey from Boston to, say, Woods Hole can actually take as long as the 300-mile drive to Canada. July begins the flood of families, predominantly to the south shore beachside motels; August brings flocks of psychiatrists, lawyers, doctors, and other professionals to Chatham, at the Outer Cape's southern extremity, and to bayside towns from West Barnstable to Wellfleet. Meanwhile, the cheapest of the old motel courts, sharing the twilight years of their owners, revert to full occupancy throughout the summer—even midweek and in bad weather—serving as housing for both seasonal workers and low-income Cape residents who are forced to do the "Cape shuffle," having been displaced by nine-month

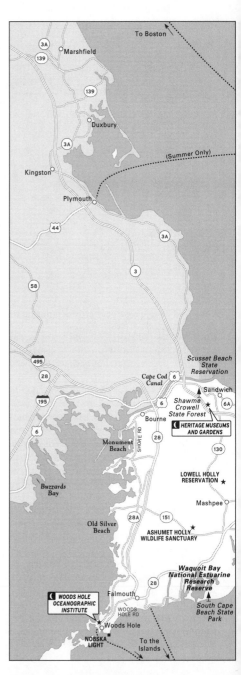

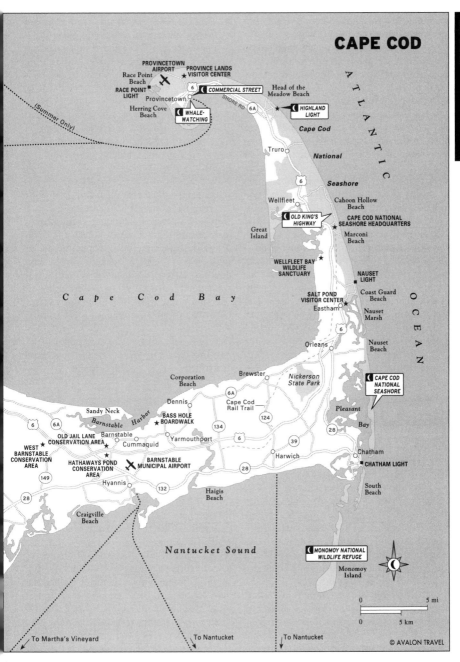

CAPE COD

PROVINCETOWN
AIRPORT
PROVINCE LANDS
VISITOR CENTER
Race Point
Beach
RACE POINT
LIGHT
Provincetown
COMMERCIAL STREET
Head of the
Meadow Beach
HIGHLAND
LIGHT
Herring Cove
Beach
WHALE-
WATCHING
SHORE RD
6A
Cape Cod
ATLANTIC

(Summer Only)

Truro

National

6

Seashore

Wellfleet
Cahoon Hollow
Beach
OLD KING'S
HIGHWAY
CAPE COD NATIONAL
SEASHORE HEADQUARTERS
Great
Island
Marconi
Beach
WELLFLEET BAY
WILDLIFE
SANCTUARY
NAUSET
LIGHT
SALT POND
VISITOR CENTER
Coast Guard
Beach
Eastham
Nauset
Marsh

Cape Cod Bay

Orleans
Nauset
Beach

6

OCEAN

Corporation
Beach
Brewster
Nickerson
State Park
CAPE COD
NATIONAL
SEASHORE
Dennis
Cape Cod
Rail Trail
Pleasant
Sandy Neck
Barnstable Harbor
BASS HOLE
BOARDWALK
134
124
Bay
6
6A
OLD JAIL LANE
CONSERVATION AREA
Barnstable
Cummaquid
Yarmouthport
28
Chatham
WEST
BARNSTABLE
CONSERVATION
AREA
HATHAWAYS POND
CONSERVATION
AREA
BARNSTABLE
MUNICIPAL AIRPORT
6
39
Harwich
CHATHAM LIGHT
149
28
Hyannis
132
South
Beach
28
Haigis
Beach
Craigville
Beach

Nantucket Sound

MONOMOY NATIONAL
WILDLIFE REFUGE

Monomoy
Island

0   5 mi
0   5 km

To Martha's Vineyard   To Nantucket   To Nantucket   © AVALON TRAVEL apartment leases and temporary fivefold summer rent increases.

Yet, despite the disadvantages, high season is also when everybody is open for business—seven days a week, morning, noon, and night. Don't be surprised, though, if some businesses are still closed when high season kicks in. This is usually because owners are still trying to hire the necessary summer staff. A veritable army of Caribbean islanders and Eastern Europeans on temporary visas, many working two or more jobs, is all that keeps the Cape's summer economy from seizing up like a car without oil, but since the visa process is guided by national politics, it is prone to arbitrary change.

Vacationers with more leeway in their schedules may prefer the spring and fall **shoulder seasons,** which are quite popular with a discerning few hundred thousand people. These are the months when prices are a tad lower—the 30-percent-off signs start appearing in front of T-shirt and beachwear shops as early as the last weekend of August, and many lodgings offer Sunday–Thursday discounts—and the wait for a table at top dining spots is tolerable. Many repeat visitors regard fall in particular as the Cape's best

season because the water and weather remain warm but the crowds largely disappear.

The exact lengths of the shoulder seasons greatly depend on the weather and location. The spring shoulder begins at Easter and ends in late May. The fall shoulder is more elastic, running from Labor Day through October across most of the Cape, and from Columbus Day to early November in selected pockets that have romantic B&Bs, such as Provincetown and areas along the Old King's Highway.

By Thanksgiving in most places, and by New Year's everywhere, the **off season** has tightened its grip across the region, and won't let go until the daffodils bloom in April. Businesses close up, or start keeping malleable hours. If nobody comes in the door, off go the lights and down come the shades, regardless of the stated schedule on the window, answering machine, and website. While traditional tourist attractions during the off season are few, you'll discover great scenic beauty and a gregarious community spirit as year-round residents turn out for nightlife, gallery events, and to support the local restaurants that dare to stay open throughout the winter.

The Upper Cape

One of the great attractions of the Cape is the diversity of its towns. Behind the uniform weathered-gray shingles and simple little saltbox houses, clam shacks and soft-serve ice cream machines, pitch pine and scrub oak forests, and subscriptions to *Bassmaster* and *Modern Maturity,* lie such fundamental differences in history, politics, and demographics that a taxonomist could easily find evidence for separate species. This certainly holds true of the four Upper Cape towns, which by turns either embrace or ignore tourism, are highly commercialized or nearly rural, and can feel either country-clubbish or working class. With about one-third fewer lodgings than any of the other parts of the Cape, it's

an area often bypassed by visitors bound for the motel-lined shore of the Mid-Cape and inn-saturated streets of Provincetown, and by all the hopefuls headed to the Woods Hole ferry. Which only means that the people who do stop here can start enjoying a Cape vacation while other travelers are still stewing in traffic on U.S. 6.

The Upper Cape also benefits from having a nearly forgotten side to it: the Buzzards Bay shore. Although only a couple of the beaches here are open to outsiders who come by car (one, Monument Beach, even has free parking!), simply driving or cycling the route closest to the bay is as good an introduction as you can get to the sedative charms of the Cape landscape. Though it led the region in catering to summer tourists in the late 1800s, with fancy beachfront hotels along the then-new railroad to Woods Hole, the area has since slid gently into a lower gear. A few garish new suburban-style subdivisions have slashed into the hills offering water views, but more often the road passes modest old homes tucked behind trees, marsh-edged inlets, undeveloped woods, and signs for boatyards. Bumper boats, miniature golf, T-shirt stores, taffy shops, and other cheesy Cape cud are nowhere to be found—arguably because low-clearance railroad bridges keep buses and RVs away. (The bridges are something to keep in mind if you have bikes mounted on your car roof—there's only 11.5-foot clearance at Cataumet.) And while four-lane Rte. 28 effectively draws southbound drivers more intent on their destination than on the scenery, this is one of the few places on any of the Cape shores where puttering along won't instantly produce a 25-car entourage of impatient tailgaters.

snow-covered branches in Sandwich

© JEFF PERK

SANDWICH AND BOURNE

Sandwich, settled by a group of 60 families from north of Boston in 1637, was the first town to be established on the Cape; adjacent Bourne, which split from Sandwich in 1884, was the last. The area also had one of the only Indian settlements to have survived to the end of the colonial era, a place called Comassekumkanet until its residents, members of the Herring Pond band of Wampanoags, succumbed to the preaching of missionaries. Although the resulting "praying Indian" reservation was eventually absorbed by Sandwich, the band is memorialized on the north side of the canal by the namesake Herring Pond Recreation Area, a small turnout with parking and picnic tables off U.S. 6 in Bournedale. The site is popular in spring when thousands of alewives (members of the herring family) return to the pond to spawn; come in mid- to late April to watch the run at its peak.

Despite the proximity of generally intolerant authorities in nearby Plymouth, early Sandwich became a haven for Quakers and other religious groups who disagreed with the Pilgrims. This acceptance became a hallmark across Cape Cod, whose various towns were about the only ones in provincial Massachusetts to let go ministers who didn't suit their congregations (off-Cape ministers usually served lifetime appointments). Perhaps it also foreshadowed an aloofness from the orthodoxy of the following century, too, when the strong patriotism boiling over in Boston and elsewhere in New England failed to kindle much passion on the Cape.

As the terminus of the Plymouth stagecoach line in the early 1800s, Sandwich was one of the earliest towns on the Cape to attract tourists. These early pioneers of the region's now-dominant industry were usually men of wealth or consequence from nearby southeastern Massachusetts or Boston (like Daniel Webster), who were drawn to Sandwich for sport hunting in its deep woods. The town now has its sights set on motorists flocking over the Sagamore Bridge, and it snares them with its exceedingly well-turned, almost manicured historic district on the banks of Shawme Pond, at Main and

Water Streets (take U.S. 6 exit 2, or turn south at the traffic light on the Sandwich stretch of Rte. 6A).

Cape Cod Canal

The Cape used to be separated from the rest of the state by a valley with two opposite-flowing rivers, the Manomet and the Scusset, whose headwaters came to within a mile of each other. Indians portaged between them, and so did the Pilgrims—who recognized as early as the 1670s that a canal between them would be a good idea. Over the next 200 years, it seems as if every engineer and surveyor in the U.S. was hired or consulted at one time or another to review the prospects for a canal between the Cape Cod Bay and Buzzards Bay. All praised its suitability, but it wasn't until 1884 that anyone ventured to actually start digging. A couple of decades of stops and starts, political slapstick, lawsuits over contracts, and other diversions ensued, but finally, in 1909, construction began in earnest, fully financed by private capital. The first vessels passed through the completed eight-mile canal in July 1914. The passage never proved profitable for its builders—navigating the narrow channel was dangerous, and vessels kept hitting the drawbridges. The federal government bought the canal in 1928, nearly doubled its width, and built the two huge highway bridges that now provide the Cape's principal link to the rest of the nation.

Operation and maintenance of the canal is overseen by the U.S. Army Corps of Engineers, which also runs the **Cape Cod Canal Visitors Center** (60 Ed Moffitt Dr., Sandwich, 508/833-9678 or 508/759-4431 exit 622, www.nae.usace.army.mil, 10 A.M.–5 P.M. Thurs.–Sun. mid-May–late June, daily late June–Aug., Wed.–Sun. Sep.–mid-Oct., closed mid-Oct.–mid-May, free) at the eastern end of the canal. Drop by to learn about the canal's history and wildlife, view traffic video and radar monitors, and shop for Cape-related books at the small gift shop. For a more extensive selection of regional titles, head up Rte. 6A to the excellent **Titcomb's Book Shop**

(432 Rte. 6A, 508/888-2331, www.titcombs bookshop.com, 10 A.M.–5 P.M. Mon.–Sat., noon–5 P.M. Sun. year-round), a little ways past the Beehive Tavern in East Sandwich.

The 6.5-mile **Cape Cod Canal Bike Path**—comprising service roads on the banks of both sides of the canal—is paved for use by skaters, joggers, and cyclists; expect lots of slowpokes and great views of the canal's ship traffic. When you tire of battling headwinds as stiff as the currents through the canal (the tidal difference between the bays at either end is over five feet), consider hooking up with Shore Road in Bourne (parallel with the west end of the Cape-side path) and bicycling a short distance west to the beaches at Gray Gables, facing the canal, or Phinney's Harbor, on the causeway to Mashnee Island. Parking is limited to residents at the former and is nonexistent at the latter, so biking is about the only way to experience either beach in summer.

Parking lots that give access to the canal's north side are mostly located beside speedy U.S. 6 westbound, and appear with so little warning that you'll probably have to turn around and try a second time. On the Cape side, parking is available at the east (Sandwich) end beside the big, boxy electricity-generating station off Rte. 6A (turn on Tupper Road and follow signs with the U.S. Army Corps of Engineers logo), and at the west (Bourne) end off Shore Road, by the railroad lift bridge that resembles the two towers of London's Tower Bridge. Bike rentals are available from **Cape Cod Bike Rental** (508/833-2453) at 60 Rte. 6A a jot west of the Stop & Shop plaza.

Aptucxet Trading Post

Wall Street may be the seat of America's capital markets today, but if you want to see the "Birthplace of Free Enterprise in America," you'll have to pay a visit to the Aptucxet Trading Post Museum (24 Aptucxet Rd., 508/759-9487, Tues.–Sun. May–early Oct., $4 adults, $3.50 seniors, $2 children, $10 family) beside the canal bike path in Bourne. There, off Shore Road west of the Bourne Bridge, is a replica of the seasonal 1627 trading post where

COURTESY OF THE CAPE COD CHAMBER OF COMMERCE

There are plenty of paved trails for biking on the Cape.

Pilgrims, Native Americans, and Dutch from New Amsterdam dickered, bargained, and bartered to change wampum into furs and vice versa. There's also a saltworks, windmill, and the minuscule private depot President Grover Cleveland had built when he escaped malarial Washington, D.C. to visit his "summer White House," the home he bought and named Gray Gables, at the mouth of what was then the Manomet River.

Historic Sandwich Village

"Quaint" is a word much abused on the Cape, so to refrain from contributing to its abuse, let me define this and another important term: Places that are "quaint" are exceptionally akin to postcards come to life. They fit a romanticized image of what historic New England towns "should" look like, and often try hard to conceal how truly commercial they are. "Cute" (in these pages only) refers to a quaint place where real people live and work.

The village of Sandwich—with its restored 1640 gristmill grinding cornmeal for tourists, its classically inspired Town Hall and

meetinghouse, its Christopher Wren church on a hill, and its carefully crafted imitation stagecoach inn—almost epitomizes quaintness. By the same token, it is such a dainty morsel, such a small-scale sample, that finding fault is out of the question. There simply isn't enough there to saturate the senses, even though you could spend the better part of a day (and a fair amount of money) examining the various collections of things carefully maintained throughout the town. That doesn't just include the places that charge admission: **The Weather Store** (146 Main St., 508/888-1200 or 800/646-1203, www.theweatherstore.com, 10 A.M.–5 P.M. Mon.–Fri., 10 A.M.–1 P.M. Sat.) demonstrates as much single-minded dedication as any of the town museums with its fascinating inventory of weathervanes, whirligigs, tide clocks, sundials, rain gauges, lightning detectors, anemometers, thermometers, barometers, and the like, both new and antique.

Sandwich Glass Museum

One of the early gents who came to Sandwich for the hunting was Deming Jarves, who recognized in the woods a potential source of fuel for a glass factory's furnaces. (Daniel Webster, for one, complained that the consequently diminished forests were no longer adequate for "good sport.") For much of the 19th century, Jarves's Boston & Sandwich Glass Company dominated the nation's nascent glassmaking industry, turning an expensive import item into a domestic commodity well within the means of most Americans.

At the Sandwich Glass Museum (129 Main St., 508/888-0251, www.sandwichglassmuseum .org, 9:30 A.M.–4 P.M. Wed.–Sun. Feb.–Mar., 9:30 A.M.–5 P.M. daily Apr.–Dec., closed Jan., $5 adults, $1.25 children 6–14, free 6 and under) in the single-story clapboard building on Main Street opposite Town Hall and First Church, gallery after gallery of samples illustrates the evolution of this early mass-produced glassware. While the factory's artisans were capable of remarkable personal work, it helps to have a collector's interest in the cut saucers, plates, lamp chimneys, and other household items displayed in such great numbers.

◖ Heritage Museums and Gardens

About three-quarters of a mile south of Town Hall is Sandwich's king of collecting, the Heritage Museums and Gardens (67 Grove St., 508/888-3300, www.heritagemuseums andgardens.org, 10 A.M.–5 P.M. daily Apr.–Oct., $12 adults, $10 seniors, $6 youth 4–12, children under 3 free). Here is Americana by the acre, a diverse assemblage encompassing antique autos, military miniatures, Currier & Ives prints, landscape paintings, trade signs, and carved cigar-store figures, just to name a few of the items. A working 1912 carousel is among the larger specimens in the collection, though even the gallery buildings themselves are architectural showpieces, and the grounds are a horticultural collection of show gardens. The famous hybrid rhododendrons alone draw busloads of gawkers when in bloom (the first half of June). Added highlights include changing art exhibits and a summer concert series; call for details.

Camping

Sandwich has two state campgrounds to its credit, both of which may be booked in advance (877/422-6762, www.reserveamerica .com, $9.25 nonrefundable reservation fee). If you need a place to hook up your RV, try **Scusset Beach State Reservation,** on Cape Cod Bay due east of the Rte. 3 traffic rotary at the foot of the Sagamore Bridge; follow the signs. It may look as if you'll be plugging straight into an outlet in the wall of the hulking gas-fired power station, but it's actually on the opposite side of the canal from the camping area—just close enough so those blinking aircraft warning lights on the tall smokestacks will be as reassuring as stars twinkling in the night's dark firmament. Five tent sites are tucked in among the scrubby little trees at the back of the campground and are available mid-April through mid-October for $17 (discount for Massachusetts residents). The other 98 sites are available year-round to self-contained vehicles for $15.

If sleeping next to a utility company isn't your idea of what camping's all about, try the **Shawme-Crowell State Forest** (off Rte. 130 on Main Street in Sandwich proper, 508/888-0351). No RV hookups are available, but the campground has a disposal station, full restrooms with hot showers and modern conveniences, and even a store selling firewood and minor supplies. The 285 sites, generously spread throughout the pine woods, are available mid-April–mid-October during the week and year-round on weekends (barring blizzards) for $14 a night, $12 for in-state residents. A few dozen spaces are also open to RVs through the winter. Although overnighters are granted free day use of Scusset Beach (a savings of $2), this property's distance from the Cape Cod Rail Trail and the National Seashore ensures that it never fills as quickly as Nickerson State Park, on the Outer Cape, the region's only other public campground reachable without a boat.

Accommodations

Outside of the three hostels in Eastham, Truro, and Provincetown, some of the most affordable rooms on the whole Cape are found at the **Spring Garden Inn** (578 Rte. 6A, 508/888-0710 or 800/303-1751, www.springgarden.com, mid-Apr.–Nov., $105–130 d), a small motel near milepost 7 on Rte. 6A in East Sandwich. The 11 pine-paneled nonsmoking rooms facing a bird-filled marsh are only a half-mile walk from a bayside beach. (There's also a shallow inground pool.) Rates include complimentary bagels and fresh baked goods in the morning.

You'll find a half-dozen other small motels and cottages, none as inexpensive, along Rte. 6A west and east of the Spring Garden Inn. There's also a **Best Western** (100 Trowbridge Rd., 508/759-0800 or 800/528-1234, www.bestwesterncapecod.com, $150–170 d), in neighboring Bourne at the foot of the Cape side of the Bourne Bridge. For not too much more, you could also try one of the handful of bed-and-breakfast places in the center of Sandwich's historic village—especially if you don't need the motel-standard extra double bed for your kids, or such unromantic amenities as in-room TVs and telephones. Most of the B&Bs are found within a short stroll of the scenic gristmill on Shawme Pond.

A perfect example is the ◖ **Annabelle Bed & Breakfast** (4 Grove St., 508/833-1419, www.annabellebedandbreakfast.com, $165–235), on the crest of a hill immediately west of the pond, at the end of a long winding drive. This grand buttercup-yellow mansion would certainly have a view over the pond and town, were it not for being well screened by plenty of mature trees that, with the professionally landscaped grounds, give it the air of a secluded country estate. Though outwardly a replica of poet Henry Wadsworth Longfellow's 18th-century Cambridge home, this house was actually built in 1999 specifically as a B&B. Beneath the elegant proportions and Georgian symmetry are all the benefits of modern construction—full-sized baths (most with whirlpool tubs), climate controls for the central air and radiant-floor heat in each bedroom *and* bath, soundproofing between rooms—plus all the luxurious touches you'd expect from such a dis-

tinguished-looking property, from fine linens and flat-panel TVs to free WiFi inside and out. If you're on a diet, don't even think of staying here, as the sumptuous gourmet breakfasts will vanquish any self-control. In-room spa services may be arranged, too, and limo service from Boston's airport, for an additional charge.

Right in the heart of town is the very Victorian **Isaiah Jones Homestead** (165 Main St., 508/888-9115 or 800/526-1625, www.isaiahjones.com, $225–275 d). Behind the wicker porch furniture lie seven rooms decorated in authentic late-19th-century style—floral chintz fabric here, a full canopy bed there, and everywhere fresh flowers and candles. As a concession to modern romance, a couple of rooms have gas-fueled fireplaces and whirlpool baths. Rates include full breakfast (with a strata if you're lucky) and afternoon refreshments.

Nearby, **The Belfry Inne** (8 Jarves St., 508/888-8550, www.belfryinn.com, $180–315) exemplifies that contemporary, design-magazine blend of selected antiques, abstract art, and ultramodern plumbing. The inn occupies a former church built in 1900. Its half-dozen rooms were renovated with the Book of Genesis in mind, the colors of each corresponding with one of the first six days of creation. All preserve architectural details from the building's former ecclesiastic life, from stained glass windows to the interior oak flying buttresses, and feature private balconies, hot tubs, and fireplaces. Rates include continental breakfast served in the ground-floor bistro.

Food

A good bet for any meal of the day is the home-style **Marshland Restaurant** (109 Rte. 6A, 508/888-9824, www.marshlandrestaurant.com, 6 A.M.–8 P.M. daily, 6 A.M.–8:30 P.M. Fri.–Sat., $7–17), a combination bakery/eatery at the Citgo gas station 1.5 miles east of the Bourne–Sandwich line. (Their T-shirt logo: "Eat here and get gas!") Escarole soup, fish 'n' chips, spaghetti and meatballs, veggie stir-fry, veal parmesan, and homemade desserts (try the Pilgrim pie—apple-cranberry

THE STRANGE CASE OF THE HUNGRY GOURMET

Most people can probably remember a favorite little restaurant that promptly hit the skids as soon as it became wildly popular. At least, you thought the quality ran out the back door; the people lining up outside every night, for some odd reason, failed to notice. Many vacation resorts suffer from this syndrome on a grand scale – millions of people spend millions of dollars every year on food that no self-respecting airline would serve. For proof, look no further than the Rte. 28 side of the Cape, where cottonseed oil is king.

Of course, food may only be a mere afterthought to a day spent basking in the sun or splashing in the surf – some carbohydrates, some icy liquids, and you're a happy camper. But anyone who values both variety and quality will find it a marvel that the Cape – supposedly with more restaurants per capita than any other part of New England – is so *average*. Good, fresh seafood is a rare and delicious thing, and it should be a crime to subject it to the same salty batters and gooey sauces that are used back home solely to hide the fact that back home, the seafood isn't fresh.

Fortunately, a new generation of young chefs is changing the Cape's dining scene slowly but surely, abetted by influences from immigrant kitchen workers. Thus the future of dining on the Cape continues to brighten. It's entirely possible to stake your dining pleasure on random choice without undue worry about regretting it later, especially outside the Mid-Cape stretch of Rte. 28.

If you don't love seafood, don't worry – burgers are plentiful and poultry is always an option, albeit typically a second-rate one. Vegetarians should be prepared to consume plenty of pasta and pizza. Early-bird specials are offered by more restaurants here than in any other region of the state, making significant savings possible for those who work up an appetite before 6 P.M.

Diners with a conscience will be dismayed at the amount of plastic and paper that is casually consumed by restaurants here. If you want to minimize your contribution to the daily garbage train hauling the stuff off-Cape, firmly refuse the well-intentioned attempts to serve you better with huge handfuls of paper napkins and complete place settings of plastic – even when all you order is french fries. Those soda cans and bottles may often be returned to where you bought them, whether or not they carry a cash deposit (most do); now that most towns accept recyclables like glass and metal, many takeout counters and shops have begun in-house collections. Those that haven't may think twice about their environmental apathy if enough customers seem to expect action, so don't hesitate to speak up.

---

with walnuts—if you visit in autumn) are examples of the rib-sticking fare. Prices are low enough to produce lines of patient diners on summer weekends: Two people can eat breakfast for under $10, and other meals are just as friendly to the wallet.

Southeast Asian is one of the many ethnic food groups all but missing from the Cape's dining repertoire, so if you're looking for a fix of Cambodian or Vietnamese food, make a beeline down Rte. 28 to **Stir Crazy** (570 MacArthur Blvd., 508/564-6464, 4 P.M.–9:30 P.M. Tues.–Sun. year-round, $9–15), in the Bourne village of Pocasset. Found three miles from the Bourne Bridge in one of the small, nondescript commercial strip malls that flank the highway's southbound lanes, this tiny eatery has travel-poster decor, radio-station ambience, and a modest menu of tasty stir-fry meals. "Beef Lock Lack" (Cambodian *loc lac,* sirloin tips on a bed of watercress) and *Nhem shross* (vegetables and shrimp in rice shell appetizer) are good choices. Vegetarians can have most of the menu items prepared without meat; just ask.

A number of restaurants near the Cape Cod Canal have good water views, but if you're looking for a meal to match the panorama, you've got to go to the **Chart Room** (1 Shipyard Ln., 508/563-5350, noon–10 P.M. Thurs.–Fri.,

11:30 A.M.–10 P.M. Sat., 11:30 A.M.–4 P.M. Sun., May–mid-Oct., $5–35), overlooking Red Brook Harbor from the Kingman Marine boatyard in the Bourne village of Cataumet. The place serves traditional surf and turf, from broiled swordfish and baked stuffed lobster to steaks and lamb chops, but prepares them to a higher standard than most Cape waterfront places, which seem to believe that you pay for the view rather than the food. Entrées are in the $20 and up range, but sandwiches, served all day, are quite a bit cheaper. Reservations are nearly essential; ask for a porch table if you want the best seat for a Buzzards Bay sunset.

Another option that's more likely to feature grilled fresh fennel than french fries is **The Belfry Inne & Bistro** (8 Jarves St., 508/888-8550, www.belfryinn.com, 5 P.M.–10 P.M. Wed.–Sun., $25–34), inside a church-like building in the heart of historic Sandwich. The seasonally changing but always cosmopolitan dinner menu is served year-round; reservations are advisable in summer.

FALMOUTH

Steamer connections to Nantucket and Martha's Vineyard made Falmouth a conduit for both island-bound Sunday day-trippers and resident "summer folk" as early as 1836—the dawn of offshore tourism. But it wasn't until the railroad came down the Buzzards Bay coast to Falmouth's portside village of Woods Hole in 1872 (ostensibly to serve the guano industry based there) that the town started to capture a piece of the tourism pie for itself. When the railroad inaugurated "Dude Train" service from Boston in 1886, Falmouth siphoned off even more of the summer trade, prompting construction of a series of grand Victorian resorts, mostly along Grand Avenue overlooking the Vineyard Sound. Visitors would come for weeks or months at a time, many traveling from New York via the luxurious Fall River Line, disembarking across Buzzards Bay and completing their journey by train. Side by side with the tourists came the summer-home owners, who invested in property along the shore. All of

the old hotels are gone (along with the railroad they relied upon for customers), but the turn-of-the-20th-century real estate developments remain and are a defining visual element of the town's south shore.

If you want to read more about the town's history, drop by **Eight Cousins** (189 Main St., 508/548-5548, www.eightcousins.com, 9:30 A.M.–6 P.M. Mon.–Sat., 10 A.M.–6 P.M. Sun.), the award-winning downtown bookstore that, in addition to specializing in children's books, carries adult fiction and nonfiction (they stock the full Book Sense list of independent-bookstore best-sellers), and devotes several shelves up front to titles about Falmouth.

Waquoit Bay

If you study the Upper Cape shoreline on a map, you'll notice how the sea, rising after the end of the Ice Ages, has pushed up the water table and flooded the valleys carved by glacial meltwaters through the coastal sandplain along Falmouth's southeastern coast. The largest of these fingerlike valleys breached by Vineyard Sound is now largely protected within the state-owned **Waquoit Bay National Estuarine Research Reserve** (Rte. 28, 508/457-0495, www.waquoitbay reserve.org), whose visitors center is down the road from Edwards Boatyard. A vast open-air laboratory of ponds, salt marsh, barrier beaches, and a large wooded island, the reserve is used in part to study the effects of non-point-source pollution. That is the collected runoff from a wide area of petroleum-stained pavement, over-fertilized yards, and leaky septic systems—which adds up to a major environmental hazard, as serious as any pipeline spill or untreated factory discharge. The effects are ominous: algae blooms, fish kills, and declining eelgrass beds, for a start. (Eelgrass is a vital nursery habitat for shrimp, crabs, and over a dozen fish species, including such commercial varieties as flounder, pollack, and hake. If there's no eelgrass, there are no baby fish.) Waquoit Bay is hardly alone in these problems—from sea to shining sea, the nation's wetlands and the fisheries they

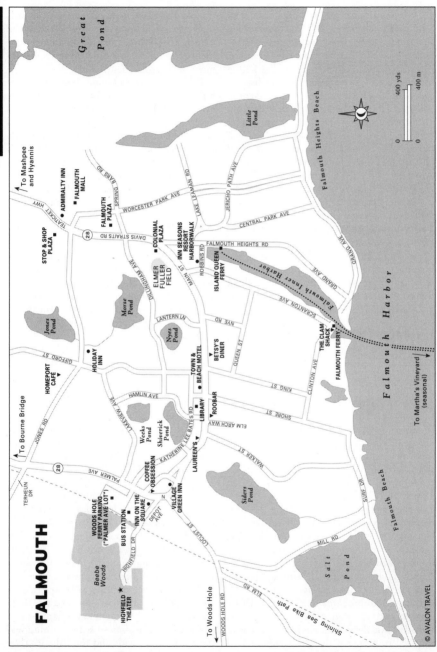

FALMOUTH

Great Pond

Little Pond

Jones Pond

Morse Pond

Nyes Pond

Weeks Pond

Shiverick Pond

Siders Pond

Salt Pond

Beebe Woods

Falmouth Heights Beach

Falmouth Harbor

Falmouth Inner Harbor

Falmouth Beach

400 yds
400 m

To Mashpee and Hyannis

TEATICKET HWY

To Bourne Bridge

To Woods Hole

To Martha's Vineyard (seasonal)

ADMIRALTY INN

FALMOUTH MALL

FALMOUTH PLAZA

STOP & SHOP PLAZA

COLONIAL PLAZA

INN SEASONS RESORT HARBORWALK

ISLAND QUEEN FERRY

ELMER FULLER FIELD

HOLIDAY INN

HOMEPORT CAFE

TOWN & BEACH MOTEL

BETSY'S DINER

THE CLAM SHACK

FALMOUTH FERRY

LIBRARY

ROOBAR

LAUREEN'S

COFFEE OBSESSION

VILLAGE GREEN INN

INN ON THE SQUARE

BUS STATION

WOODS HOLE FERRY PARKING ("PALMER AVE LOT")

HIGHFIELD THEATER

WORCESTER PARK AVE

CENTRAL PARK AVE

FALMOUTH HEIGHTS RD

DAVIS STRAITS RD

SPRING BARS RD

LAKE LEAMAN RD

JERICHO PATH AVE

GRAND AVE

GRAND AVE

ROBBINS RD

SCRANTON AVE

DILLINGHAM AVE

MAIN ST

LANTERN LN

NYE RD

QUEEN ST

KING ST

CLINTON AVE

SHORE ST

GIFFORD ST

HAMLIN AVE

LAKEVIEW AVE

KATHERINE LEE BATES RD

ELM ARCH WAY

WALKER ST

JONES RD

PALMER AVE

TERHEUN DR

HIGHFIELD DR

DEPOT AVE

LOCUST ST

MILL RD

ELM RD

SURF DR

WOODS HOLE RD

Shining Sea Bike Path

28

28

N

© AVALON TRAVEL

support are seriously threatened—but it's one of the few subjected to careful study. On the outreach side, the reserve sponsors a number of seasonal interpretive programs to inform visitors of the bay's special qualities and raise awareness about watersheds. You can also explore on your own—some five miles of trails run through the place, including boardwalks in the marshes.

WOODS HOLE

Woods Hole has the distinction of being Massachusetts's only seaside college town. This isn't just any college, either—the tiny village at the Cape's "other tip" is home to the Woods Hole Oceanographic Institution (WHOI, or "hooey"), a private, largely federally funded research center known most widely for the work of its pioneering little deep-sea submersible, *Alvin*. The U.S. Geological Survey (USGS), the National Marine Fisheries Service (NMFS), the Marine Biological Laboratory (MBL), the undergraduate Sea Education Association, and Woods Hole Research Center (an environmental think tank) are also based here in whole or in part, making Woods Hole the 800-pound gorilla in the world of marine science and education. Though the presence of the Martha's Vineyard ferry gives the village all the trappings of the Cape's other tourist towns in summer—overflowing parking lots, scores of cyclists, strolling shoppers, eateries crowded with out-of-towners—during the off-season, the community of some 1,500 scientists and students reveals its true nature—essentially that of one big academic campus.

That heavy volume of summer traffic to the Steamship Authority ferry, along with the dearth of even paid parking around the village, can make a peak-season visit frustrating for drivers. One solution is to take advantage of the acres of free daytime parking back in Falmouth at the Falmouth Plaza (on Rte. 28, east of downtown, park on the Starbucks side) and from there hop aboard **The Sealine,** the regular Hyannis–Falmouth/Woods Hole bus. Running daily until early evening (and until

COURTESY OF THE CAPE COD CHAMBER OF COMMERCE

Woods Hole

COURTESY OF THE CAPE COD CHAMBER OF COMMERCE

biking the Shining Sea Path

10 P.M. Fri.–Sat. late June–early Sept.), Breeze buses and trolleys are a service of the Cape Cod Regional Transit Authority (www.cape codtransit.org), meaning that all-day CCRTA passes are valid (standard adult fare is $1 otherwise). A second option is to bike to Woods Hole via the three-mile **Shining Sea Path,** a paved rail trail beginning at the intersection of Woods Hole Road and Mill Street (south of Main) in the heart of Falmouth and ending right at the Steamship dock.

◖ Woods Hole Oceanographic Institute

The work of Woods Hole's scientific community isn't concealed entirely behind closed lab doors or beneath distant oceans. The **WHOI Exhibit Center** (15 School St., 508/289-2252, www.whoi.edu, 10 A.M.–4:30 P.M. Mon.–Sat. May–Oct., 10 A.M.–4:30 P.M. Tues.–Fri. Nov.–Dec., closed Jan.–Mar., open by appointment Apr., call 508/289-2663, $2 donation requested), in a chapel-like clapboard building a block north of Water Street, has two floors of displays and videos on coastal ecology and discoveries made through WHOI-sponsored research, from understanding the lives of jellyfish in local Atlantic waters to strange life-forms around the ocean floor's hydrothermal vents. The center also showcases the tools of the oceanographer's trade, including a full-sized mock-up of the remarkable titanium-sphered *Alvin,* a 30-some-year-old pioneer of deep-sea exploration, discoverer of the *Titanic,* and doorway to the world of 4,500 meters (14,700 feet!) under the sea. A small gift shop sells selected books, magazines, and journals. As a complement to these exhibits, the WHOI News and Information Office, downtown on Water Street, sponsors guided 75-minute walks around its campus, giving a general overview of the institution's history while taking in the dockside ship operations and even, if you're really lucky, a laboratory. Offered from late-July through August, the walks commence at the Information Office (508/289-2252) at 10:30 A.M. and again at 1:30 P.M., and reservations are strongly recommended, as space on tours is limited.

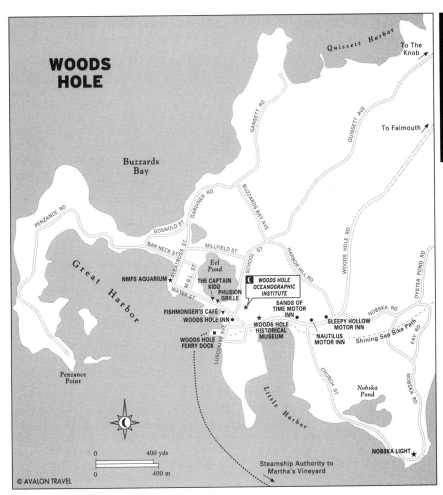

WOODS HOLE

Marine Biological Laboratory

The village center is shared by shops, restaurants, and the buildings of the Marine Biological Laboratory (7 M.B.L. St., 508/289-7623, www.mbl.edu), a private nonprofit that hosts marine-related undergraduate and graduate programs for students of two East Coast universities, as well as the sponsored research of hundreds of scientists from around the world. Free tours are available weekday afternoons at 1 P.M. and 2 P.M. late June–August, starting at the Pierce Visitors Center (100 Water St.); look for the half-hulled ship model poking out of the facade. Reservations are required. The visitors center also offers exhibits and features live animals during its hours of operation, which are generally from 10 A.M. to 3 P.M. or 4 P.M. depending on the time of year. The center is open every day in July and August; Mon.–Sat. in June; Mon.–Fri. in May and October; Tues.–Fri. in November and December; and closed from Christmas until the end of April.

© JEFF PERK

Marine Biological Laboratory

Woods Hole Science Aquarium

At the end of Water Street stands the National Marine Fisheries Service's Woods Hole Science Aquarium (Albatross St., 508/495-2001, 10 A.M.–4 P.M. Tues.–Sat. mid-June–mid-Sept. and 11 A.M.–4 P.M. Mon.–Fri. off season, free, http://aquarium.nefsc.noaa.gov). You've seen their names on laminated menu cards at sushi bars, but here's where you can see what cod, haddock, yellowtail flounder, salmon, octopus, and other denizens of local waters really look like. The creatures in this exhibit of the village's oldest science institution (the NMFS's forerunner established a collecting station in Woods Hole in 1871) are all the subjects of the facility's research into fish biology and fisheries resource management—so they may change to reflect what's turning up on twice-weekly sampling trips. There's usually at least one scene-stealing harbor seal in the outdoor pool by the entrance, too. Which creature is featured depends upon who's been rescued from shore stranding and is being fattened up or allowed to regain flipper strength before being released again into the wild.

OceanQuest Discovery Cruises

If you're not content just looking, you can get wet with a hands-on 90-minute tour by OceanQuest (100 Water St., 800/376-2326, www.oceanquest.org, $22 adults, $17 kids 4–12, $5 children 4 and under, infants free, purchase tickets at the dock but advance reservations are highly recommended, reservations required on Sat.). Making the rounds of collection points in the harbor, naturalists use handling tanks aboard the vessel to bring up critters for examination—and the day's catch serves as an introduction to topics in marine ecology. Weather permitting, up to four departures are scheduled each weekday in summer from the dock opposite the Marine Biological Laboratory Candle House, next to the pleasant waterfront park filled with salt-spray roses. Two additional cruises leave each Saturday.

Woods Hole Historical Museum

A fine overview—literally—of the community at the end of the 19th century is offered by the Woods Hole Historical Museum (579 Woods Hole Rd., 508/548-7270, www.woodsholemuseum.org, 10 A.M.–4 P.M. Tues.–Sat., mid-June–mid-Oct., free admission), for among the exhibits providing a local angle on maritime history in the main house is a scale model of the village circa 1895, complete with operating Z-scale railroad. The barn adjacent houses the museum's ship models and small wooden boat collection, which is highly recommended for learning the difference between a catboat, knockabout, dory, and dinghy—useful knowledge in this region, where many kids still learn to sail not long after they learn to walk. The museum publishes an attractive quarterly journal, *Spritsail*, and has produced a number of award-winning books, from collections of historic photos to a cookbook, all of which are available on the premises. Every Tuesday at 4 P.M. in July and August, you may also join museum volunteers on a free walking tour around the historic village center.

Beaches

Thanks to shallow underwater topography and the nature of off-shore currents, Falmouth is blessed with the warmest average water temperatures of any town on the Cape. Eight of the town's dozen or so beaches are public, with parking available for a daily fee of $10–20 in season. Visitors can also purchase stickers for a week or longer at the Surf Drive bathhouse. Beaches are free by alternate means of access (foot, bike, taxi).

By far the most popular of the public beaches is **Old Silver Beach,** off Quaker Road in North Falmouth. This wide curving half mile or so along the edge of Buzzards Bay has a front-row seat for the setting sun, and the stone breakwaters that bracket it make for interesting exploration anytime. Come early or late or be prepared to find the parking area filled to overflowing.

Two other public parts of the shore face the more wind-whipped waters of Vineyard Sound: centrally located **Surf Drive Beach** (follow Walker St. to its end from downtown), and **Menauhant Beach,** at the end of Central Avenue in East Falmouth. The last public beach is **Grew's Pond,** in Goodwill Park bewteen Rte. 28 and Gifford Street, a little over a mile north of downtown.

Bike Rentals
Several shops in Falmouth rent bicycles, including downtown **Corner Cycle** (115 Palmer Ave., 508/540-4195, www.cornercycle.com, 9 A.M.–6 P.M. daily), a quarter-mile north of the path on Rte. 28; and the seasonal **Holiday Cycles** (465 Grand Ave., 508/540-3549, 8:30 A.M.–dusk daily mid-May–mid-Oct.), among the inns and motels along Falmouth Heights. More dedicated cyclists may want to try the longer, equally scenic route along Buzzards Bay, following Sippewisset Road from West Falmouth to Woods Hole. Along the way are houses nestled in trees like elfin cottages, glimpses of the bay through people's backyards, and **The Knob**—a.k.a. the Cornelia L. Carey bird sanctuary—at the end of Quissett Harbor Road, notable for the breathtaking views out at the end of its causeway. Rent a bike for this route at **Art's Bike Shop** (75 County Rd., 508/563-7379 or 800/563-7379,

8 A.M.–5 P.M. daily May–Sept., 8 A.M.––5 P.M. Mon.–Sat. Sept.–May), on the corner of Old Main in North Falmouth (slightly west of Rte. 28A).

Camping
The most easily accessible camping in the Falmouth–Woods Hole area is **Sippewissett Campground and Cabins** (836 Palmer Ave., 800/957-CAMP or 508/548-2542, www.sippewissett.com, mid-May–mid-Oct.), in a well-wooded semi-rural residential area 1.5 miles northwest of downtown Falmouth. Most of the 100 sites are for RVs or tents, with water and electric hookups available ($2 extra), but a few exclusive tent sites are set aside near the front of the campground under tall pines, shielded from the road by a high wooden fence. A small camp store, launderette, game room, tot lot, and volleyball net are all on the premises, and gentle Wood Neck Beach on the Buzzards Bay shore is less than a mile away. Rates vary from $25–63 per site, depending on the number of adults and the season (late May–August is peak season), with discounted family and weekly rates available. The 11 rustic cabins are only rented by the week ($275–875 depending on number of bedrooms and date of rental); all include at least a private bathroom, microwave, and some sort of refrigerator, and most have hot-water showers and full kitchens.

Alternatively, there are 10 primitive, public campsites on 300-acre Washburn Island in the **Waquoit Bay National Estuarine Research Reserve** (Rte. 28, 508/457-0495, $8), but you'll need a boat to reach them (depending on where you put in your boat, it's at least a 20-minute paddle), all fresh water has to be packed in, and no campfires of any sort are permitted (the risk of their getting out of control on the windblown island is just too high). Reservations are required (877/422-6762 or 877/422-6762, www.reserveamerica.com, $9.25 nonrefundable reservation fee). Unfortunately, canoe and kayak rental isn't available nearby, but these may be rented from **Cape Cod Sea Sports** in Hyannis (309 Iyanough Rd., 508/790-1217, www.capecodseasports.com,

$45–65 per day), which includes a car-topping kit in the rental price. Sea Sports can also deliver a boat to the East Falmouth Town Landing, a block from the reserve, for the hefty price of $49 each way.

Accommodations

The only year-round accommodations within Woods Hole sit smack dab in the village center: **The Woods Hole Inn** (6 Luscombe Ave., enter from Water St. side, 508/495-0248, $225–290 June–Aug., rates are lower Oct.–May), a stone's throw from just about everything. It's a sweet little family-run place with just a handful of sunny rooms, most featuring a double bed and small private bath, and a pleasantly modern decor in keeping with the year of its renovation (2002) rather than the age of the building (1890). Rates include morning beverages and baked goods in the lobby, and guests are entitled to a discount at the street-level restaurant under the same ownership.

A trio of small seasonal motels flanks Woods Hole Road as it enters the village from Falmouth: the **Sleepy Hollow Motor Inn** (527 Woods Hole Rd., 508/548-1986, www.sleepy hollowinn.com, $140–185 d); the **Nautilus Motor Inn** (Woods Hole Rd., 508/548-1525 or 800/654-2333, www.nautilusinn.com, $118–225 d); and the **Sands of Time Motor Inn** (549 Woods Hole Rd., 508/548-6300 or 800/841-0114, $150–200 d). All three are open mid-April through October or early November.

About three miles away from the heart of the village—conveniently close to the start of the Shining Sea Path just south of Falmouth center, and right on the route of the summer WHOOSH trolley to Woods Hole—is the year-round **Woods Hole Passage B&B Inn** (186 Woods Hole Rd., 508/548-9575 or 800/790-8976, www.woodsholepassage.com, $125–195). This century-old carriage house and attached barn, formerly belonging to an adjacent private estate, were fully renovated for B&B use, so the guest rooms, all with queen beds and modern private bathrooms, are furnished in a tasteful contemporary country style. A huge yard and acres of conservation

The Woods Hole Inn

land surround the property. Full breakfast is included, and bikes are available for guests. Innkeeper Deb Pruitt can point you to a variety of pleasant walks in the vicinity—including to a pair of residents-only beaches—and she has good taste in restaurants, too.

Up the road, Falmouth proper oozes with accommodations. For the absolute lowest prices in high season, about your only option—outside of those cabins for rent at Sippewissett Campground—is one of the small motels found between downtown and the Inner Harbor, like the **Town & Beach Motel** (382 Main St., 508/548-1380, www.townandbeach motel.com, $75–88 d). There's some unfortunate truth, however, to the maxim that you get what you pay for. A night at the Flagship Motel on Scranton Avenue, for instance, yielded this author a room with no closet, no towel rack, no phone, no hot water pressure, not even a Gideon Bible, all for about $100. So, be prepared to rough it somewhat if your budget is tight, and to pay cash, too—not all of these establishments take plastic.

A much better value is found on the shore of finger-shaped Green Pond in East Falmouth at **Green Harbor Cape Cod Waterfront Lodging** (134 Acapesket Rd., 508/548-4747 or 800/548-5556, www.gogreenharbor.com, mid-Apr.–Nov., $162–350 d), about a third of a mile south of Rte. 28. All units overlook the water (conservation land opposite preserves the scenic view), come with two beds, and have at least a microwave and refrigerator if not a complete kitchenette. Most pets are welcome, but confirm when booking. Two outdoor pools (one for kids), volleyball, shuffleboard, croquet, badminton, and free rowboats and paddleboats ensure there's nary a dull moment. With charcoal grills and laundry facilities, too, you might never need to budge from the premises once you put away your groceries. Since resident flocks of Canada geese have fouled the shallow waters of the pond, swimmers will want to use those free boats to venture farther from shore, or head two miles down to Acapesket Beach, the barrier beach beside the pond's outlet to the sea. Expect a three- to five-day minimum stay

requirement in high season, depending on the unit, and full week minimums during selected summer holidays and special events. Inquire about the three-bedroom cottage if your clan needs lots of elbow room.

Another good bet much closer to town—and without the minimum stay requirement—is **The Admiralty Inn** (51 Teaticket Hwy., 508/548-4240 or 800/341-5700, www.the admiraltyinn.com, $135–195), on Rte. 28 opposite the Stop & Shop plaza at the east end of town. Rooms, most with two queen beds, a refrigerator, and all the standard chain motel amenities (color cable TV, ironing board, hair dryer, etc.), run from large to larger, with some "townhouse suites" comprising two levels connected by spiral stairs. Both indoor and outdoor swimming pools are on site. Up to two kids stay free. There's a nightclub in the main building over the entrance, so if thumping music isn't your idea of a lullaby, be sure to ask for a room away from the front.

Several familiar national chains or their near-equivalents are found on or near Rte. 28 as it bends through the center of town, including, from north to southeast, **Holiday Inn** (291 Jones Rd., 800/465-4329 or 508/540-2000, www.capecodhi.com); **Inn on the Square** (40 N. Main, 508/457-0606, www.innonthesquare .com); and **Inn Season Resorts HarborWalk** (26 Robbins Rd., 508/548-4300 or 800/528-1234, www.innseason.com), off East Main a few hundred feet from the *Island Queen* ferry to Martha's Vineyard. All are open year-round and meet or exceed the $200 mark mid-June to Labor Day—though rates may fluctuate up to $60 higher from midweek to weekends.

Food

In Woods Hole, around the corner from the Steamship Authority ferry ("262 leisurely paces" from the gangplank), is **Fishmonger's Café** (56 Water St., 508/548-9148, 7:30 A.M.–10 P.M. daily Mar.–Oct., call for hours in the off-season, $18–28)—despite its name, this is one of those extremely rare Cape establishments that openly embraces vegetables. The regular dinner menu initially looks like your typical college-town cross-cultural blender—a bit of Cajun influence here, Middle Eastern there, Thai spring rolls, fish and chips, broiled sirloin with garden salad, steamed veggies and brown rice. But daily specials push the menu into eclectic New American territory, with offerings such as pumpkin-sage ravioli, osso buco, and grilled tuna with Barbados black beans. The owner has an admirable way with pies, and the breakfasts are outstanding: thick, moist French toast, well-stuffed omelets, and terrific homemade sausages richly reward those who arise before noon. Open for lunch, too.

Other good options abound. Just across the street is the year-round **The Captain Kidd** (77 Water St., 508/548-8563, www.the captainkidd.com, 11 A.M.–9 P.M. daily, $15–25), half casual dining, half turn-of-the-20th-century sailors' bar on the edge of Eel Pond. Next door is the more ethnically influenced **Phusion Grille** (71 Water St., 508/457-3100, www.phusiongrill.com, 11:30 A.M.–2 P.M. and 5–10 P.M. daily, Apr.–Dec., $19–30), whose seafood and meat dishes are likely to be paired with ginger-garlic-sake broth, lemongrass coconut sauce, lemon-cumin beurre blanc, or spicy chipotle aioli. Even the scrumptious chocolate torte is laced with traditional Chinese five-spice blend. Terrific views overlook the pond's yacht anchorage.

Falmouth likewise is favored with good dining options, no matter what meal you're hungry for. **Betsy's Diner** (457 Main St., 508/540-0060, 6 A.M.–7:30 P.M. Mon.–Thurs., 6 A.M.–8 P.M. Fri.–Sat., 6 A.M.–2 P.M. Sun., $5–13) is a good place to begin—breakfast is served all day long and most dinner entrées are under $10. It's a classic stainless steel 1950s Mountain View diner, in perfect shape inside and out. The omelets are tasty and the coffee refills are free, of course. In true diner fashion, there are a half-dozen varieties of pie, but alas, they taste of canned filling, and the crusts are made tough by microwaving. Stick to the puddings instead. Lunch is served daily, and early dinners every day but Sunday. For just a muffin and cuppa joe to get your motor running, head straight for **Coffee Obsession**

(110 Palmer Ave., 508/540-2233, 6 A.M.–6 P.M. Mon.–Thurs., 6 A.M.–6:30 P.M. Fri.–Sun.) in the Queen's Buyway set of shops at the corner of North Main, next to Johnson's String Instruments. It has hands-down the best coffeehouse atmosphere on the Upper Cape: There's the community bulletin board papered with notices and business cards by the door and a range of local and national newspapers for reading, the walls are a gallery for local artists, the seating is comfortable, and there's a five-cent trivia question on the blackboard by the register. Oh, and in addition to all the customary espresso concoctions, there are premium-quality whole-leaf loose teas and delicious baked goods (the cookies are big enough to be meals in themselves).

A good bet for a healthy and satisfying lunch is **Laureen's** (170 Main St., 508/540-9104, 11:30 A.M.–9 P.M. daily July–Aug., 11:30 A.M.–3 P.M. daily mid–late June and Sept–mid-Oct., 11:30 A.M.–3 P.M. Mon.–Sat. mid-Oct–mid-June, $7–16), a specialty food shop and Mediterranean/Middle Eastern café opposite the Town Hall parking lot. I won't mention the **Ben & Bill's Chocolate Emporium** (209 Main St., 508/548-7878, year-round) on the corner across the street, since your mom probably frowned on the notion of calling ice cream and candy a meal, too. But just for future reference, they make a fine dark chocolate—try the satin-smooth truffles or nut-filled bark and see if you don't agree.

For local flavor, you can't beat **The Clam Shack** (227 Clinton Ave., 508/540-7758, 11:30 A.M.–8 P.M. daily late May–early Sept., "market" prices), in the old shed overlooking the Inner Harbor at the Patriot Party Boats dock. True to its name, this worthy purveyor churns out heaps of the little bivalves, enrobed with batter and sealed with the kiss of hot oil, unmarred by fine linens, fancy decor, or faddish ethnic spices. And the menu isn't limited to fried clams—the Fryolators here tackle whatever the fishermen bring home.

Had enough of fried fish? Then consider some palate-clearing Korean-style home cooking from the **Homeport Café** (316 Gifford

St., 508/540-0886, 11:30 A.M.–2:30 P.M. and 5–9 P.M. Tues.–Fri., $8–20), incongruously tucked away in the small business office park at the corner of Jones Road, opposite The Coonamessett Inn. Large portions, low prices, and a welcome acceptance of vegetables make this worth a detour. Or try the wood-fired brick-oven pizzas from **RooBar** (285 Main St., 508/548-8600, www.theroobar.com, 5–10 P.M. Sun.–Thurs., 11:30 A.M.–10 P.M. Fri.–Sat., year-round, $10–25), washed down with a pint from their good collection of craft beers and imports, or one of the creative, colorful martinis that fuel the happy buzz in the crowd around the bar up front. If the manchego cheese, caramelized onions, artichoke hearts, and other gourmet toppings on those thin-crust pies whet your interest in the entrées, you won't be disappointed—whether encrusting free-range chicken breast with macadamia nuts or presenting miso-roasted organic salmon in a rice-paper wrapper over jasmine rice and a thai red chili broth, the chefs here know how to please both the eye and the palate. Excellent desserts, too.

Another fine choice for folks who care about good food is the **Chapoquoit Grill** (410 W. Falmouth Hwy., 508/540-7794, 5 A.M.–10 P.M. daily, $11–20) in the village of West Falmouth, near the eponymous beach on the Buzzards Bay shore. Creative and attractive menu choices—such as horseradish-rubbed tuna with smoky plum tomato vinaigrette, or sesame-encrusted pork tenderloin with sun-dried cherry-rhubarb chutney—good artisanal house breads for dipping up sauces; fine freshly made desserts; and casual, warm-toned surroundings mean that there's almost *always* a line out the door. Wear comfortable shoes, get a libation from the bar, and settle in. Once you finally get to lift your fork, you'll find that good things do indeed come to those who wait.

MASHPEE

Of the several Cape towns with an Indian name, this is the only one that still has many residents who take personal pride in that fact. Mashpee (*massa* and *pe,* meaning "great" and "water," an eastern Algonquian variant of "Mississippi") is one of two towns in Massachusetts with a significant Native American population; like the other, Aquinnah on Martha's Vineyard, the tribal affiliation is Wampanoag. After decades of requests, the U.S. government finally recognized the Mashpee band in February 2007—though the tribe's quixotic quest to open up an Indian casino in Massachusetts is another story. Mashpee was historically a Christianized Indian town right up until the 19th century, when legalistic claptrap was used by whites to finally gain ownership of whatever land hadn't been appropriated in prior centuries. It remained largely rural until relatively late in the 20th century, when a burst of development created a town within a town—New Seabury, a resort community along Popponesset Beach on the south shore—and giant shopping malls at the junction of Rte. 28 and Rte. 151. Mashpee has been engaged in a residential and commercial building boom ever since; between 1980 and 2000, its population growth made Mashpee the fastest growing town in Massachusetts.

Recognizing the threat of unbridled development on the town's character, a coalition of private and public entities has fostered an ambitious plan for land preservation, leading to the creation of a new national wildlife refuge covering parts of both Mashpee and next-door Falmouth. Mashpee has thus become one of the best places on the Cape to see firsthand such globally rare habitats as pine barrens, cedar swamps, and salt marsh. So, although there are no museums, next to no accommodations, and relatively few restaurants, you'll want to pay Mashpee a visit if you have any interest in exploring the outdoors.

Mashpee National Wildlife Refuge

Currently comprising a patchwork of land holdings, waterways, and easements across private property, the 2,000-acre Mashpee NWR (Great Neck Rd., 978/443-4661, www.fws.gov) hopes to ultimately protect some 5,800 acres of critical watershed for several rivers feeding the deep bays along the south shore. For now the refuge is divided into sections on the north and south sides of Rte. 151. The north section includes upland oak forest around the deep headwater ponds of the Childs, Quashnet, and Mashpee Rivers. There are several miles of walking trails and backwoods roads suitable for mountain biking, plus a popular **swimming beach** at Johns Pond, one of the deepest (87 feet) kettle-hole ponds on the Cape. The south section encompasses the riparian corridors of those three rivers and many smaller brooks, along with hundreds of acres of hot dry scrub oak and pitch pine belonging to the South Mashpee Pine Barrens. Abutting the eastern side of the refuge is the **Mashpee River Woodlands Reservation** (Quinaquisset Ave. and Meetinghouse Rd., 508/679-2115, www .thetrustees.org), a property of The Trustees of Reservations that protects the lower reaches of what experts consider to be one of the state's finest streams for anadromous brook trout, or "salters" (hatched in fresh water, but reaching maturity at sea). An interpretive trail guide covering both the woodlands and the pine barrens, available from the Waquoit Bay National Estuarine Research Reserve visitors center on Rte. 28 in neighboring Falmouth, is highly recommended for its detailed descriptions and clear illustration of trailhead access. The visitors center also carries the *Mashpee NWR Trail and Recreation Guide,* which gives precise locations of all the refuge's put-in points for canoes, kayaks, or sailboards, and parking areas for trailheads. Both guides are free.

If, after exploring the refuge on foot or bike, you need to cool off with a swim, head for the **South Cape Beach State Park** (508/457-0495) on Vineyard Sound. It's located near the end of Great Oak Road—not at the very end, that's the town beach for residents only—and parking is $7 in July and August.

Ashumet Holly and Wildlife Sanctuary

Mashpee and Falmouth sport separate preserves bearing the mark of "the Holly Man," Wilfrid Wheeler, the State Secretary of Agriculture who gained fame during the first half of the 20th century as one of the world's leading propagators of holly trees. His personal collection, donated after his death to the Massachusetts Audubon Society, is now the Ashumet Holly and Wildlife Sanctuary (508/563-6390, www .massaudubon.org, dawn–dusk daily, $3 adults, $2 seniors and children 3–12) at the corner of Ashumet and Currier Roads off Rte. 151 on the Falmouth–Mashpee line. The 65 varieties of holly from around the world now occupying the few dozen pondside acres were all planted by Wheeler, along with a number of other exotics such as Japanese umbrella pine, a Manchurian dawn redwood, and a late-flowering Franklinia, garden offspring of a Georgian native now extinct in the wild. In addition to summer natural history programs on the property, the sanctuary sponsors naturalist-guided trips to the Elizabeth Islands, including occasional outings to some islands not served by the usual public ferries or tours. Ashumet is of course free to Massachusetts Audubon members.

Lowell Holly Reservation

Wheeler's other bit of handiwork is the Lowell Holly Reservation (508/679-2115, www.trust ees.org, dawn–dusk daily) on Conaumet Neck, jutting out between a pair of joined ponds on the Mashpee-Sandwich town line. Unlike Ashumet, this 135-acre peninsula already had a large stand of native American holly, for which Cape Cod marks the northern edge of its natural range; Wheeler supplemented the indigenous population with new trees selected for their fruitfulness. But what's unique about this property of the Trustees of Reservations is that it's the Cape Cod equivalent of an old-growth forest, untouched by brush fires, chain saws, or plows since at least the American Revolutionary War. As such, it's one of the few places on the Cape whose mix of trees suggests how the region's landscape might have appeared to its early inhabitants. But the place is not wholly untouched; its previous owner introduced a number of flowering shrubs to provide a showy floral display each spring. Open year-round, the reservation is found on South Sandwich Road off Rte. 130, adjacent to Sandwich's

Ryder Conservation Lands; turn at the cursive-script white sign for Carpe Diem (the private residence shares the Trustees' driveway), and follow signs. Memorial Day to Columbus Day, parking is $6 on weekends and holidays, due to the popularity of the swimming beach on the Ryder side of Wakeby Pond.

Food

Cotuit (ko-TOO-it), the Barnstable village immediately east of Mashpee, is a great source of cheap eats, and while American diner-style fare may be overly abundant in these parts, only a few purveyors deserve particular notice. One is **Kettle-Ho** (12 School St., 508/428-1862, 4 P.M.–12 A.M. Mon.–Fri., 8 A.M.–12 A.M. Sat.–Sun., $14–17), named after the two implements allegedly bartered to the local Indians in exchange for Cotuit's first land. It will never grace the cover of *Gourmet,* but that's not what its regulars would want anyway. They consistently fill this small joint because they know they'll get a decent sandwich-or-burger lunch made to order at a bargain price (if it's a white-bread and scrambled egg breakfast you want, they serve that, too). Take any of the sign-posted turns for Cotuit off Rte. 28 east of the Mashpee Rotary; the Kettle-Ho is in the center of the village near the corner of Main.

Although as a rule in New England, malls are not good places for fine dining, Mashpee proves an exception. **Siena** (508/477-5929, $13.95–24.95), in the Mashpee Commons (at the southwest side of the Mashpee Rotary), back next to the multiplex, should top your list for upscale Italian food—it comes complete with a jazz pianist on Sunday evenings. If you don't mind a view of the parking lot, there's outdoor seating in summer, too.

Across Route 128 from the Commons, in the South Cape Village (a.k.a. the Roche Brothers shopping plaza), is **◖ Heather** (20 Joy St., 508/539-0025, www.heatherrestaurant.com, 5 P.M.–close daily, $19–31) another mall stand-out with creative New American cuisine served up in a bright, spacious storefront dining room and bar. The inspired menu is rich in seasonal heirloom this and wild foraged that, with grace notes from the Caribbean and Far East—a silky autumnal pumpkin bisque laced with dark rum, for instance, or a perfectly crispy duckling lacquered with ginger hoisin plated with roasted baby bok choy. It's also one of the rare Cape eateries to offer organic bison tenderloin, from North Dakota—a meat rich in flavor despite being far leaner than beef. And although you'll easily be tempted to fill up on the savory courses, it's particularly advisable to leave room for a sweet finish. Especially since there's a marvelous sampler plate featuring perfectly composed portions of most of the dessert selections, further gilded by truffles and other choice sugary morsels—ah, hypoglycemia, thy name is bliss.

Mid-Cape

The geographical heart of the Cape is its most populous area, and thus appears the most suburban. It's also characterized by a wall of motels flanking the south shore on the one hand, and by the B&B-filled villages along the historic Old King's Highway (Rte. 6A) on the other. From the standpoint of both visitors and residents, the Mid-Cape region is defined largely by the nuisance value of its traffic, but that doesn't mean it should be avoided. On the contrary, there are attractions here not found anywhere else on the Cape, from mountain-biking trails and long beachcombing hikes to ethnic restaurants, affordable motels, and stores with the widest selection of whatever you're looking for. It's also the prime gateway for ferry service to Nantucket. Even the miniature golf, saltwater taffy shops, and beach gear and novelty shops along Rte. 28 can be a sensory delight, expressions of local color unlikely to be franchised across the country. The basic key to enjoying the Mid-Cape in season is to avoid taking Rte. 28 as a shortcut to anywhere else, and be open to changing where you wanted to go nexit Otherwise, you have to depend on the courtesy of oncoming drivers to make that left turn. Better yet, hop aboard a Breeze bus—these year-round public buses ply the region's south side—and become a spectator able to enjoy the passing scenery, rather than a frustrated and unhappy driver passing by it all.

HYANNIS

One of the Cape's early resort areas, Hyannis and the neighboring villages of Hyannisport and Osterville have been known since the 1920s for their oceanfront estates. Today, Hyannis is the most urban of Cape towns (despite a population of only 16,000), a major commercial center attracting Mid-Cape visitors and residents to its big shopping plazas along busy Rte. 132. Come summer, it's an absolute boomtown, filled with families spending summer at Grandma's, renting kitchenette-equipped "efficiencies" by the week, or joining the ant-like streams of island-bound passengers making their way down to the ferry docks from satellite parking lots.

It may not have much in the way of museums or historic sights, but in addition to having the most passenger rail, bus, boat, and airline connections to the off-Cape world, Hyannis boasts the region's highest concentration of guest rooms, with over 40 motels, hotels, and inns around town. It's also a hub for Cape nightlife, with bars, cafés, and nightclubs drawing the legion of young workers who flock to the region to earn next year's college money. While the party abates after summer ends, this is still just about the only Cape town where you can schmooze over some brews with the under-35 single set off season.

Kennedy Sights

Fans of the Camelot years in the American presidency—and anyone else wanting to trip lightly down the path of nostalgia—should be sure to check out the JFK photos and videos on display at the **John F. Kennedy Hyannis Museum** (397 Main St., 508/790-3077,

JFK Memorial

CAPE COD

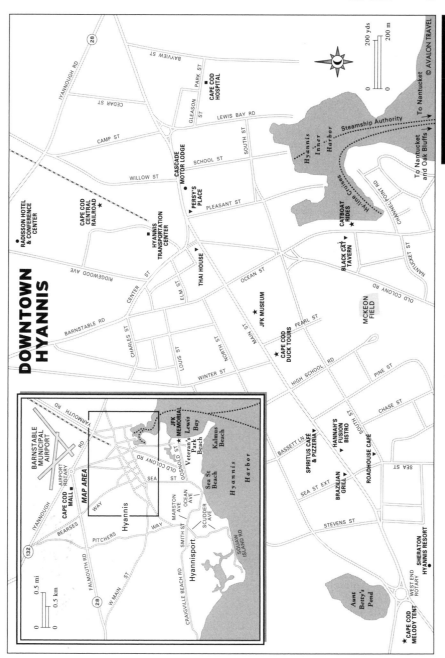

DOWNTOWN
HYANNIS

© AVALON TRAVEL

CAPE COD HOSPITAL

CASCADE MOTOR LODGE

PERSY'S PLACE

RADISSON HOTEL & CONFERENCE CENTER

CAPE COD CENTRAL RAILROAD

HYANNIS TRANSPORTATION CENTER

THAI HOUSE

JFK MUSEUM

CAPE COD DUCK TOURS

BLACK CAT TAVERN

CATBOAT RIDES

MCKEON FIELD

Hyannis Inner Harbor

Steamship Authority

Hy-line Cruises

To Nantucket and Oak Bluffs

To Nantucket

SPIRITUS CAFÉ & PIZZERIA

HANNAH'S FUSION BISTRO

ROADHOUSE CAFÉ

BRAZILIAN GRILL

SHERATON HYANNIS RESORT

CAPE COD MELODY TENT

JFK MEMORIAL

BARNSTABLE MUNICIPAL AIRPORT

CAPE COD MALL

MAP AREA

Veteran's Park

Lewis Bay

Kalmus Beach

Sea St Beach

Hyannis Harbor

Squaw Island

Hyannisport

Hyannis

Aunt Betty's Pond

WEST END ROTARY

0   200 yds
0   200 m

0   0.5 mi
0   0.5 km

www.jfkhyannismuseum.org, 9 A.M.–5 P.M. Mon.–Sat., noon–5 P.M. Sun., late May–Oct.; 10 A.M.–4 P.M. Mon.–Sat., noon–4 P.M. Sun. mid-Apr.–late May and Nov.–Dec.; 10 A.M.–4 P.M. Thurs.–Sat., noon–4 P.M. Sun. mid-Feb.–mid-Apr.; closed Jan.; $5 adults, $2.50 children 10–17, children under 10 free), on the ground floor of bunting-draped Old Town Hall, covering the years he spent vacationing at the local family spread, from the 1930s until his death in 1963. There's also a **JFK Memorial** on Ocean Street past the ferry staging area, overlooking the sheltered Veteran's Park Beach next to the yacht club (fee for beach parking in summer). The famous **Kennedy Compound**—whose nucleus is the much-expanded 1902 cottage that Joe and Rose Kennedy and their nine kids used for a summer home—is located in the well-heeled residential neighborhood of Hyannisport, south of downtown. But, given the frequent traffic restrictions, voyeurs are better off taking one of the several cruises that parade past the compound's waterfront, out by the harbor breakwater. The excursion with the most historical resonance is provided by **Catboat Rides** (164 Ocean St., #2, 508/775-0222, www.catboat.com, $30 adult, $25 senior, $10 child), with 90-minute sailing cruises to Hyannisport and beyond aboard a classic catboat, a type of sloop indigenous to the Cape. At the Ocean Street docks, look for the boat with the grinning Cheshire-like puss on the sail. The 12:15 and 2:15 excursions sail closest to the Kennedy Compound.

Entertainment and Events

Throughout the summer, you can catch up with America's aging (or ageless?) pop, rock, and country-western stars at the **Cape Cod Melody Tent** (21 W. Main St., 508/775-5630, www.melodytent.org). This in-the-round venue is certainly more intimate than any Vegas stage (no seat is more than 50 feet from the stage), and ticket prices aren't stratospheric either.

If you're in town around the Fourth of July, catch the **Cape Cod Symphony** (508/362-1111, www.capesymphony.org) on the Town Green, where they perform their annual free summer concert on the Saturday of that holiday weekend. The Boston Pops Esplanade Orchestra also puts in an annual appearance on the Town Green on the first Sunday evening in August; tickets for this special **Pops by the Sea** concert are sold in advance through the **Arts Foundation of Cape Cod** (508/362-0066, www.artsfoundation.org).

Tours

Taking the **Cape Cod Central Railroad** (252 Main St., 888/797-RAIL or 508/771-3800, www.capetrain.com, $20 adults, $18 seniors, $16 children 3–11, children under 3 free) through the varied topography of the Upper Cape is a relaxing alternative to stewing in traffic, and the railroad right-of-way is pleasantly free of the commercial clutter that increasingly mars sightseeing by car. Round-trips from Hyannis include stops in historic Sandwich and at the Cape Cod Canal; some trips include dinner or guided marsh walks. Regular scenic trips are offered Tuesday–Sunday late May–October and Mondays in July and August. Dinner trains featuring deluxe five-course meals are available at additional cost (adults only, $66) and begin on weekends in April, expand to Thursday–Saturday late-May–September, and then return to weekend operation through New Year's Eve. Trains depart from the downtown railroad station next to the Hyannis Transportation Center bus terminal and the Storyland miniature golf course.

Accommodations

Hyannis is first and foremost a motel town. The half-dozen establishments sharing the waterfront district can legitimately claim to be within walking distance of the beach, but the other 30 or so are more likely to offer views of asphalt than water. Most of the national chains found on the Cape are here in Hyannis as well, generally along mall-lined Rte. 132.

Much more affordable (and within walking distance of Main Street restaurants, shops, and all forms of local transportation, including bike rentals on the premises) is the very modest **Cascade Motor Lodge** (201 Main St., 508/775-9717, www.cascademotorlodge .com, $78–165 d, open year-round), opposite the train station.

A handful of no-frills B&Bs and guesthouses are found a little under a mile south of the downtown business district, within the residential neighborhood a few hundred yards from Sea Street Beach. **Sea Beach Inn** (388 Sea St., 508/775-4612, www.capecodtravel .com, May–mid-Oct., $90–130) is a prime example: very simple rooms with plain white bedcovers, floral wallpaper, no TVs or phones, window air-conditioning units, and common rooms that may evoke memories of grandma's house. Families are welcome (although no cribs are available), and a continental breakfast is included. An efficiency is available, although it's usually booked six months in advance.

Across the street, the **Sea Breeze Inn** (397 Sea St., 508/771-7213, www.seabreezeinn .com, year-round, $98–150 d) provides similar accommodations with a few more amenities—small TVs, radios, phones, canopy beds, all private baths—*lots* more frilly fabrics and doilies, and slightly less of a personal touch. Rates top out at $98–150 for doubles June–early September, $75–115 in the off season.

For more of a splurge, look to the village of Centerville and the luxurious ◖ **Fernbrook** (481 Main St., 508/775-4334, www.fern brookinn.com, May–Oct., $150–185). This grand, shingle-style mansion was built in 1881 by a local businessman who became Boston's leading restaurateur. Befitting a stately home with its own ballroom and 50-foot outdoor lap pool, most of the guest rooms are quite spacious, with a tasteful blend of modern amenities and just enough Victoriana to evoke the gracious comfort of summering near the seaside during the Gilded Age. Rates include a full breakfast.

A more down-home option is found in Hyannisport at **The Simmons Homestead Inn** (288 Scudder Ave., 508/778-4999 or 800/637-1649, www.simmonshomesteadinn .com, year-round, $200–260 mid-May–Oct.,

20 percent lower in the off-season), an 1820 sea captain's mansion converted into a rambling country inn. Bill the innkeeper doesn't stand for formality, so the decor won't intimidate you with matchless antiques and accessories placed *just so*. Comfort is paramount, from the evening wine to the morning's full breakfast. Free bicycles are available, and you can practice your pool-hustling moves in the billiard room when the weather is inclement. A couple of rooms have fireplaces—needless to say, they're the first to be booked in the off-season.

Iyannough Road (eye-ANN-oh), also known as Rte. 132 at one end and Rte. 28 at the other, is a veritable hotel highway entering Hyannis. Among the major chains or their nearly identical imitators are these, listed in driving order: From U.S. 6, exit 6, via Rte. 132 and Rte. 28 to Main Street, there's the **Comfort Inn** (1470 Iyannough Rd. [Rte. 132] opposite Hyannis Chamber of Commerce, 508/771-4804 or 800/228-5150, www.comfortinn-hyannis.com, $150–170 d), which is pet-friendly and offers a free continental breakfast, indoor swimming pool, and sauna.

Hyannis Days Inn (867 Iyannough Rd. [Rte. 132] next to Barnes & Noble and across from Borders Books & Music, 508/771-6100 or 800/329-7466, www.hyannisdaysinn.com, closed Dec.–mid-Feb., $120–200 d) offers free continental breakfast, indoor and outdoor swimming pools, a sauna, and exercise facilities.

Courtyard by Marriott (707 Iyannough Rd. [Rte. 132] at the south end of Cape Cod Mall, 508/775-6600 or 800/321-2211, www .marriott.com, $230–250 d) has a breakfast café and outdoor swimming pool.

Hyannis Motel/Budget Host Inn (614 Iyannough Rd. [Rte. 132] opposite Bed, Bath & Beyond, 508/775-8910 or 800/322-3354, www.budgethostinnhyannis.com, $65–120) has an outdoor swimming pool.

Radisson Hotel & Conference Center (287 Iyannough Rd. [Rte. 28], 508/771-1700 or 800/771-7200, www.radisson.com, $170–250 d) is pet-friendly, has an outdoor swimming pool, Sleep Number beds, and a fitness center.

From the Yarmouth side of the town line to the west end of Main Street, there's the **Super 8 Motel** (36 East Main St. [Rte. 28], 508/775-0962 or 800/800-8000, $90–140 d) that has an outdoor swimming pool.

Econo Lodge (59 East Main St. [Rte. 28], 508/771-0699 or 800/553-2666, www.econolodge.com, $100–160 d) is pet-friendly and has indoor swimming pool.

The **Cape Cod Inn** (447 Main St., 508/775-3000, $90–160 d) has a restaurant and indoor swimming pool.

Food

American diner-style fare may be abundant in these parts, but not all vendors of the stuff are equal. If you want to rub elbows over breakfast with residents rather than day-trippers, head up-Cape to Marstons Mills, one of the rural Barnstable villages about eight miles west of downtown Hyannis. There, you'll find the **Mills Restaurant** (149 Cotuit Rd., 508/428-9814, 7 A.M.–2 P.M. breakfast all day and lunch after 11:30 A.M. Mon.–Fri.; 7 A.M.–1 P.M. Sat.–Sun. breakfast only; $6–10), on Rte. 149 next to the Mobil station, an extremely popular place known for its solid country breakfasts (including a couple of vegetarian omelet choices), weekend brunches, and great prices. Another safe bet is is **Persy's Place** (508/447-6633, 7 A.M.–3 P.M. daily year-round, $7–16), part of a small regional chain of eateries known for their prodigious breakfast menus. A head-spinning number of pancake options, locally traditional cornmeal johnnycakes, at least four daily quiches, chipped beef on toast, *finnan haddie* (smoked haddock) for homesick Scots, omelets with or without seafood, and even catfish or trout—not to mention all manner of baked goods—guarantees there's no excuse for leaving hungry.

You can get pizza at the lighter-fare back room of the **Roadhouse Café** (488 South St., 508/775-2386, www.roadhousecafe.com, 4 P.M.–9 P.M. Sun.–Thurs., 4 P.M.–10 P.M. Fri.–Sat. year-round, $16–37), too, but most folks

wisely choose to sit up front, amid the nautical tchotchkes, and order lobster or steak. At the **Black Cat Tavern** (165 Ocean St., 508/778-1233, 11:30 A.M.–9:30 P.M. daily Mar.–Dec., closed Jan.–Feb., $19–32) across the street from the Hy-Line ferry landing, red-meat eaters seeking relief from the relentless barrage of fried seafood can also put an end to their "we're not in Kansas City anymore, Toto" lament with a thick slab of prime rib beneath the crew-racing paraphernalia decorations. Of course, seafood lovers won't go unrewarded. You can also belly up to the bar and have a simple burger or bowl of chowder while jawing with the friendly barkeep over a decent microbrew.

Though Cape Cod isn't known for multicultural dining, Hyannis is at the vanguard of what ethnic variety does exist. One example is the **Thai House Restaurant** (304 Main St., 508/862-1616, 11 A.M.–9:30 P.M. Mon.–Sat., 4–9 P.M. Sun., $8–11), next to the needle-spired Federated Church. Curries, seafood (including crispy whole fish), spicy noodle and rice dishes, and plenty of vegetarian selections are on the menu. Traditional rodizio is on the menu at **Brazilian Grill** (680 Main St., 508/771-0109, 11:30 A.M.–10 P.M. Sun.–Fri., 4–10:30 P.M. Sat. year-round, $18–26 all-inclusive), where waiters carve skewer after skewer of beef, pork, and sausage at your table.

For the best of both worlds, pop into **HannaH's Fusion Bistro** (615 Main St., 508/778-5565, www.hannahsbistro.com, 5–10 P.M. Sun.–Thurs., noon–10 P.M. Fri.–Sat., year-round) a family restaurant named after the owners' daughter. Executive chef Binh Phu brings a spicy panache to sesame-crusted ahi tuna and pan-seared scallops. But trained at fine New England restaurants for many years, he is just as skilled in mixing classic French and contemporary American dishes like prawn carbonara with crisp peas, smoky bacon, and sharp béchamel sauce. Entrées are served in a stylish but friendly bistro ambience.

Ferry from Hyannis to Nantucket

As the year-round Mid-Cape gateway to the island of Nantucket, Hyannis Harbor bustles with the horn-blasting boats of **Hy-Line Cruises** (508/778-2600, www.hy-linecruises.com), and the **Steamship Authority** (508/477-8600, www.steamshipauthority.com). If you'll be taking the bus to Hyannis, intending to connect straight to an outbound ferry, you can save yourself a wait in line by purchasing your ferry ticket when you pay your bus fare. Drivers will notice that all directional signage avoids mentioning either company's name. If you want the Hy-Line, follow signs to the Ocean Street docks; for Steamship Authority, follow signs to South Street. If you have time to kill, next to no luggage (or can drop someone off to watch it), and don't mind walking a fair piece, the cheapest in-town parking is east of the Steamship dock. Don't let the authoritative, red-flag-waving guys with the too-cool shades dupe you into turning into the super-expensive lots immediately opposite the Hy-Line passenger drop, as you can save several bucks a day (and be just as close to the ferry) by simply taking the next left. Free parking—that's right, totally free—is available from late June–mid-September in signposted visitor lots at the Cape Cod Community College, just off Rte. 6 exit 6, and across the road in the shopping plaza with the McDonald's.

Connecting bus service to both ferry docks is provided via the Villager route of the **Cape Cod Regional Transit Authority** (800/352-7155, www.capecodtransit.org, $2 adults, $1 seniors), which runs every 20 minutes throughout the day. A third satellite parking facility is located off Rte. 28/132 closer to the edge of downtown; count on signage at exit 6 to direct you to the nearest empty lot.

Both ferry companies offer a choice between fast and expensive or slow and cheap ferries to Nantucket, while Hy-Line adds a seasonal vessel to Martha's Vineyard.

BARNSTABLE TO BREWSTER
◖ Old King's Highway

Although recent decades have inundated Cape Cod with ever-increasing numbers of summer residents and retirees whose housing and shopping needs are making much of the Cape

---

STONES AND CONES

Start your eastward tour of the Old King's Highway (now Rte. 6A) in West Barnstable – or farther west – and you'll catch one of the oddest business pairings on the Cape: ice cream and gravestones. There, at the Rte. 6A junction with Rte. 149 (Exit 5 from U.S. 6), stands the **Maki Monument Co.**, cheek-to-cheek with **Old Fashioned Ice Cream & Soft Serve** (508/362-9299, 11 A.M.-10 P.M. daily, May–Sept.). The Maki family has been in the cemetery business since the 1920s; the ice cream is the latest – and most successful – of the various attempts made over the years at diversification.

---

indistinguishable from the average American suburb or strip mall, there are still a few places that capture the look and feel of yesteryear—or of two centuries ago. The Mid-Cape portion of Old King's Highway, now Rte. 6A passes through a number of these throwbacks, winding between one after another of the historic villages along the protected shores of Cape Cod Bay: West Barnstable, Barnstable Village, Cummaquid, Yarmouthport, Dennis, East Dennis, and Brewster. Shingle-sided saltbox or steep-roofed Cape houses, white clapboard churches, and fancy Federal or Greek Revival shipmasters' mansions abound—as do antiques shops, B&Bs, art galleries, pottery studios, and—surprise!—more antiques shops. Unfortunately, traffic is so heavy and fast most of the year that you won't have time to dawdle over the roadside views unless you stop and park. But the route isn't conducive to strolling pedestrians or leisure cyclists, either, as it's generally narrow and buildings abut it quite closely. So, ignore that SUV trying to climb into your back seat and just take the road at your own speed; otherwise, you'll have to take it on faith that the stuff you can glimpse through your windows is well worth a longer look.

You'll notice that each town has a historical house or museum vying for your attention along Rte. 6A, most of which suggest donations rather than charge admission. The volunteers who generally staff these places are often the very reason to stop and pay a visit; their knowledge can breathe life into otherwise rather desiccated or narrow subject matter. Visiting local historical societies is also one of the best ways to find someone who speaks with a genuine Cape Cod accent.

Edward Gorey House

Illustrator and author Edward Gorey lived beside the Old King's Highway in Yarmouthport for 14 years until his death in 2000; now his life and art are the subject of an appropriately idiosyncratic museum. Located in a traditionally gray-shingled Cape house near the town common, the Edward Gorey House (8 Strawberry Ln., 508/362-3909, www.edwardgoreyhouse .org; 11 A.M.–4 P.M. Thurs.–Sat., noon–4 Sun. mid-Apr.–June; 11 A.M.–4 P.M. Wed.–Sat., noon–4 Sun. July–Sept.; 11 A.M.–4 P.M. Fri.–

Sat., noon–4 P.M. Sun. Oct.–Dec.; $5 adults, $3 students and seniors, $2 children 6–12, children under 6 free) has both a permanent biographical exhibit—from his first baby shoes to his last sneakers and significant steps in between—and twice-yearly displays of original art, first editions of his books, and other treasures drawn from Gorey's prolific career. The museum also sells those of his books that remain in print. One of Gorey's most memorable works, *The Doubtful Guest,* is reproduced in topiary in the backyard.

Bass Hole Boardwalk and Scargo Tower

This stretch of road has the added distinction of passing by two of the more interesting places to obtain a panoramic view of the Cape. Heading east, the first is a water-level vantage point at the long Bass Hole boardwalk out over Yarmouth's bayside tidal marsh. This favorite sunset viewing spot among Mid-Cape residents is two miles north of Rte. 6A at the end of Center Street; beside it is Gray's Beach,

the one-of-a-kind Edward Gorey House

so small as to be free of charge even in high season. Farther east in Dennis is Scargo Tower, a simple stone observation tower built high atop the hill overlooking its namesake lake; turn south at the village green on Old Bass River Road, then take the next left on Scargo Hill Road and watch for the sign.

Cape Cod Museum of Natural History

Well signed on an otherwise undeveloped stretch of Rte. 6A a few hundred yards west of Paine Creek Road in West Brewster is the Cape Cod Museum of Natural History (869 Main St. [Rte. 6A], 508/896-3867, www.ccmnh.org, 9:30 A.M.–4 P.M. daily June–Sept., noon–4 P.M. Wed.–Sun. Oct.–Dec. and Feb.–Mar., closed Jan., $8 adults, $7 seniors, $3.50 children 3–12, children under 3 free). It has two floors of aquariums showcasing aquatic flora and fauna of the local waters (salt and fresh), plus a pair of interpretive trails behind the museum offering views of a salt marsh, cranberry bog, and beech grove.

Numerous items cater specifically to kids, from the live, glass-enclosed beehive to the big, rocking horse–like whale vertebrae; adults, meanwhile, should check out the museum's nature trips, scheduled throughout summer and fall. Day trips (and rustic overnights) to Monomoy Island's National Wildlife Refuge and guided full- or half-day canoe trips are among the various options; all require preregistration.

Beaches
SANDY NECK

On Cape Cod Bay by the Sandwich-Barnstable town line is the largest salt marsh ecosystem north of Chesapeake Bay and its accompanying six-mile beachfront of creeping barrier dunes. Though access to Sandy Neck isn't cheap (nonresident parking is $10 late June through early September), a visit pays many dividends: hours of potential walking along the shore, with its wrack line of tide-borne curiosities and its busy population of shorebirds; coyote tracks in the arid swale between the parallel formation of protective dunes, whose accreting sands, aug-

mented by eroded material from the western rim of Cape Cod Bay, are slowly closing off Barnstable Harbor; or the sight of tree swallows swooping through the Great Marsh behind the dunes, snapping insects out of the air (plenty of leftovers remain, however, so bring repellent). Early-summer visitors may also see the carefully monitored nests of the endangered piping plovers and least terns, two tentative but regular visitors to the Cape's shores. To reach Sandy Neck from Rte. 6A, turn north on Sandy Neck Road in East Sandwich, between the Sandy Neck Motel and the Sandy Neck Restaurant, and proceed to the ranger station and parking lot at the end.

OTHER BEACHES

Aside from those in Sandy Neck, the nicest beaches in this part of the Cape are in Dennis: **Mayflower Beach,** at the end of Beach Street; adjacent **Chapin Memorial Beach** (turn left on Taunton Ave. near the end of Beach St.); and **Corporation Beach,** at the end of Corporation Road. The first and last have concession stands in July and August, and Mayflower has seasonal restrooms.

Hiking and Biking

The town of Barnstable has much more to offer than austere coastline and spongy peat mats in tidal wetlands. Inland of Barnstable Harbor are several municipal conservation properties encompassing portions of the glacially formed moraine underlying U.S. 6. The hilly upland woods are choice spots for hiking on days too cool for the beach. You can also leave the crowds behind and find out how dry and hot a pitch pine forest can get in summer. The largest is the 1,100-acre **West Barnstable Conservation Area,** bounded by U.S. 6, Rte. 149, a small airport, and the town of Sandwich; look for parking off Rte. 149 south of U.S. 6 exit 5, on Popple Bottom Road nearly opposite the Olde Barnstable Fairgrounds golf course. (Popple is an old colloquialism for poplar trees.) Two smaller parcels sandwich the Mid-Cape Highway from beside Phinneys Lane, slightly east of Exit 6 and due south of the one stoplight on Rte. 6A in Barnstable: **Old Jail Lane Conservation Area,** with parking beside the eponymous access road on the north side of U.S. 6, and **Hathaways Pond,** a popular freshwater swimming beach on U.S. 6's south side ($5 parking fee in summer). All three welcome hikers as well as mountain bikers, and feature the kind of terrain that justifies having hiking books or a mountain bike. Since there are no rental shops in the immediate vicinity, bicyclists have the choice of tacking on a road ride or renting a car rack from down-Cape's seasonal **Idle Times Bike Shop,** on Rte. 6A two miles west of the entrance to Nickerson State Park in Orleans (29 Main St., 508/240-1122, www.idletimesbikeshop.com); call to confirm the availability of those racks. **Art's Bike Shop** (508/563-7379 or 800/563-7379, www.arts bikeshop.com, 8 A.M.–5 P.M. Mon.–Sat. year-round, 11 A.M.–4 P.M. Sun. in season), at 91 County Road in North Falmouth, also has car racks for their rental customers.

Excellent computer-generated and GPS-tested trail maps and guides to these and six other town conservation properties are available for download from the website of the Barnstable Conservation Commission (200 Main St., Hyannis, 508/862-4093, http://town. barnstable.ma.us/conservation/trailguides).

Whale-Watching

The only whale-watching excursions available between Plymouth and Provincetown are the **Hyannis Whale Watcher Cruises** (Barnstable Harbor, 508/362-6088 or 888/942-5392, www.whales.net, daily May–Oct., $45 adults, $40 seniors, $26 children 4–12, children under 4 free), off Rte. 6A in Barnstable Village. The company's speedy boat departs the Millway Marine boatyard for Stellwagen Bank off the tip of Cape Cod in search of Stellwagen's most frequently sighted species: the finback, blue, sei, humpback, and North Atlantic right whale, all of which are endangered (as is the minke whale, a seasonal visitor). Excursions are scheduled according to ocean tides and can change from day to day. Reservations for the four-hour outings are advised.

Accommodations

Most of the score of small inns and B&Bs in this area are readily visible to passing motorists along Rte. 6A between Rte. 132 in Barnstable and Union Street on the east side of neighboring Yarmouthport. No two are alike, although the prevailing theme is colonial rather than Victorian. If you want a nice romantic B&B or comfortable inn within a block of a beach, head to the south shore on the other side of Rte. 28 (but expect to pay at least half again as much as you would here).

A good example of what you'll find in this area is **The Acworth Inn** (4352 Main St., 508/362-3330 or 800/362-6363, www .acworthinn.com, open year-round, $149–169 d May–Oct.), a mid-19th-century home in the Barnstable village of Cummaquid. Light-filled rooms feature antiques and painted furniture; a few have whirlpool baths, and there's a separate fireplace-equipped suite in the carriage house. Full breakfast, too, and you couldn't ask for more congenial hosts, who are quite willing to share their knowledge and admiration of the area. A few miles away in West Barnstable is **Honeysuckle Hill Bed & Breakfast** (591 Old King's Hwy., 866/444-5522 or 508/362-8419, www.honeysucklehill.com, $179–194 d May–Oct., $30 less off season) an 1810 cottage with a handful of rooms. Innkeepers here aim to make guests feel relaxed and comfortable enough to "come to breakfast in your slippers," as Bill puts it. Queen feather beds, beach towels and umbrellas, and a full breakfast—possibly featuring fresh raspberries from their garden in summer—are all standard.

Midway between these two, in Barnstable Village, is ◖ **Beechwood** (2839 Main St., 508/362-6618, www.beechwoodinn.com, year-round), a lovingly restored Queen Anne Victorian set back from the highway behind the only weeping beech tree on Rte. 6A. The antique-filled interior runs from rare Civil War–era cottage furniture to pieces by Arts and Crafts notable Charles Eastlake. The whole effect is romantic enough that an average of three wedding proposals per year occur here. There's also said to be a mischievous resident ghost (she mostly loosens lightbulbs); some guests claim to have even chatted with her. Bicycles, beach chairs, and beach towels are all made available for guests (there are seven beaches within a five-mile radius) along with full three-course breakfasts—stay for a month and you still won't exhaust the chef's repertoire, though you'd certainly have a fine time trying). All this for $175–199 d mid-May–October, depending on the room; during the off-season, subtract about $50 (slightly less for the rooms with gas fireplaces).

In the center of Yarmouthport you can't miss the ((**Liberty Hill Inn** (77 Main St., 508/362-3976 or 800/821-3977, www.liberty hillinn.com, year-round, $140–230 d June–mid-Oct.), a distinctive 1825 Greek Revival estate atop a low hill behind the broad sloping lawn at the corner of Willow Street and Rte. 6A. Originally built by a prominent local shipwright, it's the epitome of a classic New England inn—stately white clapboard, black shutters, and wrap-around porch with wooden rocking chairs on the outside, and hardwood floors, high ceilings, and a tasteful collection of period furnishings on the inside. The bright sunlit rooms are furnished for comfort, with thoughtful attention to real traveling needs (you'll never have to leave your luggage all over the floor) and every modern amenity you would expect of a top-rated inn. Just as importantly, the innkeepers' hospitality is second to none, which explains why so many returning guests wouldn't dream of staying anywhere else. And if you pick where you stay for the breakfast they serve, look no farther: Kris's outstanding multi-course repasts and fresh-baked afternoon cookies will ensure your stay here is a memorable one.

Food

For just a snack, step into **Hallet's** (139 Main St., Yarmouthport, 508/362-3362, http://hallets.net), an 1889 pharmacy-turned-ice-cream-parlor. The apothecary cabinet along the wall is a real beauty, with Latin names inscribed on the brass drawer pulls, and the malted frappes are darn good, too. It's open spring through December, with hours varying according to the season and the owner's whim.

A few doors from Hallet's is the Japanese restaurant **Inaho** (157 Main St. [Rte. 6A], 508/362-5522, www.inahocapecod.com, 4:30–10 P.M. Mon.–Sat. year-round, $14–27), occupying the ground floor of a historic house. Perhaps no restaurant on the Cape shows off the fresh bounty of the local waters like this small establishment, whose sushi, tempura, and whole-fish dishes are served in the welcoming atmosphere of a private home. The flourless chocolate cake is one of the best desserts in the region, too—light and not too sweet.

For more traditional New England seafood, try **Mattakeese Wharf** (271 Mill Way, Barnstable, 508/362-4511, 11:30 A.M.–8:30 P.M., May–mid-Oct., $19–32), on Barnstable Harbor; turn at Rte. 6A's traffic light east of Barnstable Village. The atmosphere may be as casual as at a mall restaurant, but no mall has such a fine portside location, and few have fish of this quality. The preparations won't knock your socks off, but the dishes of no-nonsense seafood, pastas, meat, and poultry are more than competent. Enjoying bouillabaisse on the covered deck while watching the small marina in late evening's golden light is the quintessential way to end a Cape summer afternoon. Not that foul weather should be any deterrent—moody gray becomes the harbor as much as brilliant sun, and the porch seating areas can be enclosed, if necessary.

Sitting in a wooded stretch of Rte. 6A between the Barnstable town line and Willow Street (the access point to U.S. 6 Exit 7) is ((**Abbicci** (43 Main St. [Rte. 6A], Yarmouthport, 508/362-3501, www.abbicci.com, 4–10 P.M. daily, noon–3 P.M. Mon. and Fri.–Sat., 11 A.M.–3 P.M. Sun., year-round, $27–45), whose yellow 18th-century colonial facade belies the sleek, contemporary northern Italian restaurant within. With its cosmopolitan atmosphere and exceptional cuisine, this place is deservedly counted as one of the best dining spots along Rte. 6A. Jars of extra virgin olive oil sit on every table; the crusty white house bread is served with a head of roasted garlic. The dessert list is about as long as the main menu, and the outstanding wine list is adjusted a couple times a week with uncommon selections from California, Italy, and France, a dozen of which are served by the glass. In a nice gesture to neighbors and regulars, early-bird suppers (actually three-course prix fixe dinners) are also offered at a very reasonable price. Reservations, needless to say, are all but essential much of the year.

Reservations would be essential for **Brewster Fish House** (2208 Main St. [Rte. 6A], Brewster, 508/896-7867, 11:30 A.M.– 9:30 P.M. daily year-round, $19–29) as well— if they took them. But since they don't, your only hope is to show up early (by 5:30 at least) to snag one of the 30-some tables at this unassuming Brewster establishment. Once you snag a seat, however, you can sit back and relax with some of the best seafood on the Cape. The restaurant eschews the same old fried fish and lobster combos that typify so much of Cape "cuisine" to offer the freshest fish in simple preparations that bring out, rather than obscure, the fishes' flavors. If the bluefish are jumping, don't hesitate.

Another restaurant that is slowly dragging the Cape into the 21st century culinary light is **C Gracie's Table** (800 Main St. [Rte. 6A], Dennis, 508/385-5600, www.gracies tablecapecod.com, 5–9:30 P.M. Wed.–Mon., May–Sept., call for hours in the off-season, $18–30), an authentic Spanish restaurant featuring tapas and "petite entrées" from the Basque region of Northwestern Spain and Southwestern France. It features both traditional tapas items such as *patatas bravas* (fried potatoes in spicy sauce) and *bacalao* (salt cod), with more unexpected offerings—pork adobo and frog's legs provencal. Situated in Dennis's arts complex, a stone's throw from the Cape Cod Playhouse, Cape Cod Cinema, and Cape Cod Art Museum, it's the perfect place to catch a bite and a glass of wine before or after the show.

The Outer Cape

Most of the human settlement of the Outer Cape, right up to this century, has come from its proximity to excellent fishing grounds. (The Cape's name, of course, reflects this.) Native Americans spent summers fishing and gathering shellfish, 15th- and 16th-century European fishing vessels put ashore to dry fish and engage in minor trade, and post-*Mayflower* colonists built a fishing industry from these exposed shores. But what the sea giveth, it can also taketh away—like a video on fast forward, the effects of wind, tide, and erosion are probably more visible on the Outer Cape than anywhere else along the Massachusetts coast, not only from year to year, but sometimes from day to day. The barrier beaches and backshore cliffs that bear the brunt of this process comprise the region's crown of natural wonders: the 44,000-acre Cape Cod National Seashore, extending the length and sometimes the breadth of the Outer Cape. Small museums and historic sights are peppered throughout the area, too. Most of the former are best characterized as houses of memory—idiosyncratic collections of commonplace objects now rendered rare or unusual by sheer passage of time. Other sights are relics of some long-vanished skill or town specialty, such as translating Morse code or coopering barrels. Little effort is made at giving context, academic or otherwise, but jumble-shop browsers will feel particularly at home. Generally, these local spots are all more rewarding when stumbled upon by accident rather than intent.

CHATHAM

Situated at Cape Cod's "elbow," Chatham presides over the hazardous waters whose "dangerous shoulds and roring breakers" sent the *Mayflower* scurrying for the protection of

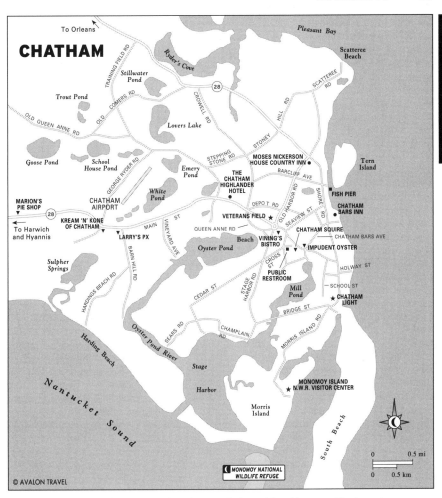

CHATHAM

Provincetown harbor, according to her chronicler William Bradford. Now that the Cape's economy has shifted from harvesting cod and trading with Cathay to marketing quaintness, this old sea captains' town of about 6,500 year-round residents has become one of the Cape's best gifts to the tourist trade, with clapboard mansions, boutiques, art galleries, summer concerts in the old bandstand, and historic lighthouses. Nor does it shut down and turn out the lights when the tourists go home. But while it's one of the Cape's most fashionable addresses, Chatham is even coveted by the sea itself; unfortunately for oceanfront homeowners, negotiating with Poseidon is an extremely one-sided deal. Since the protective outer barrier beach was breached in a 1987 winter storm, the town's coastline has been more dramatically altered than perhaps anywhere else on the Cape; see the results for yourself at the vast South Beach, in front of the Coast Guard station and lighthouse on Shore Road, which once was separated from town by the harbor.

◖ Monomoy National Wildlife Refuge

Monomoy Island (actually two separate islands) used to be a peninsula connected to town, as South Beach is now, with bus service down to the lighthouse station at its tip. A 1958 storm breached the sandy strand, and today the only residents of this 2,700-acre National Wildlife Refuge are birds, a winter colony of harbor seals, and several hundred gray seals, who have been year-round residents since 1991. Like some tourists, these seals seem to have liked what they saw, and not only came to stay, but told a lot of their friends—most of whom seem to be Canadian bachelors from Nova Scotia's Sable Island, home to 90 percent of North America's gray seals. Needless to say, Monomoy is great bird-watching territory—two-thirds of all avian species recorded in Massachusetts have been sighted here—and good for strolls on the beach without stepping over thousands of sunbathers.

The refuge's **headquarters and visitors center** (508/945-0594, http://monomoy.fws.gov) are located on Morris Island, south of Chatham Lighthouse and Coast Guard Station; follow Morris Island Road until you see the refuge entrance sign. Open 8 A.M.–4 P.M. daily from late May through Labor Day, and weekdays off season (staff availability permitting), the one-room center offers displays about the natural forces that influence the refuge, interpretive brochures for the short trail looping along the shoreline marsh behind the building, and information sheets on some of the significant wildlife protected here. You can also pick up an annotated bird-watcher's list of nearly 300 species sighted on Monomoy.

As a property of the U.S. Fish and Wildlife Service, the islands are open to the public so long as you observe certain guidelines with respect to their ecology and inhabitants. Massachusetts Audubon's Wellfleet Bay Wildlife Sanctuary (508/349-2615, www.massaudubon.org) offers trips to North Monomoy ($35) and South Monomoy ($70). Simple but informative wildlife-watching cruises around the refuge are offered by **Monomoy Island Excursions** (508/430-7772, www.nantucketislandferry.com, $35 adults, $30 children 4–12), departing from Saquatucket Harbor in Harwichport. Their ticket office on Main Street (Rte. 28) is shared with the Nantucket Island Ferry.

If you don't have your own boat and don't wish to tramp about with a naturalist guide and company, you can hire someone to ferry you across, or even rent a boat of your own. For transit to the beaches of North Monomoy, Keith Lincoln's **Monomoy Island Ferry** (508/945-5450, $20 adults, $15 children 15 and under), departs three times daily in summer (weekends in spring and fall) from the beach below the refuge headquarters on Morris Island Road. Simply head down and look for the red shuttle van to check in and get tickets. Passage takes less than 10 minutes. He also offers 90-minute seal-watching trips to the far tip of Chatham's South Beach in season ($32 adults, $28 children 15 and under). Located about a half-mile south of the Chatham Lighthouse, **Outermost Harbor Marine** (83 Seagull Rd., 508/945-2030, www.outermostharbor.com, $15) also operates a shuttle to North Monomoy ($20 all ages) on demand daily late May through early September, and 8 A.M. and noon Monday–Saturday spring and fall. They also run a shuttle for bathers, fishermen, and seal watchers to South Beach ($20 adults, $10 children 12 and under) and can give referrals to boats in the marina that conduct private fishing charters.

A final note: Between early June and the last full moon in August, the north island in particular is overrun by greenhead horse flies, whose voracious appetites are not to be underestimated. Take all the usual precautions—covering every inch of exposed skin with clothing and bug repellent, for example—but recognize that no matter what you do, you're likely to meet that one cloud of greenheads who lap up DEET like slugs do beer.

Accommodations

Quaintness enhances the price of lodgings everywhere on the Cape, and Chatham is no exception. The dozen small inns and B&Bs within a reasonable stroll of downtown almost all charge well over $150 for a double room in summer, though before mid-June or after Labor Day rates on some of the larger properties dips under $100. For example, **The Chatham Highlander Motel** (946 Main St., 508/945-9038 or 877/945-9038, www .chathamhighlander.com, Apr.–early Dec.), a family-friendly motel on Rte. 28 west of the rotary, has double rooms for $89–129 in the pre- and post-season shoulder months. Even during the height of summer, double rooms are $159–209 (kids $10 extra). There's an outdoor pool, the children's beach at Oyster Pond is nearby, it's an easy half-mile up the sidewalk to Main Street, there are breakfast cafés within walking distance, and the British-expatriate owners, Mike and Pauline, are warm and friendly hosts (whose ties to the U.K. explain the electric kettles). Two efficiency units are available, too, for stays of five nights or more.

Another country inn with spacious, comfortable rooms and full breakfasts is the **Moses Nickerson House** (364 Old Harbor Rd., 508/945-5859 or 800/628-6972, www .mosesnickersonhouse.com, year-round), a sprawling 19th-century whaling captain's mansion well under a mile from downtown and within walking distance of the Fish Pier on the harbor. Rates are $209–259 late May–October, $179–219 during shoulder season, and $119–169 the rest of the year (the two rooms with gas fireplaces are, of course, at the high end of that off-season range). The decor runs from the Oriental carpet, blue-velvet upholstery, and hand-painted antiques of the "regal" room opening out onto the front porch through variations on country, Victorian, and painted-wicker summer cottage styles. Owners Linda and George make innkeeping look like fun, too, which adds to the pleasure of any stay here.

Arguably the premiere resort on all of Cape Cod, ◖ **Chatham Bars Inn** (Shore Road, Chatham, 508/945-0096, www.chathambars inn.com, $400–755 d), pulls out all the stops on subdued luxury. It's one of the area's most lauded—and with a full-service spa, a restaurant serving food that's nothing short of impeccable, and a breezy spot on gorgeous Pleasant Bay, it's easy to see why.

The **Chatham Chamber of Commerce** (www.chathaminfo.com) can give you the skinny on what else is available—and usually even has an idea about who has last-minute availability; visit their seasonal information booth next to Chatham Town Hall at 533 Main Street or their year-round visitors center at 2377 Main Street (10 A.M.–5 P.M. Mon.–Sat. noon–3 P.M. Sun., June–mid-Oct.; 10 A.M.–2 P.M. Mon.–Fri., closed Sat.–Sun., mid-Oct.–Dec.; closed Jan.–May), or call 508/945-5199 or 800/715-5567.

Food

If you aren't staying in a B&B and need an eye-opening meal, you could grab some overpriced croissants from one of the gourmet bakeries in the center of town, or you could drive west on Rte. 28 to **Larry's PX** (1591 Main St., 508/945-3964, 5 A.M.–3 P.M. mid-June–early Sept., 6 A.M.–2 P.M. early Sept.–mid-June, $3–13) in West Chatham's Ship Ahoy plaza, and join the local fishermen over an early breakfast. If it's lunchtime or later, consider a visit to that king of the fried clam, **Kream 'N' Kone of Chatham** (1653 Main St., West Chatham, 508/945-3308, "market" prices), up the road. This signature Cape dish may have been born in Essex, on Boston's North Shore, but it tastes as if it's achieved nirvana in the fryers of this small fast-food joint across from the A&P supermarket. The place is open April–October, or as long as the customers keep coming.

For a sweet finish, head farther west to **Marion's Pie Shop** (2022 Main St., 508/432-9439, www.marionspieshop.com, 8 A.M.–6 P.M. Mon.–Sat., 8 A.M.–5 P.M. Sun., late May–early Sept.; 8 A.M.–5 P.M. Tues.–Sat., 8 A.M.–4 P.M. Sun., early Sept.–late May), in South Chatham. Fruit pies, pecan pies, and lemon meringue pies are among the offerings (all for takeout only), from family size down to mini two-person portions. (If you have a kitchen at your disposal, Marion's also serves heat-and-serve quiches, casseroles, and savory meat pies.) To say the lemon meringue is Massachusetts's best is awfully faint praise given the lack of competition, so let's be more specific: The crust is perfectly crisp and flaky; the filling has a nice custardy texture, not too sweet; and the meringue is lofty enough to reach from your chin to your nose. In sum, it's as good a commercial variety as exists outside of the Midwestern Pie Belt.

The menu at **€ The Chatham Squire** (487 Main St., 508/945-0945, http://thesquire.com, 11:30 A.M.–10 P.M. Mon.–Thurs., 11:30 A.M.–10:30 P.M. Fri., noon–10:30 P.M. Sat., noon–10 P.M. Sun., open year-round, closes 30 minutes earlier mid-Oct.–mid-May, $11–20) isn't as fancy as some other local restaurants, but its village tavern atmosphere enhances any meal. Selections include center-cut sirloins, linguine with clams, shrimp scampi, and chicken piccata. The Squire has a fine raw bar for oysters and other shellfish, and it makes an earnest effort at offering attractive vegetarian selections.

Another all-season option is **The Impudent Oyster** (15 Chatham Bars Ave., 508/945-3545, 11:30 A.M.–1 A.M. daily, year-round, $18–34), steps off Main Street near the bandstand. This creatively named place is sure to be recommended by your innkeeper or B&B host, which is partly why dinner reservations are absolutely mandatory throughout high season. The seafood selection is quite good, portions are more than generous, and the soothing classical music, sable-hued wood, and white linen makes for a delightful setting. Whether all this will compensate for the iceberg salads, plain presentation, and bread pudding–textured pies is up to you; the popular vote, though, is a resounding yes.

For a place that prefers preparing its fresh fish and fine meats on a wood grill rather than in a sauté pan, and for herb-infused reductions instead of rich cream sauces, look for **Vining's Bistro** (595 Main St., Chatham, 508/945-5033, 5:30–9 P.M. Sun.–Thurs., 5:30–10 P.M. Fri.–Sat., Apr.–Dec., $17–30), on the second floor of a small shopping arcade near the Rte. 28 rotary. If the contemporary decor doesn't assure you that this isn't your father's Cape Cod restaurant, the multi-

a leisurely afternoon in Chatham

ethnic influences and attention to vegetables certainly will.

ORLEANS AND EASTHAM

Two of the smallest towns on the peninsula, Orleans and Eastham (pronounce both syllables; it's not "East'm"), share the pivot point in the Outer Cape, where the tributaries of Cape Cod Bay and the Atlantic come within half a mile of each other and all the major up-Cape highways merge into the single strand of U.S. 6. Both towns were once united with their neighbors in a much larger township named after the native Nauset Indians, one of several bands residing around inlets on the Cape's back shore. The Nausets' home turf was much visited by European explorers and would-be colonists in the early 1600s, partly because of a navigational impediment that once stretched eastward from today's shore, forcing vessels to take shelter in the area from unfavorable winds or to make repairs to broken rudders. "Tucker's Terror," as it was branded by English captain Bartholomew Gosnold

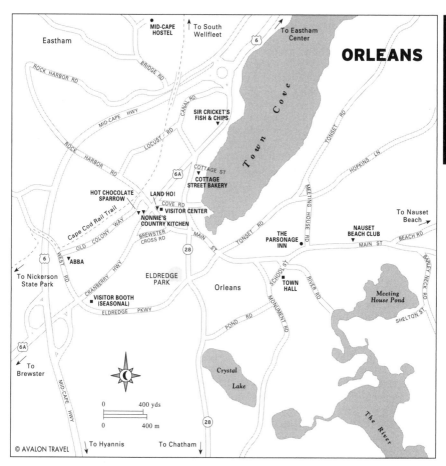

Eastham

MID-CAPE HOSTEL

To South Wellfleet

To Eastham Center

ORLEANS

ROCK HARBOR RD

BRIDGE RD

CANAL RD

MID-CAPE HWY

LOCUST RD

ROCK HARBOR RD

SIR CRICKET'S FISH & CHIPS

Town Cove

TONSET RD

HOPKINS LN

COTTAGE ST

COTTAGE STREET BAKERY

HOT CHOCOLATE SPARROW

LAND HO!

COVE RD

VISITOR CENTER

NONNIE'S COUNTRY KITCHEN

Cape Cod Rail Trail

OLD COLONY WAY

BREWSTER CROSS RD

MAIN ST

TONSET RD

MEETING HOUSE RD

THE PARSONAGE INN

NAUSET BEACH CLUB

MAIN ST

BEACH RD

To Nauset Beach

BARLEY NECK RD

WEST RD

ABBA

CRANBERRY HWY

ELDREDGE PARK

Orleans

SCHOOL ST

TOWN HALL

RIVER RD

Meeting House Pond

SHELTON ST

To Nickerson State Park

VISITOR BOOTH (SEASONAL)

ELDREDGE PKWY

MONUMENT RD

POND RD

To Brewster

MID-CAPE HWY

Crystal Lake

The River

0   400 yds

0   400 m

© AVALON TRAVEL

To Hyannis

To Chatham

in 1602, may even have been the reason the Pilgrims were forced to abort their southward journey along the Outer Cape shore en route to the mouth of the Hudson. The Nausets' encounters with these various newcomers neatly synopsizes their experience with Europeans in the New World: amicable relations soured by the newcomers' prejudice and greed; kindness and hospitality repaid with suspicions; amends made and strained again; and, ultimately, the combination of microbes and weapons reducing an indigenous population to a bunch of poetic place names.

Lacking sufficiently deep harbors to attract the shipbuilding and other maritime industry adopted by many other Cape towns, this area remained invested in agriculture well into the early 1900s. Eastham, in particular, enjoyed a reputation for being the farmer among its seafaring neighbors, with its farms supplying produce, dairy products, and even grain to the region. Today, Orleans provisions and outfits the area with its shopping centers, while Eastham has become the gateway to the National Seashore, whose main visitors center is within the town limits. Between them, the two towns boast dozens of accommodation options and a range of fine beaches.

Nauset Marsh

The salt marsh estuaries protected by the Nauset barrier beach are a world often unseen by Cape visitors: calm and unpaved, with nary a traffic tie-up in sight. The vast majority of this large salt marsh is actually in neighboring Eastham, but seasonal boat access is available from the Town Cove in Orleans, courtesy of guided two-hour pontoon-boat trips sponsored by the Massachusetts Audubon Society (508/349-2615). The price is $40 and preregistration and advance payment are required.

You can experience the marsh even more closely with a four-hour guided kayak tour from **Goose Hummock** (Rte. 6A, Orleans, 508/255-0455 or 508/255-2620, www.goose .com, $60) on Town Cove, Cape Cod's leading outdoor outfitters for over half a century. If you're a paddler bringing your own gear, the good folks at Goose Hummock can also give pointers on where to go and what to avoid. Or download a guide to the marsh from the website for **Cape Cod Water Trails** (www .kayakcapecod.com), dedicated to promoting low-impact recreation on the Cape's inshore waterways.

◖ Cape Cod National Seashore

Begin your visit to the Cape Cod National Seashore at the **Salt Pond Visitors Center** (508/255-3421, www.nps.gov/caco, 9 A.M.–4:30 P.M. daily year-round, extended hours in summer), beside U.S. 6 about three miles north of the big Orleans rotary. This center and its helpful staff and handy publications will orient you to what's available in the park's 44,000 acres, from historic lighthouses to abandoned cranberry bogs and from beautiful beaches to rigorous bike trails. Inform yourself with a briefing on the park's natural history from the museum exhibits, pick up a field guide from the small shop, and most definitely inquire about the tempting lineup of ranger-guided activities. Wading around playing amateur naturalist in muddy salt marshes, learning to surf cast, canoeing one of the park's kettle ponds, listening to campfire storytelling, and taking part in after-dark

wildlife searches are among the many activities offered daily and weekly in high season. Reservations are occasionally required, and fees may be charged, especially where equipment is provided; call for advance details.

One of the attractions that northbound drivers will pass prior to reaching the visitors center is the 1867 **Captain Edward Penniman House** (open daily in season), on Fort Hill Road off U.S. 6. In sharp contrast to the plain Cape houses that were the prevailing standard, this whaling captain's fancy Second Empire–style mansion and its ornamental carpentry illustrates how lucrative a seaman's career could be in the days when the nation's lamps were lit with whale oil. And yes, that front gate is indeed a pair of whale jawbones. Bird-watchers and anyone curious about what remains of the Nauset tribe that once lived here should walk the short trail around panoramic Fort Hill just beyond the mansion, overlooking Nauset Marsh.

Beaches

Orleans has one beach on its ocean side and one on its bay side, and both are available to visitors for a parking fee of $15 per day or $50 for a weeklong sticker (the beaches are free to cyclists and walkers). Bayside **Skaket Beach** is the warmer and calmer of the two. **Nauset Beach,** on the other hand, is considered one of the best on the Cape—mile after mile of sandy shore, with nothing beyond those waves until you hit the Iberian peninsula. In summer, it often appears as if every day-tripper on the Cape has ended up here, but determined walkers can generally find some space way down the beach.

Unlike many Cape towns, Eastham also permits visitors to use all nine of its freshwater and saltwater beaches, provided you purchase a weekly sticker for $55. The town also permits day use at a rate of $15 per car at four of its beaches (First Encounter, Campground, Cooks Brook, and Wiley Park). Its bayside shore, while boring for anyone hoping to do some bodysurfing, can be lovely, especially as the sun gets low over the water and the crowds head home for

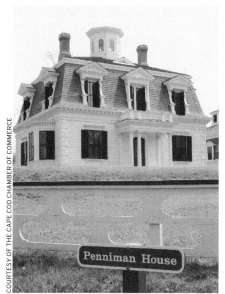

Penniman House

Captain Edward Penniman House

dinner. **First Encounter Beach,** named for the initial meeting of the Pilgrims and the locals back in 1620, has the most parking, plus restrooms, but others that are not as well signposted on U.S. 6 are equally deserving. Turn off on Massasoit Road in North Eastham to access **Campground Landing Beach, Cooks Brook Beach,** and **Sunken Meadow Beach,** for instance (restrooms at Cooks Brook only). If you're cycling the Rail Trail, consider detouring to **Kingsbury Beach** or **Thumpertown Beach,** and turn the lack of public parking to your advantage.

Erosion off Eastham's backshore beaches is fierce—loss of a dozen feet a year in the vicinity of Nauset Light is not uncommon. Most erosion goes to build up offshore sandbars, some of which become visible at low tide. Because of these bars Eastham is one of the only places in Massachusetts that attracts serious surfers. From the clifftop parking lot at **Nauset Light Beach,** located a mile north of the National Seashore's Salt Pond Visitors Center, you can often watch them among the breakers, looking like board-riding seals in their full-body wetsuits. Nauset Light is managed by the National Park Service, which has a lifeguard during summer months and charges a $10 parking fee in season. The National Park Service also runs nearby **Coast Guard Beach** on the Atlantic, a mile and a half east of Salt Pond Visitors Center on Nauset and Doane Roads. Note, however, this beach has such limited parking that during high season, cars must use the satellite lot on Doane Road and take the bus shuttle or walk the remaining half mile.

Camping

The only public campground in the Outer Cape is in Brewster's **Nickerson State Park** (508/896-3491, www.mass.gov, mid-Apr.–mid-Oct., $15–17), west of Orleans on Rte. 6A. The 420 sites are broken up into many small cul-de-sac clusters throughout the park's dense pine- and oak-covered hills, whose stones and sand are well carpeted with a comfortable mat of pine needles. Though a number of sites are rather too close to their neighbors, most are adequate—you won't feel as if you're sleeping under the flags, signs, and laundry lines some of the more settled-in residents use to stake out their perimeters, and a few choice spots—#32 in Area 7, for one—are quite secluded indeed. Though no hookups exist, a disposal station is available, along with full restrooms, showers, a camp store, and bike rentals (next door) for use on the park's many paved trails or the on Cape Cod Rail Trail, which crosses Rte. 6A beneath Nickerson's front entrance. If you don't have a tent, inquire about renting one of Nickerson's yurts ($30–40). To reserve any site in advance, call 877/I-CAMP-MA (877/422-6762), or reserve online at www.reserveamerica.com ($9.25 fee per reservation).

Accommodations

Accommodations in Orleans are about evenly split—half are on Rte. 28 south from downtown toward Chatham, and half are in East Orleans, near the popular Nauset Beach. Eastham's are concentrated along U.S. 6, with a dozen others scattered close by. For the most affordable digs in the area, check out Hostelling International's **Mid-Cape Hostel** (75 Goody Hallet Dr., Eastham, 508/255-2785 or 888/901-2085, www.usahostels .org, mid-May–mid-Sept.). Tucked into the woods off Bridge Road near Rock Harbor on the Orleans-Eastham line, next to the fancy Whalewalk Inn and one-quarter mile from the Cape Cod Rail Trail, the hostel comprises eight small bunk-filled cabins. Cozier than they are rustic, the cabins sleep eight people each. There are two outdoor showers in addition to the indoor facilities. Reservations are definitely recommended—the cabin with the double bed is snatched up quickly by families—but outside of July and August weekends, anyone looking for same-day accommodations may get lucky. (Given the distance to the nearest transit, don't just walk in without calling ahead.) Rates are $32–35 for a dorm bed and $128–175 for a private room. As at most HI-affiliated hostels, the registration office is closed during the day, 10 A.M.–5 P.M.

There's a year-round **Sheraton Four Points Hotel** (508/255-5000 or 800/325-3535, www .starwoodhotels.com, $245–300 d June–early Sept.), on U.S. 6 in Eastham about a mile north of the Salt Pond Visitors Center—the "best available" rack rates off season start at a very reasonable $85 for a double.

In addition to B&B homes found through reservations services—some of which still fall below $90 for a double with a shared bath in high season—a number of highly regarded B&B inns are also found in this area. One that is sure to please is **The Parsonage Inn** (202 Main St., Eastham, 508/255-8217 or 800/422-8217, www.parsonageinn.com, open year-round, $135–180 d June–Oct., down to $95–105 d in winter) in Orleans opposite Fancy's Farm, 1.5 miles from Nauset Beach. Friendly, casual comfort is the rule at this 1770 Cape-style house and its rambling additions, amid country antiques and fascinating souvenirs of East Africa. No vicar could make you feel more welcome and at ease than owners Ian and Liz Browne, either. Rates include full breakfast and happy hour refreshments. Also

high on the hospitality index is the **Nauset House Inn** (143 Beach Rd., Orleans, 508/255-2195, www.nausethouseinn.com, mid-Apr.–Oct.) a mile farther east toward the beach. With a plant-filled conservatory, painted furniture, whimsical trompe l'oeil, and extensive quilts, this place has an insidious fun streak running through it—the kind that gives rise to dangerous thoughts about quitting your job and moving to the Cape to putter around enjoying yourself, entertaining friends, and sharing your life with tourists. If you catch yourself thinking what a delight it would be to run an inn like this, you'd better pack up and leave right away—don't even think of staying around for that big breakfast smorgasbord. Rates run $115–175 for a double with a private bath, $85–95 for a double with a shared bath, and $75 for the small single room with a shared bath—an excellent value for solitary travelers.

For out-of-town seclusion with beautiful views out over Nauset Marsh to the ocean, nothing beats the **Fort Hill Bed & Breakfast** (75 Fort Hill Rd., Eastham, 508/240-2870, open year-round, $235–325 d May–Oct., $200–275 off season). This attractive 1868 Greek Revival farmhouse (built by the brother-in-law of Captain Penniman, whose own home across the street now belongs to the National Seashore) has been converted into an all-suites property with charm and amenities to match its unique location (one three-room suite even has a piano).

Additional B&B accommodations, both local and elsewhere on the Outer Cape, can be booked (for a nominal fee) through **Bed & Breakfast Cape Cod** (508/255-3824 or 800/541-6226, www.bedandbreakfastcape cod.com).

Food

Wake up to a tried-and-true white-bread breakfast at **Nonnie's Country Kitchen** (Rte. 6A, 508/255-1415, 4:30–11:30 A.M., Mon.–Sat.), opposite the Mobil station at Main Street in downtown Orleans, where the only questions needing any reply are, "How d'you want those eggs?" and, "Need a refill on that?" Though hunched with age, Nonnie is as dedicated as ever. The decorative plate collection on the walls will turn flea-market archaeologists pea green with envy.

When it comes to batter-dipped seafood cooked in hot oil, Orleans has two of the Cape's best purveyors. Try the perfectly fried sweet scallops at **Sir Cricket's Fish & Chips** (Rte. 6A, 508/255-4453, 11 A.M.–8 P.M. daily, year-round, $8–15), for example, a hole in the wall south of the rotary and next to the Nauset Lobster Pool.

If your heart pauses at the thought of another day's dining on fried anything, repair to the tiny **(Cottage Street Bakery** (5 Cottage St., 508/255-2821,, www.cottagestreetbakery .com, 6 A.M.–6 P.M. daily, year-round), just off downtown Rte. 28 a block south of its junction with Rte. 6A. Enjoy breakfast items such as French toast or the bakery's own granola with fruit, or lunch on sandwiches, soups made from scratch, quiches, and vegetable pies. Owner JoAnne Kenney knows not to ruin her fine handiwork in the microwave, either—she warms the savory pastries in an oven, preserving the tender crusts. If you're on any sort of sugarless diet, stay away—JoAnne bakes up a fragrant storm of meringues, tarts, cookies, cakes, fruit danish, pies (generally sold whole), and luscious buttery croissants (try the almond crème with rum and frangipani). Luckily for off-season visitors, this place has a strong local following, so its delights can be savored year-round.

Another Orleans eatery that doesn't live and die by the tourist trade is **Land Ho!** (Rte. 6A, 508/255-5165, www.land-ho. com, 11:30 A.M.–10 P.M. Mon.–Fri., 5 P.M.– 10 P.M. Sat., noon–10 P.M. Sun. daily year-round, $8–10 sandwiches, "market" prices for seafood), a genuinely local joint smack-dab in the center of Orleans, at the corner of Main Street. Charbroiled burgers, deli sandwiches, beer-boiled knockwurst, fried and broiled seafood, and an excellent kale soup are among the casual menu items available day in and day out, all at prices aimed at attracting neighbors more than gouging visitors. For dessert, step over to **The Hot Chocolate Sparrow** a block and a half away next to the Cape Cod Rail Trail (5 Old Colony Way, 508/240-2230, 6:30 A.M.– 11 P.M. daily July–Aug., 6:30 A.M.–10 P.M. Mon.–Thurs. and 6:30 A.M.–11 P.M. Fri.–Sat. Sept.–Oct., 6:30 A.M.–9 P.M. mid-Oct.–June). Fudges, nut barks, truffles, caramels, toffee crunch, cream-filled and solid chocolates, cranberry cordials, chocolate-dipped dried fruits and ginger, chocolate-covered espresso beans—you get the picture. The place is half bakery and half café, so your companion who pretends not to like sweets can have a complete meal while you experimentally reevaluate whether you prefer milk or dark chocolate. Just be warned, the heady aromas of cocoa butter, coffee beans, and baked goods are impossible to resist, so don't think you'll get away with "just looking."

For a bit of fine dining, try to land a table at the year-round **Nauset Beach Club** (222 Main St., 508/255-8547, 5–8:30 P.M. daily year-round, $18–34), in East Orleans. Though after 6:30 P.M. in season there's almost invariably an hour's wait for a table (no reservations for parties of fewer than six), the food is worth it. Robust dishes like veal saltimbocca, lobster vermicelli, and risotto are prepared with fresh, high-quality ingredients (no iceberg lettuce here), accompanied by good wines and imported brews, and served in an attractive, intimate dining room free of pretense.

In the right hands, melding ingredients and dishes from different cultures is an act of revelation, the familiar and foreign combining to produce tastes that you simply can't get enough of. Israeli-born Chef Erez Pinhas exhibits exactly this kind of intuition at **(Abba** (89 Old Colony Way, 508/255-8144, www .abbarestaurant.com, 5–10 P.M. daily July– early Sept., 5–close Tues.–Sun., $18–34), creating unforgettable Mediterranean-Asian dishes like Thai saté duck breast with herbed gnocchi, filet mignon with green coconut curry, and grilled sushi-grade tuna in a pool of balsamic miso mustard sauce. Given the artfully arranged dishes, consummately professional service, and cozy dining room accented with embroidered pillows and silky fabrics, it's hard not to feel like you are experiencing a modern cosmopolitan version of feasting in a pasha's tent.

WELLFLEET

As one of the least commercialized towns on the entire Cape, Wellfleet is a window to what must have been the rule rather than the exception as recently as a single generation ago. Once the home port for one of the largest cod fleets in 19th-century New England, and a top oyster producer for over 40 years, the town is now more of an enclave for writers and psychiatrists than fishmongers. Most tourists, anchored by the more extensive accommodations in neighboring Provincetown or Orleans, know only of Wellfleet's ocean beaches—if they know the town at all—but those who do make the short detour from the highway will find a pleasantly becalmed community of small art galleries, a working pier, and almost no T-shirt shops.

Instead of competing with the motel rooms and retail capacity of its neighbors, Wellfleet prefers to be an oasis for the long-term rental crowd, with restaurants and shops sprinkled among—or in—old houses and town offices on narrow, winding streets. You won't find much artificial quaintness here either—like fading jeans worn chamois-soft, this place feels lived-in.

While Wellfleet had some early ups and downs in fishing, shipbuilding, and coastal trading, its lasting fame has come from its oysters. The foot-long specimens gathered by Native Americans—so plentiful that Champlain named the harbor after them when he charted Wellfleet waters in 1606—died off before the American Revolution, but imported stock kept "Wellfleet" synonymous with "oyster" well into the Victorian era (quite appropriate for a town whose namesake was an English village known for its bivalves). Virtual monopoly over New England's supply of this alleged aphrodisiac was attained in the middle decades of the 1800s, abetted by the newly arrived railroad, fast schooners, and fussy tycoons who could afford to be particular about their Wellfleets on the half shell. The oysters' popularity was such that by 1870, as many as 40 vessels were engaged in ferrying Virginia seed to the Outer Cape for a proper upbringing. Chesapeake's partisans may choose to focus on this Southern pedigree, but chefs and gastronomes claim Wellfleet's water imparts the agreeable and incomparable flavor to its shellfish. A deadly parasite known as the oyster drill devastated the industry in the early 1900s, but renewed interest in aquaculture may restore the Wellfleet *Cassostrea virginica* to its lost throne.

Songs of praise for the oyster aside, the town was no slouch in the fishing industry back in the days when cod and mackerel outnumbered tourists. A few working boats still exist, along with plenty of good clam-digging mudflats (required permits are sold at the Town Pier), but these days Wellfleet is better known for its cluster of art galleries and pottery studios than for what it fetches from the sea. Fortunately, despite shifting demographics, the town retains some of the look and feel of a place in which mending nets is more important than peddling knickknacks to tourists—a true anachronism on the Cape.

Besides more than a dozen galleries—almost all of which lie within the triangle formed by Main, Commercial, and Holbrook—a couple of interesting bookstores, shops stocking items such as used silk kimonos or Afrocentric art (**Eccentricity,** on Main, 508/349-7554), and an exceptional fish market, **Hatch's** (behind Town Hall, 508/349-2810, www.hatchsfish market.com, mid-May–mid-Sept.), this place is also summer home to the small **Wellfleet Harbor Actors Theater (WHAT)** (box office 508/349-9428, www.what.org). Favoring topical contemporary drama over retreads of old Broadway chestnuts, WHAT performs in two theaters. One is a simple black box space in a plain building on Kendrick Avenue between the Town Pier and Mayo Beach, while the thoughtfully designed, state-of-the-art main stage is near the post office on Rte. 6. The company also sets up a tent in summer for children's shows.

If you spend much time within earshot of the First Congregational Church, listen carefully whenever its bells chime, and perhaps you'll figure out how to use "ship's time." According to *Ripley's Believe It or Not!*, this is the only town clock in the world that uses this two-, four-, six-, and eight-bell system for marking the hours.

Beaches

Between the third weekend in June and Labor Day, most of Wellfleet's 10 saltwater beaches are off limits to anyone without a beach sticker (available to visitors with proof of Wellfleet lodging from the booth at the end of Commercial Street in the Town Pier parking lot; $70 a week or $225 for the season). Exceptions include three of the five long backside beaches—**Marconi, White Crest,** and **Cahoon Hollow** ($15 parking fees in season)—and the always-free **Mayo Beach** along Kendrick Avenue near the Town Pier. Windsurfers, by the way, aren't particularly welcome here; Wellfleet restricts sailboarding to certain hours in only one area—Burton Baker Beach, which is restricted to resident sticker holders. Likewise, surfboards are allowed only on the Atlantic's White Crest Beach.

Permit or no, parking is never guaranteed—unlike the ticket you'll get if you ignore the No Parking signs. Since parking restrictions don't have to be posted in rural areas, confirm where it's safe to stash your car when buying your beach sticker.

Great Island

Thanks to the continual reshaping of the Outer Cape, this former island has developed a link to the hilly shore west of Wellfleet's village center, and has thus become one of the more exceptional hiking spots in the National Seashore. Since walking the length of the island can easily take a full afternoon, visitors generally enjoy great solitude even on the most frenzied summer holiday weekends. It's a good place for bird-watching, and an excellent spot to play amateur naturalist, like Thoreau. The farthest part of the trail, out to Jeremy Point, gets submerged at high tide; know when this occurs or be prepared to do some wading. Since

THE LAST DRIVE-IN SHOW

Drive-in movies have become an endangered species across America, but even more so in New England, where spiraling real-estate values have sped the demise of many once- memorable drive-ins. Luckily for Cape visitors, one fine local example not only still survives, but also thrives: the **Wellfleet Drive-In Theatre** (51 Rte. 6, South Wellfleet, 508/349-7176, www.wellfleetcinemas.com), right beside the highway at the Eastham-Wellfleet town line.

Built in 1957, the Wellfleet shows first-run double features nightly almost year-round, rain or shine ($8 adults, $5 seniors and children 4-11, children under 4 free). Come summer, you can spend your entire day here: play mini-golf on the 18-hole course; dine on burgers, fish and chips, and ice cream at the Dairy Bar & Grill (508/349-0278); browse the giant flea market that takes over the parking lot during the day (8 A.M.-3 P.M. Sat.-Sun. and Mon. holidays Apr.-Oct., plus Wed.-Thurs. July-Aug., 508/349-0541); shop at the arts and crafts gallery (Mon.-Tues. July-Aug.); and knock back some brews at the cocktail bar (nightly July-Aug.). Finally, after the sun has fully set, park in front of the giant screen, tune your car radio to the FM stereo sound system (door-mounted mono speakers still available upon request, too), and enjoy the show.

Be sure to come early – not only to avoid hunting for a spot in the dark, but also to see the pre-show animated countdown, a piece of retro '50s Americana almost worth the price of admission all by itself.

summer's prevailing southwesterly winds can be brisk and unabating, extended wading isn't as pleasant as you might think, unless it's a really hot day. The National Seashore visitors centers can help plan an outing, or you can join Park Service rangers for their free guided tours in season; call 508/255-3421 or visit www.nps.gov/caco for a schedule.

Marconi Station

In 1903, President Theodore Roosevelt sent greetings to King Edward VII of England via the magic of Guglielmo Marconi's wireless telegraph—a historic event made possible by an enormous set of radio masts erected two years earlier at this Wellfleet cliff. The antennae are long gone—coastal creep has undermined the site, although a couple of the concrete anchor posts remain at the cliff's edge—but a small pavilion managed by the National Seashore holds a model and interpretive signs recalling the facility and explaining the scientific achievement it represented. Here, too, is the trailhead for the National Seashore's Atlantic White Cedar Swamp Trail, an easy 45-minute ramble through an ecosystem more typical of the wetlands along the southern New England coast than the Cape's well-drained, sandier glacial moraine. Along with the towering native pines, the rot-resistant white cedars were aggressively harvested by European settlers as building material. Imagine the specimens along this trail replaced by mammoth trees five feet wide, and you'll appreciate why the early colonials felt their prayers had been answered.

Numerous ships have been wrecked on the shoals off this stretch of shore, but none as famous as the *Whydah,* a pirate ship that sank here in 1717. "Black Sam" Bellamy and over 100 of his crew washed up, dead, but no treasure was recovered until 1985, when salvager Barry Clifford located the first of the ship's artifacts. (You can see some of the millions of dollars worth of recovered coinage and hardware in Provincetown at the Expedition Whydah museum).

Wellfleet Bay

Salt marsh, ponds, and moors, home to numerous species of terrestrial and marine animals, are part of the landscape found within Massachusetts Audubon's **Wellfleet Bay Wildlife Sanctuary** (291 State Highway/Rte. 6, West Rd., 508/349-2615, www.mass audubon.org, 8:30 A.M.–5 P.M. daily late May–mid-Oct., 8:30 A.M.–5 P.M. Tues.–Sun.

mid-Oct.–late May; trails dawn–dusk daily year-round, $5 adults, $3 seniors and children 3–12), whose entrance and parking are located off U.S. 6 just north of the Eastham-Wellfleet town line. Turtles, horseshoe crabs, migratory and nesting birds, bats, and owls are among the denizens of the sanctuary's 1,000 acres, which include what was once part of President Grover Cleveland's favorite duck-hunting habitat. Brush up on your wetland ecology at the visitors center, or join one of the guided walks or bird-watching programs scheduled during the busiest months of the year (prepaid reservations required). More active events are also sponsored, such as snorkeling around the bay in search of crabs and snails, twilight canoeing, and various off-site excursions to places like Pleasant Bay estuary south of Orleans, Monomoy Island, and offshore to the fishing grounds of the Atlantic aboard a commercial trawler. All require advance registration; fees run from $10 to $70 depending on the program.

Camping

Are you a tenter tired of ending up sandwiched between a pair of patio furniture collectors equipped with enough lanterns and charcoal lighter fluid to outshine a Texas oil refinery? Relief is at hand at **Paine's Campground** (180 Old County Rd., 508/349-3007, www .campingcapecod.com, mid-May–early Sept., $40 for two, $15 per additional adult, $5 per additional child; early Sept.–late Sept. $30 for two adults, $10 per additional adult, $3 per additional child), east of U.S. 6 in South Wellfleet. Located in pine woods a few minutes' ride north of the Cape Cod Rail Trail terminus, most of Paine's 150 sites are strictly for tenters and pop-up trailers. Better yet, they provide wholly separate areas for families, groups, couples, and singles and young couples. Reservations recommended.

Accommodations

Wellfleet has scores and scores of weekly rental cottages and kitchen-equipped efficiency units, about a dozen B&Bs (most with one or two rooms), and a half-dozen motels, all of which are along U.S. 6. Moderate room rates are fairly abundant in these parts, too, although minimum-stay requirements are as widespread as everywhere else. Before mid-June and after early September, most motels go straight into their inexpensive off-season rates—ideal for the budget traveler. The **Wellfleet Chamber of Commerce** (508/349-2510, www.well fleetchamber.org) will happily provide you with a brochure that lists every one. Call to request a copy or drop by their seasonal information booth (9 A.M.–6 P.M. daily in summer; 10 A.M.–6 P.M. Sat.–Sun. in spring and fall) along U.S. 6 in South Wellfleet, beside the northern end of the Rail Trail.

Among the motels on U.S. 6, South Wellfleet's **Even'tide Resort Motel & Cottages** (650 Rte. 6, 800/368-0007 in Massachusetts or 508/349-3410, www.even tidemotel.com, late Apr.–Oct.) is both attractive and reasonably priced. Located near mile marker 98, it's right on the Rail Trail, which makes it possible to get to local beaches without messing with either highway traffic or resident parking restrictions. In-room mini-fridges and all the usual motel amenities are standard, plus there's a heated, indoor, 60-foot pool. Peak-season rates for double rooms are $98–155, mid-June through Labor Day; after Labor Day rates drop back to $75–85. A variety of two- to four-bedroom cottages, some with housekeeping, some without, are also in the woods at the back of the property; rates are $950–2,800 per week depending on size and season.

For something more like a low-key country inn, with simple furnishings, claw-foot tubs, nappy white bedspreads, and rustic rough pine walls in some quarters, check out the 1813 **Inn at Duck Creeke** (70 Main St., 508/349-9333, www.innatduckcreeke.com, May–mid-Oct.) just off U.S. 6. Overlooking Duck Pond under half a mile from the center of town, this breezily informal place has its own tavern and is next to two restaurants. Phone- and TV-free double rooms with private baths are $115–135 in the peak period (late June through Labor Day), and $90–130 in spring and fall. Rooms with shared baths are $10–20 less. All rates include continental breakfast.

Food

While a location a step or two off the beaten track has its advantages at the height of summer, off season it almost guarantees everything is shut up tight for the duration. This is certainly true of Wellfleet, where one of the few winter eating options is the local branch of **Box Lunch** (50 Briar Ln., 508/349-2178, www.box lunch.com, $4–12), the Cape chain of rolled-pita sandwich shops. Fortunately, there's also **Finely JP's** (554 Rte. 6, 508/349-7500, 5 P.M.–10 P.M. daily June–early Sept. and Thurs.–Sun. in the off-season, $15–26) in South Wellfleet about a mile north of the Wellfleet Drive-In theater. Despite being a Yankees fan, the chef/owner knows his way around seafood: delicious local oysters or clams on the half shell, warmed spinach and scallop salad, spicy calamari or garlicky sautéed shrimp over pasta. In fact, he does a great job across the board, from the hearty vegetarian lasagna to pork medallions with apples and goat cheese. Even the pizzas are made with a gourmet flair. Nothing too fancy, but darn good—and darn good value, too. The restaurant is open nightly for dinner late June–early September, dropping back a day at a time through the shoulder season until reaching the off-season Thursday–Sunday schedule.

To judge by the plain brown Formica-top tables in unpretentious elbow-to-elbow rows inside **Mac's Shack** (91 Commercial St., 508/349-6333, www.macsseafood.com, 4:30 P.M.–10 P.M. Tues.–Sun., late May–mid-Oct., $19–32), a barn-like building with a big wooden dory on the roof, you might presume the menu is simply the typical fried and broiled seafood found up and down the Cape. Such traditional fare is indeed available, and the simple preparations showcase just how impeccably fresh the ingredients are (not so surprising when you find out that all the fish dishes at Mac's are sourced through the side of the business that runs three eponymous retail fish markets and a regional wholesale operation).

But where the kitchen truly excels is with more stylish offerings—a grilled lobster tail with wild mushrooms and Thai sauce, clam fritters with chimi-churri sauce, even braised Kobe beef short ribs. Or treat yourself to arguably the best sushi on the Cape, generously cut, accompanied by a small but well-chosen selection of cold sakes. The reasonably priced sashimi platter alone is worth a pilgrimage.

Outside of Provincetown, **The Wicked Oyster** (50 Main St., Wellfleet, 508/349-3455, 11 A.M.–1 P.M. and 5–10:30 P.M. Thurs.–Tues. June–Aug., call for off-season hours, $10–30) is about as cool as Cape Cod gets. The casual spot jumps with young, well-dressed patrons supping on fennel-infused oyster stew and spinach-and-scallop salads.

TRURO

When regular visitors to the Cape think of Truro, the image that usually comes to mind is of Beach Point, the nearly treeless low-lying stretch of the bayside shore visible from the highway. More precisely, the image is of

Days's Cottages on the beach, classic green-shuttered white-clapboard Depression-era rental cottages all in a row right above the tide. These are the most photographed lodgings in the state, some say.

The most sparsely populated town on the Cape (just over 2,000 year-round residents), Truro is also the most varied topographically. From the Pamet River valley, barely above sea level, it rises to over 120 feet and then back down to its narrow neck in the north, again barely above sea level. In addition to its prominent headlands towering over its backside beaches, Truro has the most visible of the Cape's five major dune systems (best viewed from the Pilgrim Heights picnic area, but also clearly seen from U.S. 6 along Pilgrim Lake in North Truro). The sculpting force of the wind is clearly evident in their form, the centers scooped out as if by a giant bucket. These parabolic dunes also demonstrate the continuing evolution of the Outer Cape landscape as they slowly shift west, invading the waters of Pilgrim Lake.

Truro's splendid isolation and striking sea-

Days's Cottages

© JEFF PERK

scapes have been a major attraction for artists for much of the past century. Before World War II, artists built a colony of shacks in North Truro's dunes, some of which still remain—preserved not only as a historic relic of that era, but also to be made available to working artists today under a residency program administered by partners of the National Park Service.

🄲 Highland Light

Truro's most prominent attraction is Highland Light, a.k.a. the Cape Cod Light, built high atop what was once known as the Clay Pounds in North Truro. Sitting 123 feet above the waves, its light visible for 23 miles out to sea, this important beacon was first lit in 1798, warning mariners away from one of the Atlantic coast's most hazardous shipping lanes. Moved and modernized 60 years later, the lighthouse was again threatened by erosion in the late 1980s, having lost over two thirds of its original 10-acre clay hill to the ravages of waves and storms. Local fundraising to save the structure resulted in the 1996 move to its present location. Though still operated as an automated U.S. Coast Guard aid to navigation, the property is maintained by the **Truro Historical Society** (508/487-3397, www.truro historical.org), which provides access to the very top of the light daily 10 A.M.–5:30 P.M. mid-May–October (you must be willing to climb steep winding stairs). This is the only functioning lighthouse on the Cape that's regularly and completely open to the public. The former keeper's house at the base contains the Society's gift shop and displays photographs of that '96 relocation effort. Back near the parking lot is the **Highland House,** the Society's highly eclectic museum (10 A.M.–4:30 P.M. Mon.–Sat., 1–4:30 P.M. Sun., June–Sept.) in what was once a summer hotel on the railroad line from off-Cape. While the lighthouse grounds are free and accessible year-round, there is an admission fee for the Highland House and to go up the lighthouse ($4 each).

Surrounding the lighthouse is **Highland Links** (508/487-9201), an 1892 descendant of the rough Scottish links. Between April 1 and mid-December, a nine-hole round costs $33 and 18 holes costs $55 (add $8.40 per person for cart rentals).

Beaches

Of the town's several beaches, only those belonging to the National Seashore are open to nonresident day use: **Head of the Meadow Beach** on the Atlantic and **Corn Hill Beach** on Cape Cod Bay (both $10 for parking).

A couple of hard-to-find little historical plaques testify to the town's small but vital part in the saga of the Pilgrims' brief stay on the Cape at the end of 1620. One is at Corn Hill, namesake for that National Seashore beach, where the hungry immigrants pilfered a stash of buried Indian corn. The other marks Pilgrim Spring, where they first found fresh water, although since the spring was only located in 1920 during the town tercentenary, authenticity is a matter of trust.

Camping

Truro is about as far from city lights as you can get on the Cape, so clear night skies are always filled with stars. You'll certainly be able to appreciate the constellations at the **North of Highland Camping Area** (52 Head of the Meadow Rd., 508/487-1191, www.capecodcamping.com, mid-May–mid-Sept., $30 for up to two people, $11 each additional adult, $3 per child), two-tenths of a mile from Head of the Meadow Beach, on Truro's back shore. Amid the gnarled pitch pine woods are over 200 sites for tents and pop-ups. Peace and quiet is the guideline here, since there are no electrical hookups, no motor homes, no motorcycles, no open fires, and no pets. Slightly farther south is **Adventure Bound Camping Resort Cape Cod** (46 Highland Rd., 508/487-1847, www.ntcacamping.com, year-round, $35–50, half-price during shoulder season), also known as North Truro Camping Area, located between U.S. 6 and Highland Light, which favors RVs with its electrical and water hookups and free cable TV. Nearby is **Horton's Camping Resort** (71 S. Highland Rd., 508/487-1220 or 800/252-7705, www.hortonscampingresort .com, May–mid-Oct., $30–41 d, $12 each

SHIPWRECKS

"Who lives in that house?" I inquired.
"Three widows," was the reply.

– Henry David Thoreau, *Cape Cod*

As evidenced in Thoreau's quote, throughout its recorded history, Cape Cod has been a dangerous place for mariners. On the journey from Europe, a quarter-point error on the compass in a dead-reckoned course to Boston could fetch a sailing vessel up against the shoals along the back of the Cape. Before the availability of the mass-produced chronometers that enabled ships to accurately plot their longitude, a course from the southern Atlantic to Boston was well-nigh impossible; instead, so as to avoid running afoul on the shallow rocks and sandbars scattered around the entrance to Nantucket Sound, vessels had to head toward Long Island and then creep up the coast around the Cape. Bad weather also greatly contributed to the litter of wrecks, with thick fogs that robbed navigators of their bearings and wind-lashed seas that could drive ships aground, if not swamp them outright. An 1864 survey identified nearly 500 wrecks in Cape waters during the 17-year period prior to the Civil War. An even greater number was recorded during the last two decades of the 19th century.

Local fishing fleets have historically been the hardest-hit victims of the weather. The region's 19th-century annals are filled with fierce storms that made widows by the score. The October Gale of 1841, in which 57 fishermen from Truro alone were lost, is among the more infamous examples. Another, the Portland Gale of 1898, was responsible for

sinking hundreds of vessels all around the Cape over three days.

Of all the Cape's threats to navigation, Peaked Hill Bar ("PEEK-id"), about a mile northwest off Truro's back shore, has been the worst. It has claimed more ships than perhaps any other single spot along the Atlantic coast outside of Cape Hatteras. One of its most notable wrecks was that of the HMS Somerset in 1778; this was the same British man-o'-war that helped blockade Boston's harbor before the Revolution. (Paul Revere was ferried across Boston Harbor right under her nose, so to speak, on that April night in 1775 when the pair of lights in the Old North Church steeple signaled the marching orders of the British Redcoats.) Every few decades, shifts in the sand open up the old ship's grave and let the hull mutely remind beachcombers of the dangers in these waters. There's a 19th-century ironclad, the Francis, that still bares her bones every now and again, too.

Now that Cape Cod no longer sends the greater share of its able-bodied citizens to labor at sea, the human toll of lost ships and their crews is not nearly as grim as in Thoreau's day. Technology, too, has helped make navigation safer in fogs and storms. But the risks aren't wholly erased, as high-profile marine accidents in recent years have clearly demonstrated. In 1994, for instance, a cruise ship ran aground in Nantucket's South Channel. And in 2003, an oil barge headed to the Cape Cod Canal struck a rock in Buzzards Bay, causing one of the worst oil spills in New England history.

---

additional adult, $4 per child). Horton's 220 sites include a generous number for tenters, as well as some reserved spots for campers without children. There's even a fully accessible bathroom for visitors with disabilities. Reservations are essential during the June 15–September 15 peak season, and a three-night minimum is required on holiday weekends. Located between Highland Light and the FAA's big transatlan-

tic air traffic control radomes east of U.S. 6; turn at the blue "Camping" sign about 5.5 miles north of the Truro-Wellfleet line and proceed another mile. It's worth noting that between June and mid-October both North Truro and Horton's campgrounds are connected to downtown Provincetown and Herring Cove Beach (as well as to the market in the center of Truro) by the **Provincetown Shuttle,** a seasonal dollar-a-ride route of the regional transit authority (800/352-7155, www.capecodtransit .org; North of Highland Camping Area is about a mile from U.S. 6, where the shuttle can be flagged down).

Accommodations

Truro has plenty of small motels that look like throwbacks to the era of Kerouac's road trip across America, although more and more of them are being used as housing for low-wage seasonal workers in Provincetown's service economy. It also has spartan cabin and cottage colonies on the highway and all along Beach Point, but most of these are for weekly rentals only, with prime summer weeks often booked a year in advance.

The area's only non-camping budget option is Hostelling International's **Truro Hostel** (508/349-3889 or 888/901-2086, www.usa hostels.org, late June–Aug., $35 dorm bed, $125–150 private room), at the end of North Pamet Road. Take the Truro Center–Pamet Roads exit from U.S. 6, and stay to the east of the highway. Though hardly convenient to any local transit—both the seasonal local bus shuttle from Provincetown and the P&B bus from Hyannis stop two miles away near the Truro post office, and Provincetown's ferries are a windblown 10-mile trek to the north—this 42-bed hostel packs a full house throughout its short, 11-week season, and no wonder—the former oceanside Coast Guard station in the Pamet River valley is a two-minute walk from beautiful Ballston Beach, where parking is otherwise restricted to residents with beach stickers. (Geographical aside: The beach is a few hundred yards from the headwaters of the Pamet River, which drains west to the Cape Cod Bay; when the ocean succeeds in breaching this gap—as it temporarily has during past winter storms—the northern tip of the Cape becomes an island.) It's also got plenty of common space, a decent kitchen, and superb second-floor views (for the women, that is; men get to share two basement rooms big enough to ensure at least one snorer in each). So, have your credit card handy when you call or visit

their website. No private rooms for couples here, and no family rooms unless space is available. The registration office is open 8–11 A.M. and 3–10 P.M.

PROVINCETOWN

Where once the sea sustained Provincetown—as trading center, whaling village, and fishing port—now the summer does. Clinging to the inside shore of the outermost arm of Cape Cod, contemporary "P'town" is a salty mix of tourists, artists, fisherfolk, and a thriving gay and lesbian community. It's a place whose population mushrooms by a factor of 12 between the off-season calm and the high-season carnival. Here is where the *Mayflower* Pilgrims first came ashore, plundered caches of Indian corn, and then left for the mainland in search of an adequate source of fresh water. Subsequent centuries saw a hardscrabble fishing village take hold amid the dunes—a place whose bargain cost of living and beautiful light proved a big draw to painters and playwrights in the decades before World War II.

In 1901, Charles Hawthorne, fascinated by the Mediterranean feel of the dilapidated harbor village and all its Portuguese fishermen, opened an art school here. Greenwich Village Bohemians followed, a fashionable flock that included the likes of John Reed and Eugene O'Neill, whose Provincetown Players made theater history. John Dos Passos, e. e. cummings, Edward Hopper, Sinclair Lewis, Jackson Pollock, Mark Rothko, and Norman Mailer are some of the other luminaries who have lived here at one time or another. Since at least the 1970s, Provincetown has also been known for its active gay and lesbian community. Rainbow flags are flown proudly here, and it's not unusual to see singing drag queens on roller-skates along Commercial Street.

Now that the cottage-filled town has become a major seaside resort, its streets overflowing each summer with T-shirt-shopping, taffy-eating, Teva-wearing sunseekers, bargains are more scarce than parking spaces. At least the sunsets are free—and still one of the best shows in town.

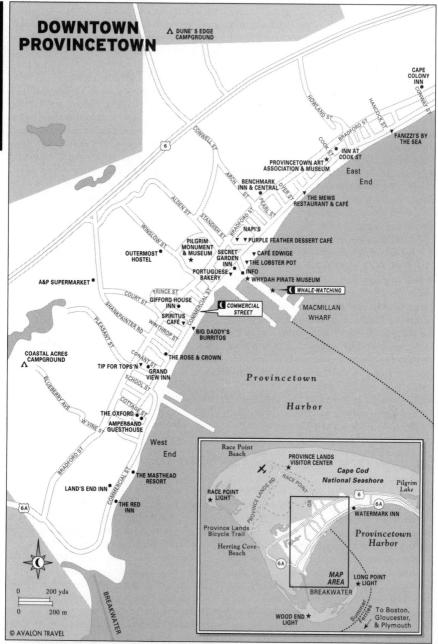

DOWNTOWN PROVINCETOWN

DUNE'S EDGE CAMPGROUND

CAPE COLONY INN

HOWLAND ST

HANCOCK ST

CONWAY S

BRADFORD ST

COOK ST

FANIZZI'S BY THE SEA

CONWELL ST

INN AT COOK ST

PROVINCETOWN ART ASSOCIATION & MUSEUM

East End

ARCH ST

BENCHMARK INN & CENTRAL

DYER ST

PEARL ST

STANDISH ST

THE MEWS RESTAURANT & CAFÉ

ALDEN ST

WINSLOW ST

BRADFORD ST

NAPI'S

PURPLE FEATHER DESSERT CAFÉ

PILGRIM MONUMENT & MUSEUM

SECRET GARDEN INN

CAFÉ EDWIGE

THE LOBSTER POT

OUTERMOST HOSTEL

PORTUGUESE BAKERY

INFO

WHYDAH PIRATE MUSEUM

A&P SUPERMARKET

COURT ST

PRINCE ST

COMMERCIAL ST

WHALE-WATCHING

COMMERCIAL STREET

MACMILLAN WHARF

GIFFORD HOUSE INN

SHANKPAINTER RD

PLEASANT ST

SPIRITUS CAFÉ

WINTHROP ST

BIG DADDY'S BURRITOS

Provincetown

COASTAL ACRES CAMPGROUND

CONANT ST

THE ROSE & CROWN

Harbor

TIP FOR TOPS'N

GRAND VIEW INN

SCHOOL ST

BLUEBERRY AVE

COTTAGE ST

THE OXFORD

W VINE ST

AMPERSAND GUESTHOUSE

West End

BRADFORD ST

COMMERCIAL ST

THE MASTHEAD RESORT

LAND'S END INN

THE RED INN

6A

0   200 yds
0   200 m

BREAKWATER

© AVALON TRAVEL

Race Point Beach

PROVINCE LANDS VISITOR CENTER

Cape Cod National Seashore

Pilgrim Lake

RACE POINT LIGHT

PROVINCE LANDS RD

RACE POINT RD

6

6A

WATERMARK INN

Province Lands Bicycle Trail

Herring Cove Beach

6A

Provincetown Harbor

MAP AREA

LONG POINT LIGHT

BREAKWATER

WOOD END LIGHT

Summer Ferries

To Boston, Gloucester, & Plymouth

◖ Commercial Street

Running the length of town, Commercial Street is made for strolling: One lane wide, with only one sidewalk, it all but requires pedestrians to take command of the road, in turn forcing vehicles to slow almost to a walker's pace. Lovingly tended gardens, gallery windows, and architectural variety ensure that no two blocks are alike. Cape Cod Bay plays hide and seek between the houses, sometimes bringing walkers up short in their tracks at the sudden sight of a momentarily perfect composition of light, water, and moored yachts. Discreet, nearly hidden artifacts—the marker for Eugene O'Neill's house, a plaque commemorating the fish-shed-turned-theater where O'Neill's playwriting career was launched, the private garden of allegorical creatures and deities, Chiam Gross's potbellied sculpture *Tourists*—are only ever noticed by pedestrians. In short, this is a town where walking one mile merely whets the appetite for one more, and where both may be traced and retraced twice a day for a week without ever growing stale or predictable.

Pilgrim Monument

Only one place in town combines both a figurative overview of local history and a literal overview of local geography: **Pilgrim Monument and Provincetown Museum** (High Pole Hill Rd., 508/487-1310 or 800/247-1620, www .provincetown-monument.org, 9 A.M.–5 P.M. daily Apr.–Nov., 9 A.M.–7 P.M. mid-June–mid-Sept., $7 adults, $5 seniors and students, $3.50 children 4–14, children under 4 free). The hill is off Bradford Street behind Town Hall; the monument is the thing on top visible from 40 miles away. Displays remind modern visitors that Provincetown, not Plymouth Rock, was where the Pilgrims spent their first five weeks in the New World, and modest exhibits range from a model of the original Provincetown Playhouse, which launched Eugene O'Neill's career, to artifacts gathered during the 15 Arctic expeditions of native son Donald MacMillan. Sticklers should be forewarned that the museum's depictions of Native Americans and assertions about Norse explorers are a bit dubious, and in general the early-history exhibit suffers

Commercial Street in Provincetown

from sloppy editing (discrepancies in the number of *Mayflower* passengers, misnamed vessels, that sort of thing). Take it as a gentle reminder that so-called history is almost invariably less a collection of facts than a point of view.

A view that's indisputable is the one from atop the 255-foot granite tower rising over the museum, which in clear weather unequivocally makes up for the lack of an elevator.

Provincetown Art Association and Museum

P'town is chock full of art—even without counting artist-run boutiques selling unique clothing, jewelry, cards, and other artifacts. Galleries range from experimental spaces to familiar storefronts featuring established local artists, and well-attended openings year-round demonstrate the vitality of the local visual arts. To check out both the deep roots of this community and its emerging new shoots, visit the Provincetown Art Association and Museum (PAAM) (460 Commercial St., 508/487-1750, www.paam.org, 11 A.M.–8 P.M. Mon.–Thurs., 11 A.M.–10 P.M. Fri., 11 A.M.–5 P.M. Sat.–Sun. late May–Sept., noon–5 P.M. Thurs.–Sun. Oct.–May, $5) in the East End. Founded in 1914, PAAM has a large permanent collection representing both famous American artists who've worked in P'town over the decades, as well as others who've lingered less forcefully in the annals of art history. Changing exhibitions drawing from this repository are staged throughout the year, mixed with exhibits of new work by living local artists.

Whydah Pirate Museum

Open up and say "argggh!" Anyone who liked the Pirates of the Caribbean ride at Disney World will love the **Expedition Whydah Sea Lab & Learning Center** (Macmillan Wharf, 508/487-8899, www.whydah.com, 10 A.M.–5 P.M. daily, May–Oct., open until 8 P.M. June–Aug., open by appointment Nov.–Mar., $10 adults, $8 children 6–12, children under 6 free). Johnny Depp is the only thing missing from this cool museum that follows the dual swashbuckling stories of the pirate ship *Whydah* and its subsequent discovery in 1984 off the shoals of the Outer Cape, the only pirate shipwreck every authenticated. The museum does a great job tracing the history of the ship from its origins as a slave vessel to its command under "Black Sam" Bellamy in the early 1700s, using many of the original artifacts from the wreck to illustrate the tale.

Provincetown Public Library

Come view the 62-foot half-scale replica of the Grand Banks fishing schooner *Rose Dorothea,* its masts stretching up in to the vaulted ceiling of the landmark home of the town library (356 Commercial St., 508/487-7094, www.ptownlib.org) formerly a Methodist Episcopal church built in 1860. The 1907 winner of the regionally renowned Boston–Gloucester Fisherman's Race, the *Rose* provides a glimpse into P'town's long legacy as a commercial fishing port.

Come, too, for the excellent (and free) views of town from the top-floor reading areas within the steeple of the former church; frequent book readings and a free WiFi hotspot can be found here, as well. The building opens at 10 A.M. on Monday, Wednesday, Friday, and Saturday; noon on Tuesday and Thursday, and 1 P.M. on Sunday. It closes at 5 P.M. on Sunday, Monday, and Friday, 8 P.M. Tuesday–Thursday, and 2 P.M. on Saturday.

The Province Lands

The northernmost of the three National Seashore visitors centers overlooks the Province Lands, whose name is a reminder of the Province of Massachusetts's explicit title to the area both before and after the town's 1727 incorporation. Now lightly wooded or covered in beach grass, the Province Lands' wind-driven dunes once upon a time threatened to bury the settlement at their watery margin. When the Pilgrims landed in 1620 they found "excellent black earth" when they probed with their shovels, "all wooded with oaks, pines, sassafras, juniper, birch, holly, vines, some ash, [and] walnut." In defiance of laws enacted as early as 1714 to save it, this tree cover was so thoroughly clear-cut by colonists that the topsoil blew away, freeing the sand to migrate toward the harbor. Two centuries after the Pilgrim landfall, Thoreau claimed there wasn't enough black earth to fill a flower pot, "and scarcely anything high enough to be called a tree." Efforts to stabilize the dunes were begun a generation prior to Thoreau's visits and continue to this day. Along with visitors center exhibits on the landscape's fragility, a variety of ranger-guided activities are scheduled throughout the summer, from beach walks and mountain-bike rides to talks at the Old Harbor Life Saving Station on the back shore; call 508/487-1256 for a schedule. Staff dispense advice and interpretive brochures, too, for trails in the vicinity. Located on Race Point Road, the visitors center is open 9 A.M.–5 P.M. daily, early May through late October, weekdays the rest of the year. National Seashore information is available from the Race Point ranger station, at the end of the road.

Most visitors to the Province Lands, like Cape visitors generally, come for the beaches. Mile after mile of coarse sand pounded by the long breakers of the open Atlantic Ocean make **Race Point Beach** a great spot for walking, bodysurfing, and just lazing under a summer sun. Walk far enough west and you'll reach **Race Point Light** (Race Point Beach, Rte. 6, 508/487-9930, www.racepointlighthouse.net), a short cast-iron tower whose steady white flash—now visible from some 11 miles at sea—has warned vessels away from the northern end of the infamous Peaked Hill Bars since 1876. Though its predecessor was undermined by storms, this is the only backside lighthouse not threatened by erosion—P'town's beaches are actually the beneficiaries of sand swept up the coast from the south.

Right at the end of U.S. 6 close to town is **Herring Cove Beach,** whose westerly orientation makes it the best place to watch the sun setting fire to the waters of Cape Cod Bay. When the sun's up, it's also a nice spot for swimming in gentle surf. Lifeguards are present and bathhouses are open at both beaches July through early September, at which time the National Seashore charges $10 for parking. The rest of the year, the beaches are free.

◀ Whale-Watching

The southern edge of Stellwagen Bank, a prime feeding area for finback, right, minke, and humpback whales, happens to be just offshore of Provincetown's breakwater—making it a prime destination for whale-watchers from mid-April through the end of October. Two different outfits offer the three- to four-hour excursions, each for the same price of $37 for adults and $29 for kids. At the start and finish of the season, you'll find just one or two trips a day, but by summer, operators run as many as nine daily departures from MacMillan Pier. The **Dolphin Fleet of Provincetown Whale Watch** (508/349-1900 or 800/826-9300, www.whalewatch.com) originated East Coast whale-watching in 1975 and stands out among local excursion operators for its use of naturalists from the local Center for Coastal Studies—one of New England's handful of cetacean research organizations. Or choose the **Portuguese Princess Whale Watch** (508/487-2651 or 800/442-3188, www.provincetownwhalewatch.com), which offers free all-day parking at their main office on Shank Painter Road by the A&P market.

Dune Tours

If you have the appropriate kind of vehicle (and no, a rental car doesn't count), it's possible to obtain an off-road vehicle permit ($50 for seven days) for driving along the backshore oversand driving corridor from the Park Service at the Race Point ranger station. Alternatively, you can not only experience the scenery of the town's Atlantic coastline, but also learn about its history and ecology, by instead joining one of **Art's Dune Tours** (4 Standish St., 508/487-1950 or 800/894-1951, 10 A.M.–sunset, $25 adults, $17 children 6–11).

Camping

Two private campgrounds are on the edge of town: **Dunes' Edge Campground** (Rte. 6, 508/487-9815, www.dunes-edge.com, May–Sept., $40 d, $14 per additional adult, $5 per child), and **Coastal Acres Camping Court** (508/487-1700, Apr.–Oct., $27–43 d, $10 per additional adult, $6 per child). Reservations at both are highly recommended July–August. Dunes' Edge is beside mile marker 116 on U.S. 6, at the perimeter of the National Seashore and a short distance from Nelson's Bike Shop, Deli, & Market, on Race Point Road, a seasonal rental outfit just yards from the Province Lands bike trails. Among the 100 mostly wooded sites is a secluded tent area, and electrical and water hook-ups for RVs. Rates drop slightly beyond peak summer months. Coastal Acres is beside Shank Painter Pond, near the very end of both U.S. 6 and Rte. 6A; turn at the sign at the Bradford Street Exit (Rte. 6A) in the West End, next to Gale Force Bike Rentals, and proceed past the riding stables. Catering more to RVers than tents—almost two-thirds of the 120 sites have power and water hookups—this campground also has one of the longer seasons around.

Accommodations

Provincetown is the only place on the Cape whose accommodations run the gamut from campgrounds and hostels to resort motels, hotels, timeshare condos, guesthouses, fancy B&Bs, and romantic, spare-no-expense little inns.

If you're on a tighter budget, be advised that during peak season, mid-June through Labor Day, rustic pine-paneled charm is about all you'll be able to find for under $100. Come spring and fall, when the weather still makes being outside—if not in the water—tolerable, and restaurant lines have all but vanished, prices everywhere start to come back to earth. A high proportion of places stay open year-round, too, if you need a winter getaway at a good price—and a few even offer in-room fireplaces.

Be forewarned that P'town hosts a number of annual special events that, unfortunately, inspire innkeepers to demand minimum stays of up to seven days. In addition to the customary Memorial Day, July 4th, Labor Day, and Columbus Day holidays, P'town celebrations that routinely cause outbreaks of No Vacancy signage include the week-long Portuguese Festival in late June, week-long Carnival in mid-August, and Women's Week in mid-

October. Minimum two-day stays throughout the summer are the rule rather than the exception, and some inns have gone so far as to require four- and five-night minimums June–September.

UNDER $50

The absolute cheapest choice for summer visitors is the bare-bones **Outermost Hostel** (28 Winslow St., 508/487-4378) just past the entrance to the Pilgrim Monument's parking lot. Comprising four historic cabins—epitomizing the height of tourist convenience back before Holiday Inn revolutionized the business— each with six or seven beds and a full bath, the Outermost is undeniably short on frills, but for $25 pp with free parking, it's also an unbeatable value. Anyone who's ever enjoyed the hospitality of the Huck Finn hostel in St. Louis may be surprised to find that owner Tom Cochran is the man behind this joint, too, but you may be sure he's as reliable a guide to P'town as to the Gateway City of the West.

$100-150

Outside of camping or hostel bunks the next least expensive summer lodging option is at the centrally located **Grand View Inn** (4 Conant St., 508/487-9193, www.grandviewinn.com, open year-round, $90–125 d in season with shared bath; rooms with a private bath run up to $155 d).

Throughout the off-season, many of the cozy waterfront efficiencies, suites, and motel rooms at **The Masthead Resort** (31–41 Commercial St., 508/487-0523 or 800/395-5095, www.the masthead.com, year-round), in the quiet West End, are within a wink of $100 for a double, making them—and their 450-foot bayside beachfront—one of the better values in town. Between mid-June and Labor Day weekend, however, most of the rates nearly triple.

A painted figurehead greets guests arriving at **The Rose and Crown** (158 Commercial St., 508/487-3332, www.provincetown.com/rose crown, $95–165 d), a unique guesthouse located in the center of town. Rooms are small but imaginatively designed; one is decked out with purple fabrics and Victorian antiques, another features exposed beams and a stately brass bed. Three less expensive rooms upstairs share a bath.

The **Secret Garden Inn** (300A Commercial St., 866/786-9646, www.secretgardenptown .com) is truly one of P'town's best-kept secrets, with affordable *and* attractive rooms full of four-poster beds and country quilts in a sun-spattered Captain's House in the East End. Breakfast is included, as is use of a five-person hot tub. Some of the rooms even have a shared balcony overlooking Commercial Street. The only downside is that most of the rooms also share a bath—but with rates of $90–165 in the high season and rooms as low as $50 in the off-season, you may find that's an inconvenience you can live with.

$150-250

Once the last stop for the stagecoach from Boston, **Gifford House Inn** (9 Carver St., 508/487-0688, www.giffordhouse.com, $105–195) has hosted Ulysses S. Grant and Theodore Roosevelt. The airy guesthouse features spacious guest rooms, and cocktails served nightly on a wraparound front porch. While the guesthouse goes out of its way to advertise that it caters to gay and lesbian guests (as if that's necessary in P'town), the friendly staff is equally accommodating to folks of all persuasions.

Another good mid-range option (for P'town) is the West End's **Ampersand Guesthouse** (6 Cottage St., 508/487-0959, www.ampersandguesthouse.com, year-round), whose high-season rates are $140–200 for bright, attractively unfussy double rooms that come with private bath, TV/VCR, plenty of cross-ventilation, and homemade continental breakfast. The only drawback is a five-night minimum throughout high season. Off season, rates drop to $95–125 for a double.

For about the same price, consider a standard motel-style room—and only a two-day summer minimum—at the East End's **Cape Colony Inn** (280 Bradford St., 508/487-1755 or 800/841-6716, www.capecolonyinn.com, mid-May–late Oct., $159–190 d).

$250 AND UP

Although definitely in the higher range of lodging prices, ◖ **The Oxford** (8 Cottage St., 508/487-9103 or 888/456-9103, www .oxfordguesthouse.com, year-round, $180–350 d), deliberately tries to cater to guests of varied means with a range of room configurations and prices. In practice, this means that every guest, including the frugal ones who save a few bucks by sharing a bath, is provided with amenities more frequently associated with deluxe business-class hotels than B&Bs: terry cloth bathrobe, minibar, TV/VCR, phone with voice mail and modem port, CD player, and individual climate control. Not to mention the bottomless supply of fresh coffee or tea at any hour, sherry in the parlor, afternoon English tea service, and bountiful fresh-baked breakfast goodies. Or the fact that the steep-pitched roof of this 1850s Greek Revival home conceals a stylish contemporary interpretation of English Country decor, next to which most of the rooms in town start to seem drab and tawdry. And need I mention the beautiful flower-filled English gardens? In short, depending on room size and whether the bath is shared, this is truly one of the most attractive places in town to bed down for the night. Although here, too, there's a five-night minimum throughout high season, I suspect that for most guests even that length of stay will end up seeming far too short. Also, it never hurts to call about shorter stays—there may be gaps in the bookings.

Over in the East End, about 10–15 minutes' stroll from the ferry, is **The Inn at Cook Street** (7 Cook St., 888/266-5655 or 508/487-3894, www.innatcookstreet.com, year-round), a carefully restored 1836 home, combines lots of decks, an inviting pocket-sized garden with a fishpond, and a variety of rooms and suites, as well as a cottage with kitchenette and loft bed. Attractively furnished, with mattresses and towels of perceptibly better quality than is customary, this inn also features a more substantial breakfast than is typical around town. June through mid-September, rates are $279–289 for a double, and go up to $339 for cottage and suites.

If the only point to a stay in P'town is waking up to water views, check out the East End's **Watermark Inn** (603 Commercial St., 508/487-0165, www.watermark-inn .com, open year-round, $205–470 weekly May–Sept., $85–280 nightly Oct.–Apr.), a harborfront property that rents exclusively in-suite accommodations. Lower rates are for rooms facing the street; be sure to inquire about midweek discounts. The bright, comfortable, modern rooms each come with a kitchenette, and all but four have access to private or shared sundecks overlooking the water.

At prices such as these, why settle for a sea-level view of the harbor? At **C Land's End Inn** (22 Commercial St., 508/487-0706 or 800/276-7088, Apr.–New Year's weekend), guests have a panoramic view of both Cape Cod Bay and the Atlantic Ocean from the summit of Gull Hill in the far West End. The top-floor loft suite—a 550-square-foot apartment, really—enjoys 360-degree views from its rooftop observation platform, as well as private wraparound wooden decks from which you can spot whales feeding offshore. The shingle-style mansion is tastefully decorated with Victorian art and antiques, much of it from the collection of the Boston merchant who built the place in the early 1900s. To say that all 17 rooms and efficiencies are unique is a gross understatement; suffice to say, if you have the slightest affinity for richly ornamented fabrics, Arts and Crafts wallpapers, stained glass, and carved wood in the fantastical oriental art nouveau style of Aubrey Beardsley, you'll love this place. That loft suite runs $570 at the height of summer, and $370 off season; other rooms and apartments are $305–480 for a double in summer, $185–280 the rest of the year.

Adult gratification has never looked better than at **C Benchmark Inn & Central** (6 & 8 Dyer St., 508/487-7440 or 888/487-7440, www.benchmarkinn.com, year-round, $225–460 d), a handsome inn that crosses contemporary Scandinavian design with the sensibilities of a cosmopolitan American spa. Drop your libations into the wetbar ice bucket filled for your arrival, plug your iPod into the stereo next to your bed, and refresh yourself in the sauna or pool before stepping out to one of many fine restaurants within a short stroll.

Food

If popularity is any measure, P'town's best breakfast is at **Café Edwige** (333 Commercial St., 2nd floor, 508/487-2008, 8:30 A.M.–10 P.M. daily July–Aug., 6 P.M.–midnight Thurs.–Sun. and 9 A.M.–1 P.M. Sat.–Sun., mid-May–early June and Sept.–mid-Oct; closed mid-Oct–Apr.; $18–36). Given the food-savvy palates in this town, acclaim like this is no small thing. Among the touches that explain the approving chorus are a choice of tabouli or home fries with the big fluffy omelets, pots of honey for tea drinkers, broiled flounder among the usual pancake and egg options, and fresh flowers on each table. Though it's only seasonal, if you miss a table for breakfast, you can try again at dinner Thursday–Sunday. (Ask for a window table—it's one of the best people-watching seats in town.) The other way to start your day off right is to make a beeline for **Carreiro's Tip for Tops'n** (31 Bradford St., 508/487-1811, 7 A.M.–8:30 P.M. daily Mar.–mid-Nov., breakfast served until 3 P.M., $10–20) in the far West End. It's a P'town version of a classic breakfast diner: mounted fish above the big picture windows, nautical tchotchkes, $5 omelets, and regulars who come in for the exact same meal at the exact same hour every day.

For a snack, sip, slice, or salad, it's hard not to like **Spiritus Café & Pizzeria** (190 Commercial St., 508/487-2808, 11 A.M.–2 A.M. in summer, open Apr.–early Nov., pizzas $17–27), which is even more funky than its Hyannis progenitor. The chrome proboscis of a cherry-red Caddy pokes out of the ceiling, the tables are adorned with painterly decorations, and the wide front steps are perfect for fraternizing. Around closing time in the busy season—when the bars are emptying out and the last pizza slices are being scarfed up by dance-happy club-goers—the pheromones are nearly as thick as the ice cream.

Another satisfying fast-food choice is **Big Daddy's Burrito** (205 Commercial St., 508/487-4432, www.bigdaddysburritos.com, 11 A.M.–11 P.M. daily May–Oct., reduced hours in fall, $4–12) in the Olde Aquarium Building. For a sample of local tradition, check out the **Portuguese Bakery** (299 Commercial St., 508/487-1803, 7 A.M.–6 P.M. daily Mar.–Oct., $4–5). Despite the impression given by restaurants around town, Portuguese cuisine isn't all tomato, onion, and cumin-flavored fish stews, simmered slowly all day. A good dessert tradition exists within the cuisine, too, as this storefront bakery amply and ably demonstrates. Try the *trutas* (sweet potato fritters) or the almond meringues for a real Portuguese treat.

Speaking of fish stews, don't leave town without trying one. **The Lobster Pot** (321 Commercial St., 508/487-0842, 11:30 A.M.–9 P.M. daily Apr.–Nov., $9–29), just east of MacMillan Pier, is a fine place to start, especially since it offers two immediate advantages: its waterfront view and the fact that upon entering you must pass the kitchen, inhaling a foretaste of the palate-tickling fare that awaits. Platters of seafood in bread-sopping sauces more than measure up to that evanescent preview, as do the clambakes, lobsters, and vegetarian pastas. If you change your mind about a sweet ending to your meal after walking out the door, step down the street and into the **Purple Feather Dessert Cafe** (334 Commercial St., 508/487-9100, www.thepurplefeather.com, 11 A.M.–9 P.M. Apr.–Oct., reduced hours in off-season), dedicated to fine homemade chocolates, gelato, fudge, and other confections.

Other waterfront options worth recommending are found deep in the East and West Ends of town. The former is **Fanizzi's by the Sea** (539 Commercial St., 508/487-1964, www.fanizzisrestaurant.com, 11:30 A.M.–10 P.M. Mon.–Sat., 10 A.M.–2 P.M. Sun., year-round, $10–25), whose dining room is so close to the water that at high tide, you may wonder if you'll get your feet wet going back out to the street. It's a casual spot with swift service where you'll eat well—char-grilled burgers, hefty fish and chips platters, roasted vegetarian lasagna, seafood over pasta, grilled fresh fish, and even meatloaf with mashed potatoes fill out the menu. At the opposite end of town and a couple rungs up the foodie's ladder is **The Red Inn** (15 Commercial St., 508/487-7334, www.theredinn.com, 5:30 P.M.–1 A.M. Thurs.–Sun. mid-Apr.–mid-May, daily mid-May–Oct., Fri.–Sun. Nov.–mid-Dec., and 10 A.M.–2:30 P.M. Sat.–Sun. mid-May–Oct., Thurs.–Fri. 10 A.M.–2:30 P.M. July–Aug., $21–38), a historic lodging property whose elegant, contemporary dining room has but two walls of large picture windows between it and the bay. Here, you can choose to dress your Caesar salad with oyster brochettes instead of anchovies, your mashed potatoes will likely have been laced with truffle oil, the mushrooms are all flavorful wild ones, and every plate is an edible painting.

If you want to take advantage of P'town's healthy variety of creative cuisine at somewhat less cost, you would do well to consider **Devon's** (401 1/2 Commercial St., 508/487-4773, www.devons.org, 8 A.M.–1 P.M. and 6–10 P.M. Thurs.–Tues. June–Sept., and Fri.–Sun. in May and Oct., $20–30). A tiny converted fishing shack with under 40 seats, this place is nothing if not cozy. The one-page menu is similarly intimate, featuring fewer than a dozen entrées each night. Seafood is emphasized, of course, but your waitperson is just as likely to recommend the organic pork tenderloin with rhubarb compote or the Bordelaise filet mignon. In short, everything is given careful personal attention, from the fish on the grill to the customer at the back. Terrific breakfasts, too—the blueberry pancakes are a particularly nice treat.

One of the few all-year stalwarts of the local dining scene is **Napi's** (7 Freeman St., 508/487-1145, 5 P.M.–10 P.M. daily year-round, 11:30 A.M.–5 P.M. Oct.–April), tucked away behind the Tedeschi convenience store on Bradford. The local king of cross-cultural blending, it offers a diverse globe-trotting menu, including spicy Oriental noodles, Greek caponata, Thai chicken, Brazilian steak, and, of course, plenty of seafood. Though not cheap ($13 for a veggie burrito dinner, for example, and generally $15–25 for entrées), it's also one of the few spots to please serious vegetarians. Pass on the forgettable, overpriced desserts. Decor reflects the owners' passion for objects with a past—from art to building timber.

◖ **The Mews Restaurant & Cafe** (429 Commercial St., 508/487-1500, www.mews .com, 6 P.M.–10:30 P.M. daily year-round, 11:30–2 P.M. Sun. brunch mid-May–Oct., $11–32) is revered by local residents for staying open 363 nights of the year. But this venerable beachfront institution also happens to serve some of the best meals on the outer Cape. Choose between creative gourmet dining or a casual yet upscale café menu in the always-lively bar. Don't miss sampling from New England's largest collection of vodkas: over 230 from 28 different countries.

Imagine Mexican–Continental fusion, then imagine it being delicious. That's what you'll find at **Lorraine's Restaurant** (133 Commercial St., 508/487-6074, 6–11 P.M. daily, Apr.–Nov., $18–30), which goes beyond burritos to offer items such as rack of lamb with roasted garlic chipotle and cognac demi-glace. The dark-wood barroom also features 100 different sipping tequilas.

Information

Get the latest word about goings-on around town at the year-round Chamber of Commerce office in Lopes Square (307 Commercial St., 508/487-3424, www.ptown-chamber.com), and have a look at their racks of colorful brochures and flyers for information on possible diversions and amusements. Or peruse a copy of *Provincetown Magazine*, a free weekly published April–September and distributed next to many local cash registers. The magazine's restaurant ads, gallery listings, and community calendar page will give you a rather complete snapshot of the town's commercial, retail, and entertainment possibilities.

Getting Around

Since P'town is a couple of miles long and barely that many blocks wide, one of the best alternatives to driving is using your feet. In warmer weather, bike shops also open for rentals. The best selection is found at **Arnold's** (329 Commercial St., 508/487-0844, May 15–late Oct.), where beach cruisers, 18- to 21-speed hybrid all-terrain bikes, and front-suspension mountain bikes rent on a sliding scale for $5 an hour $16 for four hours, or $20 for a workday (9 A.M.–6 P.M.). **Ptown Bikes** (42 Bradford St., 508/487-8735, www.ptownbikes.com, Apr.–Oct.) has comparable rates ($10 for up to 2 hours, $20 for 24 hours) and comparable bikes, but longer business hours (8 A.M.–8 P.M.), plus limited hours into the off-season. If, for some reason, you can't find satisfaction at either of those shops, try **Gale Force Bike Rentals** (144 Bradford Street Exit, 508/487-4849, www .galeforcebikes.com, May–Oct.) in the far West End, whose selection of 3-, 10-, and 18-speed bikes are available at least 9 A.M.–5 P.M. daily for roughly the same rates everyone else charges. All shops provide locks and helmets (free–$2 per day).

If you want someone else to do the driving, look for the **Provincetown Shuttle** ($2 ride, $4 all-day pass), a seasonal service of the Cape Cod Regional Transit Authority (800/352-7155). Between Memorial Day weekend and the third week in October, it loops around P'town, North Truro, and Herring Cove, the nearer of P'town's two National Seashore beaches, from 7:15 A.M. until a quarter past midnight Monday–Saturday, and 7:15 A.M.–8:15 P.M. Sunday. Buses run every half hour except before 12:15 P.M. and after 8:15 P.M. Monday–Thursday, when the frequency drops to hourly. As with all Cape Cod RTA buses, the shuttle vehicles are equipped with bike racks.

Alternatively, call a cab: **Cape Cab** (508/487-2222); **Martin's Taxi** (508/487-

0243); **Mercedes Cab** (508/487-3333); or **Provincetown Taxi** (508/487-8294). All are theoretically open year-round, but some of them do take breaks between bar closing and daybreak, or leave their phones un-answered at their whim in the depths of winter.

Provincetown Parking
On-street spaces are at a premium in this small town, so drivers should anticipate paying big-city rates to park in one of the flat-rate or per-hour lots within walking dis-tance of all the good stuff. You can slowly circle the Town Hall waiting for someone to give up a precious metered space—if you're patient, winter will roll around, everyone will go home, and you'll get lucky. If you do, note that most of the town's quarters-only meters run 8 A.M.–midnight daily.

However, you *can* feed them for a full 10 hours ($5) at one pop. If you cave in and are willing to pay for a space in an attended lot, expect anywhere from a flat rate of $5–8 for all-day farthest from downtown to $2 per hour (up to a daily maximum of $20) at the largest and most central municipal lot on MacMillan Pier. Although they're the most expensive, the city-owned lots are the easiest to find—electronic signs at key intersections point the way, with LED dis-plays to redirect drivers from the pier to secondary lots on Prince Street as necessary. Note that the summer shuttle bus includes nearly every major parking lot on its route, from far-flung lots on Bradford Street to MacMillan Pier, making it doubly conve-nient for summer visitors to leave the car in one spot and flag down a shuttle for trips around town.

Festivals and Events

APRIL
The bayside town of Brewster spends three days over the last weekend of the month (or the first in May) celebrating **Brewster in Bloom** (800/399-2967, www.brewsterinbloom.org), with a parade, golf tournament, five-kilome-ter road race, and tour of more than a dozen local B&B inns.

MAY
Ignoring whatever lingering chill may be in the air, Chatham launches its **Maritime Festival** (508/945-5199) on the first weekend of the month. Activities include lighthouse tours, a Coast Guard rescue demonstration, a "zany boat race," and various contests for professional fish-ermen and their would-be imitators, including clam shucking, fish filleting, and a "boot-in-the-bucket" test of tossing skills. Since Chatham is one of the handful of towns in Massachusetts that still has a commercial fishing fleet, a high-light of the festival is, of course, the food caught fresh from local waters.

Pre-season visitors will also find oo-dles of activities to enjoy during **Cape Cod Maritime Days,** the following week. This local observance of National Historic Preservation Week is celebrated across the Cape with lighthouse tours, slide talks, boatbuilding demonstrations, musical per-formances, narrated walks, guided kayaking tours, and open houses at historic structures normally off-limits to the public. The busy week, sponsored in part by the Cape Cod Chamber of Commerce (508/362-3225, www.ecapechamber.com), kicks off with a day-long symposium on maritime history (call 508/775-1723, or visit www.capecod maritimemuseum.org to register). A calendar of events is distributed around regional visi-tor booths, or visit www.ecapechamber.com and print your own.

JUNE
The side of Provincetown's heritage that is inextricably bound to the glory days of

its commercial fishery is on display during the **Portuguese Festival** (508/487-0500, www.provincetownportuguesefestival.com, Thurs.–Sun. on the final weekend of the month). Known primarily for the Blessing of the Fleet that takes place on Sunday afternoon, the festival also includes plenty of live music, dancing (including exhibitions of traditional Portuguese dance), and food, including soups, seafood, and sweets.

JULY

On Wednesday evenings throughout July and August, head down to the Wellfleet Town Pier for free **square dancing** under the stars (7:30–10 P.M., 508/349-0330, exit 116).

For nine days in the latter half of the month, the **Barnstable County Fair** (508/563-3200, www.barnstablecountyfair .org) enthusiastically makes residents and visitors alike forget the fact that Cape Cod has lost nearly all its traditional farmland to development. Barnyard animal displays, beekeeping exhibits, a petting zoo, blacksmithing demonstrations, circus performers, live music, and of course a full midway of carnival games and rides round out this charming celebration of agrarian tradition, held every year since the end of the Civil War at the Barnstable County Fairgrounds on Rte. 151 in East Falmouth.

AUGUST

The first Sunday of the month marks the return of the Boston Pops Esplanade Orchestra to the Hyannis Village Green for their annual **Pops by the Sea** concert (508/362-0066, www.artsfoundationcape cod.org) to benefit the Arts Foundation of Cape Cod.

Flea markets, church suppers, a jazz picnic, old-fashioned field games for kids, an antique car parade, and even free ice cream are among the many goings-on around the Mid-Cape town of Dennis during the community-wide **Festival Days** (508/398-3568, www.dennis chamber.com), which last most of the third week of the month.

SEPTEMBER

The weekend after Labor Day, the **Bourne Scallop Festival** (508/759-6000, www.bourne scallopfest.com) is held in the Bourne village of Buzzards Bay on the mainland side of the Cape Cod Canal. Games, children's rides, crafts, and of course all manner of scallop-themed cuisine fill the village's canalside park near the entrance to the Massachusetts Maritime Academy.

The second weekend of the month is also when Harwich holds its annual **Cranberry Festival** (508/430-2811, www.harwichcran berryfestival.org) in recognition of its leading role in the Cape's cranberry industry.

Around the Vernal Equinox—the third weekend of the month—the Outer Cape town of Truro ends the summer season with a suitably colorful and eclectic party. **Truro Treasures** (508/487-6464, www.trurotrea sures.org) includes live music, arts, crafts, a road race, and a sandcastle competition, and culminates in the locally famous Sunday-night "Dump Dance" at Truro's transfer station, a.k.a the town dump. (Since all refuse has been hauled off-Cape for years, town dumps up and down the region have evolved from garbage heaps into well-tended outdoor swap shops.)

OCTOBER

Mashpee Commons, the green beside the Mashpee Rotary at the junction of Rtes. 28 and 151, hosts **Oktoberfest** (508/539-1400) on the Saturday of Columbus Day weekend. In addition to the requisite beer garden, there are displays of arts and crafts, games for kids, and sidewalk sales at shops throughout the complex. (And for those who like to earn their beer, a 10K road race the same day.)

DECEMBER

Provincetown's annual—and the world's only—Gay and Lesbian Holiday Festival, better known as **Holly Folly** (508/487-2313 or 800/637-8696, www.ptown.org), livens up the first weekend of the month with nightclub dances, open-house tours of local inns, a holiday concert at Town Hall, festive menus at area restaurants, and a "shop hop" among local retailers.

For something a tad more traditional, join Santa and his elves for **Christmas in Sandwich** (508/888-0251, www.sandwich glassmuseum.org), from the first through the second weekends of the month. Enjoy music and caroling, open houses at local museums and inns, and special treats from local merchants. The historic part of the town already looks the part of the 19th-century New England village, but the holiday decorations make it fit the role even more.

Getting There and Around

BY AIR

The major point of entry into New England for commercial airline passengers is **Logan International Airport** in Boston. Any hour of day or night you can obtain the latest fares and schedules of all the buses and boats that will be available to you after arriving at Logan—plus up-to-the-minute traffic reports on airport roadways—by calling the automated **Massport Ground Transportation Information Service** (800/235-6426).

The leading year-round airline to the Cape is **Cape Air** (508/771-6944 or 800/352-0714, www.flycapeair.com), whose fleet of nine-passenger Cessnas flies to **Barnstable Municipal Airport** in Hyannis (the middle of the Cape) and **Provincetown Airport** at the very tip. A regional code-sharing partner of JetBlue Airways, Cape Air offers discounted one-day round-trips on nearly all its routes and joint fares with nearly all major foreign and domestic airlines flying into Boston and Providence, its principal gateways to the region; as well as year-round direct flights from New York City (LaGuardia)

The only other regular carrier offering year-round nonstops to the region is **Colgan Air/ US Airways Express** (800/428-4322, www .usairways.com), serving Barnstable Municipal Airport from New York City (LaGuardia).

BY RAIL

While there's no direct rail service to Cape Cod, it's possible to connect from **Amtrak** (800/872-7245, www.amtrak.com) to year-round Cape-bound bus service in either Boston or Providence, Rhode Island.

BY BUS

The most affordable year-round alternative to driving to the region is to take a bus. No matter where you're coming from in the U.S. or Canada, you can reach Cape Cod and the Islands using a major interstate bus company, such as Greyhound or a member of the Trailways network, in conjunction with the two regional companies that cover the final New England leg of the journey.

Peter Pan (888/751-8800, www.peterpan bus.com) also provides service from New York via Providence, Fall River, and New Bedford to Hyannis. To reach Hyannis from Logan Airport or Boston's South Station, however, you must take one of the dozen daily buses of the **Plymouth & Brockton Street Railway** (508/746-0378, www.p-b.com). The Hyannis Transportation Center at which all buses arrive is about a 15-minute walk from either the Hy-Line or Steamship ferry docks. A free Steamship Authority shuttle van swings by the transportation center as it makes its rounds between satellite parking lots and the South Street ferry terminal, but frankly walking is often just as quick.

After stopping at the Hyannis Transportation Center, 1–3 daily selected P&B buses from Boston continue to Provincetown and five towns in between—at least a four-hour trip from the big city all the way to the outermost tip of the Cape. Given the possible connections in Hyannis to Peter Pan buses from Providence and points west, with optimum scheduling a trip from Manhattan's Port Authority to P'town would take about eight hours and cost just under $65. An intrepid rider from Toronto could make it in about 20 hours.

BY FERRY

Crossing Cape Cod Bay off season requires a friend in the fishing fleet, but come summer several passenger ferries make the 90-minute dash between Boston and the South Shore to Provincetown, at the tip of the Outer Cape.

Bay State Cruise Company (617/457-1428 or 508/487-9284, www.provincetownfastferry .com) offers the *Provincetown III*, a high-speed catamaran that makes the three-hour round-trip three times daily from mid-May until mid-Oct. It disembarks from the Commonwealth Pier in South Boston, beside the World Trade Center, across the street from that building's eponymous Silver Line bus rapid transit station. (The Silver Line puts the ferry within minutes of both Amtrak service at South Station and Logan Airport.) Tickets are $48 one-way, $77 round-trip.

Boston Harbor Cruises (617/227-4321, www.bostonharborcruises.com) also makes the Boston–P'town run with their flagship, the 600-passenger high-speed catamaran *Salacia*. It casts off from downtown Boston's Long Wharf, next to the New England Aquarium, every morning daily from early May through early October. For Memorial Day weekend and then mid-June through early September, additional afternoon and weekend evening departures are added to the schedule, with the last boat back to Boston scheduled late enough to allow a leisurely P'town dinner and dessert.

BY BOAT

If you're coming on your own boat, you'll find nearly every Cape harbor has at least a couple of anchorages or berths for visitors. Marinas and yacht yards able to accommodate at least a few dozen cruisers are found at Cataumet, on Buzzards Bay; Falmouth, Osterville, and Hyannis, on the south shore; and Provincetown.

You'll want to call ahead and reserve a slip at the **Hyannis Marina** (508/790-4000, www .hyannismarina.com). There, on the inner har-

bor across from all the island ferries, you'll find all the repair, rigging, pump-out, hook-up, shower, and laundry facilities you could want. Trolley service to Main Street, too, aboard the CCRTA bus.

BY CAR

On most interstates and some state highways within Massachusetts, the speed limit is 65 mph, but along the Mid-Cape Highway—U.S. 6—it's 55 mph or less. You'll soon see—from traffic in most areas—that these are more polite suggestions than true limits.

PUBLIC TRANSIT

If you don't have a car, don't worry. The region is well served by public buses and tourist park-and-ride trolleys. Many operate year-round (Nantucket excepted), although of course the greatest quantity of service to the widest number of destinations is offered in summer.

With just a little patience and a few dollar bills, it's possible to reach almost every town on the Cape with the **Cape Cod Regional Transit Authority** and its collection of year-round bus lines and summer trolleys—in combination with the all-season Plymouth & Brockton (508/746-0378, www.p-b.com) and Peter Pan (888/751-8800, www.peterpanbus.com) buses. (The most notable missing link is Sandwich. When it comes to bus travel, you can't get there from here.)

The Plymouth & Brockton provides local service from the Mid-Cape (Hyannis) to Provincetown via U.S. 6, with stops at all the Outer Cape communities from Orleans north, while Peter Pan makes local stops in towns along the Buzzards Bay side of the Upper Cape, from the Cape Cod Canal down to Woods Hole. Every south shore and backside town between Woods Hole and Orleans is served by a combination of the **Hyannis-Falmouth/Woods Hole Sealine** and **Hyannis-Orleans H2O** bus routes, which operate daily from late June through early September and Monday–Saturday otherwise, plus **The Shuttle** between North Truro and Provincetown, which runs seven days a week right through mid-October. Though Hyannis is the hub of the system, connections in Orleans make it feasible to do a circle trip around most of the Mid-to-Outer Cape area.

Fares on the Hyannis-area routes and both summer shuttles are $2 per ride or $6 for an all-day pass. While the shuttles run well past sundown—past midnight in some cases—year-round buses favor daylight hours. Pick up a complete system timetable at the Hyannis Transportation Center, town information booths, or almost anywhere you see racks of tourist brochures, or visit their website (www .capecodtransit.org). You can also call the CCRTA directly (508/385-8326 or 800/352-7155) and press the appropriate buttons to get prerecorded schedules.

The Hyannis Transportation Center serves as an endpoint for all three year-round Cape Cod Regional Transit Authority bus routes: the **SeaLine,** running west to Falmouth and Woods Hole; the **Villager,** heading north to Barnstable Harbor via the Rte. 132 malls; and the easterly **H2O Line,** connecting Hyannis to Orleans via Rte. 28 through Yarmouth, Dennisport, Harwich Port, and Chatham. Saquetucket Harbor in Harwich Port, the departure point for the Freedom Cruise Line boat to Nantucket, is one of the possible stops along this last route. All routes operate daily late June–early September, and then mostly Monday–Saturday the remainder of the year. Call the CCRTA toll-free at 800/352-7155 for schedule and fare information, pick up their system timetable at the bus terminal, or download everything you need to know from www.capecodtransit.org.

MARTHA'S VINEYARD

Forget about Martha—it's "The Vineyard" to everybody in the know, or simply "the Island" to those longtime residents who barely acknowledge the existence of nearby Nantucket. By any name, it's a peach: big enough to have quiet spots even in the busiest season, small enough that you can get to know it quickly, slightly more democratic than its neighbor in matters of room and board, and far more accessible to day-trippers. This is the island of seaside naps and lazy days in chaise lounges, of sailboats and bicycles, lighthouses and gingerbread cottages, artists and professors, carpenters and movie stars, presidential advisors and, occasionally, presidents. Water sports, historical exhibits, and nature trails provide alternatives to the beach, while abundant seafood and all manner of sweets lay to rest that austere summer diet you fleetingly considered in order to fit into last year's swimsuit.

The Vineyard's 100-plus square miles are neatly divisible into "up-island" and "down-island." As on Cape Cod, this holdover from days of whalers and sailors makes sense if you remember that degrees of longitude ascend from east to west.

Down-island is the Vineyard's pedestrian-friendly threshold: Vineyard Haven, Oak Bluffs, and Edgartown. Along with a near monopoly on knickknack shops, sweet treats, and Black Dog T-shirts, down-island is where good food, nightlife, and accommodations are all within walking distance of each other. Car-free visitors also have the flexibility of catching a ferry at almost a moment's notice. While you are more likely to find the comforting glow of streetlights rather

HIGHLIGHTS

◖ **Oak Bluffs Campground:** Stroll curvy lanes amid a postcard-perfect collection of colorful Victorian gingerbread cottages (page 106).

◖ **Historic Downtown Edgartown:** Stately waterfront mansions and a stunning Greek Revival church frame the charming shop-filled blocks and narrow garden-lined lanes of the island's oldest town (page 116).

◖ **Edgartown Lighthouse:** Beautiful harbor and town views await at both the beach around the base and the railed deck at the top of this historic 45-foot tower a short stroll from downtown (page 117).

◖ **Sailing Katama Bay:** Water rats know nothing is half so much worth doing as messing about in boats, a maxim proven doubly true when lolling under sail aboard one of the Vineyard's beautiful windjammers or wooden yachts (page 123).

◖ **Mytoi:** The serenity of a Japanese-style landscaped garden provides an oasis amid the pines of rural Chappaquiddick (page 124).

◖ **Wasque Point and Cape Poge:** Swim, surf-cast, kayak, bird-watch, take tours to a remote lighthouse, or do nothing but lay listening to the steady beat of the Atlantic Ocean upon miles of barrier beach (page 125).

◖ **Gay Head Cliffs:** Watching the sunset from the upper edge of this many-shaded clay scarp is rivaled only by trekking amid the mussel-fringed boulders, mermaid purses, and other marine curiosities fetched up along the rough shore at its base (page 134).

◖ **Long Point Wildlife Refuge:** Comb the beach, let the strong surf scour your summer cares away, take a paddle tour of Tisbury Great Pond, or just saunter through the heaths of this ecologically rare coastal sandplain grasslands (page 138).

◖ **Cedar Tree Neck:** Easy trails through a varied woodland habitat lead to a beautiful scenic shore along Vineyard Sound (page 139).

MARTHA'S VINEYARD

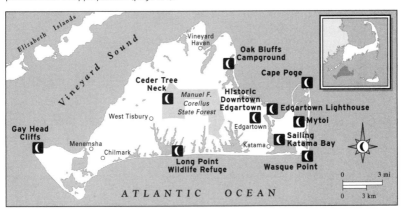

LOOK FOR ◖ TO FIND RECOMMENDED SIGHTS, ACTIVITIES, DINING, AND LODGING.

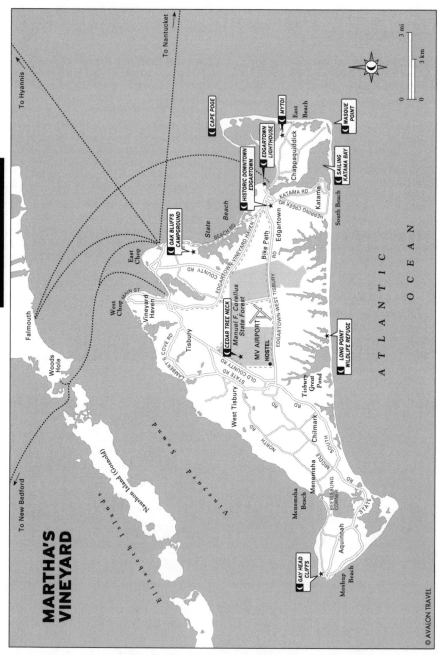

MARTHA'S VINEYARD

To Hyannis

To Nantucket

To New Bedford

Elizabeth Islands

Woods Hole

Falmouth

Naushon Island (Gosnold)

Vineyard Sound

Moshup Beach

Aquinnah

■ GAY HEAD CLIFFS

Menemsha

Menemsha Beach

Chilmark

BEETLEBUNG CORNER

NORTH RD

MIDDLE RD

SOUTH RD

STATE

West Tisbury

Tisbury

Vineyard Haven

West Chop

East Chop

MAIN ST

LAMBERT'S COVE RD

STATE RD

OLD COUNTY RD

EDGARTOWN-WEST TISBURY

Tisbury Great Pond

■ LONG POINT WILDLIFE REFUGE

MV AIRPORT

HOSTEL

■ CEDAR TREE NECK

Manuel F. Correllus State Forest

EDGARTOWN COUNTY RD

State Beach

BEACH RD

■ OAK BLUFFS CAMPGROUND

Bike Path

Edgartown

■ HISTORIC DOWNTOWN EDGARTOWN

■ EDGARTOWN LIGHTHOUSE

■ CAPE POGE

KATAMA RD

HERRING CREEK RD

Katama

Chappaquiddick

■ MYTOI

East Beach

■ MASQUE POINT

■ SAILING KATAMA BAY

South Beach

A T L A N T I C   O C E A N

3 mi

3 km

© AVALON TRAVEL

than a chorus of crickets outside your bedroom window at night, down-island offers plenty of scenic beauty and is home to more than half of the Vineyard's two dozen public beaches.

Up-island is the island's southwestern corner farthest from the Cape Cod ferries. It comprises the predominantly rural towns of West Tisbury, Chilmark, and Aquinnah, home to only a smattering of small restaurants, stores, and galleries. Many of the area's undulating country roads are lined by great allées of oak, like antebellum plantation driveways, and the woods are filled with the drystone walls of bygone sheep farms. The up-island hills—the Vineyard's highest ground—offer great views en route to their abrupt tumble into the sea beneath the steady sweep of the beacon in red-brick Gay Head Light.

While even this section of the Vineyard heavily depends on "summer people," it also relies on agriculture and fishing. Its working roots are especially visible in picturesque Menemsha harbor—home to more ground-fish draggers and lobster trappers than luxury yachts—and at the seasonal biweekly farmers' market in West Tisbury. To experience up-island at its best generally requires owning or renting a set of wheels (two or four), although every town is linked to down-island throughout the year by public transit.

HISTORY
Early Visitors

Martha's Vineyard is generally said to take its name from an abundance of native wild grapes and the daughter of Bartholomew Gosnold, the English captain who spent the late spring of 1602 around Buzzards Bay and the Elizabeth Islands (which he named in honor of his Queen), in what was then known as "the North part of Virginia." However, given that Gosnold didn't have a daughter named Martha and that his mother-in-law, Martha Goulding, helped finance his voyage, it is more plausible he was honoring her. According to the "Briefe and true Relation" of the voyage, by one of its members, John Brereton, Gosnold actually applied "Marthaes

THE LEGEND OF MOSHUP

(As told by Thomas Cooper, Gay Head Indian, to Englishman Benjamin Basset in 1792)

The first Indian who came to the Vineyard, was brought thither with his dog on a cake of ice. When he came to Gay Head, he found a very large man, whose name was Moshup. He had a wife and five children, four sons and one daughter; and lived in the Den [Gay Head's circular depression]. He used to catch whales, and then pluck up trees, and make a fire, and roast them. The coals of the trees, and the bones of the whales, are now to be seen. After he was tired of staying here, he told his children to go and play ball on a beach that joined Noman's Land to Gay Head. He then made a mark with his toe across the beach at each end, and so deep, that the water followed, and cut away the beach; so that his children were in fear of drowning. They took their sister up, and held her out of the water. He told them to act as if they were going to kill whales; and they were all turned into killers [killer whales]. The sister was dressed in large stripes. He gave them strict charge always to be kind to her. His wife mourned the loss of her children so exceedingly, that he threw her away. She fell upon Seconet [Sakonnet Point, RI], near the rocks, where she lived some time, exacting contribution of all who passed by water. After a while she was changed into a stone. The entire shape remained for many years. But after the English came, some of them broke off the arms, head, &c. but most of the body remains to this day. Moshup went away nobody knows whither. He had no conversation with the Indians, but was kind to them, by sending whales, &c. ashore to them to eat. But after they grew thick around him he left them.

(Simmons, William S., Spirit of the New England Tribes)

vineyard" to a very small, uninhabited island overgrown with various fruit-bearing shrubs and such "an incredible store of Vines…that we could not goe for treading upon them." Probably this was what's now aptly called Noman's Land, a naval gunnery-range-turned-wildlife-sanctuary off Aquinnah's south shore. By 1610, cartographers assigned the name to the much larger adjacent island. There it remains today, having outlasted "Capawack" (probably from the Algonquian word for harbor, *kuppaug*), which was for decades the most widely used appellation of the first English settlers.

The lure for Gosnold, as for other captains who ranged the New England coast in the early 17th century, was sassafras. The safrole in the leaves is now known to be a carcinogen, but to Gosnold's contemporaries the plant was widely believed to be a cure-all. "The roote of sassafras hath power to comfort the liver," enthused one 1597 herbal encyclopedia, "and to dissolve oppilations, to comfort the weake and feeble stomacke, to cause a good appetite, to consume windiness, the chiefest cause of cruditie and indigestion, stay vomiting, and make sweete a stinking breath." Perhaps more important to the gentlemen of Europe—whose demand for the stuff kept the price (and profit margins) so high—was the belief that it could cure "the French Poxe" (i.e. syphilis).

They Came, They Saw, They Converted

When Gosnold's ship, *The Concord,* anchored in local waters, the Vineyard was well inhabited by Native Americans related to the Wampanoags of coastal Massachusetts and Rhode Island—a federation of Algonquian-speaking bands whose ancestors had occupied *Noe-pe* (the land "amid the waters") for at least 9,000 years. The 17th-century Wampanoags were farmers and fishermen organized in close-knit villages around *sachems* (hereditary leaders) and *pauwaus* (religious leaders and physicians, or medicine men). When the first white settlers arrived, in 1642, four sachems presided over the island's estimated population of 3,000.

These first immigrants were farmers and shepherds from the Boston area led by Thomas Mayhew, Jr., a missionary, and his father, a merchant. For 40 pounds and a beaver hat (about three times the price allegedly paid for Manhattan 15 years earlier), Mayhew, Sr., had purchased from the Earl of Stirling the patent to all islands then unoccupied by the English off the south shore of Cape Cod—and, importantly, beyond the boundaries of both the existing Pilgrim and Puritan colonies. Bypassing the sandy heaths of Nantucket and the too-small Elizabeth Islands as ill suited to the homesteading needs of their party, the Mayhews settled on the Vineyard.

The Wampanoags accepted them, despite previous experience that included an English captain's kidnapping a sachem for zoolike display in London. Mayhew, Sr., assured the Indians that his master, King James, though superior to their sachems, "would in no measure invade their Jurisdictions." Surprisingly, he kept his word, paying for property rights as his settlements expanded or—as in the case of Nantucket—before he resold possessions granted him under his original royal patent.

Such honesty merits special mention because it stands out so much from the shameless deceits of Mayhew's mainland contemporaries, but tolerance may have begun as a form of détente. The Wampanoags could not have forgotten the ruinous Pequot War, ended just five years before, and the devastation it brought that tribe in nearby coastal Connecticut for getting in the way of the English. And Mayhew's thirty-odd homesteaders would have been conscious of being far from the assistance of authorities in either the Massachusetts Bay or Plymouth colonies.

In any event, the Indians' mortality rate and acculturation made hostilities or illegal land grabs wholly unnecessary. Beginning with a nasty plague outbreak a few years after the settlers' arrival, European diseases reduced the Wampanoag population by over 70 percent within as many years. Devoted missionary work by both Mayhews (capitalizing in part on the *pauwaus'* inability to stem disease-related deaths) converted many more Indians into model subjects of English law. Some were so thoroughly assimilated that the English islanders paid to send them to Harvard to be trained for the ministry.

After Mayhew, Jr., was lost at sea on a fundraising trip to England, Mayhew, Sr., effectively ran the island as the private Manor of Tisbury, with himself as Lord and Chief Justice. Intolerant of dissent, the Governor-for-Life jailed or exiled his fellow landowners as he saw fit, until finally succumbing to nature's term limits at the age of 85. Nine years of squabbling later, in 1691, the Vineyard was annexed to the new Province of Massachusetts formed by monarchs William and Mary after the various colonial charters were revoked by an English parliament impatient with their subjects' unruliness.

Population Pressures

Frothy politics aside, the remainder of the 17th century and most of the 18th were marked most by rapid population growth among whites—more from new births than new immigrants. Predictably, this had side effects. When J. Hector de Crèvecoeur wrote, in his *Letters from an American Farmer,* that travelers to the Vineyard couldn't avoid becoming acquainted with all its principal families, he was complimenting island hospitality, but he might as well have been satirizing the islanders' inbreeding. At the time of his visit, in the 1770s, almost every new island marriage was between cousins of some kind; by the mid-1800s, half the island's population had one of only a dozen surnames. Until settlement by off-islanders in the 20th century introduced new blood (and disapproval of marriage between cousins), there was no stigma attached to the high incidence of deafness among newborns—particularly in the rural up-island towns. Until after World War I, not surprisingly, sign language was widely spoken here.

The most pressing problem posed by the high birth rate, though, was that, like an infestation of weevils in a small garden, people proceeded to strip their patrimony bare, forc-

ing a shift from sheep-shears, milking stools, and plowshares to oars, nets, and harpoons. Turning from their deforested, overgrazed hills (and later from an economy completely KO'd by English raids and embargoes during the American Revolution), an estimated 20 percent of the Vineyard's men—Wampanoag and white alike—became expert whalers and merchant seamen, as highly prized by captains and ship owners as their Nantucket brethren. "Go where you will from Nova Scotia to the Mississippi," wrote de Crèvecoeur, "you will find almost everywhere some natives of these two islands employed in seafaring occupations."

But this didn't last, either. By the 1840s, local whale-oil merchants faced stiff competition from mainland producers (who were closer to their consumers), and local wool producers were edged out by cheaper foreign imports. In the year of John Brown's pre–Civil War raid on the federal arsenal at Harpers Ferry, whale-oil prices were shot down by cheaper Pennsylvania crude; by the end of the war, the whale fleet had been scrapped, sunk, or was rotting at the wharves. The Vineyard's whaling days were over.

"We'll Camp Awhile in the Wilderness"

As seafaring fortunes waned, the newest and most lasting transformation of the Vineyard was taking root in the Second Great Awakening, a nationwide resurgence of Methodist revivalism. In 1835, southern New England Methodists began holding revival tent meetings in an oak-shaded meadow they christened Wesleyan Grove, erecting a small village of huge "society tents" each August to house the crowds who came to experience a week of Bible-thumping preaching and religious conversion. The year the market for whale oil nosedived, 1859, some 12,000 souls turned up at the camp meeting, seeking salvation in 400 tents.

These tent revivals were such a magnet for tourists that they were featured in the *New York Times* travel section and in illustrated weeklies such as *Harper's.* The great congregation-sponsored tents were gradually replaced

VINEYARD ETIQUETTE

The list of past and present Vineyard residents includes Spike Lee, Harvey Weinstein, Mike Wallace, Carly Simon, Denzel Washington, Alan Dershowitz, Judy Blume, Diane Sawyer, David Letterman, James Taylor, Bill Murray, Walter Cronkite, Art Buchwald, John Belushi, and Jackie O. Maybe the sun does shine a little brighter on these people, but don't come to the Vineyard expecting to bask in it yourself.

Local wisdom holds that the Vineyard attracts celebrities precisely because locals have either too much Yankee sense or Puritan humility to make a fuss over cultural icons in the flesh. This legendary discretion has become the cornerstone of Vineyard etiquette, which declares that celebrities are to be allowed to go about unmolested by photographers or autograph-seekers. Should you see Somebody, you should feign indifference instead of, say, crossing the street to get a better look. If Somebody sits at the next table in a restaurant, you are requested to act nonchalant instead of playing paparazzo with your camera.

You can do otherwise, of course, but then many trees' worth of *Vineyard Gazette* newsprint will be expended by local vigilantes clucking their tongues over another tourist who "just doesn't get it." Anyway, you're wasting your time driving Chilmark's back roads hoping to catch some box-office headliners shmoozing over a barbecue; most of those Very Important People stay so well out of sight that the closest you'll get is the airport, within earshot of their chartered jets.

by fanciful wooden family cottages whose occupants soon set aside as much time for parlor entertainment, croquet, and promenading along the seashore as for hymns, gospel, and prayer. A speculative group of investors, the Oak Bluffs Land and Wharf Company, began constructing a summer resort around Wesleyan Grove, deliberately mirroring the camp meeting grounds' informality, capitalizing on the impeccable reputation and high moral character of the revival gathering (as opposed to the liquor-soaked haven of high society across Vineyard Sound at Newport) and targeting the same sober Christians as the camp meetings. Out of this emerging middle class of shopkeepers, blacksmiths, carpenters, watchmakers, and other artisans seeking both a hard-earned reprieve from sweltering cities and safe recreation for their families, "Cottage City"—eventually renamed Oak Bluffs— was born.

Over the last century, the Vineyard has continued to cultivate its reputation as a summer resort, although the demographics of both the visitors and their hosts have changed. The 1960s and '70s saw a rise in VW owners and McGovern voters coming to roost here permanently, accompanied by a handful of celebrities looking for a place to avoid the limelight. Both have been followed by the seasonal tide of college students seeking good parties and a wave of professionals, academics, and business execs on a spree of second-home buying. These days, media moguls and A-list movie stars are plunking down millions for secluded beachfronts and pedigreed estates. Besides sending high-end property values toward the moon, this latest trend has drawn stargazers who either don't know or don't care about the local etiquette. Old-timers may rightly wonder whether the "good and happy grocer" of the camp meeting years would see the Vineyard of today as the piece of heaven he had sought or the profligate high-rolling resort he had sought to escape. But if you weren't here in the mellow hippie years, you have nothing to mourn. Local letter-to-the-editor writers may perennially wring their hands over the changes, but until all the old stone walls crumble to dust and the lighthouses fall into the seas, there will be enough uniquely New England flavor here to keep comparisons with Vail, Sun Valley, or Beverly Hills firmly at bay.

PLANNING YOUR TIME

Although the Vineyard is in New England, instead of four seasons to the year there are just two: in-season and off-season. The first is the big mixed-blessing phenomenon of the summer, which has carried the Vineyard economy now for more than a century. It's a fairly well-rehearsed course: After a practice gallop over the Memorial Day weekend, *in-season* does a few light warm-up laps through June before finally bolting out of the gate in a breakneck frenzy on the Fourth of July. Careening like a tornado through Labor Day, it finally slows to a canter by Columbus Day—the semiofficial end of the race and the point at which most owners retire to tally up their winnings.

Lingering momentum and clement weather can prop up *off-season* weekends through Thanksgiving, but then the island finally becomes again the property of its year-round residents, who savor the calm until their memory of the last blockbuster summer becomes so distant that they grow impatient for the sequel. (Not all locals cope well with the annual shift from traffic jams to cabin fever: the drought–flood–drought resort economy, coupled with intense isolation, is believed to strongly contribute to the high local incidence of alcoholism.)

The biggest difference between in-season and off-season is, as you might expect, a sudden increase in the availability of just about everything. By the same token, it's also at this point that the restaurants, buses, ferries, accommodations, and shops all start to scale back their operating hours. Beach buses and hourly public shuttles between up- and down-island are the first to cease, stopping promptly after Labor Day weekend, not to resume until the following mid- to late June (the shuttles still run, but not nearly as often). By mid-October, most up-island restaurants and half the B&Bs in West Tisbury, Chilmark, and Aquinnah have followed suit. By autumn, down-island towns start to roll up the rugs, cover the furniture, and forward the mail, too—but they have enough year-round resi-

© BRIAN JOLLEY

cottages that formed the original town of Oak Bluffs

dents to at least keep a few restaurants open all year. Last, but not least, there's Vineyard Haven; thanks to four-season Steamship service, it actually retains a passing resemblance to a fully functioning small town, even at the nadir of winter.

The off-season brings with it certain requirements—double-check restaurant hours, for example, and rely more on driving than you would in the longer and warmer days of summer. But these are more than outweighed by advantages such as choosing lodgings upon arrival (rather than sight-unseen three months in advance) and dining when ready, without waiting in line for an hour or making do with a fifth-choice reservation. While the *early* off-season (Apr.–June) is most prized, anyone looking for a cozy weekend escape to an austere Winslow Homer landscape shouldn't rule out December, or even February.

What you should *not* expect from the off-season in the Vineyard is significant savings. Innkeepers' supply costs are as high in winter as

MARTHA'S VINEYARD

in summer, and off-season business is too sparse to be worth a price war. Yes, some room rates may drop almost 50 percent between summer and winter, but that simply reflects the fact that July prices are stratospheric; they return in January to the realm of the average Marriott hotel.

Like resort destinations all over the country, the Vineyard struggles with the pressures of popularity. Realtors talk about three-acre minimum lots as the balm for fears of over-development, but look closely as you come in on the ferry from Woods Hole and you'll see what land conservationists are concerned about—the wooded Vineyard shore is filling with rooftops. The development issue grows ever more urgent as summer traffic in down-island towns approaches your average metropolitan rush-hour gridlock. You can be part of the solution rather than the problem by leaving your car on the mainland if at all possible, and taking advantage of the year-round public transit, extensive bike paths, taxis, and your feet.

Those using foreign currency must make their cash exchanges prior to arriving—none of the banks here handle such transactions. You won't ever be far from an automated teller machine in the down-island towns, but up-island is a different story—beyond Beetlebung Corner, there's nothing, so come prepared.

Vineyard Haven

This is the island's largest year-round community and only year-round ferry port. But by all appearances, it's just your average small seaside town of about 2,000 stalwart souls, with a little light industry near the wharf, tree-shaded residential streets overlooking the harbor, and a small commercial downtown. White clapboard and gray shingle descendants of the venerable, sharp-gabled, Cape-style house rub shoulders with old captains' mansions. The automotive spectrum ranges from rust-flecked American sedans to teenagers in their parents' hand-me-down foreign imports, from oversized pickup trucks that clearly earn their mudflaps to mirror-polished SUVs. Whatever its varied occupations the rest of the year, come summer, the town has its hands full playing host and maître d' to the million-plus visitors swarming through it.

Once known by the Wampanoags as "Nobnocket" (place by the pond), the port was known to later generations of sailors as Holmes Hole, after a 17th-century landowner. Early in the Victorian era, image-conscious citizens changed the name after deciding they preferred living in a place that sounded closer to heaven than hell. Since then, the harborside village has grown indistinguishable from Tisbury, the 17th-century township of which it was once just a part—but, aside from legal documents and town stationery, both general usage and the U.S. Postal Service now favor "Vineyard Haven" for the whole.

Visitors disgorged by the ferries will find restaurants, shops, accommodations, car and bike rentals, ATMs, and (in the Steamship Authority Terminal beside the pier and, seasonally, above the Stop & Shop parking lot across the street) public restrooms—all within a few blocks' walk. The one amenity you needn't bother looking for is a liquor store; by law, Vineyard Haven, like all the up-island towns, is dry.

SIGHTS
Historic Architecture

Since "the Great Fire of 1883" destroyed its center, the town's oldest buildings are found on upper Main Street north of the Bank of Martha's Vineyard building (whose distinctive facade, a cross between Craftsman-style stone and Mediterranean tile bungalow, occupies the grounds of the harness shop where the fire may have begun) and a block farther up from the harbor along William Street. Many of the fifty-odd houses included in the Historic District along this quiet street were built as a result of the whaling and trade industries. Befitting the wealth of their builders, some of these houses typify the Greek Revival style now most commonly associated with old banks.

Plenty of New England's most attractive civic architecture has been inspired as much by religion as commercial profit, as some of this town's present and former churches attest. Tucked along side streets crossing Williams are three worthy examples: the classically inspired **Tisbury Town Hall,** a former Congregational and Baptist Church on Spring Street that's also known as Association Hall; the newer United Methodist **Stone Church,** on Church Street, built early this century to replace its demonstrably flammable predecessor; and, opposite, the former 1833 Methodist meetinghouse, now **The Vineyard Playhouse,** the island's only professional theater. Association Hall is also home to a performance center, the **Katharine Cornell Memorial Theater,** a fully accessible space used by various local groups. During Town Hall's regular business hours it's worth stepping inside the theater for a peek at the

large island-themed murals by the late Stan Murphy, a Vineyard artist known for his luminous paintings of people and nature.

West Chop

Vineyard Haven's V-shaped harbor is protected on either side by jaw-like hunks of land known as East and West Chop. Upper Main Street runs along West Chop to a separate village of Tisbury, located at the end; East Chop belongs to neighboring Oak Bluffs.

About two miles up Main from the downtown shops is the 19th-century **West Chop Lighthouse,** sitting beside the road for photographers' convenience, though not open to the public (it's a private Coast Guard residence). The current 1891 brick tower is the third incarnation in a series of lights at this location that have guided seafarers since James Monroe sat in the White House. The white beacon, visible on the mainland, shows red if you get too close to the shoals off the end of the point.

West Chop Park, near the turnaround loop at the end of Main, is favored for watching the

view of Vineyard Haven Harbor

ISLAND TOURS

Want to start off your Vineyard holiday with a 2.5-hour narrated trip around all six towns? The white, pink, and turquoise old school buses of **Martha's Vineyard Sightseeing**, a.k.a. Island Transport (508/627-8687, www.mvtour.com, $26 adults, $14 kids 12 and under), rendezvous with all incoming ferries in both Vineyard Haven and Oak Bluffs 9 A.M.–4 P.M. daily mid-May–late October, and with the 10:30 and 11:30 A.M. ferries from April 15–November 1. You can buy your tickets at the Steamship Authority terminal in Woods Hole, or aboard the Hy-Line, Falmouth, and New Bedford ferries en route to the island.

The all-island buses pay only a cursory visit to the down-island towns, since the vehicles are too large to negotiate narrow downtown streets, but they do include a 25-minute stop at the Aquinnah Cliffs. The tour guides are typically off-island college students whose knowledge of the Vineyard comes from scripts, so when it comes to identifying celebrity driveways or explaining what happened at Chappaquiddick in 1969, take what they say with a good dash of salt.

Alternatively, consider taking a walking tour with a real historian. **Vineyard History Tours** (508/627-2529, $12, free to kids under 12) conducts a "Ghosts, Gossip, and Downright Scandal" 75-minute tour in each of the down-island towns – Vineyard Haven, Oak Bluffs, and Edgartown – typically two or three times a week in season as well as by appointment year-round. Call for current departure times and starting points.

sunsets over Vineyard Sound, but any time on a clear day, it offers a nice view out over what was once one of the world's busiest coastal waterways. Before railroads and the 1914 completion of the Cape Cod Canal siphoned away most of the cargo and passengers, this area was second only to the English Channel in boat traffic. Two hundred years ago, you could have counted scores of sails belonging to coastwise packets bound for Boston or New York and merchant vessels bearing West Indies molasses, South American hides, Sumatran spices, and Arabian coffee. Until technology enabling precise calculation of a ship's longitude became widely available, in the 19th century, most "East-Indiamen" put in at Vineyard Haven or Woods Hole before negotiating the great extended hook of Cape Cod; to set a course for Boston or Salem directly from the Caribbean or South Atlantic would have otherwise risked a fatal snag on Nantucket South Shoals.

ENTERTAINMENT

A variety of groups keep the performing arts alive on the island, often in casual surroundings such as local churches and school auditoriums. Professional theater, however, does have a home of its own: **The Vineyard Playhouse** (10 Church St., box office 508/696-6300, Oct.–June 508/693-6450, www.vineyardplayhouse.org) presents some half-dozen mostly contemporary works by mostly American playwrights on the main stage between late June and Labor Day (performances 8 P.M. Tues.–Sun.), followed by such perennial off-season events as a fall new-play competition, a winter holiday show, and a spring short-play festival. Rush tickets and previews of all shows are sharply discounted, so if you happen to catch an early dinner in town, it's a cinch to stroll by after and see if there's a pair of good seats left for dessert.

The Playhouse also stages Shakespeare in the outdoor **Tisbury Amphitheater,** near the corner of West Spring Street and State Road, beside beautiful Lake Tashmoo, in July and August (5 P.M. Wed.–Sun., $15), weather permitting.

Named after the local resident and Broadway star whose philanthropy made it possible, nearby **Katharine Cornell Memorial Theater** (51 Spring St.) in Vineyard Haven's Association Hall hosts community theater and chamber music. Consult the island papers or check the display case in front of the building to find out what's currently going on.

The home of the summer blockbuster is the intimate **Capawock Theater** (Main St.,

508/627-6689), one of the island's two year-round cinemas showing first-run features and occasional foreign films. Truly independent arthouse fare—anything with subtitles, documentaries, and favorites from the Sundance/Cannes festival circuit—is screened on a regular basis throughout the year at the Katherine Cornell Memorial Theater on Spring Street by the **Silver Screen Film Society** (www.mv filmsociety.com). Schedules are always listed in the weekly papers.

The eclectic side of the local music scene can be heard live on Saturday nights at **Che's Lounge** (38C Main St., 508/693-8555, year-round), or at their weekly open mic on Wednesday. Che's also features regular poetry slams and weekly salsa dancing (lessons provided).

The Vineyard's creative community includes plenty of writers, poets, and scholars who take to the bully pulpit of the Vineyard Haven Public Library (200 Main St., 508/696-4211, www.vhlibrary.org) on a fairly regular basis, or pop up for the occasional reading at Bunch of Grapes bookstore. The weekly calendar section of the *Martha's Vineyard Times* (www.mvtimes .com) is the best resource for specific announcements of such upcoming events.

SHOPPING

An abundance of craftspeople and commercial artists consider the Vineyard their year-round home, and Vineyard Haven has its fair share of galleries displaying their work. It has also become the island's center for home furnishings, with an eclectic collection of retailers offering very personal visions of how to beautify your nest, from kilims to English country antiques. There are unique specialty stores, too—aromatherapy potions here, Native American jewelry there—and enough apparel shops to keep a clotheshorse occupied for hours. No need to shop on an empty stomach, either—you can grab a quick sandwich or snack around almost every corner.

One of the first sights to greet passengers disembarking from the Woods Hole ferry is **The Black Dog Bakery** (11 Water St., 508/693-

4786, www.theblackdog.com, 5:30 A.M.–6 P.M. daily), across from the Stop & Shop Market. Although the muffins seem to have shrunk in proportion to their popularity, the Dog is still a mighty contender in the island's baked goods sweepstakes. The related tavern on the beach behind the bakery was famous even before President Clinton and family stopped in for a bite while vacationing here in the '90s, but the place now seems determined to clothe half the planet in its trademark T-shirts—which is why part of the bakery may at first glance resemble a sportswear store. If you're interested in seeing what, besides clothing, the owners have chosen to put their logo on, from black lab dinnerware to paw-print drawer pulls, stop in at the **General Store** (508/696-8182, 9 A.M.–5 P.M. daily, off-season hours vary) behind the bakery. If you manage to somehow escape Vineyard Haven without paying this place a visit, don't worry—like an increasing number of other island retailers, the Black Dog General Store has branches in all three down-island towns.

Opposite the Black Dog Tavern, on the dead-end lane headed toward the harbor, is **Stina Sayre Design** (13 Beach St. Ext., 508/560-1011, www.stinasayre.com, year-round by appointment or chance), a small atelier of women's couture. If you're on the island around Thanksgiving you can catch Sayre's annual fashion show at the Mansion House, but she welcomes drop-ins, too, as she enjoys meeting potential clients in person.

The very presence of **The Devil's Dictionary** (9 Main St., 508/693-0372, 10 A.M.–10 P.M. Mon.–Sat., noon–7 P.M. Sun. mid-June–mid-Sept., off-season hours vary, closed Feb.–Mar.) on Main Street is one of those defiant gestures proving that the Vineyard is not just your parent's family resort. Barware, cigar-smoking accessories, pin-up calendars, pool- and poker-playing necessities, leather gameboards, and assorted gadgets are among its "defining products for men." There is also a smokers' club in the back complete with pool table, plus hookahs and loose tobacco for all you louche Paul Bowles wannabes.

Decorative wares of subtle beauty fill **Nochi**

(29 Main St., 508/693-9074, www.nochimv .com, 10 A.M.–5 P.M. Mon.–Sat. Apr.–Dec.), from fine table and bed linens to distressed furniture. European ceramics, selected clothing for women, French soaps, and fresh flowers round out the many items of interest, but this shop is also noteworthy for carrying the delectable and inspired confections of Vosges Haut-Chocolat *and* Mariebelle, two of America's outstanding boutique chocolate makers.

Worth a detour down at the end of the little courtyard across the street from Nochi is the flagstone-floor studio of local artist **Richard Lee** (behind 34 Main St., 508/693-4156). His hallucinogenic style of reverse painting on glass is whimsically zoomorphic—imagine the Ramayana illustrated by Hieronymus Bosch and you'll get the idea. He also paints and gilds animal skulls and furniture. If, as is often the case, Richard is out enjoying summer at the beach rather than laboring over his workbench, a great spot to relax and bid your time waiting for him is **Che's Lounge** (38C Main St., 508/693-8555, noon–7 P.M. Sun.–Mon., noon–9 P.M. Fri.–Sat. year-round) just opposite, a coffeehouse-cum-hangout par excellence, with excellent teas, chai, and of course coffee, plus mighty fine baked goods from the Scottish Bakehouse on State Road.

The **Shaw Cramer Gallery** (76 Main St., 508/696-7323, www.shawcramergallery .com, 10 A.M.–5 P.M. daily May–mid-Oct., hours vary Oct.–Apr.) is the place to go to put some serious pizzazz into your dinnerware or furnishings; among the functional and decorative contemporary housewares are locally made pillowcases.

Quite the retro blend of new, old, and new reproductions of the old are found at **Mix** (65 Main St., 508/693-8240, 9:30 A.M.–6 P.M. Sun.–Mon., 9:30 A.M.–7 P.M. Fri.–Sat. July 4–early Sept.; 10 A.M.–5 P.M. daily the rest of the year), a store that more than lives up to its name. There are trays made from recycled magazines, hula-girl highball glasses, antique cameras, vintage diner signage, and whimsical onesies and other baby clothing. There's colorful melamine and acrylic tabletop goods from

Precidio (the Canadian company that brings you Rachael Ray's line of hipster products), sake sets cast from Limoge porcelain, and a broad line of quality ceramics by Mud Australia, as well as quilts, scarves, sunhats, and floor mats, canisters of gourmet loose teas, and first-edition Golden Books for kids. The gift possibilities are, as you can see, virtually endless.

Turn down the lane beside Bowl & Board to find **Midnight Farm** (Cromwell Ln., 508/693-1997, www.midnightfarm.net, 9 A.M.–9 P.M. Mon.–Sat. and 10 A.M.–6 P.M. Sun. late May–Aug., 9:30 A.M.–5:30 P.M. Mon.–Sat. and 10 A.M.–5 P.M. Sun. the rest of the year), widely known as Carly Simon's store, although she's just one of the business partners. It's full of very beautiful and very expensive art, housewares, barefoot-in-the-park casual clothing, eco-friendly personal care products, and one-of-a-kind tchotchkes.

If $80 scarves or $2,000 hand-finished wooden sideboards aren't in your budget, there's always the **Thrift Store** (38 Lagoon Pond Rd., 508/693-2278, www.mvcommuni tyservices.com, 9 A.M.–5 P.M. Mon.–Fri. and 9 A.M.–2 P.M. Sat.–Sun.) between Island Color and Tisbury Printers, a block from the post office. Some surprisingly high-quality merchandise has been known to turn up on the racks amid all the old record albums, used clothing, and household jetsam, making shopping there a little like playing the lottery.

As a port of some renown, Vineyard Haven has the usual complement of marine-related services on Beach Road around the many boat repair shops. It isn't all outboard motors and anti-fouling paint, though, as illustrated by the flea-market array of consignment material at **Pyewacket's Flea Circus** (63 Beach Rd., 508/696-7766), in the yellow clapboard house between the shipyards and the Tisbury Market Place mini-mall.

If you paid attention to the upper stories of the downtown streetscape, you probably noticed the pterodactyl weathervane adorning the building opposite the Bank of Martha's Vineyard on Main. That little woman grasped in the dinosaur's talons is, of course, Raquel

Welch, but if you remember the '60s cult classic *One Million Years B.C.*, you already knew that. If you wonder where that 'vane came from—and whether you can get one like it—head to the studio-cum-gallery of **Tuck & Holand Metal Sculptors**, about 10 minutes' walk out of town along State Road (275 State Rd., 508/693-3914, www.tuckand holand.com, 9 A.M.–5 P.M. daily). There's about a two-year waiting list for the firm's unique *repoussé* (French for "pushed from the back," referring to how they're made, not how they work) weathervanes, which sell for prices starting in the low five figures for custom designs. But a few stock items are typically for sale in the display room. Browsers are warmly welcomed, and it's always fun just to watch Andy Holand tattooing a good mambo on his latest work-in-progress, or to flip through the portfolio books of his and his late partner Travis Tuck's past work. Many of their unique works adorn off-island homes and buildings, from a Steven Spielberg–commissioned velociraptor to the Nittany Lion over Penn State's Beaver Stadium. You'll also find Tuck's designs atop a couple of local town halls, supermarkets, the *Gazette* offices in Edgartown, and the hospital.

Past Tuck & Holand, State Road is the province of a strip of shops geared mostly toward errand-runners, but past the dry cleaning and home appliance center you'll also find the island's only miniature golf course, opposite Cronig's Market: **Island Cove Mini-Golf** (386 State Rd., 508/693-2611).

When all your window-shopping and art-critiquing requires more substantial sustenance than ice cream from **Mad Martha's** on Union Street, or butter-smooth fudge from **Murdick's,** at the corner of Union and Main Street, try a sandwich from **M.V. Bagel Authority** (96 Main St., 508/693-4152), or dig into a hefty turkey sandwich from **Bob's Pizza** (22 Main St., 508/693-8266), or nosh on a panini from **Beetlebung Coffee House** (32 Beach St., 508/6936-7122) between the Chamber of Commerce Visitor Center and Five Corners.

RECREATION
Beaches

Vineyard Haven has five public beaches, three of which are within a mile of downtown. Tiny **Owen Park Beach** is only a block from the Steamship Authority (SSA) dock, but it gets more use as a boat launch than as a serene spot for catching rays. Since the breakwater keeps the surf away, it's probably best appreciated by really small kids—but if you have some time to kill before catching the ferry, it's good for soaking tired feet. The area to the left of the wooden town pier is private, by the way. From the SSA, either cut through the parking lot behind the bank, or step up to Main and follow the one-way traffic one block to the bandstand; that's Owen Park. The beach is at the bottom of the hill.

Farther up Main Street, about three-quarters of a mile from the cinema, is the **Tisbury Town Beach** (also called Bayside), an 80-foot sliver of sandy harbor shoreline between stone jetties at the end of Owen Little Way, from which you can watch the comings and goings at the Vineyard Haven Yacht Club next door. Free swimming lessons are given here in summer. On the other side of the harbor, about three-quarters of a mile along Beach Road toward Oak Bluffs, is **Lagoon Bridge Park,** on Lagoon Pond. Here, too, sunbathers are outnumbered, this time by water-skiers and windsurfers. (It's also the only one out of the town's four beach parks without any parking.)

Vineyard Haven's most attractive swimming beaches are about two miles from downtown near the west end of Lake Tashmoo. Facing Woods Hole and the Elizabeth Islands across Vineyard Sound (that's big Naushon stretching away to the left and tiny Nonamesset almost opposite), the ocean portion of **Wilfrid's Pond Preserve** is exemplary of the north shore: little to no surf, light winds (if any), no audible motorized boats, and water that stays relatively warm and shallow for some distance from shore. It's also quite small, which is why parking (free) is limited to space for five cars. Wilfrid's Pond itself is not open to swimmers, but the bench overlooking its brackish waters is a fine spot to forget worldly cares.

Another half mile past Wilfrid's, at the end of the same heavily gullied and potholed lane, is **Tashmoo Beach** or Herring Creek Beach (also with free parking). At first glance, it's disappointingly small, but walk back along the sandy lakeshore and you'll find the part favored by regulars. To reach either beach, make a right at the end of Daggett Avenue on the better-maintained of the two sandy tracks there by the fire hydrant.

Water Sports

The island's best all-around source for buying or renting sailboards, sea kayaks, canoes, surf- and bodyboards, and just about anything else that can skim across water under power of wind, wave, or paddle is **Wind's Up!** (199 Beach Rd., 508/693-4252, www.windsupmv.com, 9 A.M.–6 P.M. daily late-June–Aug., 10 A.M.–5:30 P.M. daily mid-June and Sept. and Tues.–Sat. Apr. and Oct., hours vary Nov.–Mar.) past the big gas tanks on Vineyard Haven's harbor. The friendly folks at this we've-got-everything emporium at Lagoon Harbor Park also offer lessons for nearly all the equipment they stock, provide car racks if you want to try the waters in another town, and for $50 will deliver to anywhere on the Vineyard for stuff you rent by the week. Sailboard rentals range from $29 an hour to $195 a week (more for expert-level boards). A small-group introductory windsurfing lesson is $60, while a full eight-hour "certification" course—two days of coaching plus three additional practice hours scheduled at your leisure—runs $110. Sea kayaks rent for $16 per hour to $150 per week (slightly more for tandem and expedition models); lessons are $50 per hour. Canoe rentals run $25 per hour to $195 per week. Half-day (4 hours), full day (24 hours), and three-day rentals are available for most items. Lifejackets are included in the rental prices—and so are wet suits, for windsurfing lessons and hourly rentals (they can be rented separately, too).

Surfers—including kitesurfers—should also check out **Corner 5 Surf** (5 Water St., 508/693-

VINEYARD BEACH BASICS

When it comes to beaches, the Vineyard has a little something for just about everybody, from bodysurfers to wading toddlers. Most, but not all, of the island's more than two dozen beaches are free and open to the public. Several on private conservation land charge seasonal access fees, and five town-owned beaches are restricted in summer to local residents and specific guests. Parking is not a given – some places have little or none, and some charge up to $20 for the privilege.

There's no nude beach per se, although discreet naturists are tolerated in select areas. Private ownership extends down to the low-water line, though, so please respect beach fences, No Trespassing signs, and community standards for shedding your Speedo.

As a rule, the strongest surf is found along the Atlantic-facing south shore, since there's no land between here and Hispaniola to dampen the ocean swells. These beaches are the first to close during foul summer weather, when prevailing southwesterly winds propel huge waves up the shore. In their wake are new underwater sandbars that build the kind of tall breakers beloved by serious boogie boarders, but hazardous to windsurfers and their equipment. Parents and timid swimmers should also be mindful of this shore's strong undertow.

Until the onslaught of winter northeasters, the east shore (facing Nantucket Sound) and the north shore (facing the Vineyard Sound) are milder. As a rule, they're also warmer. North shore beaches are reputed to have the clearest water and definitely feature the best sunsets.

3676, www.cornerfive.com, 9 A.M.–5 P.M. daily late May–early Oct., 9 A.M.–9 P.M. daily July–Aug., off-season hours by appointment), right at Five Corners next to the Black Dog Bakery. Whatever your gear needs, from board shorts to board wax, you can find it here or they'll be happy to special order it. Surfboard rentals are also available by the half or full day ($20–25).

Lagoon Pond is one of the best spots on the island for beginning and intermediate windsurfers. It's great for kayakers, too. Good winds and safety from big ships make it a two-mile-long playpen—although it sometimes buzzes with water-skiers. Access is from the adjacent public beaches. If you brought your own rig to the island by car, Sailing Park Camp in Oak Bluffs is the only Lagoon Pond public access with parking.

Sailing

Local waters are a day-sailor's delight. If you've left your yacht in San Diego, you can rent or charter something here, from a little Sunfish to a big sloop—or catch a scheduled cruise with one of several operators.

The most visible cruising outfit is undoubtedly Coastwise Packet Company, a.k.a. **Black Dog Tall Ships** (Beach St. Ext., 508/693-1699, www.theblackdogtallships.com), owned by Captain Robert Douglas, founder of the Black Dog Tavern and its spinoff merchandising empire. Coastwise has three windjammers dedicated in whole or part to daytrips ($60) and charters from mid-May through mid-October, with all three in peak service June–August.

The company flagship is the square topsail schooner, *Shenandoah,* a 152-foot (sparred length) motorless wooden ship built in 1964 specifically for passenger service. Only slightly smaller is the meticulously restored gaff-rigged pilot schooner, the *Alabama,* originally built in Pensacola in 1926. The latest addition to the fleet is the *Chantey,* an intimate 38-foot gaff-rigged schooner built in 1927 to a design by William Atkin, whose boats are highly regarded for their seaworthiness.

Both of the bigger ships dedicate several weeks in the height of summer to six-day hands-on cruises for youngsters between the ages of 9 and 16 ($850), so in July and August the only opportunity for adults to catch a sched-

MARTHA'S VINEYARD

windsurfing on Vineyard Haven Harbor

uled cruise on the *Shenandoah* or *Alabama* may be on Saturday. Fortunately each has room for dozens of passengers, so it's rare to be turned away even on the day of sailing, although reservations are strongly encouraged.

Day sails on the big vessels last three hours, and of course go wherever the wind blows. You'll be able to lend a hand in raising the thousands of square feet of sail, if you wish, and can share the wheel with the captain, too. Or simply enjoy the salt-sea breeze, the slap of waves on the hull, the hum of the wind through the rigging, and the curious gulls overhead while enjoying a complimentary glass of wine. Trips aboard the *Chantey,* which takes a maximum of only six passengers, are two hours (1–3 P.M. and 5–7 P.M. June–Aug). For reservations or information on the fleet's current sailing schedule, drop by the office at the foot of the wharf beside the Black Dog Tavern.

A variety of other options exist for leisure sailing out of Vineyard Haven Harbor during the summer. You could, for instance, call and see if there's a space aboard the

HIKES AND RAMBLES

Nearly a thousand Vineyard acres are available for your recreational use, mostly in the form of small preserves with simple trail systems winding through fields and forests, around ponds and wetlands, and along shorelines and streambeds. All but a handful are free, and nearly all are open dawn to dusk year-round, except during deer hunting week (beginning after Thanksgiving). An excellent, free, island-wide map identifying all accessible conservation properties is available by mail from the **Martha's Vineyard Land Bank Commission** (P.O. Box 2057, Edgartown 02539), or you can pick up a copy in person from their office in Edgartown (167 Main St., 508/627-7141, www.mvlandbank.com).

Trail maps to individual properties are usually posted at the trailheads nearest car and bike parking; if no map is present, the trail is most likely a straightforward loop or something equally self-evident. For the ultimate peace of mind, pick up a copy of Will Flender's thorough *Walking Trails of Martha's Vineyard* in local bookstores or directly from the **Vineyard Conservation Society** (VCS), an advocacy group headquartered at the Mary Wakeman Conservation Center off Lambert's Cove Road in Vineyard Haven (18 Helen Ave., 508/693-9588, www.vcsmv.org).

Two other land-saving organizations – the Sheriff's Meadow Foundation and Vineyard Open Land Foundation – share office space with the VCS at the Wakeman Center; besides selling Flender's book and dispensing free information about their individual missions, the center hosts workshops and fundraisers and is the starting point for anyone interested in hiking around the adjacent 22 acres of ponds and cranberry bogs.

In addition to guided programs held in season at the selected properties included here, both the VCS and the Land Bank conduct off-season monthly walks on island conservation land. The VCS series (every second Sunday, Oct.-Mar.) typically includes at least one hike on privately owned, undeveloped land not otherwise open to the public; the last event of the season is an island-wide beach cleanup on Earth Day in April. The Land Bank series (every first Sunday, Nov.-May) showcases the organization's own fine properties until their culminating full-day cross-island hike on National Trails Day, the first Saturday in June. Both island weeklies, the *Vineyard Gazette* and the *Martha's Vineyard Times*, announce starting times and meeting places a few days before each walk, or you can get the skinny straight from the friendly staff at either organization. When choosing your apparel, by the way, remember that these hikes are often wet or muddy.

The Trustees of Reservations (508/693-7392, www.thetrustees.org), which preserves several of the most noteworthy island properties through both outright ownership and conservation restrictions (CRs) held on otherwise still-private land, offers off-season hikes and walks, too, although usually for Trustees members only. Led by the staff naturalist, such "CR walks" give members a peek at not-yet-public parcels like "the Brickyard" and Squibnocket Point. Instructions for becoming a Trustees member ($45 for individuals, $65 for families) can be found on their website.

Final notes: While some conservation properties ban mountain biking on their trails, the State Forest allows it, and in many cases, so does the Land Bank. You'll find each property's policy about bikes – and pets, too – at bulletin boards near the trailhead parking areas. And anyone interested in gathering live shellfish at any of the pond or bayside properties must obtain a town license from the shellfish warden at the appropriate town hall.

Ena (508/627-0848, www.sailena.com, $60 per person for three hours), a 34-foot John Alden–designed wooden sloop. Or consider the **Liberty** (508/560-2464, www.sloop liberty.com, $55 per person for three hours), a 40-foot gaff-rigged sloop built by the Vineyard's very own specialists in wooden boat construction, Gannon & Benjamin. Both are also available for full-day private sailing trips in local waters.

If you want more than just a little half-day cruise on which someone else plays skipper while you feel the wind and spray, you're looking for a term charter. ("Bareboat charters," the arrangement whereby you flash your skipper's license and sign a lot of expensive pieces of paper and walk away with a big boat at your command for a week, aren't available on the Vineyard.) One of the more notable charter opportunities available in July and August is aboard the 64-foot Alden-designed schooner, *When and If* (201/739-8810, www.schooner whenandif.com), built for General George Patton in 1939. Whether you want to sail by for a few days or a few weeks, New Jersey–based Ruitenberg Charters provides the captain, crew, cook, and all housekeeping gear; you simply provide the passengers (up to 15) and your own beach towels.

Would you prefer solo sailing—or beginners' lessons on something you can haul out of the water without a crane? **Wind's Up!** (119 Beach Rd., 508/693-4252, www.windsupmv .com) rents Sunfish and similar-sized boats for $35 per hour, $110 per day; or slightly larger catamarans for $40 per hour, $125 per day. Instruction runs $90 or $100 per hour for two or three learners, or splurge on five private lessons for $320.

ACCOMMODATIONS
Under $50

The Vineyard's best budget option for overnight stays is camping. Since the island doesn't offer much of a backcountry wilderness experience, fiscal austerity is about the only reason to camp. The only place to do it is **Martha's Vineyard Family Campground** (Edgartown Rd., 508/693-3772, www.campmvfc.com, late May–mid-October). It mostly attracts RV-style campers, but tenters are tolerated. Rates start at $48 for tent sites for two adults, $4 per child, or $54 for a trailer or RV and two adults. They rent pop-up campers, too. No dogs or motorcycles are permitted.

$100-150

In summer, the pickings in this price range can be counted on your thumbs. One is the **Kinsman House** (278 Main St., 508/693-2311, $125 d), built in 1880 as the rectory of a local church. Located at the corner of Tashmoo Street, on the quiet end of Main where big homes sit behind stone walls and large lawns. The three rooms here provide simple comfort with shared bath and no breakfast (one room actually has an en suite toilet, but must still share the shower). The proprietor, Doreen—only the property's third owner—keeps her prices low partly as a deliberate act of resistance against the economics of exclusion that have turned the Vineyard into a playground for the super wealthy (she herself is a school teacher).

Built back when President Jefferson was welcoming Lewis and Clark home from their river trip, **The Look Inn** (13 Look St., 508/693-6893, year-round, $125 d), at the corner of William Street, offers a casual antidote to the stereotypical B&B's dust-ruffled, four-poster decor. "No bows" vow hosts Catherine and Freddy of their restored farmhouse. Their aesthetic leans instead toward futons and contemporary prints in tasteful, chintz-free rooms with sinks tucked in corners to make sharing the bath that much easier. The serenity of the breakfast table beside the garden's little ornamental fish pool will make Main Street's bustle seem much farther away than the few blocks it really is—which is only fitting for the home of a yoga teacher and massage therapist.

Outside of high season, many of the pricier larger inns—including nearly all those cited in the higher price categories to follow—offer something in this range until at least mid-May and again after late October.

MARTHA'S VINEYARD

ADVICE ABOUT ACCOMMODATIONS

Any skeptic who doubts the Vineyard's hot-spot reputation obviously hasn't tried to book a room here in summer, when the island's 100-plus inns, B&Bs, motels, hotels, guesthouses, and resorts are as full as Las Vegas on a Saturday night. Demand is strong enough to keep many innkeepers busy playing their annual game of brinkmanship with visitors, ratcheting up room rates and lengthening minimum-stay requirements until customers cry uncle. So far, most visitors aren't blinking, so scores of the island's rooms now easily top $200, and few accept single-night bookings (not only in high season, but also on weekends and holidays most of the year).

If these stats make you blink, don't give up hope – just modify your expectations. Staying flexible with your travel dates, sharing a bathroom, accepting smaller quarters, and settling for rooms without views are all tactics for maximizing your chance of locating lodging. Leaving children at home may help, too, since most B&Bs and small inns cultivate a kid-free atmosphere. As a rule, the fewer antiques and the larger the establishment, the more likely it welcomes families.

Speaking of expectations, traditional B&B lovers should be warned that full breakfasts are possibly the island's rarest amenity. If waking up to eggs Benedict, fresh fruit pancakes, or crêpes is why you're choosing a B&B, inquire carefully about what's for breakfast *before* guaranteeing that three-night reservation with the nonrefundable deposit.

Looking for a place with a private beach? You can count the number of candidates on your hands. Most of the beaches are like small sandboxes on busy boat-filled harbors anyway. As an alternative, consider up-island accommodations that afford guests the privilege of visiting large, beautiful, town beaches restricted to local residents – or try for one of the many rooms across the street from Oak Bluffs' or Katama's broad public beaches.

Off-season's popular object of desire – the bedroom warmed by a nice crackling winter fire – is likewise available at just a dozen or so properties, although a score more have hearths in living rooms or other common areas. Can you sit by the fire and watch Neptune hurl waves against the shore outside? Only from a distance. This island is made of sand, not stone; outside of the tranquil confines of Vineyard Haven's inner harbor, any lodging built that close to any coastline not reinforced by concrete would wash away in a year. Private fireplaces and full breakfasts? Again, mostly no, but there is one notable exception – the Jonathan Munroe House in Edgartown.

$150-250

The vast majority of the Vineyard's lodging choices are small inns and adult-oriented B&Bs. If you're a family of four or just prefer free HBO to small talk over breakfast with strangers, make a beeline for the **Vineyard Harbor Motel** (60 Beach Rd., 508/693-3334, www.vineyardharbormotel.com, $150–190 d). It's one of the few properties on the island with its own private beach, a short stretch of sand fronting the boat-filled harbor. Some rooms come with a full kitchen, too, including the penthouse king-bedded suite, which is a comparative bargain at $210.

A contemporary bed and breakfast with distinctive character, **Marni's House** (122 Holly Tree Ln., 508/696-6198, www.marnishouse.com, May–Oct., $175–220 d) sits in tranquility at the edge of the West Chop woods, some 80 acres of conservation land frequented by deer and birds. A 20-minute walk along Old Lighthouse Road, a now-disused ancient way through the trees, brings you right to the heart of town. The trio of modern rooms are each quite different from one another (one even has an enameled Japanese *ofuro,* a barrel-shaped soaking tub), but all have outdoor wooden decks among the trees, and of course guests share in the bountiful homemade breakfasts, including Marni's daily handmade breads.

a king suite at the Mansion House

At the corner of State Road and Edgartown Road about 10 minutes' walk from downtown is the **Twin Oaks Inn** (20–28 Edgartown Rd., www.twinoaksinn.net), comprising two distinctly separate properties. The more traditional B&B of the pair is the **Clark House** (508/693-6550 or 866/493-6550, $150–235 d), whose enclosed front porch is well equipped with comfortable rocking chairs. Its five rooms, all with private baths, come in sizes suitable for families as well as couples. The other half is the adjacent **Hanover House** (508/696-6099 or 800/696-8633, $185–245 d), a perfect example of a classic New England country inn. Dating to the 1860s, this spacious property offers a dozen rooms and a trio of suites, including two with full kitchens. It coddles guests with antiques, an inviting porch, sunny decks, and an atmosphere that makes you feel right at home. A bunch of complimentary bicycles are available for Twin Oaks guests—"the early bird gets the bike"—along with beach towels, beach chairs, and even sandcastle-building tools for anyone who would like them. There is WiFi if you truly are jonesing to catch up on email from the office, and a continental homemade breakfast is included.

Some Vineyard accommodations seem to target people who would sooner empty their wallets than sit on the same porcelain as strangers. Others earn their higher rates with more than just a private commode and complimentary basket of tiny shampoo bottles. One of the more attractive values in this category is the **Greenwood House** (40 Greenwood Ave., 508/693-6150, www.greenwoodhouse.com, $199–269 d), two doors away from the public library on Main Street. The handful of rooms are all decorated with one eye toward period appearances—the house dates to 1906—and the other toward creature comforts: air-conditioning, color cable TV, mini-refrigerator, hair dryers, phones, and, of course, private baths. A full breakfast is included, too.

East of downtown is a quiet residential area occupying high ground overlooking the harbor. Here just minutes' walk from shops and restaurants sits **The Doctor's House Bed & Breakfast** (60 Mt. Aldworth Rd., 508/696-0859 or 866/507-6670, www.doctorshouse .com, $200–285 d), on two landscaped acres above wooded Cat Hollow. Built in 1906, this Arts and Crafts mansion offers over half a dozen rooms to guests seeking period decor and traditional B&B comforts, from the little welcome gift of locally-made chocolate to the full cooked-to-order breakfast.

$250 and Up

The most stylish and luxurious property in town is the (**Mansion House** (9 Main St., 508/693-2200 or 800/332-4112, www .mvmansionhouse.com, $279–319 d), right smack in the center of town. While outwardly resembling a classic clapboard "painted lady" Victorian resort, it is in fact thoroughly modern, having risen from the ashes of the 2001 fire that burned its historic predecessor to the ground. The gables, bays, verandas, balustrades, and lofty cupola are all an architectural tip of the hat to the past, but inside the decor eschews frills and lace in favor of a clean Californian sun-drenched look. New construction means no creaking 19th-century floors, wafer-thin walls, or plumbing shoehorned into former closets— instead the spacious rooms feature central air, soundproofing, and full-sized bathrooms. Some deluxe units and suites ($359–516) also come with oversized plasma TVs, gas fireplaces, and porches that look out over the harbor, and all guests can relax on the rooftop deck with its lovely panoramic views. Rates include breakfast at the inn's restaurant, and there is a full spa and health club on the premises, complete with 75-foot indoor pool and enough fitness equipment to keep up with your customary cardio or free-weight regimen.

FOOD

Easily the most famous Vineyard restaurant is **The Black Dog Tavern** (21 Beach St. Extension, 508/693-9223, www.theblackdog .com, 7 A.M.–10 P.M. daily mid-May–Dec., 7 A.M.–3 P.M. daily and 5–close Fri.–Sun. Jan.–early May, $14–31), next to the ferry staging area in Vineyard Haven, behind the Black Dog bakery-cum-clothing-store full of Black Dog brand wearables. The T-shirts have been sighted around the world, from Patagonia to Nepal, and if you're grabbing a snack at the bakery counter, you may marvel that global

fame hasn't brought about tremendous price hikes. The tavern's prices, on the other hand, are more typical of the island's best dining spots, although it isn't one of them—not for dinner, at any rate. Better to come for breakfast, when you can enjoy the harbor view and nautical mementos without breaking the bank. It's absolutely mobbed in summers; no reservations accepted. While it doesn't have the full menu of the downtown location, the Black Dog's satellite Bakery Café, on State Road at the southern edge of town, nearly opposite the turnoff for the Tisbury Park & Ride, is a good alternative for up-island visitors who want to sample the muffins, chowder, or burgers but avoid the morass of Five Corners traffic.

Named after its original owners, the (**ArtCliff Diner** (39 Beach Rd., 508/693-1224, 7 A.M.–2 P.M. daily Thurs.–Tues. year-round except April) is now presided over by a former White House pastry chef—but don't think that means the menu is all sweetness and light. *Au contraire,* you'll find hearty choices from steak 'n eggs to potato pancakes, although admittedly everything is done up with a Vineyard touch: fresh-squeezed OJ, fine herb and nut breads, plenty of vegetarian options to complement the burgers and lobster rolls, organic yogurt with the granola, and fine Vermont cheddar for the grilled cheese. Breakfast mavens can order their favorite egg dishes right up till closing. So, what are you waiting for?

When dinnertime rolls around, most diners seem to head to Oak Bluffs and Edgartown, where liquor licenses are in ready supply. If you don't miss having alcohol with your evening meal—or if you've come prepared, bottle-filled brown bag in hand—consider cruising the Mediterranean from the comfort of your dinner table at (**Mediterranean** (52 Beach Rd., 508/693-1617, www.med-mv.com, 6 P.M.–close Thurs.–Sat. mid-Apr.–mid-May, daily late May–mid-Oct., Thurs.–Sun. late Oct.–early Nov., $28–33), opposite Ace Hardware on the industrial side of busy Five Corners. This charming waterfront restaurant overlooks the swaying masts in the boat anchorage just outside the big picture windows and draws on the culinary traditions of countries from North Africa and Spain to the Levant. The menu artfully blends familiar local ingredients with preparations found nowhere else on the Vineyard.

If these prices leave no room for risk-taking, make a beeline for **Nicky's Italian Café** (395 State Rd., 508/696-2020, www.nickys italiancafe.com, noon–2 P.M. Mon.–Fri., 5:30 P.M.–close daily July–Aug., 5:30 P.M.–close Mon.–Sat. the rest of the year, $12–28), located behind Radio Shack in the commercial block adjacent to Cronig's Market, on the very busy stretch of State Road almost a mile from the harbor (take VTA bus 2, 3, or 10). Nicky's is a casual lunch-and-dinner spot favored by locals both for its reliable cuisine and its prices.

For the ultimate seaside vacation meal, try a bluefish sandwich and soft-serve ice cream from **Sandy's Fish & Chips** (State Rd., 508/693-1220, 11 A.M.–7 P.M. Mon.–Sat. late Apr.–Sept.), at the corner of Martin Street in the same building as John's Fish Market. While Sandy's can certainly fill your beach basket, picnickers who prefer to play Dagwood and build sandwiches from scratch are best served by the friendly **Tisbury Farm Market,** across from Cronig's Market. You'll find imported cheeses, olives, and other fixings—and high-quality baguettes, focacia, and other fresh loaves to put 'em on.

VINEYARD DINING

Unlike Cape Cod, the Vineyard doesn't consume its weight in frying oil each day. Fish and chips are available if you want them, but most Vineyard eateries compete for either the country-club surf-and-turf set or upscale palates accustomed to fine comestibles at high prices. Local epicures have come to expect fresh herbs, organic greens, bottled water, and meat-free menu selections (if it isn't on the menu, ask). Even delis and fried-seafood shacks cater to health-conscious herbivores with veggie burgers. If you enjoy wine with your dinner, remember that Oak Bluffs and Edgartown are the only Vineyard communities where you can buy alcohol in stores or restaurants. If you're dining in one of the island's dry towns, be sure to bring your own – and expect a small corkage fee to be added to the bill.

Most places stay open seven days a week in season, then cut back days and hours when business becomes more uneven. Before or after the June-August season, confirm that your destination restaurant is open before making any pilgrimage.

Oak Bluffs

Although even the meadow voles in the most remote acre of the island must by now recognize the tremors of The Season, possibly no place is as utterly transformed by the summer crowd as Oak Bluffs. From its chaste beginnings as host to great Methodist tent revival meetings, "OB" has evolved into the most honky-tonk town on the Vineyard, thanks to its after-dark appeal to the under-25 crowd.

Blue-blooded Nantucketers, raised to see the Vineyard as a mongrel cross between Coney Island, Kmart, and a sailors' bar, get goose bumps just thinking of what goes on here, but it's no Fort Lauderdale or Virginia Beach—or even Santa Cruz. Compared to the rest of the Vineyard, though, there's no denying that on summer evenings, this joint jumps. Cars prowl along "the Circuit" (Circuit Avenue, downtown's main drag), the small handful of nightclubs and bars pulse with music and pheromones, and even underage kids get giddy in the swirl of yearning, strolling up and down the Avenue with gossipy enthusiasm, eyeing members of the opposite sex, and lapping up lots of ice cream. Weekenders and tourists, meanwhile, shop and enjoy the carnival atmosphere. At summer's end, the instigators of all the fun vanish as quickly as they arrived, returning to school yards and campus quads and leaving the town as quiet as a banquet hall after a big wedding. Gone are the gaggles of teenagers, the guitarists gently strumming Kurt Cobain songs, the cross-legged rows of young sidewalk sitters. Gone are the lines at the two cinemas, and the crowds spilling out of the amusement arcade. Although the music still blares and the doors stay open until at least Columbus Day, more often than not it feels as if staff outnumber patrons as the end of daylight saving time rolls around. The rapid exodus of the town's spirited lifeblood makes OB the first down-island town every year to roll up its summer finery and shutter its colorful facades. Restaurants and accommodations nearly all close by the middle of October, with the pleasant exception of the least expensive eateries, several of which remain open year-round.

But OB's appeal isn't confined to the young. On the contrary, all but the most rural-minded travelers may find it to be the best base for exploring the whole Vineyard. By bus, car, or bike, it's as favorably connected to the rest of the island as you can get, and has ferry connections to more ports—including Nantucket and Rhode Island—than any other island town. Its restaurants and accommodations fit nearly all price ranges—which is more than can be said of any other place on either the Vineyard or Nantucket. It offers some of the most interesting street fairs and special events, from winter's Chili Contest to summer's Jazzfest. It has the most number of ice cream parlors, including **Carousel Ice Cream Factory** (15 Circuit Ave., 508/696-8614, 10:30 A.M.–11 P.M. daily July–early Sept., daily hours vary March–Nov.), possibly the best, and, across the street, **Ben & Bill's Chocolate Emporium** (12 Circuit Ave., 508/696-0008, 11 A.M.–midnight daily July–early Sept., daily hours vary May–mid-Oct.), possibly the most fanciful—try the lobster flavor for proof, or "moose droppings." Even the beach and brewpub are but a stroll from your most accommodations. All this is wrapped in a fanciful Victorian frame of Gothic Revival and Queen Anne architecture.

SIGHTS
Flying Horses Carousel
It doesn't take a kid or a carousel buff to appreciate the craftsmanship of the landmark **Flying Horses** (508/693-9481), a contemporary of Coney Island's first merry-go-round. The 22 colorful steeds, adorned with real horsehair, were carved in 1876 by C. W. F. Dare. (Although it claims to be the nation's oldest working carousel, Rhode Island has an 1870 contender for the title.) Rides are $1.50, and if you grab one of the brass rings at the right time, you get another ride for free. (You can tell which kids have been on-island for a while by the number of rings they're able to grab at once.) Located on Lake Avenue smack between downtown and the harbor, the carousel is open 11 A.M.–4 P.M. weekends from Easter Sunday through early May and then daily through early October; between Memorial Day and Labor Day, it stays open until 10 P.M. nightly.

◖ Oak Bluffs Campground
Just behind the commercial storefronts along Circuit Avenue lies a carpenters' jigsaw fantasia of the former Wesleyan Grove, now formally known as the M. V. Camp Meeting Association grounds, whose tent revivals begat both OB and the island's tourist industry. Stroll through the Arcade on Circuit Avenue and you'll discover a riot of colorful little cottages encircling Trinity Park and its large, open-sided Tabernacle like wagons drawn up around a campfire—hidden from downtown by design.

The tall fence and limited entry points were originally intended to restrict the secular influences of the resort community springing up right in the pious campers' backyard. The closely packed cottages—which truly deserve the name, unlike the extravagances perched upon the seaside cliffs of Newport—evoke the intimacy of the tent encampment, whose early years were dominated by big tents shared by whole congregations. The steeply pitched roofs and twin-leaf front doors are deliberate allusions to the A-frame tents and their entrance flaps.

If the Campground seems too neighborly for comfort by modern suburban standards, re-

MARTHA'S VINEYARD

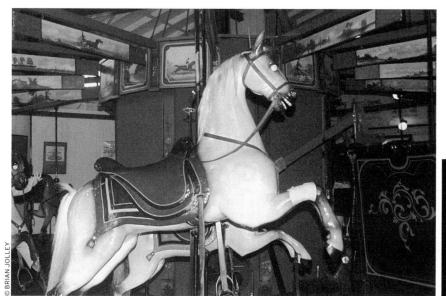

© BRIAN JOLLEY

Flying Horses Carousel is the oldest continually operating carousel in the country.

member that in the 1860s, when most of these were built, the average huge hotels in America's most popular resorts were about as communal as you could get, with just about every waking hour spent in the company of fellow guests. For these happy campers, the mutual lives and close ties to their neighbors were not only customary, they were a source of their security. The ethos of the private car and private bath was still over half a century away when most of these little houses were built, and it shows.

With the exception of the 1879 wrought-iron and sheet-metal Tabernacle, the Campground is a celebration of the power woodworking tools newly available in the latter half of the 19th century. The gingerbread, porch railings, and window shutters are a catalog of imagination, from the decorative (arabesques and French curves) to the narrative (a hunter and hound chasing a hare). Stop by the **Cottage Museum** (1 Trinity Park, 508/693-0525, www.mvcma.org, 10 A.M.–4 P.M. Mon.–Sat. and 1–4 P.M. Sun. mid-June–mid-Oct., $2) for some free advice on locating the architectural highlights. Pony up the nominal admission fee and you can also check out the mu-

seum's collection of furnishings—typical of the Campground's Victorian heyday. Some nights in summer, the Tabernacle is used for musical performances, from Wednesday evening community sings to weekend concerts; if you're visiting in August, check the events listings in the local papers for information.

One of the early secular alternatives to gospel preaching was **Illumination Night,** begun by the Oak Bluffs Company in 1869. Houses in both that company's resort development, outside Wesleyan Grove, and the Methodist Campground itself were bedecked with Japanese lanterns and banners that humorously commingled the sacred and the profane in such messages as, "We Trust in Providence, Rhode Island." Now, on the third Wednesday each August, Trinity Park and the surrounding cottages perpetuate the lantern-hanging tradition as part of a community event sponsored by the Camp Meeting Association.

Ocean Park

Fronting Nantucket Sound, surrounded by the turrets and balconies of OB's most spacious

STRAWBERRY FIELDS FOREVER

One of the increasingly rare chunks of down-island open land that hasn't been turned into house lots, **Whippoorwill Farm** (80 Stoney Hill Rd., 508/693-5995) deserves special mention because it's the only place on the island where you can pick a basket of succulent strawberries.

Strawberries are usually ready for picking around the second week of June and continue at least until the end of the month; depending on the timing of their crops, some plants bear fruit throughout July as well. Call ahead to check on the pickings.

Straddling three townships – West Tisbury, Tisbury, and Oak Bluffs – Whippoorwill Farm is most easily reached from the OB side. Take the signposted turn off the Edgartown-Vineyard Haven Road (about a 0.25 mile northwest of Barnes Road) and follow Stoney Hill Road another 0.5 mile west. Don't pay attention to the Private sign at the gates of the fancy Iron Hill Farm housing development, by the way – maybe it helps to justify adding another digit to the value of those pondside estates, or is a minuscule deterrent to the moped-riding six-pack-toting teens who used to hang out here, but the road is most assuredly public.

mansions, seven-acre Ocean Park is the focal point of many festivities. An ornate bandstand, built in anticipation of President Grant's 1874 visit, sits on the huge lawn like a fancy stickpin on a bolt of green felt; here in July and August, **free concerts** by the Vineyard Band are held on alternate Sunday evenings. Here, too, are the best seats in the house for August's end-of-season **fireworks display,** which doubles as a fundraiser for the local fire department. Other times in summer, it harbors basking couples, Frisbee players, and small kids running themselves silly. Admirers of **Victorian architecture** can stroll the park boundary and find a textbook of picturesque styles: hints of a Tuscan villa here and a Swiss chalet there, Queen Anne towers and piazzas, Craftsman- and Shingle-style influences, and the ubiquitous fancy roof and porch trim deriving from the town specialty—carpenter gothic.

In the small portion of the park near the police station stands a monument to the end of the Civil War—"The Chasm is closed," begins its inscription. Though it definitely depicts a bronze Union soldier (notice the "U.S." on his belt buckle), the local resident who bestowed the statue as a gift to the town was also a veteran of the 21st Regiment of Virginia, which is why there's a tablet dedicated "in honor of the Confederate soldiers" on the pedestal.

East Chop Light

At the suburban tip of East Chop along East Chop Drive sits the East Chop Light, originally the island's only private lighthouse. In 1869, Captain Silas Daggett ventured his own money to build the navigational aid, then solicited contributions for its support from fellow captains, ship owners, and marine insurance companies. Besides alleged difficulty collecting after vessels had arrived safely, the civic-minded captain's first tower also burned down and had to be replaced—at no small expense. Eventually, the U.S. government bought the whole thing off Daggett. Finding his lantern building to be "little better than a shanty," the Federal Lighthouse Board approved construction of the cast-iron present structure in 1878. The name on the sign, Telegraph Hill, predates the light by a generation. In the early 19th century, a semaphore tower occupied the spot and sent shipping news from the island to Woods Hole for relay to owners and underwriters in Boston. In the middle of the century, that tower was replaced by an underwater telegraph cable.

Now leased from the Coast Guard by the local historical society (508/627-4441, www.marthasvineyardhistory.org), the light is open to the public for sunset viewing on summer Friday evenings late June through early

October, from 90 minutes prior to sundown to 30 minutes after; admission is $3.

ENTERTAINMENT

A frequent contributor to summertime cultural performances is Oak Bluffs' octagonal **Union Chapel** (508/693-5350) on the upper end of Circuit Avenue. Free organ recitals fill the warmly resonant wooden interior on summer Wednesdays at noon, while a variety of other musical offerings—from Shaker songs to piano jazz—fills up many an evening between the end of June and the end of August.

Clubs and Pubs

With one significant exception in Edgartown, nearly all the nightclub action on the island occurs on Circuit Avenue in Oak Bluffs. Case in point: stand at the foot of Circuit Avenue and you can have your pick of **The Lampost,** which also contains **The Dive Bar** in the basement and **Sinners & Saints** on the second floor (6 Circuit Ave., 508/693-4032, www.lampostmv.com, 4 P.M.–12:30 A.M. Mon.–Fri., 12:30 P.M.–12:30 A.M. Sat.–Sun., closed in the off-season); **The Ritz Café** (4 Circuit Ave., 508/693-9851, 4 A.M.–midnight daily); and **Seasons** (19 Circuit Ave., 508/693-7129, www.seasonspub.com, 5:30 P.M.–close daily). All are bars that do their utmost to uphold lower Circuit Avenue's reputation as a party street, sometimes against a background of live music by local bands, but more often against ESPN, jukeboxes, and loud conversation fueled by cheap drinks.

For more of a piano-bar atmosphere—albeit an occasionally rockin' piano bar—check out the lounge at **The Island House** (11 Circuit Ave., 508/693-4516, www.islandhousemv.com, 5 P.M.–close June–Sept., call for off-season hours), opposite The Lampost. **Offshore Ale House** (30 Kennebec Ave., 508/693-2626, www.offshoreale.com) has Irish *sessiuns* and other live acoustic performances. After the summer crowds abate, Seasons trades some of its dining tables for pool tables; the Lampost and its associated club rooms close down completely.

While several island restaurants are known for their musical offerings, **Lola's** (15 Island Inn Rd., 508/693-5007, www.lolassouthernseafood.com, 5 P.M.–close daily), the Southern-styled restaurant at the Island Inn off Beach Road on the southern outskirts of OB, is the king of the lot. Its pub offers plenty of live blues, roots, funk, R&B, and jazz year-round (nightly July–Aug., at least weekends otherwise). In July and August there's live tunes during Sunday brunch, too—including, a couple times each summer, rousing spirit-raising soul-saving Gospel music.

Note that island-wide ordinances ban smoking in all restaurants *and* bars.

SHOPPING

Anyone disembarking from the ferries at Oak Bluffs Harbor will be forgiven for initially thinking that T-shirt, postcard, and candy shops are the only retail trade on offer in downtown OB. In spite of the fact that some of the stores contain the word "gallery" in their names, the only art in the Dockside Market Place by the Hy-Line pier is strictly of the tourist variety. Away from the harbor, past the bars and cafés, the main drag becomes slightly more recognizably part of a real town, with diner-like lunch counters and general merchandisers holding back-to-school sales in the fall.

Amid all the shops competing for your attention, it isn't hard to pick out the vivid and whimsical window display at **Craftworks** (42 Circuit Ave., 508/693-7463, www.craftworksgallery.com, 11 A.M.–5 P.M. daily Mar.–May, 10 A.M.–9 P.M. daily June–Aug., 10 A.M.–5 P.M. daily Sept.–Dec. and Sat.–Sun. Jan.–Feb.). From bold Marisol-style folk art to the kind of pottery Keith Haring might have kept around his loft, even their functional crafts exude fun.

If brass temple bells, Peruvian woolens, or things made of kinte cloth are more your style, check out the **Third World Trading Company** (52 Circuit Ave., 508/693-5550, www.thirdworldtrading.com, 10 A.M.–10 P.M. daily June–Aug., daily hours vary Sept.–early Nov. and Apr.–May, noon–4 P.M. Thurs.–Mon.

mid-Nov.–Mar.), a few doors up the block. There's apparel at **Cousen Rose Gallery** (71 Upper Circuit Ave., 508/693-6656, www.cousen rose.com, 5–9 P.M. Fri. and 11 A.M.–5 P.M. Sat.–Sun. Memorial Day–June, 10 A.M.–9 P.M. Mon.–Sat. and 11 A.M.–5 P.M. Sun. July–Labor Day, daily hours vary through mid-Sept.), past the pottery store at the top of the avenue, but it earns its name with its range of monoprints, pastels, watercolors, and other small painterly work. Don't miss the collection of children's books, either.

Arts District

Located about a quarter mile from the harbor on Dukes County Avenue, around the corner of Vineyard Avenue, the Arts District comprises a small cluster of artsy businesses, from interior designers to a recording studio. A good first stop is the **Allison Shaw Gallery** (88 Dukes County Ave., 508/696-7429, www.allisonshaw .com, by chance or appointment year-round), in a renovated wood-shingled fire station painted a dusky cerulean blue. Inside you'll find posters, notecards, and fine-art giclée prints of the owner's striking photography, along with Vineyard-themed books she has illustrated, from coffeetable volumes of sumptuous color to cookbooks celebrating local products.

The adjacent **Periwinkle Studio** (92 Dukes County Ave., 508/696-8304, by chance or appointment year-round) is a working artist's space that periodically also turns itself into a gallery for solo or group shows. Across the street is the **Dragonfly Gallery** (91 Dukes County Ave., 508/693-8877, www.mvdragon fly.com, noon–6 P.M. Thurs.–Sun. May–mid-Oct. plus Wed. July–Aug.), whose exhibitions of contemporary fine art usually reflect more ethnic and international diversity than is usual in this business. Sharing the other half of the same building is a cozy little boutique, **Red Mannequin** (93 Dukes County Ave., 508/693-2858, noon–7 P.M. Wed.–Mon. mid-June–early Sept., noon–5 P.M. Fri.–Sat. and varied other days mid-Sept.–mid-Oct. and Apr.–early June, closed mid-Oct.–Mar.), featuring fashions and jewelry with a funky SoHo-style flair.

Judy, the proprietor, favors designers a little out of couture's mainstream—from the UK and Boston, for instance—whose lightweight knits and washable silks prove that dressing up need never be dull.

The Arts District ends with Isabella Stewart Gardner eclecticism at **Pik-Nik** (99 Dukes County Ave., 508/693-1366, www.piknikmv .com, daily by chance or appointment late May–early Oct., and by chance or appointment rest of the year, too), in the large clapboard home of professional fashion stylist Michael Hunter. Clothing for men and women, from edgy European designers such as Vivienne Westwood, doyenne of punk and darling of Mayfair couture, to shoes from Timberland UK, is juxtaposed with home goods—think modern Bauer stoneware, as bright and festive as the classic collectible originals; radical porcelain forms by the Czech design shop Qubus; and re-interpretations of iconic English china patterns by Wedgwood artist Robert Dawson. Toss in contemporary and abstract paintings and sculpture and you have a mashup of art and apparel unlike anything else on the Vineyard. A highly selective collection of vintage housewares occupies the breezeway behind the house, while the barn in back is where you'll find rotating art shows with an Island focus.

Thirsty shoppers and cyclists will find plenty of refreshment in the coolers at **Tony's Market** (119 Dukes County Ave., 508/693-4799), just down the street. Tony's has good pizzas and huge double-stuffed deli subs, too.

RECREATION
Beaches

Running discontinuously below Seaview Avenue's sidewalk promenade is the **OB Town Beach,** the most central of OB's four. Except when low tides expose a decent swath of sand, it's narrow and often gravelly—especially at the northern end, between the harbor entrance and the ferry pier at Ocean Park. Near the foot of huge, grassy Waban Park is the most pleasant and popular part, nicknamed the Inkwell, with lifeguards and swimming lessons in summer. South of the Inkwell, the **Joseph A. Sylvia**

State Beach stretches in a broad two-mile crescent between OB and Edgartown (which calls its end **Bend-in-the-Road Beach**). Backed by the windsurfing haven of Sengekontacket Pond, facing the gentle kid-friendly waves of Cow Bay, and easily accessible by the paved OB-Edgartown bike path, State Beach is deservedly one of the island's most popular.

Facing Vineyard Haven Harbor is calm, clear little **Eastville Beach** (minimal parking) beside the Lagoon drawbridge and riprap-lined channel underneath. Although lacking the sheer beachcombing breadth of State Beach, it's a good dipping spot for cyclists or neighboring cottage renters, and a prized spot for sunset views. The handkerchief-sized beach at **Sailing Camp Park** (a former Lagoon Pond Girl Scout camp off Barnes Road in the wooded residential edge of town), is only recommendable as a put-in for windsurfers—despite the diving raft offshore.

Kayaking

Try your hand at paddling around in local inshore waters with **Island Spirit Sea-Kayak Adventures** (508/693-9727, www.islandsspirit.com). Choose from half- or full-day outings, in ponds or the ocean, under the midday sun or the full moon. Everything is provided: quality boats, dry bags for your gear, safety instruction…all you need do, basically, is show up willing to work out, perhaps get a little wet, and have some fun.

Parasailing and Power Boating

Got an itch to sail *over* water? Consider parasailing with **Martha's Vineyard Ocean Sports** (Dockside Marina, Oak Bluffs, 508/693-8476, www.mvoceansports.com, daily late May–mid-Oct., $110). It's a cinch: you're rigged up on a platform on the back of a turbo-powered boat and towed up 400 feet or more in the air for a good 15-minute ride. Since dips in the water upon returning to earth are entirely optional, you can bring your camcorder without fear of submerging it and give the folks back home a satellite view of New England, including the Newport Bay Bridge in Rhode Island on the western horizon, 25 miles away.

© JEFF PERK

MARTHA'S VINEYARD

kite-surfing in Oak Bluffs

If you'd rather stay on the water's surface, MV Ocean Sports can take care of that, too, with water-skiing, Jet Skiing, kneeboarding, Bump & Ride inner tubes…you name it, starting at $135 for the first hour. Guided two-hour sightseeing Jet-Ski rides to Chappaquiddick are available starting at $200 for one person. Alternatively, outboard-equipped six-seat Boston Whalers may be rented for $125 per hour, $325 per half day, or $550 per eight-hour day, not including fuel.

ACCOMMODATIONS
$100-150

At first blush, Oak Bluffs visitors are among the island's most fortunate, since a handful of the town's accommodations squeak in under $150. What do these lucky super-savers get for their money? B&Bs and guesthouses with shared bathrooms; usually fans in place of air-conditioning; and fewer frilly fabrics, antique furnishings, and soundly insulated walls than typically found at higher prices.

One of the most central of all the town's

available lodgings is also one of its least expensive: the **Nashua House** (30 Kennebec Ave., 508/693-0043 or 888/343-0043, www .nashuahouse.com, $99–159 d), at Healy Way across from the Offshore Ale Company. Shared baths and simple, clean, cozy rooms with the painted wood-slat walls so typical of Oak Bluffs' lodgings are the order of the day, with AC in summer. Six of the 16 rooms have an ocean view—the beach is just 150 yards away across Ocean Park—while others share a pleasant second-floor balcony looking out over the small plaza in front of the post office.

The side streets off Seaview Avenue, near the town beach and Edgartown bike path, are lined with modest gingerbread cottages, including a number of lodgings. **Titticut Follies** (37 Narragansett Ave., 508/693-4986, www.titticutfollies.com, May–mid-Oct., $115–125 d) is a prime example: no TVs, phones, or AC here, just simple wood-floor quarters painted cheery colors a few hundred yards from the beach. A couple rooms share a cedar shower house outside. If you have an appreciation—or nostalgia—for the early postwar decades, you may especially enjoy Titticut's trundle-bed, partial-bath apartment units ($145–160 per night, $650–700 per week), whose kitchens wouldn't look out of place on *Leave It to Beaver.*

The next step up over the bare-bones guesthouse is one of the neighborhood's rustic B&Bs. Consider, for instance, **The Narragansett House** (46 Narragansett Ave., 508/693-3627 or 888/693-3627, www.narragansetthouse .com, mid-May–mid-Oct., $125–185 d), a block and a half from Circuit Avenue. Built as a hotel in the 1870s, the main building offers 13 rooms decorated in summery pastels and painted white wicker, most with a single queen bed, all with private baths and AC. The most popular rooms have private little porches from which you can sit and watch the world go by, but the wraparound front porch also has plenty of comfy rocking chairs to coax you into practicing the art of enjoying the moment. The family-reunion atmosphere engendered by reg-

ular patrons is quite fitting for such a casual throwback to a pre–Holiday Inn era.

$150-250

The name of **Brady's NE SW Bed & Breakfast** (10 Canonicus Ave., 508/693-9137 or 888/693-9137, $137–157 d shared bath, $195 d private bath) reflects the blend of New England's seaside cottage-style, white wood-slat walls and the owner's penchant for Southwestern poster art. This porch-wrapped Victorian just steps from the beach has private verandas, shared baths for three of its four rooms, fans rather than AC, and a warm welcome. Traveling with your pet? Brady also welcomes dogs.

In Oak Bluffs, proximity to the beach comes at a premium price. That means if you have more on your agenda than just basking by the water's edge below the town's seawall, you can get more for your dollar by choosing lodgings on the inland side of downtown. In some cases, much more: the **◖ Admiral Benbow Inn** (81 New York Ave., 508/693-6825, www .admiral-benbow-inn.com, $165–215 d), about 15 minutes' walk from the harbor, is a beautiful Victorian B&B with seven graciously appointed rooms, all with private bath. The decor favors the clean aesthetic of light, soothing colors and simple Eastlake-style furnishings rather than chintz and cabbage roses, underscoring just how modern 19th century taste could be. The VTA bus route between Vineyard Haven, Oak Bluffs, and Edgartown passes right in front of the inn. Guests needing a respite from island exploration will find the parlor and gardens to be inviting places to relax over a book or conversation. The hospitality of the owners, Bill and Mary, will have you planning your return before your stay is over.

Several inns are smack in the center of town. In my opinion the most attractive is the **Madison Inn** (18 Kennebec Ave., 508/693-2760 or 800/564-2760, www.madisoninnmv .com, May–Oct., $179–269 d), which is as centrally located as you could ask for, being surrounded by restaurants and but a block from the Flying Horses carousel and Ocean Park. Half the rooms have two double beds, perfect for families. Clever construction and carefully selected furnishings, such as flat-panel TVs, maximize the available space, and a warm Southwestern palette gives this place a comfortable atmosphere. Peak rates are mid-June–August.

Facing the Hy-Line ferry landing at the edge of the harbor, **The Dockside Inn** (9 Circuit Ave. Ext., 508/693-2966 or 800/245-5979, www.vineyardinns.com, Apr.–Oct., $200–250 d) tips its hat to the Victorian beach resorts of a century ago and the colorful Carpenter's Gothic cottages all around town. Wide, wraparound verandas, detailed woodwork, period fabric prints, and furniture styles all allude to the belle Époque (without succumbing to chintz), but modern amenities and spaciousness abound, thanks to the inn's true age (it was built in 1989). Put this within just minutes' walk of all downtown, a beach, and four summer ferries, and its high-season rates (mid-June–August) compare favorably to all the equally expensive places purporting to swaddle their guests in luxuries. Come in the shoulder months, when rates drop $50 across the board, and you'll receive an even better bargain. Pets are welcomed in several of the rooms, too.

The strikingly beautiful **(Iroquois Cottage** (Samoset Ave., 508/693-3627 or 888/693-3627, www.narragansethouse.com, May–Oct., $200–275 d), the sister property to the neighboring Narragansett House, was built as a Victorian guest house in the 1870s. Completely gut-renovated in the late 1990s, its six spacious, elegant guest rooms are a far cry from the 19th century's cramped and spartan lodgings. Now you'll enjoy luxury linens, oriental carpets, antiques, stained glass transoms, rich woodwork, fully modern baths, and private porches—plus the soundproofing afforded by modern construction. Rates, which are at their peak from Memorial Day through Labor Day, include a continental breakfast.

If want resort activities—tennis courts, swimming pool, proximity to golf and beaches—without paying a premium for 24-hour staff and room service, consider the **Island Inn** (Island Inn Ln. off Beach Rd.,

508/693-2002 or 800/462-0269, www.island inn.com, late Mar.–Oct., $210–245 d, discounts for stays of four days or more), about a mile and a half from downtown. The decor is comparable to modern motel rooms found along every interstate in the country, with comfortable furnishings and forgettable framed art. However, there are also kitchenettes or full kitchens in every room. Families will appreciate the spacious two-bedroom suites and two-story townhouses ($285–375). Prices are at their peak only from late June–August, so even better deals may be had in the early or late days of summer. If you like traveling with your pet, note that outside of high season the inn also accepts canine companions, one of the few properties on the Vineyard to do so.

$250 and Up

At the quiet end of downtown, **The Oak Bluffs Inn** (Circuit Ave. and Pequot, 508/693-7171 or 800/955-6235, www.oakbluffsinn.com, May–Oct., $215–300 d) honors the town's decorative pedigree downstairs, but upstairs a soothing lack of Victoriana reigns, making the comfortable, high-ceilinged rooms seem even more spacious. A four-story tower with a rooftop cupola gives late-August guests a sky-box seat for the town's end-of-season fireworks display (and simply a great view at any time). The rates, which peak mid-June–Labor Day, do not include an 11 percent tax and "gratuity" surcharge.

(The Oak House (79 Seaview Ave., 508/693-4187 or 866/693-5805, www.vine yardinns.com, mid-May–Oct., $240–330 d) between Narragansett and Pequot is a former summer home of the state's fourth Republican governor. It's been turned into the quintessential B&B—a seaside Victorian with a picket fence and peaked roof, rocker-filled porches for afternoon tea and lemonade, and sunny balconies overlooking the beach across the street. Whether clad in solid oak paneling or coordinated around more feminine yellows and pinks, the 10 rooms and suites are almost exactly as you'd imagine a B&B should look, from antiques and gauzy curtains to the occasional painted brass bed or

Oriental rug. (They also come with TVs and telephones.) Two-room suites run $360–370 for up to four people in high season.

FOOD

When dyed-in-the-wool Nantucketers threaten their offspring with visions of the bogeyman, chowing down on pub grub on Oak Bluffs' Circuit Avenue is what they have in mind. But bars don't have a monopoly on this island's cheap eats. Instead, make your way to **Linda Jean's** (25 Circuit Ave., 508/693-4093, 6 A.M.–8 P.M. daily, $6.95–14.95), where sturdy breakfasts, lunches, and early dinners transport patrons back to simpler days and square meals, when coffee came only as decaf or regular and Cool Whip had cachet.

Hearty, thick-crusted pizza is available at **Giordano's Restaurant, Clam Bar & Pizza** (Circuit Ave., 508/693-0184, www.giosmv .com, 11:30 A.M.–10:30 P.M. daily late May–early Sept., $9.95–21.95, cash only) filling the entire block opposite the Flying Horses Carousel. But the real reason to come here is the robust and inexpensive red-sauce Italian meals. Another enjoyable, affordable Italian option—and the only one for off-season visitors—is **Pomodoro** (53 Circuit Ave., 508/696-3002, 11:30 A.M.–9:30 P.M. daily, $8.95–15.75), also serving up inexpensive pastas and pizzas in a high-ceilinged, contemporary space with a casual, family-friendly atmosphere.

Across the street is the ever-popular **◖ Slice of Life** (50 Circuit Ave., 508/693-3838, www .sliceoflifemv.com, 8 A.M.–9 P.M. daily, till 10 P.M. in summer, $7.50–22), a cozy little cafe and bakery featuring simple fare made from scratch with the best ingredients available. That means breakfast dishes with quality meats and cheeses (no bright orange American cheese slices here), buttermilk pancakes with real maple syrup, a flavorful lunch assortment of grilled panini, pizza, and salads, and dinner staples of roasted organic chicken, local fish, grilled or barbecued meats, and their lean half-pound burger on a rustic roll. Leave room for the scrumptious desserts.

OB is home to the island's sole brewpub,

the **Offshore Ale Company** (30 Kennebec Ave., 508/693-2626, www.offshoreale.com, 11:30 A.M.–close daily, $10.95–25.95), where a half-dozen housemade beers are always on tap. While the rustic building and peanut shells strewn on the plank flooring set the tone, the food is above average: generous salads, wood-fired brick-oven pizzas, hearty burgers cooked to order, fresh local oysters, beer-battered fish and chips, even a kid's menu. Come summer the Offshore also features live music four times a week, including a weekly Irish sessiun on Wednesday evening.

While there's no shortage of other taverns in town where you can slake your thirst for brews and burgers while ESPN plays on the TV over the bar, a special nod is due to **Seasons Eatery & Pub** (19 Circuit Ave., 508/693-7129, www .seasonspub.com, 11 A.M.–11 P.M. daily, $8.95–23.95). Beside the standard menu of burgers, sandwiches, chicken wings, salads, pasta, steak, and seafood, there's a full sushi bar incongruously adjacent to the main dining area. The extensive menu of maki rolls and nigiri pieces can be accompanied by cold sake, or just one of the nearly two dozen beers on tap at the regular bar. If there's a pro sport that you want watch while dining, this is a good place to come, as there are TVs just about everywhere you look. Kids get free tokens for the next-door game room with their meals, and if you couldn't leave your laptop at home, the place is a WiFi hotspot, too. Good thing there's so much else to do on the island or there might not be any reason to leave the premises.

The man behind the Seasons sushi concession has his own little restaurant nearby: **O-Sun Asian Kitchen** (5 Oak Bluffs Ave., 508/696-0220, 11 A.M.–9:30 P.M. daily, $11–28) mixes tasty Japanese noodle, rice, and tempura dishes with a modest menu of Chinese items, all at low prices not often seen on the Vineyard. The view from seats facing the windows takes in the nearby Steamship Authority pier, the long arm of Chappaquiddick on the horizon, and usually a handful of sailboats scudding across the bay in between.

OB has its high-end eateries, too. One of the

best is **❰ Park Corner Bistro** (20H Kennebec Ave., 508/696-9922, 5–10 P.M. daily June–Sept., hours vary Oct.–May, $15–28), fronting the small downtown Post Office plaza. "Bistro" here draws more inspiration from TriBeCa than Paris—behind the mullioned windows are a small dining room and even smaller bar, stylishly decorated with dark wood, white linens, black trim, and lithesome waitstaff. The casual air is all Vineyard, though, and the food is simply excellent: assertive flavors, novel touches (a lashing of bourbon in the pan of the pork tenderloin, a splash of citrus in the garlicky steamed mussel broth), homemade pastas, ample portions, and no skimping on the wine servings if you order by the glass. In summer, breakfast and a Latino-flavored lunch are served, too.

For a real splurge, try **The Sweet Life Café** (63 Circuit Ave., 508/696-0200, www .sweetlifemv.com, 5:30 P.M.–close Thurs.–Mon. May–mid-Oct. and 5:30 P.M.–close daily mid-June–early Sept., $32–44) opposite the Oak Bluffs Inn. The elegance and intimacy of the residential interior and back garden provide the perfect backdrop for the kitchen's contemporary approach to classic continental cuisine, pairing fine meats, fresh fish, and pick-of-the-crop vegetables with flavorful herbed broths, glazes, and wine reductions. Steak frites, braised monkfish with linguini and clams, an autumnal rack of pork in port wine sauce with pumpkin risotto, or wild mushroom strudel with polenta are just a few examples—each plate arranged with an painterly flourish. The expertise also extends to the desserts—life doesn't get any sweeter than this.

In a class by itself is **Lola's Southern Seafood** (15 Island Inn Rd., 508/693-5007, www.lolassouthernseafood.com, 5 P.M.–close Thurs.–Sat. and 10 A.M.–2 P.M. Sun. starting Easter weekend and ending late Oct., varied additional days in May and Sept., daily late May–early Sept., till 11 P.M. late June–Aug., lunch noon–3 P.M. Mon.–Sat. late June–early Sept., $19.95–39.95) at the Island Inn off Beach Road. Although it's a trek from downtown OB if you're on foot (it's easier to just hop the VTA bus 13 to Edgartown), Lola's gives you more than enough reason to need that 1.3-mile walk back to Ocean Park and the Steamship dock. Lola, who is from Louisiana, has abandoned the idea of portion control. Forget ordering a full entrée for every adult—each platter comes with enough side dishes (starches and greens) to choke a horse. Pony up the fee for splitting a plate (or stick to the appetizers), and you'll still pay less and eat more than in almost any other island restaurant. Anyone lacking a teamster's appetite may want to stick to the pub, where a saner sense of proportion prevails (think 7 rather than 16 ounces of steak, for instance, or a plate rather than a platter of jambalaya) with commensurately lower prices.

Edgartown

With more than 350 years of history, staid old Edgartown is the antipode of youthfully energetic adjacent Oak Bluffs, which is why skateboarders and in-line skaters should be aware of the $20 fine for venturing downtown on wheels. Yachting is the only true sport here, and if you can't afford to maintain a boat for the season, you can still adopt the local dress code of ruddy pink pants and brass-buttoned blue blazer—or a full outfit of tennis whites prior to cocktail hour—and pretend one of those sleek-hulled vessels swinging out there on its mooring is yours.

Called Great Harbor by the English (who made it their first island settlement) and then Old Town, after a second community was carved out of Indian lands to the west, Edgartown was renamed in tribute to the young son of the Duke of York and was finally incorporated in 1671, the same year the Duke gave his approval to Thomas Mayhew, Sr.'s private Manor of Tisbury. (Getting the ducal wink and nod was crucial—just a few years earlier, the restored Merry Monarch, King Charles II, had sown great confusion by giving the Duke's Manhattan-based colony nominal control over all the dry land off the southern New England coast, from Long Island to Nantucket.) The most enduring legacy of old Mayhew's rule is Edgartown's continuing role as the seat of regional government—named with anachronistic English pomp the "County of Dukes County" and comprising both Martha's Vineyard and the Elizabeth Islands. But the Lord of Tisbury might take a pacesetter's pride in the town's per-capita income (highest in the region) and feel a kinship with the town's many registered Republicans (the largest percentage on the island). For the visitor, however, probably more interesting than the modern abundance of country squires is the town's abundant neoclassical architecture—testament to the wealth accumulated by captains and ship owners in the heyday of whaling.

SIGHTS
Landmark Buildings

Three of the town's architectural treasures are owned by the Martha's Vineyard Preservation Trust, which maintains one as a museum and keeps all three open for scheduled seasonal tours. The Trust's headquarters occupy the **Daniel Fisher House** (99 Main St., 508/627-4440, www.mvpreservation.org), an elegant Federal-style mansion built in 1840 by one of the island's most successful whale-oil tycoons. Superb though its symmetry may be, the good Dr. Fisher's home was upstaged three years later by his next-door neighbor, the **Old Whaling Church,** a Greek Revival eminence whose giant columns and broad pediment evoke the Parthenon's temple front. The Trust-owned building now does double duty as the Edgartown Performing Arts Center, with a broad variety of secular events complementing the Methodist services still conducted each Sunday beneath the graceful chandeliers. Befitting such a true community center, its 92-foot clock tower is also a landmark for boaters out in Nantucket Sound.

In utilitarian contrast to this pair's grandeur is the **Vincent House** (11 A.M.–3 P.M. Mon.–Fri., May–Columbus Day, $4), a simple, south-facing example of early New England's homegrown "full Cape" style—i.e., a steep-roofed, story-and-a-half box with pairs of windows flanking a central door. Built in 1672, it's the island's oldest surviving residence and retains its original masonry, nails, hinges, handles, and woodwork. It's also the Preservation Trust's museum of island life. During the same season, guided tours of all three Trust properties are available daily on the hour at 11 A.M., noon, 1 P.M., and 2 P.M. for $10, starting from (and including admission to) the Vincent House. If you intend to also visit the Martha's Vineyard Museum, you can purchase a joint ticket ($15) valid for as many days as it takes for you to visit each property.

◖ Historic Downtown Edgartown

Streets intersecting Main near the center of town—School, Summer, Winter—are all worth roaming for a good look at the full range of island architectural styles, from old saltboxes and half-Capes to spare Congregational meetinghouses and Tiffany-windowed Catholic churches. But Water Street is the island's premiere showcase of Federal and Greek Revival styles. Wander in either direction, north or south, past the shops and the verandas of downtown inns and you'll quickly come to numerous 19th-century captains' and merchants' houses lined up along the harbor and looking, with their black shutters and white siding, like so many piano keys.

In this street-sized textbook of neoclassical architecture, you should have no trouble spotting either the restrained Federal style of the early 1800s (pilasters framing nearly square facades; columned porticos, fanlight windows and sometimes even sidelights framing the front doors; smaller third-story windows; and fancy, turned balustrades crowning flat roof lines) or the bold Greek columns of the successive style, which came into vogue following the widely reported expeditions of British Lord Elgin to Athens's Acropolis.

【 Edgartown Lighthouse

If downtown's concrete expressions of the 19th century's love of Greek and Roman civilization don't inspire noble resolutions to read your Ovid or Aeschylus, perhaps you'd prefer to sit at the base of the 20th-century Edgartown Lighthouse at the end of North Water Street and entertain more modern sentiments about the inconstancy of sun and tide. By the time the cast-iron present tower was brought, early in World War II, to replace its 111-year-old predecessor, shifting sand had filled in around what originally was a stone pier set a short way from shore; where once the lighthouse keeper had to row to his post, now you may simply stroll through salt-spray roses.

Still an aid to navigation owned by the U.S. Coast Guard, the lighthouse is maintained by the Martha's Vineyard Museum. Renovated in 2007 to finally outfit the interior with stairs (previously, access to the top was only by ladder), the top of the light is open to the public 11 A.M.–5 P.M. Thursday–Monday ($5), with hours extended on Thursday to 30 minutes after sunset.

Martha's Vineyard Museum

Comprising a collection of buildings a couple blocks from downtown's commercial bustle, the Martha's Vineyard Museum (508/627-4441, www.mvmuseum.org, 10 a.m.–5 p.m. Mon.–Sat. mid-June–Columbus Day, 10 a.m.–4 p.m. the rest of the year, $7 in season and $6 off season) is fortunate to possess a better-than-average potpourri of historical relics—over 30,000 in all, from scrimshaw and whaling try-pots to costumes, domestic furnishings, and old farm implements. The Martha's Vineyard Historical Society curates the museum, mining this repository of artifacts for its changing exhibits, and also drawing upon the society's vast collection of historical photos, vintage postcards, and ephemera. Genealogists who fancy some connection to past islanders should visit the

© BRIAN JOLLEY

MARTHA'S VINEYARD

Edgartown Lighthouse is a popular spot for weddings and parties.

society's library to research the family tree. The library also sells copies of the Dukes County Intelligencer, the society's quarterly assemblage of articles on island history and lore.

The museum's most prominent exhibit is visible even before entering through the corner gatehouse—sitting in the yard is a large piece of lighthouse technology over 140 years old, an example of the huge Fresnel lens, whose invention revolutionized coastal navigation. The ground-level view from inside the lens may seem disorienting, but these concentric prisms totally reversed the illuminating efficiency of 19th-century lamps; whereas before, only one-sixth of a parabolic reflector's light could be seen by mariners, Augustin Fresnel's "dioptric apparatus" concentrated as much light in its high-powered beam as had previously been lost. In a reminder that red-tape bureaucracy is hardly a modern affliction, the U.S. government dithered for 30 years, despite the proven efficiency, making scientific studies and committee reports before finally adopting the French-made lens. One of the earliest Fresnels

ODE TO A VINEYARD CHICKEN

If you visit the Vineyard Museum in Edgartown, be sure to pause a moment and pay your respects at the two verse-covered headstones in the Carriage House. Nancy Luce, the West Tisbury woman who had these memorials erected before she died in 1890, would surely appreciate the visit. And so, no doubt, would the bantam hens honored by the tablets: Ada Queetie, Beauty Linna, and Poor Tweedle Dedel Bebbee Pinky.

Poor little Ada Queetie,
She always used to want to get in my lap
And squeeze me close up, and talk
pretty talk to me.
She always used to want I should hug
her up close to my face,
And keep still there she loved me so well.
When she used to be in her little box to
lay pretty egg,
She would peak up from under the chair,
To see her friendy's face.

Poor little Ada Queetie has departed
this life,
Never to be here no more,
No more to love, no more to speak,
No more to be my friend,
O how I long to see her with me, live
and well,
Her heart and mine united,
Love and feelings deeply rooted for
each other,
She and I could never part,
I am left broken hearted.

Luce was one of the island's best-known "characters," an eccentric who wrote a volume of poetry, *Poor Little Hearts,* for her beloved chickens. She sold copies of the book – and postcards of her brood – to 19th-century tourists who passed her farm (she also happily gave recitals for a small tip). Her own grave, toward the rear of the West Tisbury burying ground, off State Road, bears a simple marker without any epitaph.

installed by the U.S. Lighthouse Service, this particular lens faithfully flashed its light over Aquinnah for nearly a century before it was replaced by an electric lamp.

During the off-season, one of the major display areas—the Thomas Cooke House, that tidy 18th-century Colonial—is closed for lack of heating.

Chappaquiddick

The Wampanoags' descriptive name for Edgartown's sibling chunk of tree-covered sand means "separated island," but modern inhabitants have no time for all those syllables; it's "Chappy" now, to one and all. But the full name endures in infamy after what happened in 1969, when a car accident proved fatal to a young woman and nearly so to the career of the state's then-junior senator, who was behind the wheel. Kennedy-bashing may be a popular recreation back where you come from, but not here; nothing brands a visitor as an off-island

yahoo more quickly than chasing after vicious gossip about the nation's foremost political dynasty. Of course, plenty of Islanders privately suspect that tourists are all yahoos anyway, so questions about what happened that night in '69 are grudgingly anticipated.

Sparsely inhabited and infused with rural end-of-the-road isolation, Chappy feels far off the map even when the waiting line at the ferry clearly proves the opposite. Visitors are lured by the superb beaches at Wasque and Cape Poge, but canoeing, bird-watching, bodysurfing, surf-casting, hiking, and walking are equally good reasons to join that ferry line.

Means of access to the island (which isn't quite separated anymore) are limited to the **Chappy Ferry,** a.k.a. the *"On Time"* (508/627-9427, $12 for cars and drivers, $6 for bikes and riders, $4 pedestrians), or a good swim across the narrow entrance to Edgartown's inner harbor. The ferry runs every day of the year from the waterfront downtown, beginning at 6:45 A.M. Rates and schedule are posted at the landings, but in brief, you can count on continuous service until midnight in season (May 15–Oct. 15), and until 7 P.M. otherwise; after 7:30 P.M. off season, two periods of service are spread out over the evening with the final run leaving at 11:10 P.M. All fares are round-trip and are collected in full upon first crossing. Because of the maze of narrow one-way streets approaching the Edgartown waterfront, even bicyclists should follow the Chappy Ferry signs.

FARM Institute

The Vineyard is fortunate to have a number of dedicated individuals and organizations trying to raise awareness about the importance of preserving local farms. With homes being built at an annual rate of nearly five per week, there is unceasing pressure to turn the island's remaining agricultural land into house lots. With an eye on changing the perception of agricultural land and labor through education, the FARM Institute (Aero Ave., 508/627-7007, www.farminstitute.org) uses hands-on activities to teach kids the value of sustainable food production, responsibility for caring for and raising farm animals, and stewardship of land for the benefit of the community. Pretty radical stuff for 21st-century kids raised on Wii and fast food. Judging by the endless smiles on the faces of the young farmer-campers who lend a hand to help run the place, this 160-acre working farm is nurturing a bumper crop of educated consumers and policy-makers for the future, along with chemical-free meat and produce for local restaurants and markets.

If you are staying on the island for at least a week between June and August with a child between the ages of 5 and 14, visit the institute's website to download a program brochure describing the farm's rolling series of Monday–Friday half- and full-day summer camps and teen apprentice programs ($300–410, with discounts for early registration). There are also two-day, 90-minute programs for two- to four-year-olds ($60). On the second and fourth Saturdays of July and August the farm welcomes volunteers of all ages to help feed animals, col-

© KATHRYN OSGOOD

kids feeding the free-range chickens at the FARM Institute

lect eggs, work in the barn and garden, and perform other necessary farm chores.

You came to the island to play, not pick vegetables or care for piglets? No problem, the Institute has that covered, too, with its five-acre corn maze (dawn–dusk daily mid-July–Sept., $10 ages 14 and up, $5 otherwise). The farm's master maze designer is a wizard at crafting a challenging course, which each year is divided into two routes. One, aimed at beginners, is estimated to take under 30 minutes to complete, while the second, more advanced route is intended to keep you busy for over an hour.

The FARM Institute is located on the right side of Katama Road on the way to Edgartown's South Beach, about 1.6 miles from the fork with Herring Creek Road.

ENTERTAINMENT

Diverse is the adjective for Edgartown's **Performing Arts Center** (89 Main St., 508/627-4442), in the Old Whaling Church, whose calendar typically ranges from big names in acoustic and spoken performance to antiques auctions and assorted other community events. One regular on the church schedule is the **Martha's Vineyard Chamber Music Society** (508/696-8055), whose series of weekly concerts in July and August are performed on Monday nights in Edgartown, and then on Tuesday at the **Chilmark Community Center** (520 South Rd. in Chilmark, 508/645-9484, www.chilmarkcommunitycenter.org).

Nightlife

The Vineyard's biggest club and the only one that attracts national touring rock, reggae, funk, jazz, fusion, and folk acts sits out on the airport entrance road: **Outerland** (17 Airport Rd., 508/693-1137, www.outerlandmv.com, schedule varies late May–Sept.). The former hangar was made famous in the '80s as a low-rent tin-roofed dive featuring intimate performances by friends and contemporaries of then–co-owner Carly Simon.

After passing through other hands and eventually into bankruptcy, the club was resurrected by local luminaries whose collective influence ensures that big-name performers continue to make use of the state-of-the-art stage and sound system behind the deliberately nondescript metal exterior and wall-sized evocation of Thomas Hart Benton's Vineyard paintings. An outpost of Oak Bluffs' Smoke 'n' Bones Bar-B-Q dishes up finger-licking southern-style ribs, brisket, catfish, and other omnivorous treats 6–9:30 P.M. whenever there's a show (the music typically starts at 10 P.M.). Handicap-accessible and smoke-free, the place also offers memberships if you want to avoid being excluded by the guardians of the gate.

SHOPPING

Despite Edgartown's high-end demographics and an affected gentility unsullied by crass neon and billboards, each new season seems to find another of the city's expensive boutiques turning into another T-shirt shop indistinguishable from those found in every tourist town the world over. Holdouts against this trend include one of the island's most prominent galleries, plus a few purveyors of eye-catching, offbeat, or just plain unique gifts and indulgences.

While you'll find the most interesting gift and souvenir shopping around the harbor, long-term visitors on errands in cars prefer the commercial plazas on Upper Main Street between the Stop & Shop and The Triangle (the local name for the split between Main and the roads to Vineyard Haven and Oak Bluffs). The narrow, one-way downtown streets are great for pedestrians, but summer drivers should take an extra dose of hypertension medication before trying to do the same.

Foremost among the harborfront art venues is the **Old Sculpin Gallery** (58 Dock St., 508/627-4881, www.oldsculpingallery.org, 9 A.M.–9 P.M. Mon.–Sat., noon–8 P.M. Sun. late May–mid-Oct.) opposite the ramp for the Chappy Ferry. Housed in a former boatbuilders' workshop, this is the Vineyard's oldest operating gallery, run by the nonprofit Martha's Vineyard Art Association. The MVAA also operates their Studio School in the building, offering art classes and workshops for kids, teens, and adults throughout the summer; email mvaa@verizon.net for registration details. Drop by for a snack and a sip with the artists at the customary new show openings, every Sunday evening from 6 P.M. till closing.

A block up from the harbor is the **Christina Gallery** (32 N. Water St., 508/627-8794 or 800/648-1815, www.christina.com, 10 A.M.–5 P.M. daily Apr.–Dec., hours vary Jan.–March). The two floors of paintings and photographs are often quite predictable, but venture upstairs past all the sun-drenched beach, cottage, and sailing scenes and you'll find a trove of antique charts and maps.

Don't miss **Once in a Blue Moon** (12 N. Summer St., www.bluemoonmv.com, 508/627-9177, 10 A.M.–5:30 P.M. daily late May–Sept., hours vary off season, closed Jan.–Apr.), for its stunning yet affordable jewelry, much of it handcrafted contemporary work from predominantly European artists. The unique designs are complemented by other selected works of fine art, as well as one-of-a-kind women's clothing and fashion accessories.

Tom Demont, owner and artist of Edgartown Scrimshaw Gallery, working on a custom engraving

Next door is **The Golden Door** (18 N. Summer St., www.thegoldendoormv.com, 508/627-7740, 9 A.M.–5 P.M. daily May–Oct., hours vary in the off-season), specializing in art from the Far East. It isn't nearly as incongruous as you might think—carved pachyderms, shining Buddhas, and mandala-like print fabrics were just the sort of worldly souvenirs whaling captains brought home a century and a half ago.

Crew members on those 19th-century whalers usually couldn't afford fancy trinkets for the loved ones *they* left behind. To keep from returning empty-handed, they used slack time over the course of their three- or four-year voyages to produce handmade gifts of scrimshaw, or carved whale ivory. The **Edgartown Scrimshaw Gallery** (43 Main St., 508/627-9439, 10:30 A.M.–5 P.M. Mon.–Sat. and 10:30 A.M.–4:30 P.M. Sun. June–Oct., 10:30 A.M.–5 P.M. Tues.–Sat. Nov.–Christmas and Apr.–May, and 11 A.M.–4 P.M. Sat. Jan.–Mar.) offers both antique and modern examples of the scrimshander's art (practiced these days mostly on the fossilized tusks of Siberian wooly mammoths, American mastodons, and walruses). Nantucket lightship baskets, lightship basket jewelry, wooden whales, and nautical art also fill the walls and cases of this shop, and friendly commentary is freely dispensed to the curious.

Whaling tales of a different sort—plus sailing stories and all manner of island-related reading matter—are found across the street in **Edgartown Books** (44 Main St., 508/627-8841, www.edgartownbooks.net, 9:30 A.M.–5:30 P.M. Mon.–Sat., 11 A.M.–4 P.M. Sun.), knowledgeable suppliers of good reading for beach chairs drawn into the shade or armchairs drawn up to the fire.

RECREATION
Beaches
When it comes to public beaches, Edgartown is arguably the most well endowed on the island, with surf of all sizes and miles of sand. Plenty of athletic-looking, bronze-bodied young surfers and swimmers make **South Beach** the Vineyard's answer to Southern California, although easy access from town ensures that

© KATHRYN OSGOOD

South Beach, also called Katama Beach, is three miles of barrier beach.

everybody can see and be seen on this lively three-mile strand. (By the way, the security guard at the far western end of the beach should convince anyone skeptical of the idea that some islanders enforce their waterfront property rights rather rigidly; he no longer packs a sidearm, but that's a small improvement.)

Swimmers who don't want to battle the undertow may prefer the warmer waters of Katama Bay, accessible from **Norton Point,** the narrow barrier that divides bay from ocean at the eastern end of the beach, or **Katama Point Preserve,** a small, sandy chunk of Land Bank property adjacent to the town landing on Edgartown Bay Road. County-owned Norton Point, by the way, is the only part of the Vineyard outside of Chappaquiddick that allows driving on the beach. Required oversand vehicle permits ($30/day or $100 for Apr. 1–Mar. 31, discounts for county residents) are available from the Treasurer's Office (9 Airport Rd., 508/696-3845), or in summer at South Beach at the Norton Point gatehouse.

Facing Nantucket Sound on the combined outer shores of Chappy's Cape Poge Wildlife Refuge and Wasque Reservation, **East Beach** and **Chappaquiddick State Beach**—still known to many locals as Leland Beach—constitute Edgartown's other breathtaking waterfront. Over four miles of austere, unspoiled barrier beach backed by fragile grass-covered dunes, salt marsh, and salt ponds await swimmers and beach walkers. Swimmers should stay far from the Point itself due to the dangerous riptides.

Expect to pay admission in season ($3 adults, free for ages 15 and under, May 30–Oct. 15), and expect to find some bird-nesting areas roped off in summer. Each end of the shore has its own access point: the northern end via Dike Road, and the southern end at Wasque Point. Oversand vehicle permits are a flat $180, valid for a year (Apr. 1–Mar. 31), and may be purchased 9 A.M.–5 P.M. daily May 30–October 15 from the Wasque Reservation gatehouse (508/627-3255), the Dike Bridge gatehouse (508/627-3599), or from a patrolling ranger. Out of season the permits are available from the Trustees of Reservations office in Vineyard Haven (860 State Rd., 508/693-7662), or from Coop's Bait & Tackle in Edgartown (147 West Tisbury Rd., 508/627-3909, about a mile from Main Street).

Anyone seeking an escape to the water within easy walking distance of downtown should consider **Chappy Point Beach,** a narrow outer harbor strip of sand on Chappaquiddick, within a short stroll of the *"On Time"* ferry. Flanking the squat tower of Edgartown Light on Starbuck Neck are two more beaches— **Lighthouse** and **Fuller Street**—half a mile of mostly sand, weather depending, as suited to views of the historic Edgartown Inn or close-up portraits of the lighthouse as to sunbathing or swimming.

Private property ownership prevents anyone on South Beach from venturing farther west, but there is in fact a short amount of public beach on the barrier dunes between the ocean and Edgartown Great Pond. Owned by the Land Bank and named, appropriately enough, **Edgartown Great Pond Beach,** the property is only accessible by boat, which can only be put in at the Turkeyland Cove town landing on the Great Pond (all ponds of sufficient size are public waterways). This landing is at the end of an unsignposted dirt turnoff from Meetinghouse Road just opposite the white fence marked 145. From the West Tisbury–Edgartown Road, it's 1.3 miles south on Meetinghouse to the turnoff (the only one with a Y on the right side of the road), and another 0.8 miles to the actual landing; if coming from Road to the Plains, it's 0.2 miles north on Meetinghouse to the turnoff. After you've set out by boat, aim for the left side of the barrier beach and watch for the Land Bank's boundary-marking signs.

Water Sports

Sengekontacket Pond, shared between Oak Bluffs and Edgartown, is an excellent spot for windsurfers, kayakers, and canoers. Although Sengekontacket can get too shallow at really low tides, it typically has steady winds and is free of motorized craft. Access is from the boat ramps off of Beach Road. Strong currents and prevailing offshore winds make Cow Bay (in front of State Beach) and enclosed Katama Bay (accessible from the town boat ramp on Katama Bay Road in Edgartown) the province of more experienced windsurfers and paddlers.

Whether you bring your own boat or the means to transport a rental, you'll find several fine saltwater and freshwater ponds worth exploring, including Poucha Pond, at Wasque Reservation, and Edgartown Great Pond, via the Turkeyland Cove town landing off Meetinghouse Road.

Guided canoe outings (including canoe) are scheduled in summer by the **Massachusetts Audubon Society** (508/627-4850, www .massaudubon.org), and the **Trustees of Reservations** (508/627-3599, www.thetrust ees.org), at Felix Neck and Cape Poge Wildlife Sanctuaries, respectively.

🌊 Sailing Katama Bay

In 2007 a storm cut through the barrier beach at the southern end of Katama Bay, roiling Edgartown's formerly mild-mannered Katama Bay with steady, occasionally swift currents previously quite alien to the well-protected inner harbor. Despite the new challenges to slipping in and out of docks—which could last for decades before the breach is naturally sealed, as hydrographers predict—Edgartown remains one of southern New England's most popular sailing spots. You, too, can experience the beautiful bay and adjacent outer harbor waters off Cape Poge with one of the sailing vessels that call this town home.

For scheduled outings, contact **Mad Max Sailing Adventures** (25 Dock St., 508/627-7500, www.madmaxmarina.com, 2 and 6 P.M. daily late May–early Sept., call for schedule through Oct. 1, $55), which offers daily two-hour cruises, rain or shine, aboard its sleek 60-foot catamaran. Or consider the *Magic Carpet* (Memorial Wharf, 508/645-2889 or 627-2889, www.sailmagiccarpet.com, daily June–early Oct., $65), a beautiful all-wood teak and mahogany European-built 56-foot Bermudan yawl designed by Sparkman and Stephens, naval architects renowned for their racing yachts. Join this pedigreed former New York Yacht Club flagship for two-hour public sails four times a day from morning till sunset. Calling on short notice—even the same day—is perfectly acceptable, given that you may change your mind about sailing in uncertain weather, although reservations are preferred. Both accept bookings for private sails, too. Bring your own snacks and beverages, alcoholic or otherwise.

Felix Neck Wildlife Sanctuary

This Massachusetts Audubon Society property (Felix Neck Dr., 508/627-4850, www.mass audubon.org, trails daily dawn to dusk, $4) lies on a neck of land jutting out into Sengekontacket Pond, a large windsurfer and waterfowl habitat whose saltwater ebbs and flows with the tides in adjacent Cow Bay. A good cross section of the Vineyard's landscape is found here, from open meadows to woodlands. There's a small freshwater pond attractive to black ducks and mallards, and a bird blind to make their nesting and feeding easier to watch. Similarly, patient observers can spy on the spring nesting of fast-diving ospreys—also known as buzzards—atop poles strategically placed in the open margin of the peninsula's pine groves.

Throughout summer and fall, there are various scheduled walks with naturalists to introduce you to the sanctuary's wildflowers, birds, turtles, and marine life. Other program highlights include canoe trips, stargazing, snorkeling in Sengekontacket Pond, and even cruises to the Elizabeth Islands. Ask at the nature center (8:30 A.M.–4:30 P.M. Mon.–Fri., 9:30 A.M.–4:30 P.M. Sat., and 10 A.M.–3 P.M. Sun. June–Aug.; 9 A.M.–4 P.M. Mon.–Fri., 10 A.M.–3 P.M. Sat., and 12:30–3 P.M. Sun. Sept.–May) about these and other current activities.

The entrance is a sandy lane signposted on the Edgartown–Vineyard Haven Road.

North Neck Highlands Preserve

One of the least strenuous, yet most rewarding hikes is found at this diminutive Land Bank parcel, where one side of Chappy narrows to the point of being just some hundreds of yards in width. From the first parking lot, a short trail west leads to a sharp bluff with panoramic views over Edgartown Harbor, the lighthouse, State Beach, Oak Bluffs, and the long thin arc of Cape Poge Elbow. Wooden stairs descend to the narrow beach below, with benches helpfully placed on the way down. When the beach is in the lee of the prevailing breeze, a remarkable stillness may be found here—and since swimming is not allowed, the quiet is usually only shared with folks casting lines into the narrow gut through which Cape Poge Pond empties into the harbor. The eastern side of the preserve lies along the much rougher, rockier pond shore. Both sides afford fine bird-watching, as migrating species take a rest in the preserve's low, scrubby trees after crossing Vineyard Sound. Access to the property is along a very bumpy sand road—North Neck Road—a little over a mile from Chappaquiddick Road, and a total of about 2.5 miles from the Chappy Ferry.

◖ Mytoi

Midway along Chappaquiddick's sandy Dike Road, the scaly trunks and tangled branches of pitch pine suddenly give way to the improbable sight of a little Japanese-style garden. The creation of Mary Wakeman, a well-known local conservationist, Mytoi is now one of the small gems in the crown of the Trustees of Reservations (www.thetrustees.org). The garden exudes tranquility. Even at the zenith of summer, the pond inspires philosophical thoughts; cross the arched bridge to the islet at its center and feel them rise up like morning light. In spring—when the slopes are blanketed with bold daffodils, rhododendrons, dogwood, azaleas, and roses—the windswept, beach-grass-covered dunes at the end of the road might as well be halfway around the world. Though entry is free, contributions toward the site's upkeep are encouraged (note the metal dropbox before you get to the pond). A water fountain and restroom provide amenities rarely found on such rural properties; also, take advantage of the recycling bins for disposing of those empty cans and bottles rolling around your backpack or back seat.

🧭 Wasque Point and Cape Poge

The Trustees of Reservations also own nearly the entire east shore of Chappaquiddick, from the southern end of Katama Bay to Cape Poge Bay, from whose waters are taken some 50 percent of the state's annual bay scallop harvest. **Cape Poge Wildlife Refuge** encompasses over four miles of this barrier beach, accessible via Dike Bridge at the end of Dike Road, while **Wasque Reservation** (WAY-skwee) protects a couple more miles of dunes and grassland around Wasque Point. Admission to either or both is $3 (free for ages 15 and under, $3 parking June–Sept., parking free the rest of the year). Restrooms, drinking water, and recycling bins for beverage containers are all found at Wasque; at Dike Bridge there is nothing but a pay phone beside the attendant's shack.

Oversand vehicle permits are necessary for driving beyond the Cape Poge parking area ($180, valid Apr. 1–Mar. 31). Purchase from gatehouse attendant 9 A.M.–5 P.M. daily May 30–Oct. 15, or from a patrolling ranger. Out of season the permits are available from the Trustees of Reservations office in Vineyard Haven (860 State Rd., 508/693-7662), or from Coop's Bait & Tackle in Edgartown (147 West Tisbury Rd., 508/627-3909, a little over a mile from Main Street). Air for reinflating tires is available year-round at Mytoi. Even with the requisite permit, be aware that access may be totally denied if the endangered piping plover and least tern are nesting on the beach. The dunes are quite fragile, too, anchored by those wisps of beachgrass; since destabilized dunes are more likely to wash or blow away—or choke up the salt marsh that helps support the rich shellfish beds—you'll notice many warnings posted to stay on existing Jeep tracks and boardwalks. If you hate having your freedom circumscribed by such silly-sounding restrictions, be warned that nature is the enforcer here as much as any ranger—the beachgrass is riddled with poison ivy.

The summer crowds come mostly for the swimming and surf fishing (beware of the undertow), but any time of year, this shore is unmatched for the simple pleasure of walking until there's nothing but breaking waves and scuttling little sanderlings to keep you company. Bird-watching has gained a steady following, too, with osprey nesting on the pole at the northern end of the refuge, great blue herons stalking crabs through the tidal pools behind the dunes, oystercatchers foraging with their flashy orange bills at the edge of the surf, and ragged formations of sea ducks skimming across the winter ocean. The cedar-covered portions of Cape Poge provide browse for deer and small mammals, most of whom remain out of sight but for the occasional footprint or scat pile; if you're lucky, you may catch a glimpse of one of the resident sea otters slipping into a pond on the way up to the 1893 **Cape Poge Light.**

Thanks to the unremitting erosion along Chappaquiddick's outer shore, this is the Vineyard's most transient lighthouse; the present wooden tower has already been moved three times in the last century, most recently in 1986. Before it was automated in World War II, this lonely post was one of the many spoils available to the political party controlling the White House; whenever the presidency changed hands, so, too, would the nation's lighthouses. (Cape Poge's first keeper was appointed by Thomas Jefferson.)

Ninety-minute **lighthouse tours** are offered between Memorial Day and Columbus Day (daily at 9 A.M., noon, and 2 P.M., $25 adults and $12 kids). The beacon is also included on 2.5-hour **Cape Poge natural history tours** (508/627-3599, 9 A.M. and 2 P.M. daily Memorial Day–Columbus Day, $40 adults and $18 kids). Trustee members receive discounts on both trips. Joining the Trustees also makes it possible to sign up for the members-only **fishing discovery tours** out to a selected stretch of either Cape Poge or Wasque, where a fishing guide will teach you to surf cast (8:30 A.M. and 1:30 P.M. daily Memorial Day–Columbus Day, $60 adults and $25 kids). Special half-priced membership is available on the spot for anyone not yet belonging to the Trustees. Preregistration is required for all of these—space is limited. All three tours use special "safari" vehicles that depart from the Mytoi parking area (free van shuttle from the Chappy side of the *"On Time"* ferry).

Naturalist-guided canoe trips around Cape Poge Bay or Poucha Pond (POACH-a) are another option, priced and scheduled exactly the same as the natural history tours. Members-only **canoe rentals** (9 A.M.–5 P.M. daily June–Sept., $25 per half day and $35 per full eight-hour day) are also available for the do-it-yourselfer at the Dike Bridge gatehouse for use in Poucha Pond. Here again, would-be renters can instantly obtain special half-price Trustees' memberships.

Flying

Katama Airfield, off Edgartown's Herring Creek Road, is the nation's largest all-grass airfield. Established in 1924, its three runways see quite a bit of use from small private planes. It's also where you'll find **Martha's Vineyard Glider Rides** (508/627-3833 or 800/762-7464, www.800soaring.com, Mon.–Fri. early July–early Sept., $65–140 depending on the length of the ride), the island affiliate of Soaring Adventures of America, a national outfit with 150 locations coast to coast. On clear days, your enthusiastic pilots, Rob Wilkinson and Bob Stone, will give you a gull's-eye view of the Vineyard from a self-propelled sailplane or motorglider.

More airborne thrills are available from **Biplane Rides by Classic Aviators Ltd.** (508/627-7677, www.biplanemv.com, $149–399 for two depending on length of ride), offering open-cockpit flights in a Waco-UPF-7 acrobatic biplane. Loops, dives, barrel rolls, and other aerobatic maneuvers can be included for an extra fee.

When you return to earth, stop in at **The Right Fork Diner,** the airfield's diner, for a burger and fries, a taste of the owner's sweet rolls—from her grandmother's recipe—or just some Ben & Jerry's ice cream.

ACCOMMODATIONS

When it comes to accommodations, Edgartown costs more than any of its neighbors—witness the $300 summer rates for standard doubles in the island's only chain hotel. As a result the only time you will find rooms in the $100–150 range (or lower) is November through April.

$150-250

Located at the quiet edge of downtown, the **Edgartown Commons** (Pease's Point Way, 508/627-4671 or 800/439-4671, www.edgartowncommons.com, May–mid-Oct., $195–235 d, two-bedroom units $290–315) targets families seeking affordable lodgings with its 35 guest rooms—ranging from studio units to one- and two-bedroom suites—all featuring fully equipped kitchen areas. There is an outdoor pool and playground on the premises. Note that there is no air conditioning in any of the units—fans are provided instead—and there is no maid service, either.

$250-350

Stately old Edgartown has a number of large, luxurious inns carved out of elegant 19th-century homes. For example, canopy beds abound at **The Victorian Inn** (24 S. Water St., 508/627-4784, www.thevic.com, $255–425 d), which captures the spirit of its namesake era in both decor and in the utter absence of any TVs or phones. (WiFi, however, is available.) Thoroughly contemporary, however, is the dedication of the hands-on owners and well-trained staff to your comfort and enjoyment of the island, from the complimentary cut-glass decanter of vintage sherry in your room to an ever-ready willingness to help make arrangements for whatever sport or diversion suits your fancy. As for the generous four-course gourmet breakfasts, they are topped only by the views from the third-floor private balconies overlooking the garden court and harbor beyond the timeshare resort across the street. Predictably, rates peak between Memorial Day and Columbus Day; for real bargains visit in winter.

More of a B&B-style warm welcome is featured opposite the Old Whaling Church at the **Jonathan Munroe House** (100 Main St., 508/627-5536 or 877/468-6763, www.jonathanmunroe.com, $200–285 d). Its handful of generously sized rooms (half with fireplaces and whirlpool tubs), ample full breakfasts (choose from four entrées), afternoon wine and cheese, and dedicated staff offer year-round comfort. Like nearly every comparable property around, Jonathan Munroe House has a two- or three-night minimum in season. A snug two-floor, one-bedroom cottage in the rear garden, with fireplace and whirlpool bath, is a relative bargain at $375 d in summer.

The **Ashley Inn** (129 Main St., 508/627-9655 or 800/477-9655, www.ashleyinn.net, $250–375 d) occupies a shipshape old captain's home opposite small Cannonball Park. Rooms in the main house are a comfortable size (no tripping over your traveling companion's belongings) with unpretentious, tasteful decor; wonderfully friendly innkeepers; TVs and telephones; and a huge yard that invites curling up in the hammock with summer reading, far from the madding crowd. Prices are of course lower before June and after Columbus Day, bottoming out at $125–195 January–April; the three-night minimum only applies to high-season weekends, too. One- and two-bedroom townhouse suites with whirlpool tubs are also available by the week for anyone wishing to lie in the lap of luxury.

Plenty of elbow room comes standard at (**The Lightkeepers Inn** (25 Simpson's Ln., 508/627-4600 or 800/946-3400, www.thelightkeepersinn.com, $275–375), whose five suites and private cottage are all large enough to include a queen four-poster bed, double pull-out sofa, and kitchen or kitchenette with dining area. (Room #3, the smallest, has a single-burner electric range, microwave, and mini-fridge rather than a full-sized four-hob range oven and refrigerator.) A family of four will find this place to be one of the best deals going given how few accommodations on the island have rooms designed with more than just couples in mind. If you find yourself stuck indoors, the pleasant and comfortable furnishings include TV, DVD, CD-radio,

and WiFi, and one upstairs suite has a delightful umbrella-shaded deck with charcoal grill. The inn manages to feel sequestered from the town's summer bustle even though it is located steps from downtown's shops and restaurants, and just a block and half from the harbor.

Nineteenth-century antiques aren't out of place at **The Shiverick Inn** (5 Pease's Point Way, 508/627-3797 or 800/723-4292, www.shiverickinn.com, $270–375 d, suites up to $550), one of the state's relatively rare Second Empire mansions, although the mansard roof and cupola are actually additions to the original 1840 house. The grace and simple refinement of that earlier age are borne out in the high-ceilinged rooms, cozy library, and formal gardens—where one may take one's afternoon tea (or morning granola, toast, and fruit) when weather allows. The inn's many fireplaces make it a romantic winter retreat (Nov.–Apr. rates start at under $140 d); but even in summer, its modest size and the innkeeper's deft personal touch keep the high-season pandemonium at bay.

The only national chain represented on the Islands is the modern **Clarion Martha's Vineyard** (227 Upper Main St., 508/627-5161 or 800/922-3009, www.clarionmv.com, $279–379 d). The full-sized, two-bed, air-conditioned rooms are exactly what you'd find nationwide. The prices, however, are all Vineyard.

$350 and Up

An atmosphere of relaxed but graceful welcome infuses the parlor registration area of the (**Hob Knob Inn** (128 Main St., 508/627-9510 or 800/696-2723, www.hobknob.com, $350–525 d, suite $600). Thanks in part to the country decor, there is neither starched nor flowery formality here. Instead, wicker chairs and rockers on the wraparound porch and comfy seating in the common rooms invite guests to socialize or simply hang out as if visiting the manorial seat of some posh but down-to-earth godparent. The staff are clearly pros—warmly courteous, efficient, and prepared at the drop of a pin to help make your stay positively memorable. The individually-decorated rooms are larger than average and equipped with air purifiers and white-noise generators in addition to such standard amenities as flat-panel TVs, WiFi, terrycloth robes, and high-end bath amenities. Generous made-to-order breakfasts are included, and there are sauna, fitness, and spa facilities on the premises. You can rent bicycles on site, too.

Providing the perfect backdrop to the beachfront view of the Edgartown Lighthouse, the **Harbor View Hotel & Resort** (131 N. Water St., 508/627-7000 or 800/225-6005, www.harbor-view.com, $375–700 d, suites $780–1,600) is the epitome of a classic Gilded Age seaside resort. Built in 1891, its Shingle-style sprawl of turrets, wood railings, gables, and wide verandas looks like something out of *The Great Gatsby*. After nearly $80 million in renovations, the grand dame is once again a trendsetter in the Vineyard hotel business. In addition to high-end bath products and furnishings in all of its rooms and suites, it earns its place at the summit of local luxury properties with an emphasis on concierge services and activities programs for everyone in the family. From breakfast in bed to champagne on ice upon arrival, and from pilates classes on the lawn to fishing charters aboard the hotel's own boat, the Harbor View can pamper like no other.

FOOD

It's an old bit of folk wisdom that when you come across a botanical hazard in nature, the antidote is always growing nearby. Lo and behold, the same principle applies to the cost of eating out on the Vineyard. The **Ⓒ Dock St. Coffee Shop** (2 Dock St., 508/627-5232, 7 A.M.–10 P.M. daily year-round), a.k.a. the Dock Street Diner, is the island's hole-in-the-wall antidote to wallet-emptying restaurant prices—right in the heart of Edgartown, no less, next to R. W. Cutler's Bike Rentals at the very foot of Main Street. Postcards from customers taped to the soda fountain machine, out-of-date calendars on the wall, newspapers lying around on the counter, tasty breakfasts

for two for $10 before tip, and even decent frappes—see, there is a God.

Good-quality takeout, sit-down lunches, baked treats, and liquid refreshments are best obtained from **Espresso Love** (17 Church St., 508/627-9211, 8 A.M.–9 P.M. daily year-round), behind the County Court House on Main Street. Vegetarians will find that the **Edgartown Deli** (52 Main St., 508/627-4789, 8 A.M.–9 P.M. daily May–Oct.) makes a fine garden burger, and subscribers to the banana ice cream diet won't want to miss adjacent **Vineyard Scoops.** Fried seafood fans, meanwhile, should step down to the takeout-only **Quarterdeck Restaurant** (25 Dock St., 11 A.M.–8:30 P.M. daily May–Oct.) by the harbor.

If all it would take to make you happy is some decent pizza, stop by **Fresh Pasta Shoppe** (206 Upper Main St., 508/627-5582, 11 A.M.–9 P.M. Mon.–Sat. and 4–9 P.M. Sun.) near the Triangle as you bike in or out of town. Right at the tip of the Triangle itself is **The Square Rigger Restaurant** (Edgartown–Vineyard Haven Rd. at Beach Rd., 508/627-9968, 5:30 P.M.–close daily year-round, $26–33), the family-friendly home of surf-and-turf at prices that turn locals into regulars. If you want to sample lobster, make this your first stop (VTA bus 1, 11, or 13).

Another of Edgartown's most affordable and dependable restaurants is **The Newes from America** (Kelley St., 508/627-4397, www.kelley-house.com, 11:30 A.M.–11 P.M. daily late May–early Oct., 11:30 A.M.–10 P.M. Mon.–Thurs. and 11:30 A.M.–11 P.M. Fri.–Sun. the rest of the year, closed Christmas, $7.50–11.95) in the Kelley House inn at the corner of N. Water and Kelley Streets. Lower prices don't mean inferior food—the Newes's family-friendly menu of soups, sandwiches, burgers, and dinner-sized salads keep the casual crowd happy, as does the great selection of microbrews (in bottles and on draught). On winter weekends it's the only place for miles that serves food till 11 P.M., so night owls take note.

Across the street, behind one of the porches of the rambling Colonial Inn (where Somerset

Maugham sat out World War II), **Chesca's** (38 N. Water St., 508/627-1234, www.chescasmv .com, 5:30–10 P.M. daily mid-Apr.–mid-Oct., $24–38) serves up fine Italian-influenced cuisine with a blend of paper-napkin informality and the hardwood, clapboard dignity of an old New England resort. The dining room's contented murmurs aren't due just to the catchy mood music—the food is inspiringly fresh, seasoned with a bold hand, and prettily garnished. The restaurant doesn't stint on the desserts, either, as anyone who believes "the more sugar, the better" will happily discover. Though many entrée prices are well over $30, there are some relatively good values on the menu, particularly among the pasta dishes.

When it's time to impress your traveling companion with a fine meal at a local hot spot with the see-and-be-seen crowd—maybe lobster and chanterelle crêpes, followed by seared cod on a porcini ragout in sugar snap pea broth, or garlic-crusted sirloin on white-bean-and-truffle fondue—make a beeline for (**Alchemy**

(71 Main St., 508/627-9999, www.alchemymv. com, 11 A.M.–2:30 P.M. Mon.–Sat. and 5:30– 10 P.M. daily late May–early Oct., dinner only hours vary Oct.–New Year's and Feb.–May, $27–32.50). It also serves a less expensive bar menu—$13 burgers and fries, $9 duck confit nachos, that sort of thing. In the off-season months, the bar is a fine place to discover how island life doesn't allow strangers to stay unacquainted for long.

Out-of-the-ordinary touches abound at (**Détente** (3 Nevins Sq., 508/627-8810, www .detentemv.com, 5:30–10 P.M. daily late May– early Sept., hours vary the rest of the year, $30– 36), a hidden gem behind the Colonial House. Here you might encounter summer peaches in a savory appetizer, autumnal parsnip pierogis paired with a rich osso bucco, Sardinian fregola to soak up the jus of a rack of lamb, tropical lychee contrasting with yellowfin tuna tartare. In short, more inspiration and flavor is packed into the dozen dishes served here than is found on many menus twice as long.

Up-Island

In a place that's already about as laid-back as New England gets, up-island is where the Vineyard truly goes barefoot and fancy-free. Yet the relative seclusion of the up-island villages have traditionally meant that they are the purview more of the summer resident or cottage renter (and celebrities seeking true rural privacy) than day-trippers or weekenders (despite the hordes of bus tourists flocking to the renowned Gay Head Cliffs). "Out of sight, out of mind" seems to be up-island's best disguise—trailheads look a lot like just more private driveways, their flora and vistas hidden from view. Visitors dedicated to maximizing beach time give scant thought to the up-island forests, and people who spend the big bucks to bring their cars across seem most likely to use them to avoid exercise rather than to explore the nooks and crannies where public shuttle- and tour-bus riders can't go. In short, for a va-

riety of reasons, even many up-island regulars never bother to explore the unheralded hilltops, ponds, and meadows virtually in their own backyard. All of which means that if you're able to spare the time and expense to get around up-island at your own pace, you have the chance to still discover the quiet, down-home place that for most down-island residents exists now more in memory than in fact.

WEST TISBURY

Oak Bluffs may boast greater diversity, but the most politically liberal town on the island is this 1896 splinter from next-door Tisbury. Familiarly known as "West Tis" (rhymes with fizz), the community had no qualms about allowing hippies to set up camps in the woods back during the first reign of bell-bottoms and the fringed halter. Even today, the area sets a standard for island liberals—in addition to the still-common colonial office of fence viewer, whose modern mandate is to arbitrate boundary disputes—for example, West Tis elects a Community Right-To-Know Committee, an EPA-mandated oversight group that most towns resist on the grounds that industry has only positive attributes.

Although this was one of the fastest-growing towns in the entire state during the go-go years of the 1980s, agriculture is still a vital part of West Tisbury's economy and landscape. From onions and lettuce to strawberries and cream, if you partake of an island-grown meal there's a good chance its components were cultivated here. Most of the upscale restaurants around the island make a point of using local produce wherever possible, but for a true taste of the Vineyard's truck gardens, look no further than the **West Tisbury Farmer's Market,** in and around **The Grange Hall** (sometimes still referred to as the "Old Ag Hall"), a picture-book 1859 Gothic Revival shingled and gabled barn on State Road in the town center. There are farm stands down-island, too (Edgartown's **Morning Glory Farm,** at the corner of Machacket Road and Edgartown–West Tisbury Road, about a mile from Main Street, is in a class by itself), but between mid-June and Columbus Day weekend, The Grange is *the* place to go, as much for the ambience as for the fruits of the earth. Along with purveyors of affordable vine-ripened tomatoes and enough cruciferous vegetables to make even the surgeon general happy, there are always a few vendors selling fresh-cut flowers, a few masters of the Mason jar selling pickles and preserves, a few bakers with homemade desserts, and even fresh-spun yarn from just-sheared sheep fleece. If you have someplace to store the leftovers—not that there are likely to be many—Eileen Blake's pies are deservedly legendary. Also famous are the fresh Vietnamese spring rolls by Thi Khen Tran, who sells copies of her cookbook, *The Egg Roll Lady of Martha's Vineyard,* too. The market is held on Wednesday afternoons 3–6 P.M. and Saturday mornings 9 A.M.–noon; needless to say, Saturdays are mobbed.

Up-island's other celebration of its agrarian lifestyle, August's annual **Livestock Show and Fair,** raises the rafters of the "New Ag Hall" with a Vineyard version of the standard county fair; expect oyster shucking contests and great live music along with those horse pulls and tables of homegrown or homemade food. Also known as the Fairgrounds, the new hall is on Scotchman's Lane about half a mile north of the old one.

Like a page of Norman Rockwell's sketchbook, the village around the farmer's market is exemplary 19th-century picket-fence New England, from the handsome Congregational Church and well-trod porch of Alley's General Store to the proper old homes on tree-lined Music Street. (This leafy residential way was once known to some as Cowturd Lane; "Their savage eyes turn'd to a modest gaze by the sweet power of music"—perhaps Tisbury residents renamed the street back in the 1800s for the piano-playing daughters of a resident whaling captain and six of his neighbors). Those old ivories are long silent but the visual arts live on, in and around **The Field Gallery and Sculpture Garden** (1050 State Rd., 508/693-5595 or 800/355-3090, www.fieldgallery.com, 10 A.M.–5 P.M. Mon.–Sat. and 11 A.M.–4 P.M. Sun. May–Dec.), next door to the Council on Aging center and wonderful town library. As at most other island galleries, exhibits here are condensed for the summer rush, so each Sunday evening is opening night for the new art of the week. If you can't wait around for the wine and cheese, **Back Alley's,** across the street, has a smart lineup of reasonably priced deli sandwiches and baked goods (try those snappy ginger cookies), plus dirt-cheap coffee refills for folks who supply their own cups.

Half a mile away, facing the end of Scotchman's Lane, is the large **Granary Gallery** (636 Old County Rd., 508/693-0455 or 800/472-6279, www.granarygallery.com, daily late May–early Oct., at least weekends in shoulder season Easter–Christmas), which has the distinction of being the Time-Life Gallery of Photography's sole New England representative. So, in addition to locally produced artwork in a variety of media (paint-

© BRIAN JOLLEY

The "New Ag Hall" in West Tisbury hosts a variety of shows and fairs.

ing, sculpture, and sometimes textiles), you can browse—or buy—limited editions, mostly signed, of museum-quality prints by the likes of Alfred Eisenstadt, Margaret Bourke-White, Andreas Feininger, Carl Mydans, and others whose contributions to *Life* magazine have become some of the nation's most recognizable cultural images.

North Tisbury

Within 25 years of their arrival, the English outgrew their settlement at Edgartown and moved up-island to this fertile area between Priester's Pond and Lambert's Cove Road. It was known to the Wampanoag as "Takemmy" (place where people go to grind corn), but may actually be from *touohkomuk* (wilderness). The English shepherds called the settlement Newton (Edgartown then was Old Town), and later Middletown. Now named after the post office station sandwiched into a storefront within a small shopping plaza, this part of West Tisbury township no longer qualifies as very wild, although it's still plenty rural.

One part of the scenery worth stopping for is the **Polly Hill Arboretum** (809 State Rd., 508/693-9426, www.pollyhillarboretum.org, 7 A.M.–7 P.M. Thurs.–Tues. in season, dawn–dusk Thurs.–Tues. off season, suggested donation $5), about a half mile south of the junction with North Road (to Menemsha). Old stone walls are reminders that these 60 acres were once a sheep farm, but Ms. Hill, a famous horticulturist, turned a third of the property into an open-air laboratory for her work with ornamental trees and shrubs. The rest is kept in natural meadows and woods. Perhaps the most captivating time to visit is mid-June through July, when the dramatic allée of Kousa dogwoods is in full bloom, but there are numerous rare and beautiful species worth seeing throughout the year, as well as a variety of programs at the visitors center.

North Tisbury's commercial side includes a couple of arty shops along State Road, most notably **Martha's Vineyard Glassworks** (683 State Rd., 508/693-6026, www.mvglassworks.com, 10 A.M.–5 P.M. daily late May–early Oct.), where the art of shaping attractive, functional items out of molten glass is on view daily in season. It's also worth checking out the **Yes, We Have No Bananas Gallery** (455 State Rd., 508/696-5939, www.bananasgallery.com, 11 A.M.–6 P.M. daily mid-June–early Sept., closed Tues.–Wed. mid-Sept.–early Oct. and late May–early June, hours vary mid-Oct.–mid-May) for their unconventional clothing, jewelry, and gifts.

Christiantown

Although the Puritan founders of the Massachusetts Bay Colony had obtained their royal patent by promising that "the principall Ende" of their settlement was to convert the indigenous people to "the Christian Fayth," the evangelical magistrates in Boston were so busy prosecuting heretics and building a profitable mercantile trade that it was here on the Vineyard—outside their jurisdiction—that the first New England mission to the Indians began. The year after the Mayhews settled their parish in Edgartown, a Wampanoag named Hiacoomes became the island's first voluntary convert to Christianity. Within a decade, over 10 percent of the Vineyard's Indian population had signed a covenant with the proselytizing Thomas Mayhew, Jr.; within a generation, a majority of the Wampanoag on both the Vineyard and Nantucket had not only converted, but had also resettled themselves into a series of 15 Christian communities modeled after the English style, a move heralding the profound change colonization wrought upon both Wampanoag culture and the Indians' relationship to the land.

One such town stood in North Tisbury on what's now Christiantown Road, off Indian Hill Road. With the blessings of Thomas Mayhew, Sr., Wampanoag converts consecrated their first Christian church and burial ground here in 1659, on a parcel of land rented from a pair of up-island sachems. Besides the small number of descendants denied federal tribal recognition, all that's left of Christiantown now is tiny little Mayhew Chapel, an 1829 replacement of the original; the mostly unmarked tombstones opposite; and abandoned 19th-century cellar holes and stone walls

along the peaceful loop trail through adjacent **Christiantown Woods Preserve.** About a 0.25-mile walk past the parking lot (follow the road and take the first right; this is not driveable) is a state-maintained **fire tower.** When the tower is staffed—which is only when fire danger is high—you are welcome to go up and enjoy the fine 360° views.

Chicama Vineyards

While most island farmwork happens far from the curious eyes of off-islanders, an exception exists here, at the state's first legitimate winery, which offers tours up to five times a day in season. Year-round, taste from a variety of red and white table wines made from European *vinifera* grapes, including chardonnay, zinfandel, cabernet, a cranberry dessert wine, and the occasional sparkling wine. Chicama also bottles its own line of gourmet flavored oils, mustards, vinegars, chutneys, and other condiments. All, like the wines, are for sale in the gift shop–tasting room (80 Stoney Hill Rd., 508/693-0309, hours vary in May, 11 A.M.–5 P.M. daily June–Christmas, Sat. only Jan.–Apr.). The winery and shop are a mile down sand-and-gravel Stoney Hill Road from the signposted turn off State Road.

CHILMARK

Sparsely populated Chilmark (whose year-round population is less than 850) once resembled a little corner of New Zealand, with more sheep than humans. The resemblance stopped at labor and farm expenses, though; before Down Under's huge sheep stations put the kibosh on profitability, back in the mid-19th century, Chilmark wool had been second only to whale oil in importance to the island economy. (The whalers themselves made use of the wool in the form of heavy-duty satinet coat fabric milled in neighboring West Tisbury.) Dozens of miles of drystone walls, all built from up-island's limitless supply of glacial till, lie half-hidden in the now-forested hills, quiet reminders of the loose-footed flocks of black-faced sheep that once dominated the local landscape. If you've taken a close look at these sorts of walls elsewhere in New England, you'll notice that the Vineyard has a distinctive "lace wall" in its repertoire— a rickety-looking style with big gaps between the stones. The usual explanation has been that these perforated walls were built to accommodate stiff ocean winds raking over the once-treeless up-island hills, but Susan Allport, author of the exceptional *Sermons in Stone,* suggests the design may be a Scottish import. Although there is no written record one way or the other, a nearly identical style of see-through stone wall in Scotland—called a Galloway dike—was built to look deceptively precarious specifically to frighten bold sheep from attempting to leap over them.

Despite having its trees and vegetation shorn to the ground by its early "husbandmen," Chilmark still boasts some of the island's best soil, even if these days artists and telecommuting professionals far outnumber local farmers (though farms still seem to outnumber retail shops). The center of the village is the intersection of State (alternately known in Chilmark as South Road), Middle, and Menemsha Cross Roads (named Beetlebung Corner, after the stand of tupelo trees whose hardwood was valued by ships' chandlers for making mallets—beetles—and cask stoppers—bungs). On the east side of the intersection is the **Chilmark Library** (508/645-3360, Mon.–Thurs. and Sat.), whose "Island Room" is an ideal rainy-day destination for anyone whose appetite has been whet by the morsels of history presented here. Also hard by the corner is the **Chilmark Store** (7 State Rd., 508/645-3739, deli 7 A.M.–7 P.M. daily May– mid-Oct., market stays open till 8 P.M.) a worthy pit stop for cyclists and others in need of a sandwich or slice of pizza. If your consumer impulse runs to something more stylish than groceries and minor housewares, check out the town's popular Flea Market, on the grounds of the **Community Church** (8:30 A.M.–3:30 P.M. Wed. and Sat., end of June–late Aug. or early Sept.), where mostly professional craftspeople, artists, and antiques dealers market seconds or blemished wares passed over by regular retail

buyers at prices which, while not a steal, are generally well-discounted.

With the exception of the village of Menemsha, most of Chilmark is rather leery of tourists. Summer's hordes may pay the bills but that hasn't alleviated the Not In My Back Yard syndrome. (If you've never thought of yourself as the vanguard of the great unwashed, just attend a local town hearing the next time someone proposes creating a public beachfront reserve, and listen to the dire predictions of how you'll ruin the neighborhood. You'd think tourists are just Hell's Angels in beach gear.) But not all Chilmark's inhabitants are loath to receive visitors; nothing's going to faze Lillian Hellman or John Belushi, for example, at their eternal residences in **Abel's Hill Burying Ground,** on South Road less than three miles from West Tisbury's town line. While they're probably the most famous tenants, anyone with an eye for good epitaphs and fine stone-carving will take greater interest in the many historic 18th- and 19th-century markers.

Menemsha

Anyone who wants proof that some of the people around here make a living off something besides the tourists can come to this Chilmark village and admire the Coast Guard station poised above the water in the golden light of a late summer afternoon. But the even bigger attraction is the fishing fleet in Menemsha Basin, whose catch ends up on tourists' plates all over the island. Watching guys in rubber boots shovel fish into barrels against a backdrop of buoy-covered shacks crowned with whale-shaped weathervanes is undeniably picturesque—especially compared to downisland's retail barrage—but it resists any use of the word "quaint." If this place is an anachronism, it's only because so much of the region no longer soils its hands with old-fashioned cash register keys or Touch-Tone telephones.

Besides watching sunsets framed by the boat basin's thicket of swaying masts, Menemsha's summer visitors come for hiking, swimming, and seafood in the rough. Cyclists looking for a shortcut to Aquinnah—and a chance to avoid some of the hills and punishing headwinds encountered on State Road—won't want to miss the **Menemsha Bike Ferry** (508/645-5154, $4 one-way, $7 round-trip), which shuttles across Menemsha inlet to West Basin, near the east end of Lobsterville Beach. It operates on demand daily 8 A.M.–6 P.M. July–Labor Day, plus weekends in the shoulder months of June, September, and October, weather permitting. But before you make a descent to the Menemsha inlet, check the signs at any of the approaches in Chilmark, West Tisbury, or Aquinnah to confirm whether the ferry is indeed running.

AQUINNAH

The most remote of the island's six towns, rural Aquinnah (year-round pop. 344) seems to stand in sharp relief against the fortunes of its sister communities. Although its population rebounded in the 1990s to keep pace with the rest of the Vineyard's double-digit percentage gains, Aquinnah has an unemployment rate nearly three times the statewide average, and the lowest average household income in all of Massachusetts. By the numbers, it would seem to belong in Appalachia rather than on one of New England's most star-studded resorts. The numbers, however, don't tell the full story. Most of the town's property owners are summer people whose incomes boost the statistics somewhere else—if their accountants let the government know about it at all. Many other residents thrive on an underground economy of cottage artisanship, cash contract work, or investment income that escapes the attention of labor statisticians. With vacant land selling for $200,000 an acre and town kids tending to go to prestigious colleges and graduate schools, Aquinnah might be called many things, but "poor" isn't one of them.

Along with Mashpee on Cape Cod, Aquinnah is one of two Massachusetts communities with a significant Native American population—almost 30 percent, according to the last national census. Most are Wampanoags of the Aquinnah (Gay Head) band, one of the

remaining handful of the 50 or so bands that once made up the Wampanoag nation; descendants of two other bands, the Christiantown and Chappaquiddick, also live in the community, although their cultural identity hasn't been maintained well enough to receive the same recognition. If every tribal member lived in Aquinnah, they'd outnumber their non-Indian neighbors by more than four to one, but more than half of the 992-member band live off-island, and most of the rest live down-island.

In the 17th century, this area belonged to the sachemship Aquinnah (high land). Most of it stayed under Indian ownership until the 19th century, when condescending schemers pressured or duped native landowners into quite literally giving away the farm. After lengthy legal action, a few hundred acres were finally returned to the local Wampanoag after they obtained federal recognition in 1987, but there's no reservation—the restored acres came with some strings attached. Not surprisingly, accepting less than full control over a parcel of ancestral land much smaller than hoped for was a controversial price to pay for tribal recognition. During most of the 19th and 20th centuries, the community was known as Gay Head, after the high escarpment on which the lighthouse still stands, but in 1997 residents voted to return to their indigenous roots.

For anyone interested in the Wampanoags' history, the **Aquinnah Public Library** (State Rd. at Church St., 508/645-9552, 2–7 P.M. Mon., Wed., and Fri.; 10 A.M.–4 P.M. Sat.), has a room devoted to books about and by Native Americans. Ask the librarian to suggest a few of local relevance.

◖ Gay Head Cliffs

Declared a National Natural Landmark in 1966, 130-foot high Gay Head Cliffs have been a tourist attraction for as long as tourists have come to the Vineyard. Cliff-climbing is *definitely* off-limits—it's dangerous and accelerates the severe erosion of the unanchored clay—but you can admire the antediluvian strata from above or below, depending on whether you take

© KATHRYN OSGOOD

the eroding cliffs at Gay Head

Although the immediate grounds of the light are fenced off from public access throughout most of the year, on summer weekends (Fri.–Sun.) between June's solstice and September's equinox, the tower and grounds are opened for self-guided sunset tours ($3, free to children under 12, free to everyone on Mother's Day). The gates open 90 minutes before sundown and close 30 minutes after. Tours are canceled if the weather is so lousy that the sun can't be seen.

With the exception of a few tacky little gift sheds and fast-food stalls on the path to the clifftop overlook, Aquinnah is blissfully lacking in commercial attractions. Hungry visitors will find breakfasts, burgers, sandwiches, fried seafood, salads, and diner-style desserts at the seasonal **Aquinnah Restaurant** loftily perched at the cliff edge (Aquinnah Circle, 508/645-3867, 8 A.M.–3 or 4 P.M. daily mid-May–Columbus Day, 8 A.M.–7:30 P.M. daily late June–Aug., hours vary Easter–mid-May). Please note that despite the declared schedule of open hours, if business is too slow due to bad weather, the eatery may not remain open past 4 P.M. even in peak season.

ENTERTAINMENT

Modern dance is the bailiwick of **The Yard** (Middle Rd. off Beetlebung Corner, 508/645-9662, www.dancetheyard.org) an up-island artists' colony founded in the early 1970s and located in Chilmark, close to Beetlebung Corner. Their Barn Theater hosts a season of dance performances by colony residents at least one weekend a month from May to September, often including premieres of improvisational works that will next appear (at much higher prices) in New York City.

Real traditional New England **contra** and **square dances,** sponsored by the Country Dance Society (508/693-5627 or 508/693-9374), take place monthly off-season, September–May, at the Chilmark Community Center and West Tisbury's Grange Hall. Beginners are welcome; call for schedule and dates, or consult newspaper calendar listings.

a five- or fifty-minute walk from the parking lot. If the ground could talk, those multihued layers could tell some mighty interesting stories, if the fossilized remains of camels are any indication. On clear or partly cloudy evenings, the clifftop overlook provides exceptional front-row seats for watching the sun extinguish itself in the ocean off Rhode Island.

Adding to the photogenic view from the cliffs is the 19th-century red-brick **Gay Head Lighthouse** (508/645-2211), whose alternating red and white flashes warn ships away from Devil's Bridge, a treacherous line of partially submerged offshore rocks that prompted construction of the original 1799 beacon. Tricky currents and bad weather still sank many a sailing vessel on these rocks, even after the dim lanterns of old were replaced with the powerful Fresnel lens now seen in the yard of the Vineyard Historical Society; worst among these various disasters was the wreck of the *City of Columbus,* on which more than a hundred of its sleeping passengers died within a few minutes on a winter's night in early 1884.

RECREATION
Beaches

For the duration of summer, up-island towns restrict most of their beaches to residents or renters who bring a copy of their lease on a local house to the requisite office at town hall. Don't think the permits apply only to cars: Chilmark's beach attendants will check them no matter how many wheels—or feet—you come in on. (Guests of Chilmark B&Bs and inns can obtain walk-in beach permits, and can take advantage of the Chilmark beach shuttle bus that services the town's handful of lodgings; inquire at check-in.) So, **Lambert's Cove,** in West Tisbury; **Lucy Vincent** and **Squibnocket Beaches,** in Chilmark; and **Philbin** and **Head of the Pond** Beaches, in Aquinnah, are thus off-limits to most visitors from June through September—although at gorgeous Lambert's Cove, nonresidents are free to come catch the sun's last golden rays 6–9 P.M. But despair not—the publicly accessible alternatives are by no means negligible.

West Tisbury, for example, has a pair of conservation properties along the south shore whose mix of pond and ocean beaches amply reward the effort of reaching them. **Long Point Wildlife Refuge** (508/693-3678, 9 A.M.–5 P.M. June 15–Sept. 15, additionally 9 A.M.–7 P.M. Fri.–Sun. July–Aug., dawn–dusk otherwise, $3 for anyone over 15 plus $10 parking June 15–Sept. 15) another property of the Trustees, has half a mile of dune-backed beach along the Atlantic that rarely gets congested—thanks to the strict limit on the number of vehicles admitted. For more elbow room on hot, clear days, arrive early and walk west from the parking lot. To get there, turn off the Edgartown–West Tisbury Road onto Waldron's Bottom Road (look for the Trustees sign) and then follow the arrows.

Just west of Long Point is the Land Bank's **Sepiessa Point Reservation,** with a small beach along the edge of Tisbury Great Pond (watch for sharp oyster shells on the beach). The pond itself is a body of saltwater and marsh now hemmed in on the ocean side by barrier dunes (private) that are breached twice

© KATHRYN OSGOOD

A father takes his children fishing at Squibnocket Beach in Chilmark.

a year to maintain the pond's salinity, vital to maintaining its shellfish population. This place is virtually unknown even to most Vineyarders, so don't be surprised if you have it to yourself. Though free, parking is extremely limited; beachgoers should use the first trailhead pull-out and leave the southerly ones for folks who have boats to schlep. The walk to the beach from the upper trailhead is just over a mile, mostly through woods.

Menemsha Beach is Chilmark's most accessible—a big, family-friendly north shore spot with plenty of parking, food, restrooms, and views of the local fishing fleet returning to adjacent Menemsha Harbor; from the village center, follow signs for Dutcher Dock. A second, concession-free north shore beach—quite a lovely one, too—is found at **Great Rock Bight Preserve,** a Land Bank property quickly reached by a short trail accessed off of North Road; look for the Land Bank sign a little under four miles south of State Road. By contrast, the Land Bank's **Chilmark Pond Preserve,** off South Road opposite Abel's Hill

Cemetery, offers what's tantamount to a private beach club, with the lesser of 10 vehicles or 40 people allowed onto the property at any one time. The preserve's small piece of the south shore lies just east of permit-only **Lucy Vincent Beach.** Lucy Vincent is regarded by some as the island's finest beach, but don't get your hopes up—to even reach the ocean dunes, you must bring a canoe or kayak and paddle diagonally across Chilmark Pond (be sure to read the lengthy posted explanations of where you can and cannot land on the opposite shore). In the end, it's one plum that may stay tantalizingly out of reach, despite being free and public.

Arguably the best public swath of south shore surf and sand is at the Land Bank's **Moshup Beach** and adjacent **Aquinnah Public Beach,** just a scant half-mile or so from the famous Gay Head Cliffs. Limited parking is available—for a punitive $20 in summer—in the lot at the State Road loop atop the cliffs, near the public restrooms (where, incidentally, the down-island shuttle bus stops). Cyclists will find free racks down Moshup Trail at the beach itself.

East of the well-marked Land Bank property line is residents-only Philbin Beach; in the other direction, toward the base of the cliffs, is the island's principal nude bathing area. Up until the '90s, it wasn't uncommon to see people painting themselves from top to bottom with the richly colored clay from the cliffs, but enforcement of the prohibition against all climbing, digging, and souvenir-taking from this Wampanoag-owned National Landmark has been sharply increased in the years since. The strict rules are not the work of mere spoilsports—clay removal artificially hastens erosion. Simply walking around the base of the spectacular marine scarp, however, is perfectly legit.

Aquinnah's only other public shore is sheltered **Lobsterville Beach,** a mecca for surfcasters. The absolute ban on parking on Lobsterville Road makes access difficult, however. Aquinnah house renters and inn guests who obtain town parking permits (and the lucky few who snatch up the three or four spaces available for nonresidents) can park a mile away in the small lot at the end of West Basin Road, just across the narrow channel from the fishing boats in Menemsha Basin; otherwise, it's a two-mile walk from the Aquinnah bus stop up at the clifftop loop.

By far the best non-automotive approach is via the Bike Ferry from Menemsha, when it's operating (June–October). Of course, if it's swimming rather than fishing that you want, save yourself a mile walk or ride and stick to state-owned **West Jetty,** at West Basin; despite the protection from prevailing southwesterly winds, Lobsterville is generally much too rocky to stretch out a towel on (although it should be pointed out that the offshore eelgrass and crab beds aren't everyone's idea of tactile pleasure).

Kayaking

If you're serious about becoming a sea kayaker, you probably want to take lessons from a serious paddler committed to the sport, such as John Moore at **Kayaks of Martha's Vineyard** (508/693-3885, www.kayakmv.com). Two- to two-and-a-half-hour beginner's lessons ($35 per hour, plus $25 for a boat) cover all the basics—equipment, strokes, safety and rescue—but lessons are tailored to suit your skills. Though based at Lambert's Cove, John's business is mobile, so just phone to arrange an appropriate outdoor classroom. Off-season requests aren't a problem, either—he's a year-round resident, and even has dry suits for arctic souls who want to play in nippy April or November.

The Trustees of Reservations offers kayak tours of Tisbury Great Pond in summer.

Manuel F. Correllus State Forest

This forest was originally set aside to protect the dwindling population of the heath hen, a relative of the prairie chicken extinguished on the mainland through hunting and habitat loss. But the gesture was undermined by a big forest fire and continued hunting. By 1932, the hen was extinct. In spite of a legacy of tree farming, a blight that's killing off the remaining stands

MARTHA'S VINEYARD

Manuel F. Corellus State Forest

of red pine, and proximity to the island's airport, some trail-savvy islanders consider the state forest a hidden gem. Hikers interested in the Vineyard's floristic communities won't find any better place to sample the island's pitch pine barrens and scrub oak bottoms, for example—and mountain bikers can crisscross the forest on miles of fire roads. If you happen to visit during a snowy winter, you'll find good cross-country skiing through the property, too. Pick up a map and advice from the helpful staff at the forest headquarters (508/693-2540), off Airport Road.

◖ Long Point Wildlife Refuge

Big waves along an exceptional South Shore beach are the draw for summer visitors to this isolated up-island spot (508/693-3678, www .thetrustees.org, 9 A.M.–5 P.M. Mon.–Thurs. and 9 A.M.–7 P.M. Fri.–Sun. June 15–Sept. 15, dawn–dusk otherwise, $3 per person over 15 plus $10 parking June 15–Sept. 15, free otherwise). Bird-watchers and wild blueberry lovers may prefer the trails around the grasslands and shrub-

covered heath opposite the high-season parking lot on Long Cove Pond. Interpretive trail guides to the mile-long barrier beach-and-grassland loop are available year-round at the parking-lot bulletin boards, and are downloadable online. The other mile-long trail visits the freshwater marsh along the edge of Long Cove, where in spring and summer, you might hear frogs singing for sex, see herons stalking their supper, or spot river otters before they spot you.

Spring is also a good time to catch migrating ducks feeding on the ponds and songbirds scouting nesting sites in the woods. Fall is impossible not to enjoy—as the last papery pink salt-spray roses start to fold, the bayberry and huckleberry bushes impart a warm burgundy glow to the heathlands, and the waterfowl stop over again on their way south. On good summer swimming days, you'd do well to consider biking in to avoid being turned away when the parking lot fills; but off-season, this is a good place to be alone with your thoughts and brisk ocean breezes.

Naturalist-guided kayak tours of Tisbury Great Pond are offered in season (508/693-7392, 8:30 A.M., 11 A.M., and 1:30 P.M. daily June 15–Sept. 15, $25). Reservations for the 90-minute excursions are strongly recommended. For an out-of-the-ordinary paddling experience, sign up early for one of the special moonlight paddling tours offered over three or four nights preceding, during, and after the full moon (dates vary June–Sept., $45).

In summer the refuge gates are locked an hour after admissions end, so don't expect to hang around for watching the sunset over distant Aquinnah or admiring the star-studded carpet of the Milky Way.

Summer access is via Waldron's Bottom Road off the Edgartown–West Tisbury Road; follow the signs to the high-season parking lot by the beach (fresh water and restrooms available). Off season, the gate at road's end is closed; mid-September through mid-June, visitors should then use the heavily potholed, single-lane dirt track called Deep Bottom Road (again, follow the signs) to get to the facilities-free parking area near the caretaker's cottage.

Sepiessa Point Reservation

Like nearby Long Point, this Land Bank reservation protects some of the planet's last remaining acres of sandplain grasslands, backed by a large swath of woodlands along the edge of Tiah's (rhymes with wise) Cove, one of many slender inlets to Tisbury Great Pond. Since the only public boat access to the Great Pond is via the reservation's cove-side canoe and boat slides, most islanders familiar with this unheralded place know of it by the cove's name instead of the peninsula's. The property sports a short stretch of hard, sandy beach along the pond edge, too, but heed the posted warnings about the broken oyster shells, which are about as friendly to tender, unshod feet as discarded metal sardine cans. At a small pull-out near the reservation entrance—the only parking available to hikers and swimmers (each boat slide has its own handful of spaces)—a signboard identifies the trails that loop through pine-oak woods and converge on the grassy meadows about a mile away. Though quite plain for most of the year, the meadows are good wildflower territory in spring—the bushy rockrose, Nantucket shadbush, and other rare sandplain plants blossom throughout May and June. Summer's insects and autumn's berries bring birds out of the woods to forage throughout the rest of the high season, and if you look carefully before they all get eaten, at the end of summer, you may spot fruit-bearing creepers of the wild grapevine that supposedly inspired the island's name. Northern harriers, another of the state's rare species, have occasionally been sighted hunting in the meadows for rodents and insects.

Free year-round, Sepiessa Point is signposted with the Land Bank logo along Tiah's Cove Road, a dead-end fork off New Lane in West Tisbury. Only about 1.25 miles from the Edgartown–West Tisbury Road, the reservation is accessible to most bikes and even up-island shuttle riders who request a stop at New Lane, almost across from the volunteer fire station. A downloadable PDF of the reservation's trail map is available from the Land Bank's website, www.mvlandbank.com.

◖ Cedar Tree Neck

Ask your innkeepers or island hosts to recommend their favorite hiking spot and nine times out of ten they'll nominate this property of the Sheriff's Meadow Foundation. Located on West Tisbury's North Shore, it fully earns its reputation with nearly two miles of looping trails through woods, wetlands, and dunes; along a brook; along a moraine ridge; and along the beach. A kid-friendly pamphlet—available in the map kiosk at the parking lot—provides interpretive details on one trail; others are summarized on memoranda posted in the kiosk by the property managers. The trails were designed in part by Anne Hale, whose locally published book *From Moraine to Marsh: A Field Guide to Martha's Vineyard* is the best natural history companion for walks around the Neck.

Swimming is prohibited along the property's gorgeous Vineyard Sound shoreline, and a summer attendant enforces this restriction—part of the terms that made the land public. As is the case nearly everywhere on the Vineyard, neighboring houses are never far from sight, but the beauty of the Neck will put them clean out of your mind. In fact, don't be surprised if a scant half-hour of soaking up the views from the beach has you forgetting your *own* home. Located at the end of Obed Daggett Road, off Indian Hill Road, Cedar Tree Neck is free all year. A bike rack is provided, but restrooms aren't.

Waskosim's Rock Reservation

Straddling the West Tisbury–Chilmark town line near the headwaters of pristine Mill Brook are nearly 200 acres almost straight out of the 19th century: abandoned farmland bordered by dry-stone walls, the ever-encroaching forest, and wetlands that feed that brook, a vital tributary of Tisbury Great Pond. The waters of the brook are so clean that they're home to the brook lamprey, a species whose hypersensitivity to pollutants has made it widely endangered.

Presumably named after a local Wampanoag, Waskosim's Rock is a giant cracked boulder that marked a 17th-century boundary between

English and Indian lands. Natural forest succession has obscured the views once afforded from the rock itself, but fine down-island vistas may yet be found by the cleared fields rising out of the Mill Brook valley and from occasional breaks in the hilltop forest. Since much of the abutting private property is equally undeveloped, trails through the reservation's varied habitats are as good for bird-watchers as for anyone looking for a glimpse of Vineyard Haven's water tower. Conspicuous summer visitors include flickers, cuckoos, blue jays, and ovenbirds (in the dry oak forest at the southern, high end of the property); cedar waxwings, swallows, song sparrows, and white-eyed vireos (out on the old pastures); and northern parula warblers (around the scrubby red maple swamp near the trailhead).

The reservation's entrance, and parking for both bikes and cars, is signposted with a discreet Land Bank logo beside North Road a few hundred feet on the Chilmark side of the Chilmark–West Tisbury boundary.

Fulling Mill Brook Preserve

Although drivers on Chilmark's Middle Road will most likely miss its small trailhead parking lot, the relaxing half-mile walk through the Fulling Mill Brook Preserve is worth turning around for. The quiet, lazy trout stream grows garrulous and boulder-strewn as it runs through mixed hardwood forest down the shoulder of Abel's Hill, part of the morainal ridge that runs between Tisbury and Aquinnah. Shrubby savanna interspersed with oaks and a spot of wildflower-filled meadow occupy some of the slopes over the stream.

The brook takes its name from the mill that used its waters in the process of "fulling" cloth—making it heavier through shrinking and pressing—back in the 1800s. In the 1700s, several tanners treated hides in this neck of the woods, too. Today, decaying leaf litter and fresh breezes have replaced the tannic scent of curing leather. In summer, woodland songbirds abound along the brook's path, but proximity to those drier upland habitats means you're as apt to hear mourning doves and song sparrows as the quiet call of the whippoorwill.

While cars are limited to the Middle Road lot, cyclists can take advantage of a second bike rack, on South Road, at the preserve's lower end, beside an impressive stone and wrought-iron gateway.

Peaked Hill Reservation

Three of the island's highest points, including Radar Hill, an old World War II garrison site, and 311-foot Peaked (PEA-kid) Hill, crown a cluster of ridges whose slopes were once nearly girdled with luxury homes. The Land Bank's timely acquisition of these Chilmark heights preserved some especially good vantage points for Aquinnah sunsets, views over the Elizabeth Islands to the Southeastern Massachusetts coast, and hawk-watching. Numerous large moss- and lichen-covered glacial erratics, chunks of granite gouged out of mountains or exposed bedrock farther north and deposited here during the last ice age, dot the wooded trails. Some of the stones form the panoramic ledges; others are distinctive enough to have their own names (such as Wee Devil's Bed) or serve as reminders of the late 18th- and early 19th-century farmers who cleared much of this land (their pin-and-feather technique for splitting huge boulders into gateposts and foundation slabs is writ large on the edges of unused stones).

The military has also left some marks here. They're mostly steel-and-concrete tower footings and broken asphalt, but notice, too, the mature tree grown up through the old Radar Hill fencing, its trunk indelibly tattooed by the rusty chain link. The reservation now plays host to a large herd of white-tailed deer, whose distinctive bite can be seen in the severed ends of lower branches on small trees and shrubs all over these 70 acres. The rich forest understory and dense thickets also provide vital cover for numerous small mammals and birds, including an array of finches, sparrows, swallows, warblers, and woodpeckers. Conspicuous but locally uncommon species such as yellow- and black-billed cuckoos, killdeer, and bluebirds have been sighted here, and the relatively high elevations attract red-winged hawks and

American kestrels during both breeding and migration seasons.

The entrance turnoff is signposted on Tabor House Road, a half mile from Middle Road. Parking, maps, and a bike rack are located eight-tenths of a mile up the potholed dirt lane—always take the right fork, or you'll have to back out of several private driveways.

Menemsha Hills

Part of the reason the vista from the shoulder of Peaked Hill is so attractive is that the wooded hills bordering Vineyard Sound on the other side of North Road are protected by the Trustees' Menemsha Hills Reservation. Several miles of trails offer walkers oak tree shade, hilltop views, and bracing winds along the lip of the 150-foot marine scarp over Vineyard Sound. Ruminate over the landscape, where sheep once grazed within the property's drystone walls; watch birds gorge themselves on the heath's summer berry crop; or pretend you're Thomas Hart Benton, the Missouri-born painter who summered here in Chilmark for 56 years, and stroll the rocky beach (no swimming!) with an artist's eye for the play of light and water upon the rough coast. In late fall or winter, you might spot harbor seals basking on the rocks or bobbing in the surf offshore.

A Trustees' white-on-green sign marks the reservation's parking lot off North Road in Chilmark, a little over half a mile west of the junction with Tabor House Road. Admission is free.

ACCOMMODATIONS

Up-island may not offer a large quantity of lodging choices, but it certainly has a wide variety, including the island's only hostel, a number of traditional home-style B&Bs, a luxurious inn built around a 1790 farmhouse, and modern lodgings built in the 1970s. Prices, however, are concentrated at the low and high ends, with a big gap between them.

Under $50

The Vineyard's only true budget accommodation is West Tisbury's **Hostelling International**

Martha's Vineyard (525 Edgartown–West Tisbury Rd., 508/693-2665 or 888/901-2087, www.usahostels.org, mid-May–early Oct., $32–35 HI members, nonmembers add $3), a rambling, cedar-shingled Cape-style structure at the edge of the state forest on an isolated stretch of the Edgartown–West Tisbury Road. For anyone unfamiliar with the concept, many hostels now offer private rooms for families and couples, but when this one was designed, in the 1950s (it's the first American youth hostel built specifically for the purpose), the prevailing ethic called for stacking hostelers like kids at summer camp—20 or more per room. So until someone endows this fine old place with a massive capital renovation budget, its big, bunk bed–filled dorm rooms, slightly rustic common spaces, and woodsy locale will remain the archetype of hostel life—especially when the huge downstairs bunk room is filled by some exuberant school group.

The bottom line is that when all 78 beds are full, it's a bit zoo-like, despite the staff's superhuman efforts. Off-season, it's one of the most welcoming—and well-run—hostels in the business. Advance reservations are absolutely essential in summer, and highly recommended off-season.

Although accessible by bike path, car, and summer shuttle buses, the hostel is three miles from the nearest decent market, so if you plan to use the spic-and-span kitchen, you may want to shop ahead for groceries. Internet access is available.

$50-100

Up-island's epicenter of affordability is West Tisbury, where nearly half the lodgings belong to various descendants of old Thomas Mayhew himself—few of whom seem interested in fleecing visitors. The price leader of the year-round lot is **The House at New Lane Bed & Breakfast** (44 New Lane, 508/693-4046, housenl@vineyard.net, $85 d cash only, $20 more for one-nighters in season) on seven attractive acres just off the Edgartown–West Tisbury Road, offering three rooms, all with shared baths.

$100-150

Writers searching for inspiration may particularly appreciate the creative vibes around **The Cleaveland House** (620 Edgartown–West Tisbury Rd., 508/693-9352, criggs@vineyard. net, $85 s or $100 d cash only) at the corner of New Lane, home to the author of a series of mysteries set on the Vineyard. The circa-1750 house is chock full of character, with lots of family heirlooms and stories to tell, and plenty of cozy places to kick back and think up excuses for your editor after the surrounding acres' beauty distracts you from your muse. In addition to a small room for singletons there are two fireplace-equipped rooms, one a king and the other with two twin beds. Please note, none of these rooms has a private bath, and there's a two-night minimum in season.

Just across the road, **The Red Hat B&B** (629 Edgartown–West Tisbury Rd., 508/696-7186, www.theredhat.com, $100–115 d cash only) has three modest yet comfortable rooms, all sharing a bath. Like its neighbors, it also features a large yard, so after your island adventures you can relax on the sunny deck or in the hammock under the trees.

$250-350

Set way back in the woods at the end of a sandy lane off upper Lambert's Cove Road, West Tisbury's **◖ Lambert's Cove Country Inn** (90 Manaquayak Rd., 508/693-2298 or 866/526-2466, www.lambertscoveinn.com, mid-Mar.–early Dec., $225–355 d, two-room suite $550) exudes informal sophistication. Fifteen guest rooms are spread among the buildings of what was once a grand residential country estate. The original 18th-century farmhouse, barn, and carriage house have all been completely renovated from the cellar to the rafters to create a secluded oasis of thoroughly modern comfort amid expansive, beautifully landscaped grounds. No two rooms are alike, but the warm palette and tasteful fabrics they have in common would be right at home on the cover of *Elle Decor*. Oriental carpets on hardwood floors here, four-poster and canopied feather beds there, a lot of private decks,

marbled baths, abundant pillows, flat-screen TVs with DVD/CD players—you get the picture (and if not, visit their website for photos of every room). This popular inn also features an all-weather tennis court, a modest outdoor swimming pool, and passes to lovely Lambert's Cove Beach (beach umbrellas and chairs provided). Complimentary made-to-order full breakfasts are served in the inn's restaurant, which happens to be one of the island's best choices for dinner, too.

The **Menemsha Inn & Cottages** (12 Menemsha Inn Rd., 508/645-2521, www .menemshainn.com, May–Oct., $280–350 d, cottages and houses $2,700–4,600 per week) offers a wide range of lodging options from modern motel-style rooms with two queen beds to houses that comfortably sleep six. It sits on 14 hillside acres—including a pasture with resident cow—above the cute little village of Menemsha, just off Chilmark's North Road immediately south of the Menemsha Cross Road junction. Contemporary in design and decor, the inn offers a choice of 15 well-appointed doubles and suites, 12 one- and two-bedroom, fully equipped housekeeping cottages, and two three-bedroom houses, nearly all facing Vineyard Sound. Rates include a complimentary self-serve breakfast of cereals and baked goods. If you have a group, the Carriage House's six ocean-facing suites and large two-story common room with big cushy sofas around a stone fireplace would serve as an ideal home base. Take advantage of the on-site fitness center, game room, playground, or tennis court, or take the path at the bottom of the hill to the public beach in Menemsha, 500 yards away. Beautiful sunset views of Aquinnah and Menemsha Bight, luggage-saving extras such as beach chairs and umbrellas, and guest passes to Chilmark's exclusive town beaches (regular shuttle bus service provided in season) make this a deservedly popular place, despite the absence of any air conditioning (fans are provided). Book early. Peak rates last from mid-July through August, dropping about 15 percent for the three or four weeks before and after, and by about a third for the first and last four weeks of the season.

$350 and Up

Just through the trees bordering the Menemsha Inn, under common ownership but managed separately, is **The Beach Plum Inn** (50 Beach Plum Ln., 508/645-9454 or 877/645-7398, www.beachpluminn.com, May–Oct., $325–450 d), with 11 rooms between its main house and three adjacent bungalows. The decor is a modern mix of solid summery colors paired with printed fabrics and flocked valances, and some rooms feature whirlpool tubs and private decks or patios. The seven landscaped acres include a regulation-size croquet lawn. Guests can use the gym and tennis court next door, and also have the pick of Chilmark's beaches, from the public one a short walk down the hill to permit-only Lucy Vincent and Squibnocket beaches a short shuttle-bus ride away on the Vineyard's south shore. A complimentary full gourmet breakfast is offered at the inn's restaurant, also highly regarded for its evening fine dining.

FOOD

Despite having a hostel full of them in its midst, the rural end of the Vineyard is not very kind to budget travelers. The foot-thick topsoil seems to yield not only fresh produce, but fancy destination dining. Next to nothing stays open past Thanksgiving out here, and most places start paring back their days and hours after September. Also remember that all three up-island towns—West Tisbury, Chilmark, and Aquinnah—are dry, so stop first at an OB or Edgartown package store if wine is vital to your dining pleasure.

Up-island's only reasonably priced eating is almost exclusively takeout. Worthwhile grocery-store deli counters include **Garcia's Bakery & Deli at Back Alley's** (1045 State Rd., 508/693-8401, noon–5 p.m.daily, year-round, $6–13) and **Fiddlehead Farm** (632 State Rd., 508/696-6700, 11 a.m.–3 p.m. Mon.–Fri., 11 a.m.–5 p.m. Sat.–Sun., year-round, $4–9) in West Tisbury, and **The**

oysters from a crab shack on the beach in Menemsha

Chilmark Store (7 State Rd., 508/645-3739, 10 a.m.–6 p.m. daily year-round, $7–8) at Beetlebung Corner.

In Menemsha, a pair of small summer-only shacks draw patrons from across the island, each with its own passionate following. For fried whole-belly clams and other shellfish, visit **The Menemsha Bite** (29 Basin Rd., 508/645-9239, www.thebitemenemsha.com, 11:30 a.m.–3 p.m.daily, May–June and Sept.–Oct., 11 a.m.–9 p.m.daily, July–Aug., $8–16), on the road to Dutcher Dock and the village beach.

For juicy burgers and soft-serve ice cream, check out **The Galley** (515 North Rd., 508/645-9819, noona.m.–8 p.m.daily year-round, $8–18), at the edge of Menemsha Channel. You can also dine for under $20 at the gift shop–eatery on the top of the Gay Head Cliffs, but come for the view, not the food.

Inquire after the best lobster on the Vineyard, and residents will most often steer you to **Larsen's Fish Market** (56 Basin Rd., 508/645-2680, 11 a.m.–6 p.m. daily

May–Oct., $13–19) in the heart of Menemsha. This is a taste of New England, deliciously unadorned. As the name makes clear, it's not a restaurant, but call ahead and order a lobster and they'll boil it for you on the spot to eat out back on the lobster traps at the edge of the dock, at one of the picnic tables nearby, or right on the beach. A variety of seafood soups and snacks are prepared daily, too, such as crab cakes, lobster bisque, seafood chowder, spicy stuffies (chorizo-stuffed clams), and seafood salad from the refrigerated cases inside the door. An al fresco picnic of Larsen's sweet tender fresh lobster chased down by steaming chowder as flavorful as fine bouillabaisse and fragrant as the sea, while the sun sets slowly into the ocean and keening gulls wheel in the evening breeze, is an ambrosial experience not soon forgotten.

Other prime up-island restaurants offer innovative, upscale cuisine in settings that range from studiously casual to stylishly contemporary. Several are found on the premises of the elegant inns tucked into the woods, such as West Tisbury's **Lambert's Cove Country Inn** (90 Manaquayak Rd., 508/693-2298, www.lambertscoveinn.com, 5:30 P.M.–close daily mid-June–mid-Sept., hours vary but at least Thurs.–Sat. mid-Apr.–New Year's Eve, $28–40). Conservative-sounding fare—roast chicken, filet mignon, poached lobster—is paired with rich accompaniments, such as salt cod ravioli, apple Madeira wine reduction, and wild mushroom ragout, such that each dish deliciously exceeds the sum of its attractively presented parts. (Too bad they don't serve tea of comparable quality.)

Plenty of island flavor—Caribbean island, that is—runs through Chilmark's **@ the Cornerway** (13 State Rd., 508/645-9300, www.atthecornerway.com, 6 A.M.–close daily late May–Sept., $28–45), a stone's throw from Beetlebung Corner. The chef-owner, Deon Thomas, puts an Anguillan spin on local ingredients. As visitors to that British West Indies hotspot know, this means gourmet preparations with eye-catching presentation and bold flavors. Seafood has a starring role, of course—mussels flambeed with rum, cod cakes with Scotch bonnet guacamole, swordfish with sweet potato fries—but carnivores will also find plenty of tantalizing choices, from steak and duck to traditional Carib favorites like jerk chicken and braised goat.

Festivals and Events

MAY

Ancient pagans helped wake up the earth from its winter slumbers with community rituals on the first of May. Find out for yourself how effective parading around a Maypole can be at shaking off the waning grip of cold weather by joining in the **May Day Celebration** at the Native Earth Teaching Farm (94 North Road, Chilmark, 508/645-3304). A potluck dinner is held following the afternoon of festivities, so bring along something to contribute if you plan on staying until sundown.

JUNE

Midmonth, sup like royalty at **A Taste of the Vineyard Gourmet Stroll,** on the Dr. Fisher House lawn behind the Old Whaling Church in Edgartown (508/627-4440, www.mvpreservation.org, $125). Proceeds from this food, wine, and beer blow-out, extravagantly catered by some 70 island restaurants and fine food purveyors, benefit the Martha's Vineyard Preservation Trust.

On the 16th, celebrate **Bloomsday** at Vineyard Haven's Katherine Cornell Memorial Theater, with a night of music, drama, and recitations inspired by James Joyce's *Ulysses* (www.artsandsociety.org, $15).

JULY

In the middle of the month, yachties swarm the Vineyard to race in the **Edgartown Regatta,** sponsored by the Edgartown Yacht Club (508/627-4364, www.edgartownyc.com).

During the second weekend of the month the **Annual Island Scoop Ice Cream Festival** (St. Augustine's Church, 84 Franklin Street, 508/693-7917) helps participants beat the heat with cool treats.

The third weekend brings a flavor of the Vineyard's Portuguese heritage to Oak Bluffs in the form of **The Feast of the Holy Ghost** (Vineyard Ave., 508/693-9875, www.mv holyghost.com), held both outdoors and at the Portuguese-American Club.

AUGUST

The first Monday of the month finds philanthropic islanders congregating under a big tent on the grounds of Outerland, a nightclub on the airport's entrance road, in order to take part in the **Possible Dreams Auction** (508/693-7900, www.possibledreamsauction .org, $25). High rollers bid on the opportunity to dine, play golf, go sailing, play tennis, or enjoy other private backstage encounters with Vineyard "dreammakers," including many A-list celebrities. Proceeds benefit M. V. Community Services, an island-wide social service agency.

For four days ending the third weekend of the month, the Martha's Vineyard Agricultural Society sponsors its annual **Livestock Show and Fair** (508/693-4343, http://mvas.vineyard. net, $8) at the West Tisbury Fairgrounds (also called the Ag Hall), with old county fair–style fun, replete with games, contests, good food, and music.

SEPTEMBER

The first Saturday after Labor Day, Edgartown's non-profit FARM Institute holds their annual fundraiser, **Corn-A-Palooza** (Aero Ave., 508/627-7007, www.farminstitute.org,

4–8 P.M., $15). Enjoy foot-stompin' live music, hayrides, games for kids, a giant corn maze, organic burgers and hot dogs, and of course, fresh corn on the cob.

On the second Saturday after Labor Day, Oak Bluffs takes its final bow of the season with **Tivoli Day** (508/696-7463), named for a once-grand but now long-gone Victorian dance hall. Circuit Avenue, closed to all traffic, is filled with a day-long street fair, including a parade, music, food, raffle tables, and such contests as the Waitperson Olympics, in which waiters and waitresses compete in carrying containers of water without spilling.

NOVEMBER

The day after Thanksgiving is traditionally reserved for America's national shopping spree. Locally this tradition translates into the annual **Vineyard Artisans' Holiday Festival** (Ag Hall in West Tisbury, 508/693-8989, www.vineyardartisans.com, 10 A.M.–4 P.M., $2), where a cornucopia of locally made crafts tempts browsers into buying something for everyone on their holiday gift-giving list. The entrance fee goes to the local high school's scholarship fund.

DECEMBER

Hardy year-round residents stoke the spirit of the holidays with Vineyard Haven's annual **Chowder Contest,** on the first Saturday of the month (508/693-1151) and **Christmas in Edgartown,** on the second weekend of the month (508/627-9510).

On New Year's Eve, Vineyard Haven celebrates **Last Night, First Day** (508/693-0085, www.mvy.com), with arts performances throughout the afternoon and evening, capped off by fireworks over Vineyard Haven Harbor at 10 P.M.

Information and Services

BANKS AND ATMS

You won't ever be far from an automated teller machine in the down-island towns, but up-island is a different story—beyond Beetlebung Corner, there's nothing. The deplorable practice of charging fees for cardholders who don't have local accounts infiltrated the Vineyard even before it took hold of the rest of the state, so count on being charged for remotely accessing your money.

Those using foreign currency must make their cash exchanges prior to arriving—none of the banks here handle such transactions.

MEDIA AND COMMUNICATIONS

For the most up-to-date arts and entertainment suggestions, check out Thursday's *Martha's Vineyard Times,* which includes nightclub live music listings in its calendar of events. Last-minute yard sales and estate auctions, on the other hand, are more likely to be found in the classifieds of Friday's more patrician *Vineyard Gazette,* regarded as one of the finest small-town newspapers in the nation—and possibly the most quaint. Its oversized page, aphoristic masthead, and columns devoted to bird sightings all betoken a bygone era in journalism.

On the radio dial, **WMVY-FM, 92.7,** is the local gentle pop and rock station and the best up-to-the-minute source for local beach and ferry reports. *All Things Considered* junkies who can't leave NPR behind, even while on vacation, can tune in the Vineyard's own community public radio station, **WCAI-FM, 90.1,** an affiliate of WGBH in Boston. Fans of freeform community radio should tune into the feisty local low-power non-commercial station, **WVVY-FM, 93.7,** "radio for the people," dedicated to the rich local music scene plus a dose of Amy Goodman's "Democracy Now" newscasts mixed in every weekday. Although this station's 93-watt transmitter limits audibility to the down-island towns, you can also catch its global beat, blues, psyche-delarrythmia, and other shows streaming live from www.wvvy.org.

The Vineyard's own **Plum TV** (Channel 76), part of a national network of resort-based cable access stations, is an engaging source for catching up with current island events, interviews with islanders, and other local-interest stories.

If you like to peruse racks of promotional flyers or want more accommodations to choose from, drop in on the **Martha's Vineyard Chamber of Commerce,** on Beach Road in Vineyard Haven, opposite the fire station. Place an order from their website (www.mvy.com) or call ahead (508/693-0085) for a free copy of their visitors' guide. In high season, staffed information booths in all three down-island towns (marked on the relevant close-up maps) are able to give directions, provide dining and lodging information, and answer most general tourist questions. Edgartown's booth also sells postcards and stamps, accepts mail, and vends snacks.

PUBLIC RESTROOMS

The only year-round restrooms open to the public are at the Steamship terminal in Vineyard Haven and the Church Street Visitors Center in Edgartown. In summer, a number of other facilities open up all over the island: in the parking lot next to Vineyard Haven's Stop & Shop market, at the Steamship dock and on Kennebec Avenue in Oak Bluffs, at South Beach in Edgartown, in West Tisbury's Grange Hall on State Road, and at the bottom of the loop drive atop Gay Head Cliffs. Showers are also available (for a fee), at the bathhouse beside Oak Bluffs Harbor and the Manor House Health Club in downtown Vineyard Haven, next to the Chamber of Commerce.

MEDICAL EMERGENCIES

For speedy clinical care of illnesses and minor injuries **Vineyard Medical Services** (611A

State Rd., 508/693-4400), opposite Cronig's Market, accepts walk-in patients weekdays 9 A.M.–noon. For medical emergencies the island's full-service 24-hour medical center, **Martha's Vineyard Hospital** (One Hospital Rd., 508/693-0410, www.mvhospital.com), is located off Beach Road at the foot of East Chop about 1.5 miles equidistant from both downtown Vineyard Haven and downtown Oak Bluffs.

Getting There and Around

In summer, all three down-island towns are connected to the mainland by ferries and to each other by shuttle buses and paved bike paths. Here the great concentration of food and lodging, mostly within walking distance of each other and transportation, makes it entirely practical (even eminently sensible) to arrive without a car.

PUBLIC TRANSIT

Year-round island-wide public transportation is provided by the **Martha's Vineyard Regional Transit Authority** (VTA, 508/627-9663, www.vineyardtransit.com). It's entirely possible to visit every village on the island, connect to the Steamship docks in Vineyard Haven, get to town—any town—from the airport, and ride to the beach, all via one of the VTA's dozen different routes. Most of the buses run on a fixed hourly schedule, although off-season some routes have less frequent service (and the trolley to South Beach is only seasonal). In summer—from the third Saturday in June to the end of the Labor Day holiday weekend in early September, to be exact—systemwide frequency of service increases significantly. For instance, buses start rolling between the three down-island towns at 6 A.M., with half-hourly service from around 7 A.M. until after midnight, and service every 15 minutes from 10:30 A.M. until 6:45 P.M. All fares are $1 per town, including the town of origin—i.e., $2 between towns, and $3–4 for full cross-island rides. One-, three-, and seven-day passes for unlimited travel are available from the drivers or at the Edgartown Visitors Center on Church Street for $6, $15, or $25, and monthly, yearly, and school-age student passes are available, too, although only from the Edgartown Visitors Center. Cyclists who underestimate the strength of the island's headwinds will be gratified to know that all VTA buses have bike racks mounted on the front.

Two of the VTA routes provide nearly continuous service mid-May through mid-September to their respective downtowns from free peripheral parking lots on State Road in Vineyard Haven, by the Triangle in Edgartown, and at the Edgartown elementary school on West Tisbury Road.

BIKE RENTALS

Vineyard Haven, Oak Bluffs, Edgartown, and parts of West Tisbury are linked by more than 15 miles of paved bike paths, so cycling around the island is a snap even for riders normally intimidated by traffic. The only major portion of the island lacking segregated bikeways is the southwest corner, but the beautiful tree-canopied roads there make for lovely riding nonetheless. And what better way to work off those calories from last night's dinner?

Over a dozen shops rent bikes—three on Circuit Avenue Extension next to Oak Bluffs' ferry docks, three within a block of Vineyard Haven's Steamship terminal, two within a stone's throw of Edgartown's central Main Street–Water Street intersection, and a couple more at the Triangle on Upper Main Street in Edgartown. Guests of B&Bs and inns away from the town centers can take advantage of the free bike delivery and pickup offered by such outfits as **Martha's Bike Rentals** (Lagoon Pond Rd., in Vineyard Haven, opposite the post office, 508/693-6593, Apr.–mid-Nov.); **Vineyard Bike & Moped** (next to the

© KATHRYN OSGOOD

You can rent bikes for the day or week from Edgartown Bicycles.

Strand movie house in OB, 508/693-6886); or **Wheel Happy** (S. Water St. in Edgartown, opposite the Harborside Inn, 508/627-5928, Apr.–mid-Nov.). Most rental fleets are trendy mountain bikes and hybrids, but retro three-speeds, tandems, lighter road bikes (perfectly adequate if you intend to stick to pavement), and trailers for towing kids are also widely available. (Wheel Happy caters to corporate outings with fully guided cycling tours from Edgartown to Oak Bluffs, too.)

If you've brought your own wheels and need repairs, several rental shops double as fix-it stops: Vineyard Haven's year-round **Cycle Works** (105 State Rd. next to Cronig's Market, 508/693-6966); **Anderson's Bike Rental** (Circuit Ave. Ext. in OB, 508/693-9346); **Edgartown Bicycles** (212 Upper Main St., 508/627-9008); or **R. W. Cutler Edgartown Bike Rentals** (1 Main St., 508/627-4052 or 800/627-2763, Apr. 1–Nov. 1).

TAXIS

For island-wide convenience, choose from among the many available taxi companies.

Since each town has its own set of regulations for taxi companies based within their borders, fares vary somewhat from one company to the next, particularly when it comes to the extras—fees for extra passengers, luggage, pets, late-night drop-offs, and driving on dirt roads. So if the same cab ride you took yesterday ends up suddenly costing more today, don't jump to the conclusion that you're being gypped.

Rates for up to two people from the Steamship docks in either Vineyard Haven or OB can run as high as $50–60 to Aquinnah, $18–20 to the hostel in West Tisbury, and $10–17 between down-island towns. Additional passengers are usually $3 each, and in the timeframe of 1–7 A.M. expect the fare to be doubled.

Taxi Services
Vineyard Haven
All Island Taxi, 800/693-TAXI or 508/693-2929, www.allislandtaximv.com
Harbor Taxi, 508/693-9611
Patti's Taxi Service, 508/693-1663
Stagecoach Taxi, 508/627-4566 or 800/299-5411, www.mvstagecoachtaxi.com
Tisbury Taxi, 508/693-7660

Oak Bluffs
Atlantic Cab, 508/693-7110, www.atlantic cabmv.com
A BIG Cab Company, a.k.a. Marlene's Taxi, 866/693-8294 or 508/693-0037, www.mar lenestaxi.com
Martha's Vineyard Taxi, 866/688-2947 or 508/ 693-8660, www.marthasvineyardtaxi .com
Your Taxi, 508/693-0003 or 800/396-0003

Edgartown
Accurate Cab, 508/627-9798
Adam Cab, 508/693-3332 or 800/281-4462, www.adamcab.com
Bluefish Taxi, 508/627-7373
Jon's Taxi, 508/627-4677

West Tisbury
Mario's Taxi, 877/627-6972 or 508/693-8399

CAR AND MOPED RENTALS

If you're staying down-island in summer, you really want to avoid driving. You may not think so, as you imagine all the luggage you have to carry and all the shopping you want to do—but if it's a vacation you're after, seriously consider your determination to drive; you're letting yourself in for a slow, stop-and-go crawl through intersections packed with 20,000 other cars, not one of which will yield to your left turn. If you're coming in the off-season or intend to spend most of your time up-island and have never ridden a bicycle, driving is a slightly better idea. Just mind all those cyclists, and the deer at night—particularly on curvy, shoulderless up-island roads.

If you decide to rent a car, be prepared for rates that fluctuate wildly. Ever-popular Jeeps and convertibles that rent for over $170 a day on any midsummer holiday, for instance, may drop by half off-season unless the weather is spectacular and demand is strong. Don't expect anyone but the major chains to quote prices over the phone—the independent operators prefer not to commit to anything that may scare off potential business. Remove any diamond jewelry you may be wearing and don't introduce yourself as a doctor, and you'll find these indie outfits are prepared to haggle—so long as you're mellow and not too pushy, and they can see that the competition across the street still has a car or two in the lot. By the way, before you pay a massive premium for renting one of those macho four-wheelers, remember that driving on Vineyard beaches is restricted to privately owned vehicles with valid permits. Oversand vehicle permits for Chappaquiddick are $160 from the Trustees (508/627-7689); for Norton Point—the only other part of the Vineyard's coast open to off-road vehicles—the requisite permits are $80 from the Treasurer's Office (9 Airport Rd., 508/696-3845), or at South Beach in the summer.

Car Rental Agencies
Vineyard Haven
A-A Island Auto Rentals, Five Corners, 508/696-5300 or 800/696-0233
Adventure Rentals/Thrifty Rent-A-Car, 19 Beach Rd., 508/693-1959

Beach Road Rentals, 95 Beach Rd., 508/693-3793
Budget, 36 Water St., 508/693-1911 or 800/527-0700

Oak Bluffs
A-A Island Auto Rentals, 31 Circuit Ave. Ext., 508/696-5211
Budget, 12 Circuit Ave. Ext., 508/693-1911 or 800/527-0700
Sun-N-Fun Jeep Rentals, Lake Ave., 508/693-5457

Edgartown
AAA Island Auto Rentals, 196 Main St., 508/627-6800 or 800/627-6333
Auto Rentals of Edgartown, 141 Main St., 508/627-7241

Airport
A-A Island Auto Rentals, 508/627-6800
Budget, 508/693-1911 or 800/527-0700
Hertz Rent-A-Car, 508/693-2402 or 800/654-3131
Thrifty Rent-A-Car, 508/696-0909 or 800/367-2277

HITCHHIKING

Despite the rips summer congestion is rending in the fabric of the Vineyard's small-town life, the island has a well-deserved and enviable reputation as a great hitchhiking spot, a small vestige of the 1970s preserved here thanks to the large proportion of pickups and sport utility vehicles and the island's small size (no need to worry about making conversation for just a couple of miles). If you've never tried thumbing a ride, this is a good place to start; if you mourn the passing of safe hitching in the rest of the U.S., you'll find this a welcome time warp. Which isn't to say you shouldn't trust your instincts; if you aren't comfortable with someone who's stopped to offer a lift, decline the ride. Since the preservation of this casual anachronism depends on visitors as well as residents, don't think that just because you don't know your way around, you aren't eligible to contribute—if you have extra capacity in your car, share it.

NANTUCKET

Known as the "Grey Lady" for the color of its cedar-shingled houses, stripped to a fine silvery gray by exposure to the sea air, Nantucket is barely more than a sandy mote in Neptune's eye. Two hours by regular ferry from the Cape, the island that was once one of the world's leading whaling ports is now a preserve of affluence, the lovely and narrow cobblestone streets of Nantucket Town lined with expensive boutiques and posh restaurants. Decades of capitalizing on its blue-chip reputation for quaintness have produced a movie-set perfection bordering on preciousness. (Heck, the whole town is a registered historic district, and the *entire island* is a National Historic Landmark.) Whereas Martha's Vineyard isn't self-conscious about mismatched chairs on the porch, peeling paint, or broken screen windows stacked up on the back step awaiting storage or rainy-day repair, the Grey Lady never appears in public without every window shutter and porch railing perfectly in place. Homeowners even supply their own cute captions—names like Serendipity, Whispering Pines, Ain Wee Hoose, and Latest Rumour decorate cottages all over the island. Yet for those who can take the time to explore it, this Ice Age remnant's 54 square miles offer a singular atmosphere of contemplative fogs, dusky green heathlands, garden gates laced with bright flowers, and picturesque lighthouses.

Sometimes, the island's port and business center is called Nantucket Town (just "town" suffices for verbal directions), to distinguish it from such named localities as

© JEFF PERK

HIGHLIGHTS

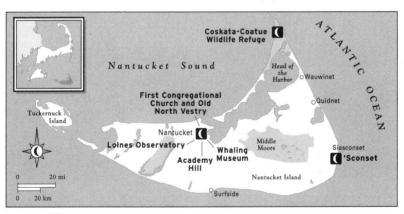

Whaling Museum: Nantucket's must-see museum, where the story of the island's meteoric rise to domination of the whaling industry is artfully told through artifacts and engaging gallery talks by interpretive staff (page 156).

Loines Observatory: See the stars as you likely have never seen them before in weekly seasonal programs describing the features of the island's night sky (page 159).

First Congregational Church and Old North Vestry: Climb to the top of a church steeple for incomparable panoramic views from the tallest observation point in town (page 161).

Academy Hill: A neighborhood just beside downtown where Nantucket's historic architectural legacy is most visibly intact (page 161).

'Sconset: Lovely little fishing-village-turned-arts-colony, now the epitome of summer leisure by the beach, where the greatest pleasure is to wander or cycle about doing basically not much (page 164).

Coskata-Coatue Wildlife Refuge: Hikes along the island's longest barrier beach are rewarded with excellent bird- and seal watching, or take an exceptional natural history tour out to the photogenic lighthouse at Great Point (page 171).

LOOK FOR (TO FIND RECOMMENDED SIGHTS, ACTIVITIES, DINING, AND LODGING.

Wauwinet, Madaket, Tom Nevers, and the tiny, mostly residential village of Siasconset on the eastern shore ("'Sconset" to locals). But town and island are actually one and the same. "Nantucket" also denotes one of the 14 counties of the Commonwealth of Massachusetts, comprising the eponymous main island and three smaller, privately owned ones to the west—tiny Esther, once attached to the main island by sandy umbilicus; Tuckernuck; and Muskeget.

HISTORY
The Good Old Days

At least half a dozen 16th-century European navigators—from Giovanni Verrazzano sailing on behalf of the French in 1524 up to English captain John Hawkins in 1565—are known to have passed in the vicinity of Nantucket, and at least a couple of them are believed to have espied its low cliffs. The earliest unequivocal evidence of an overseas visitor laying eyes on the island indicates that in 1605, George

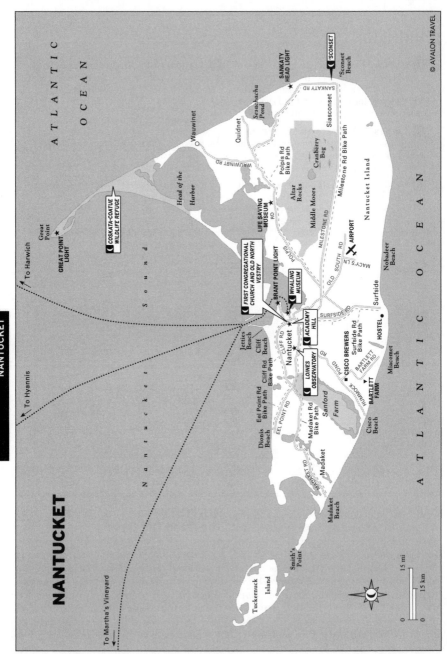

NANTUCKET

To Martha's Vineyard

To Hyannis

To Harwich

ATLANTIC OCEAN

Nantucket Sound

Tuckernuck Island

Smith's Point

Great Point

GREAT POINT LIGHT

COSKATA-COATUE WILDLIFE REFUGE

Head of the Harbor

Wauwinet

WAUWINET RD

Quidnet

Sesachacha Pond

SANKATY HEAD LIGHT

'Sconset

'SCONSET

Sconset Beach

Siasconset

SANKATY RD

Polpis Rd Bike Path

Cranberry Bog

Altar Rocks

Middle Moors

POLPIS RD

Nantucket Island

Milestone Rd Bike Path

MILESTONE RD

OLD SOUTH RD

AIRPORT

MACY'S LN

Nobadeer Beach

LIFE SAVING MUSEUM

BRANT POINT LIGHT

FIRST CONGREGATIONAL CHURCH AND OLD NORTH VESTRY

WHALING MUSEUM

ACADEMY HILL

Nantucket

Jetties Beach

Cliff Beach

CLIFF RD

SURFSIDE RD

Surfside

Miacomet Beach

HOSTEL

CISCO BREWERS

Surfside Rd Bike Path

LOINES OBSERVATORY

Sanford Farm

Eel Point Rd Bike Path

Dionis Beach

EEL POINT RD

Madaket Rd Bike Path

Madaket

MADAKET RD

Madaket Beach

POND RD

HUMMOCK RD

Cisco Beach

BARTLETT FARM RD

BARTLETT FARM

Cisco Beach Bike Path

ATLANTIC OCEAN

© AVALON TRAVEL

0   15 mi
0   15 km

Weymouth, following up on the success of Gosnold's voyage to the Vineyard, sighted the pale marine scarp at Sankaty Head. Like many a vessel—even in the age of GPS and depth-sounders—Weymouth's *Archangel* was so bedeviled by Nantucket's myriad confusing rips and shoals that he sailed clear up to Maine before making another attempt to put ashore.

Navigational hazards may have spared the island's large Native American population early contact with Europeans and their infectious diseases, but by the middle of the 17th century, land deals with Vineyard founder Thomas Mayhew brought the first permanent colonial settlement into their midst. Within a year of relocating from the Merrimack River region, Thomas Macy and Tristram Coffin had acquired most of the west end of the island for a small group of proprietors, and secured grazing rights to all Indian lands to the east.

These "first purchasers" and their partners initially believed sheep-raising would be their economic livelihood, but as the once well-wooded island was gradually denuded for crops and pasture, soil-blowing wind and leaf-drying salt air took their toll. Within a generation of settlement, the colonists (like their Vineyard compatriots) were forced by poor stewardship of the land to turn their attentions to the riches of the sea.

Gone Fishing

Nantucket wasn't the only port in Massachusetts—or New England—to outfit itself for the whaling industry. Neither did it have the biggest fleet. And it put away its harpoons and quenched its try-pot fires even as mainland neighbors were still unfurling their sails for further voyages. But no other port has come close to Nantucket in capturing the popular modern imagination with its whaling adventures—perhaps because no other port was so wholly dependent upon "blubber-boilers" for its livelihood. "The Nantucketer, he alone resides and rests on the sea," wrote Melville. "He alone, in Bible language, goes down to it in ships; to and fro ploughing it as his own special plantation . . . . With the landless gull,

that at sunset folds her wings and is rocked to sleep between billows; so at nightfall, the Nantucketer, out of sight of land, furls his sails, and lays him to his rest, while under his very pillow rush herds of walruses and whales."

The island's Nauset Indians had long been known to harpoon right whales that came close to shore—a technique English settlers also practiced through the 1600s—until they discovered the existence of the sperm whale with its head full of oil so fine that to this day no synthetic has equalled it. By 1730, Nantucketers were using a couple of dozen small ships to chase these creatures and bring them ashore for rendering. On the eve of the American Revolution, a generation later, whaling was the island's economic mainstay, employing a third of its population aboard some 150 vessels roaming the Atlantic from Greenland to Brazil.

Despite the Quaker-dominated island community's solemn declaration of neutrality during the Revolution (or perhaps because of it), both warring factions accused islanders of consorting with the enemy (which was true—with no local supplies of food or fuel, Nantucketers dealt with whomever they could to get whatever they needed). By war's end, all but one or two of the island's fleet had been burned or captured. Faced with prison or unable to return home, scores of island mariners also sailed under British and French flags; it was under the Union Jack, in fact, that Nantucketers first went whaling in the Pacific.

Government incentives to revitalize the whaling industry after the war produced competition from ports up and down the new United States; resourceful islanders responded by pushing farther than ever for their quarry, outfitting huge vessels of several hundred tons' capacity for three- to four-year voyages to "the remotest secret drawers and lockers of the world," in Melville's words. The ink was barely dry on the newly ratified Constitution before Nantucket whalers were chasing whale-spouts off the coast of Chile. One Nantucket captain discovered the whaling grounds between Easter Island and the Equator in 1818; two years later,

NANTUCKET

NANTUCKET TAXONOMY

Thanks to its size, physical isolation, and the high-minded ideals of the Victorian era, Nantucket's entire plant community – from sandplains to cedar bogs – is possibly one of the nation's best-catalogued landscapes.

Darwin's *On the Origin of Species* (1859) ushered in an age of scientific rationalism that was felt from London's Royal Academy to America's drawing rooms. As study of the natural sciences was becoming a middle-class fascination (tabloid dailies covered scientific expeditions, and Jules Verne took readers 20,000 leagues under the sea), Nantucket was becoming a popular Victorian resort, and the island's visitors heeded the encouraging call of island publicists, who promoted study of the local "vegetable and animal life." Anyone who suffered through high-school biology may find it hard to believe, but pigeonholing the natural world with Linnaean binomials was once the stuff of proper leisure.

The personification of Victorian taxonomy was probably Eugene P. Bicknell, a 19th-century New Jersey banker who amassed the island's largest inventory of plants, a ledger-perfect collection now held by the Maria Mitchell Association. Bicknell's dedication and precision are sorely missed today – a 1996 inventory of the island fell a full 26 percent short of the 1,200-plus species collected by Bicknell and others. While ecologists don't doubt that some species have disappeared over the years, it is hoped that most of the missing simply went undetected and await the arrival of a new generation of Bicknells to ferret them out. Linnaeus, anyone?

another inaugurated the hunt off the coast of Japan; and in 1835, a Nantucket ship became the first non-Inuit craft to capture right whales off the coast of Alaska. It was even a Nantucket whaler who discovered the fate of the mutinous H.M.S. *Bounty* crew by putting in at Pitcairn Island for fresh water. By the middle of the 19th century, the Pacific seemed to be crawling with Nantucketers, most of whom saw every island from the Aleutians to Tasmania before ever setting foot in Boston.

They left their names on such remote atolls as Starbuck, Howland, and Baker. They left their offspring and venereal diseases among Polynesian island women; and they left their graves, too, in places like New Zealand, where Americans who chance to examine the old cemeteries are sometimes surprised to see New England place names on the aged stones. All in the name of taking the greatest mammals of the deep and boiling them down for English, French, and American lamp oil, candle-wax, and cosmetics.

They took so many in such short order that within a few decades, the populations of a half dozen major species had been reduced to in-

significance. Profit margins on a successful voyage could still exceed 200–300 percent, thanks to the pittance paid to the crews and the lack of a reliable supply of cheaper substitutes for $1.77-a-gallon sperm oil, but in 1859, the party came to an abrupt end. A hole drilled in Titusville, Pennsylvania, hit petroleum and sank Nantucket's whaling industry. As the world lit its lamps with kerosene, Nantucket's own candle flame guttered and died.

Making Do with Quaint

After the demise of its major occupation, some of Nantucket's wealthiest citizens simply moved away. Others, seeking a return ticket to prosperity, looked to the examples of their off-island neighbors. After surveying New Bedford's textile mills, Provincetown's cod fishery, and the Vineyard's summer-cottage trade, they sank their money into resort developments. Most of these failed for a variety of reasons, not the least of which was a misunderstanding about what made the island attractive to visitors.

Nantucket's tourists, it became clear, wanted neither Falmouth's fancy seaside hotels nor

Oak Bluffs' cheek-by-jowl gingerbread cottages. Tradesmen stopped off at the Vineyard for boardwalk diversions; professionals came to Nantucket to listen to old salts tell of their whaling adventures and to soak up the primitive ambience of derelict wharves and hollowed-out villages. Amid a general revival of national interest in all things colonial, Nantucket's visitors wanted to bathe in the island's past.

If an antique-filled island frozen in the 1840s was what visitors would pay good money to see, then the island's citizens were happy to build it. And they still are; local ordinances stipulate that new houses continue to resemble centuries-old saltboxes or Capes, with cedar-shingle or clapboard siding and steep pitched roofs.

God's Country

Nantucket has taken great pains to ensure that its built environment conforms to the amalgam of myth and history it sells to visitors. Besides historic district guidelines regulating nearly every facade and fence post on the island, local bylaws and groundwater protections control growth and strictly limit new housing construction. Ten nonprofit groups and government agencies have conserved thousands of acres of open land, aided in part by the nation's first local land trust, funded by real estate transaction fees. These measures go a long way toward preventing suburban sprawl and preserving the island's image, long recognized as its most marketable commodity.

On the other hand, property values have been driven up by those who want in on this pristine economic equivalent of a gated community (over a third of the 200 wealthiest Americans, it is said, own homes here). The low forests out of town cannot fully conceal the oversized McMansions that have replaced open space or more modest homes.

Spendthrift summer tourists, wealthy second-home owners, and developers seeking to cater to both have pushed local shopkeepers out of town (over 75 percent of downtown storefronts are owned by a single real estate investment firm that also owns nearly all the island's resort hotels). This has forced many less affluent

RHYMES WITH "BUCKET"

Some folks claim that "There once was a man from Nantucket" is one of the most famous first lines in American verse. It comes from a limerick published in the Princeton University humor magazine, the *Princeton Tiger*, in November 1902:

> *There was a man from Nantucket*
> *Who kept all his cash in a bucket;*
> *But his daughter named Nan*
> *Ran away with a man*
> *And as for the bucket, Nantucket.*

More lasting fame came after several major metropolitan newspapers in Chicago and the East Coast competed to come up with additional chapters to the narrative of Nan, her man, and the purloined bucket. The two most famous sequels are the following:

> *But he followed the pair to Pawtucket –*
> *The man and the girl with the bucket*
> *And he said to the man*
> *He was welcome to Nan,*
> *But as for the bucket, Pawtucket.*

> *Then the pair followed Pa to Manhasset*
> *Where he still held the cash as an asset;*
> *But Nan and the man*
> *Stole the money and ran,*
> *And as for the bucket, Manhasset.*

Although even Shakespeare included limericks in a pair of his plays, the history of the form is steeped in the bawdy jestings of English pub patrons. The legacy of the limerick has thus been well endowed with a new body of ribald verse thanks to the obscenities that conveniently rhyme with "Nantucket."

residents to do their shopping "in America," as the mainland is traditionally known. Careful land-use planning and zoning may ultimately preserve the look, but the feel is being bruised by city-style summer traffic jams, off-island luxury retailers' colonization of local business, and off-season's vacant downtown.

PLANNING YOUR TIME

In all its jurisdictions, Nantucket is small enough and its major attractions concentrated enough so that you need not be deterred from a visit by the high tariff on either bringing a car over or staying the night—day-trippers on foot or bike can easily sample much of what the island has to offer.

Any time of year, anyone with the least bit of appreciation for American history or historic architecture will find a surfeit of both. Start with the **Whaling Museum** and then simply spend time strolling around diminutive lanes and alleyways of downtown. Throughout the high season the whole island is served by excellent public transit, so there's no excuse not to venture out to **'Sconset** to experience quaint residential Nantucket at its most picturesque. Or just go there to stroll the **Bluff Walk** and view the beautiful **Sankaty Head Light** presiding over the wild eastern shore, where Mother Nature annually exposes the impermanence of the earth beneath your feet.

Whatever your taste is in beaches, there is one here with your name on it, so visitors spending more than a day should sample the local waters. Mostly level terrain and an extensive network of paved bike paths make getting out to any of the major beaches a cinch on a bike; rental shops are all easily found within steps of the ferries. If more time is available it becomes possible to slip into the casual rhythm of island life. Make an impromptu picnic for a walk to **Brant Point Light** out of fresh-picked Bartlett's Farm berries sold right off their daily truck stand on Main Street, sample several different praise-worthy restaurants, catch a sunset at **Madaket Beach,** rent a kayak to poke around the inner harbor, learn about the constellations at **Loines Observatory,** and of course browse through the galleries on Old South Wharf. A week would be ideal, but a long weekend is a good start on sampling all that the island has to offer, too.

High season in Nantucket has a little bit of the feel of a big game of musical chairs, with far more people seemingly searching for places to eat, seats on tours, or rooms in which to stay than can possibly accommodate them all. With patience and flexibility you need not be disappointed in whatever you seek, but it helps to anticipate that everything from meals to transportation inevitably will take more time than you might have thought.

Sights

Ferry passengers disembarking from the Steamship Authority at Steamboat Wharf are greeted a block off the gangway by hints of Nantucket's two principal attractions—recreation and history. With the exception of a couple of the island's lighthouses, all the historic sights and museums are within walking distance of each other.

◖ WHALING MUSEUM

Beyond the bike shops beckoning from the foot of Broad Street is the Whaling

Museum (508/228-1736, www.nha.org, 11 A.M.–4 P.M. Thurs.–Mon. late Apr.–mid-Dec., 10 A.M.–5 P.M. daily June–mid-Oct., 11 A.M.–4 P.M. Fri.–Sun. Jan.–mid-Apr., $15), the flagship property of the Nantucket Historical Association, the highly professional steward of the island's past and tireless advocate of its thoughtful preservation. Here Nantucket's eminence in the whaling industry is recollected through art, tools, specimens, and dramatic narratives delivered with gusto by the museum's interpretive staff. Decorative

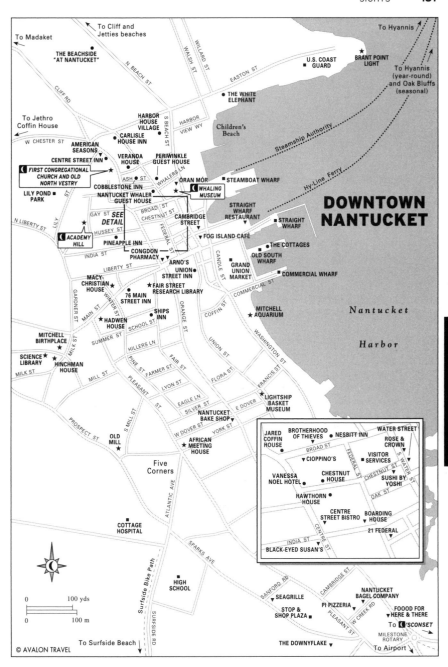

To Cliff and Jetties beaches
To Madaket
To Hyannis
THE BEACHSIDE "AT NANTUCKET"
U.S. COAST GUARD
BRANT POINT LIGHT
To Hyannis (year-round) and Oak Bluffs (seasonal)
WILLARD ST
EASTON ST
N BEACH ST
WALSH ST
CLIFF RD
THE WHITE ELEPHANT
HARBOR HOUSE VILLAGE
HARBOR VIEW WY
Children's Beach
S BEACH ST
To Jethro Coffin House
W CHESTER ST
CARLISLE HOUSE INN
AMERICAN SEASONS
CENTRE STREET INN
VERANDA HOUSE
PERIWINKLE GUEST HOUSE
Steamship Authority
FIRST CONGREGATIONAL CHURCH AND OLD NORTH VESTRY
ASH ST
WHALERS LN
ORAN MÓR
STEAMBOAT WHARF
Hy-Line Ferry
LILY POND PARK
COBBLESTONE INN
NANTUCKET WHALER GUEST HOUSE
WHALING MUSEUM
STRAIGHT WHARF RESTAURANT
STRAIGHT WHARF
DOWNTOWN NANTUCKET
N LIBERTY ST
GAY ST
BROAD ST
CHESTNUT ST
SEE DETAIL
CAMBRIDGE STREET
FOG ISLAND CAFÉ
THE COTTAGES
HUSSEY ST
ACADEMY HILL
PINEAPPLE INN
CONGDON PHARMACY
FEDERAL ST
OLD SOUTH WHARF
INDIA ST
LIBERTY ST
ARNO'S
UNION STREET INN
CANDLE ST
GRAND UNION MARKET
COMMERCIAL WHARF
MACY-CHRISTIAN HOUSE
FAIR STREET RESEARCH LIBRARY
ORANGE ST
COMMERCIAL ST
GARDNER ST
76 MAIN STREET INN
SHIPS INN
MAIN ST
WINTER ST
COFFIN ST
MITCHELL AQUARIUM
Nantucket
HADWEN HOUSE
SCHOOL ST
WASHINGTON ST
MITCHELL BIRTHPLACE
SUMMER ST
HILLERS LN
UNION ST
Harbor
SCIENCE LIBRARY
HINCHMAN HOUSE
MILK ST
PINE ST
FARMER ST
FLORA ST
FRANCIS ST
PLEASANT ST
FAIR ST
LYON ST
EAGLE LN
S MILL ST
MILL ST
SILVER ST
LIGHTSHIP BASKET MUSEUM
PROSPECT ST
NANTUCKET BAKE SHOP
E DOVER ST
W DOVER ST
YORK ST
OLD MILL
AFRICAN MEETING HOUSE
Five Corners
ATLANTIC AVE
COTTAGE HOSPITAL
SPARKS AVE

NANTUCKET

(detail inset)
WATER STREET
JARED COFFIN HOUSE
BROTHERHOOD OF THIEVES
NESBITT INN
ROSE & CROWN
BROAD ST
CIOPPINO'S
FEDERAL ST
VISITOR SERVICES
CHESTNUT ST
S WATER ST
VANESSA NOEL HOTEL
CHESTNUT HOUSE
SUSHI BY YOSHI
HAWTHORN HOUSE
OAK ST
CENTRE STREET BISTRO
BOARDING HOUSE
CENTRE ST
21 FEDERAL
INDIA ST
BLACK-EYED SUSAN'S

Surfside Bike Path
SURFSIDE RD
HIGH SCHOOL
SANFORD RD
CAMBRIDGE ST
SEAGRILLE
PI PIZZERIA
NANTUCKET BAGEL COMPANY
STOP & SHOP PLAZA
W CREEK RD
PLEASANT ST
FOOD FOR HERE & THERE
To 'SCONSET
MILESTONE ROTARY
0   100 yds
0   100 m
THE DOWNYFLAKE
To Airport
To Surfside Beach
© AVALON TRAVEL

© PETER VANDERWARKER

Nantucket's Whaling Museum

arts culled from the Nantucket Historical Association's great stash of treasures provide a glimpse into the lives of islanders past, and there are always seasonally changing exhibits, including the occasional maritime-themed show on loan from sister historical institutions, such as the Smithsonian.

Appropriately, the museum partly occupies a former candle factory, whose tapers were made from that most prized of whale oils, spermaceti. There are wonderful views over the town and harbor from the rooftop deck, too, usually accompanied by evocative sea shanties gently piped through speakers in the walls. If the trypots and whale tales whet your appetite for related books, toys, or even scrimshaw, be sure to visit the well-stocked museum shop.

MARIA MITCHELL ASSOCIATION

In 1831, the King of Denmark offered a prize to the first discoverer of a comet by telescope. Sixteen years later, Maria Mitchell (ma-RYE-a), daughter of a multitalented local educator, won the gold medal with the aid of a telescope she and her father shared on the roof of the former Pacific National Bank. At a time when, as she mused to her diary, "the needle is the chain of woman, and has fettered her more than the laws of the country," Mitchell quickly became an international celebrity.

She learned astronomy from her father, whom she aided in his sideline business of calibrating navigational chronometers (note the inscribed stone markers used for this work at the curb beside the bank at 61 Main Street, and a block south on Fair Street). After being lionized for her discovery—she became the first woman elected to the American Academy of Arts and Sciences—Mitchell undertook a career in mathematics and astronomy, eventually spending 20 years on the faculty at Vassar College before ultimately retiring to Nantucket, where she lies buried in Prospect Hill Cemetery.

Today, the Maria Mitchell Association (MMA) (www.mmo.org) promotes the study of astronomy and the natural sciences through lectures, classes, field trips, and a handful of public attractions. If you intend to visit more

COURTESY OF THE CAPE COD CHAMBER OF COMMERCE

the Maria Mitchell Association

to illustrate island flora and fauna. Among the prizes of the museum herbarium is the great amateur naturalist Eugene Bicknell's exhaustive, unrivaled collection of Nantucket plants, meticulously gathered around the turn of the 20th century.

The building also houses the association's gift shop, an excellent place to pick up field guides to everything that blossoms or breeds on the island. Or, for expert guidance in the flesh, join one of the many association-sponsored nature walks held weekly throughout the June–September season. Choose from early-morning bird-watching trips, beachcombing strolls, wildflower walks, and more.

The MMA campus also includes a **Science Library** (2 Vestal St., 508/228-9219, 10 A.M.–4 P.M. Mon. year-round) open by appointment only to both professional researchers and anyone else naturally curious about the universe.

Mitchell House

Across Vestal Street from the Natural Science Museum is Maria Mitchell's birthplace (508/228-2896, 10 A.M.–4 P.M. Fri.–Sat. mid-June–mid-Oct., $5). It's been restored with family possessions and other artifacts to illustrate the domestic life of a 19th-century Quaker family such as the Mitchells.

Vestal Street Observatory

This historic 1908 facility adjacent to the Mitchell home offers a guided tour nearly every morning (508/228-9273, 11 A.M. Mon.–Sat. mid-June–early Sept., 11 A.M. Fri. the rest of the year, $5). The tour may include a talk about the association's contributions to astronomy and sunspot observations if the clouds are cooperative. Among the permanent exhibits are photos from an extensive collection created over the course of nearly a century by MMA astronomers, plus a scale model of the solar system in the observatory's garden.

◖ Loines Observatory

Because of Nantucket's distance from the mainland, the clarity of the cool atmosphere

than one of the association's properties, invest in a combined admission pass for just $10.

MMA Aquarium

Located in the former Nantucket Railroad ticket office and a pair of adjacent buildings on Washington Street near the Town Pier, the MMA Aquarium (508/228-5387, 10 A.M.–4 P.M. Mon.–Sat. mid-June–Labor Day, $6) features a score of saltwater tanks displaying such denizens of the local marine ecosystem as squid, whelks, and shellfish. There are also a couple of touch tanks where you can get your hands wet making the acquaintance of live sea creatures up close. This is a deservedly popular place for kids.

Natural Science Museum

Live reptiles such as turtles and snakes are among the leading attractions within this museum at the 19th-century Hinchman House on the corner of Vestal and Milk Streets (508/228-0898, 10 A.M.–4 P.M. Mon.–Sat. mid-June–mid-Oct., $5). Collections of shells, preserved wildflowers, and small stuffed critters are used

NANTUCKET

over the local ocean, and efforts by town planners to eliminate unnecessary streetlights, the star-gazing conditions here rival the best desert and mountaintop observatories anywhere else in North America. So for a peek into the heavens, weather permitting, you should drop in on one of the popular **Open Nights at the Loines Observatory,** the MMA's research-oriented facility out at 59 Milk Street Extension, a short distance beyond where the town's sidewalks end (508/228-9273, 9 P.M. Mon., Wed., Fri. June–early Sept., 8 P.M. Fri. only mid-Sept.–May, $10).

Dr. Vladimir Strelnitski, the observatory's gregarious director, typically leads these events, discoursing on fundamentals of astronomy as he identifies constellations, visible planets, features of the moon, or whatever other celestial bodies are appropriate to the evening's conditions. You'll get to peer through the eyepiece of one or both of the observatory's optical telescopes, the largest of which (a 24-inch reflector) is used in the organization's ongoing research into variable stars.

HISTORICAL HOUSES

In addition to the Whaling Museum, the **Nantucket Historical Association** maintains a number of carefully restored old buildings, from one of the island's oldest surviving houses to the early 20th-century summer residence of a pair of Nantucket's most picaresque bohemians. Most are free, but the four that offer interpretive tours, each of which is outlined here, require purchase of either the NHA's all-inclusive combination ticket ($18, includes Whaling Museum admission) or the Historic Site Pass ($6, historic houses only).

Guided tours of the four are offered daily in season. All are open briefly for Memorial Day weekend, then reopen a week later and stay open 10 A.M.–5 P.M. Monday–Saturday and noon–5 P.M. Sunday through Columbus Day. Hours then change to 11 A.M.–4 P.M. Thursday–Monday until early November. For inquiries about any of the properties, call the NHA's main office (508/228-1894) or visit its website, www.nha.org.

The other structures of the NHA's collection, where visitors guide their own tours, comprise the following: the **1805 Old Gaol,** off Vestal Street past the Maria Mitchell complex; the **Macy-Christian House,** an 18th-century merchant's home at 12 Liberty Street; the island's **first public school,** on Winter Street; the **Fire Hose-Cart House,** an 1886 neighborhood fire station with antique equipment related to the Great Fire of 1846, on Gardner Street; and the restful **Greater Light garden,** a former pig and cow barn turned summer home on Howard Street.

The Oldest House

Pick up a museum guide from any of the staffed NHA properties and follow its suggested half-day walking tour for a thorough stroll through the ages, starting with the 1686 **Jethro Coffin House** on Sunset Hill, 10 minutes' walk from the center of town. Canonized more than a century ago as the island's "Oldest House," this simple farmhouse is more accurately described as Nantucket's oldest survivor on its original site, since a few older structures have all been moved and modified.

The house was built as a wedding gift for a marriage that helped end a major family feud on the island. Its design (with its central chimney, hall, and parlor) marks an ambitious improvement over that of the First Period dwellings (with one or two rooms and chimneys on the ends of the buildings) more typical of the region. Extensive refurbishment was required in the 1870s thanks to early tourists' practice of carving their names in the walls and stealing souvenir shingles.

A kitchen garden with raised beds of herbs and medicinal plants typical to the Colonial period is maintained on the property, along with a small orchard planted with an antique variety of apple tree.

Hadwen House

At the other end of the spectrum from the Coffin House is one of the NHA's youngest properties, the Hadwen House (96 Main St.). Commissioned by William Hadwen, a silversmith turned whale-oil dealer, this handsome 1845 mansion embodies 19th-century ostentation as much as the Coffin House, in its rudimentary way, set the standard for high living 160 years earlier. The Ionic-columned Hadwen and its Corinthian-columned neighbor are known as "the Two Greeks," in counterpoint to "the Three Bricks," an exceptional trio of transitional Federal-style homes built across the street by Hadwen's father-in-law.

The little dated wooden markers that identify the pedigree of many buildings on either side of the Hadwen House are the work of the Nantucket Preservation Trust (508/228-1387, 2 Union St., www.nantucketpreservation.org), one of the several island nonprofits dedicated to the protection of local historical structures, including their interiors. The NPT hosts regular **guided architectural walking tours** of these historic blocks of upper Main Street, between the Pacific National Bank and the Civil War monument, starting from in front of their office on the Union Street side of the Ralph Lauren store (9:30 A.M. every Wed. and Thurs. June–Sept., $10).

Quaker Meeting House

In the early Bay State colony under the theocratic rule of the Puritans, membership in the Society of Friends—also known as Quakers—was punishable by banishment or even death. By the time the English crown revoked the Puritan colonial charter in 1692 and established the province of Massachusetts, Puritan authority had waned enough so that Quaker preachers could travel around the region with relative freedom.

The Quaker community on Nantucket originated from the visit of such an itinerant preacher in 1701. Within a century Quakerism had become the island's dominant religion, with adherents among all the most prosperous families and business leaders. As the interpretive guide at this site will explain, eventually sectarian divisions split the community; this 1838 structure was thus originally erected by one of the splinter groups as a school.

While here, be sure to take note of the current exhibit in the one-room Whitney Gallery inside the entrance of the **Fair Street Research Library** (508/228-5205), drawn from the NHA's extensive photography and print archives adjoining the back of the Meeting House. The gallery, which is free, shares the library's hours (10 A.M.–4 P.M. Mon.–Fri. year-round, closed Wed. in winter). Library access for all you genealogists, writers, and ephemera enthusiasts is subject to a $5 usage fee.

The Old Mill

The photogenic 1746 windmill on South Mill Street is the last survivor of a collection of such grist mills that used to occupy the high ground on the outskirts of town, and the oldest windmill still in operation in the United States. Its practical mechanical design allows the cap of the mill to be rotated with a great wooden spar so that the blades can face the wind from any direction. The wind-driven millstones are still put to work producing cornmeal for sale in season whenever the weather allows.

◖ FIRST CONGREGATIONAL CHURCH AND OLD NORTH VESTRY

Outside of a trip to Altar Rock in the Middle Moors, the best panorama of the island is found atop the steeple of the 19th-century First Congregational Church and Old North Vestry (62 Centre St., 508/228-0950, www.nantucket fcc.org, 10 A.M.–4 P.M. daily mid-June–mid-Oct., $2.50 donation requested). The hike up all the stairs is amply rewarded by the view over rooftop widow's walks, a vantage from which weathered shingles, rose-covered trellises, and "catslide" roofs (shorter in back than in front) can be appreciated as textures of the landscape, rather than as architectural details.

◖ ACADEMY HILL

The visual elements that define Nantucket are certainly abundant in the downtown area, from the brick sidewalks and undulating cobblestones to the dignified wood-columned facades of library, bank, and church buildings salted amid the intimate commercial blocks and one-way streets. To truly immerse yourself in the essence of ye olde Sherburne (as the town was originally known), step away from the bustle of shoppers and steamship traffic and stroll the residential Academy Hill neighborhood around the First Congregational Church.

Spared the ravages of the 1846 Great Fire, the delightfully quiet lanes and narrow, well-shaded streets in this area—Church, Academy, Westminster, Gay, and Quince—are lined with fine shingle and clapboard homes, many retaining the character of their 18th- and early 19th-century origins. Some houses were dressed up over the years with Greek Revival entrances, Victorian porches, or bits of fancy decorative woodwork around the facades. Others sport the traditional roofwalk, large chimney, and fully enclosed front entrance that typify what is locally known as the Quaker style, named after the denomination to which so many of the shipmasters and other well-to-do families who built this neighborhood once belonged.

To the left of the Academy Hill Apartments on Westminster Street—site of the private school for which the area is named—is one of the town's few remaining historic footpaths, once called Breakneck Alley for its steep pitch down to Lily Street. Use it to reach **Lily Pond Park,** a public property of the Land Bank that offers a pleasant oasis for a picnic or snooze in the sun. Despite the name, there's no pond, but if it's late summer, there *may* be fresh edible blackberries to be found along the paths—if the large variety of resident and migratory birds haven't gotten to them first.

AFRICAN MEETING HOUSE

By the early 19th century, the area around "Five Corners"—the intersection of York Street, Pleasant Street, and Atlantic Avenue—became the heart of the free black community on Nantucket. Nicknamed New Guinea, it was similar to other black neighborhoods in towns and cities elsewhere up and down the Eastern seaboard, and included black-owned stores, homes, inns, and churches.

While houses remaining from that era have been extensively modified, the African Meeting House (508/228-9833, 11 a.m.–3 p.m. Tues.–Sat., and 1–3 p.m. Sun. July–Aug., open by appointment only Sept.–June, admission by donation), at the corner of York and Pleasant, has been restored by Boston's Museum of Afro-American History as an interpretive exhibit center. Built in the 1820s as a school for children denied access to then-segregated public schools, this modest, shingled, single-story structure went on to serve New Guinea's residents as a Baptist church and social center after a lengthy legal challenge finally opened the white schools to all island children in 1848.

The Meeting House is the centerpiece of the **Black Heritage Trail,** whose nine stops are described in a handy brochure available at the Whaling Museum or the Visitor Services office at 25 Federal Street, among other places. (You can also download a PDF copy from the Museum of Afro-American History's website, www.afroammuseum.org.) Guided walking tours of the trail are offered during the height of summer, departing from the Whaling Museum (11 A.M.–3 P.M. Tues.–Sat., and 1–3 P.M. Sun. July–Aug.).

NANTUCKET SHIPWRECK & LIFESAVING MUSEUM

Blame it on geography: Thanks to the treacherous shoals around Nantucket, certain occupations became an indelible part of island life here as nowhere else. Until the invention of navigational aids such as radio and sonar, ships were even more at the mercy of weather and waves than today. Staying safely on course and away from fatal rocks and shallows was difficult in the best of conditions; thousands failed.

Beginning in 1874, vessels that ran aground in Nantucket's alongshore waters were assisted by the U.S. Life Saving Service, which built and maintained beachfront rescue stations beside the nation's most dangerous shores. The Nantucket Shipwreck & Lifesaving Museum (158 Polpis Rd., 508/228-1885, www.nantucketlifesavingmuseum.com, 10 a.m.–4 p.m. daily June 15–Columbus Day, $5) pays tribute to this service and its surfmen with displays of equipment, numerous photos, and descriptions of their exploits—which often seemed to entail rowing out to foundering ships in open boats during brutal winter storms. Though located about three miles east of the Milestone Rotary, the museum is right on the Polpis Road bike path and NRTA 'Sconset-via-Polpis-Road shuttle route.

The original **Surfside Life Saving Station,** of which the museum building is a replica, still stands about a block behind Surfside Beach. It's now the seasonal home of the local branch of Hostelling International.

NANTUCKET LIGHTSHIP BASKET MUSEUM

Attempts were also made to keep passing ships from getting into trouble in the first place. One 19th-century solution was to anchor light-ships—essentially floating lighthouses—near various hazardous shallows. Many crew members relieved the boredom of their stationary duties with handicrafts—basket weaving in particular. In time a distinctive wood-bottomed bowl-shaped utility basket became the namesake style of the lightship crews, who supplemented their income selling them to fellow islanders and, eventually, Victorian-era tourists. In 1949, a Filipino immigrant, José Formoso Reyes, reinvented the nearly forgotten tradition for a new generation of tourists by adding decorative lids to the baskets and transforming them into women's purses. The rest, as they say, is history.

The evolution of this indigenous art form is chronicled in the Nantucket Lightship Basket Museum (49 Union St., 508/228-1177, www.nantucketlightshipbasketmuseum.org, 10 A.M.–4 P.M. Tues.–Sat. late May–mid-Oct., reduced hours Fri.–Sun. the rest of the year, $4), less than a 10-minute stroll from Main Street. The permanent collection is complemented by changing annual exhibits, live demonstrations, and Reyes's complete workshop, right down to the handwritten "Gone Fishing" sign he'd often hang outside his door. The small garden, by the way, has been planted with varieties that would have been contemporary to the 1821 construction of the building, including herbs, antique roses, and heritage apple trees.

LIGHTHOUSES

Three lighthouses grace Nantucket's coast, and if you're keen on seeing all three, you'll have your work cut out for you. Turn-of-the-20th-century **Brant Point Light** is the easiest to visit. It's the diminutive wooden nubbin at the end of Easton Street, the one around which the ferries arc into the harbor. At only 26 feet, it's the nation's shortest lighthouse, but being small hasn't spared it the ravages of the elements. Recurring fires and storms have required the original 1743 light to be rebuilt nine times.

About six miles to the east, at the end of the Milestone Road bike path, is **Sankaty Head Light,** both the island's oldest and the only one that hasn't had to be rebuilt, although it had to be moved in 2007 to avoid being fatally toppled by erosion of the scarp on which it sat. Erected in 1849, the distinctive red-

Brant Point Light

NANTUCKET

DRINK RESPONSIBLY, DRINK LOCALLY

Living on an island far away from the mainland inspires a lot of ingenuity and self-reliance. And living on an island where the long quiet winters leave you with a lot of time on your hands inspires a lot of crazy ideas. Perhaps that's partly why Nantucket has for some time now been proud home to a winery, microbrewery, and small-batch distillery – **Nantucket Vineyard, Cisco Brewers,** and **Nantucket Triple Eight Distillery,** – combined now under one metaphorical roof at 5 and 7 Bartlett Farm Road (508/228-5929 or 800/324-5550, www.ciscobrewers.com).

The vineyard was started in 1981, but summer conditions on the island were not good for the vines, so since the late 1990s the company's nine different red and white wines are carefully blended from varietal grapes primarily imported from the West Coast.

Cisco's brewing operations began in the '90s, and, thanks to the great taste of the flagship English-style amber Whale's Tale Pale Ale, have expanded rapidly. The microbrewery now produces over a half-dozen ales, lagers, porter, and barleywine. From there it was a short leap to making fine spirits – as the owners realized, whiskey is basically just distilled beer. Premium single-malt bourbon whiskey also takes a helluva long time to make, so the

inspired crew at Cisco et al., turned to distilling vodka and other spirits, like gin and rum.

The results of the micro-distillery experiment, begun in 2000, can be tasted at bars and restaurants all over the island, and on the mainland, too, for the lucky residents of some dozen states, mostly in the northeast. Their namesake Triple Eight vodka, triple distilled from a base of organic corn and Nantucket sand-filtered well water, has acquired a devoted following for its smooth taste and slightly sweet finish. Ever the upstart, it has also beaten far better-known international brands at the annual World Spirit Championships.

Tours of this "alcohol amusement park" just off Hummock Pond Road, midway between town and Cisco Beach, are offered on Saturday or by appointment. They are also open Monday–Saturday 10 A.M.–6 P.M. and Sunday noon–5 P.M. for tastings and direct purchases. If you want to anchor your drinks with some good food, turn right out of the driveway and follow the road for about a half mile to **Bartlett's Farm** (33 Bartlett Farm Rd., 508/228-9403, daily Mar.-Dec., Tues.-Sat. Jan.-Mar.) where you'll find great made-to-order sandwiches and panini, plus salads, soups, and freshly baked desserts.

belted light towers 150 feet over some of the region's most treacherous waters, its flashing beacon nearly reaching Cape Cod, 30 miles away. Although it kept mariners away from the beach, during the 50 years after its construction many of the 2,000 ships that went aground on Nantucket's shoals did so off this shore—on Rose and Crown, Great Rip, Old Man, and other of the many named hull-scraping rocks and shallow bars. These days, it makes a prominent target for landlocked navigators cycling across the hummocky Middle Moors, suspended on the windblown horizon like a tantalizing heat-mirage.

Most difficult of all to see close-up is **Great Point Light,** way out at the northernmost tip

of Nantucket. The newest of the island's lights, the present youthful incarnation is the replacement for the historic stone tower utterly destroyed by a violent winter tempest in 1984. So that this one may possibly beat its predecessor's 166-year tenure, its reinforced concrete walls are five feet thick at the base. Tours to the light are available in season.

◖ 'SCONSET

This charming little village sits at the lip of Nantucket's eastern edge. Once a collection of fishermen's shanties barely more substantial than the beach from which they launched their dories, the village has evolved into a summer cottage colony whose grand oceanfront homes buffer the island's most exclusive golf courses from the hungry Atlantic. Pretty and serene, during the brief high season it comes alive with short-term residents and visitors who appreciate outdoor activities over shopping.

From the rotary within the village center all of 'Sconset's attractions are within walking distance: restaurants, galleries, Sankaty Light, and the seemingly never-ending beach. Start by strolling among the dainty little "dollhouses" along residential Front Street, a narrow grass alley with century-old vehicle tracks of crushed shell and sandy soil. In summer the local palette of weathered gray shingle is brightened by roses climbing up trellised walls and roofs, and hydrangeas grown wherever there's enough room for a garden. Midway along the street a side path angles down to Codfish Park, the tiny neighborhood at the foot of the bank, facing the public beach. A second steeper path descends to Codfish Park from the street's north end, just past the "Footpath Only, No Bicycles" sign.

This path's left fork is also the beginning of the **Bluff Walk,** a public way skirting the very edge of the heights above the beach, hat-tipping distance from the back porches of the large Queen Anne shingle- and stick-style mansions that face Baxter Road. Here is where the sun rises on America; to the east is nothing but water until Portugal. The undertow along this stretch of shore is fierce, which is why the beach far below is usually so sparsely populated, even in the heat of summer. If the bluff's seaward edge is cliff-sharp and bare of vegetation rather than having a stable angle of repose covered in wild beach rose, you are looking at the latest loss of land to Mother Nature. These ever-eroding acres are among the most transitory on the island, relentlessly gnawed away by winter storms that swallow up to a dozen feet a year on average, and have at times suddenly reduced house lots to sandbars in the surf.

The Nantucket Preservation Trust (508/228-1387, 2 Union St., www.nantucketpreserva tion.org) conducts periodic **walking tours** of the village with a focus on the architectural heritage of its houses, some of which predate the American Revolution. Call or check out the website for the current schedule.

Festivals and Events

APRIL

On the last full weekend of the month, Nantucket trumpets the real arrival of spring with its annual **Daffodil Festival** (508/228-1700, www.nantucketchamber.org). Garden Club and Art Association events, inn tours, an antique and classic car parade, a tailgate picnic, and some three million daffodils are among the highlights.

MAY

Mid-May is a delightful time to be on the island. Buoyed by spring sun and fair breezes, islanders happily prepare for Memorial Day weekend, the first taste of the coming high season. What better time to celebrate **National Historic Preservation Month,** observed locally with tours of historic island properties and public lectures about preservation projects. Sponsored by the Nantucket Preservation Trust (508/228-1387, www.nantucketpreser vation.org).

Around the middle of the month every year, the **Nantucket Wine Festival** (508/228-1128, www.nantucketwinefestival.com) brings in big-name chefs and a full stable of international wine sellers, pouring and serving for a grand tent full of revelers. Increasingly popular, the festival is a weekend-long celebration that includes a formal gala, seminars and tastings galore, and plenty of parties.

Each Memorial Day weekend, the **Figawi Race** (508/420-1400, www.figawi.com) covers the waters between Hyannis and Nantucket with the largest sailboat race on the East Coast. The race's current size and respectability belies its rum-soaked origins, the only remnant of which is the name (an homage to the slurred morning-after query of hungover racers: "Where th' figawi?").

JUNE

After Memorial Day weekend, the island is given back to its year-round residents, now busily recruiting and training the seasonal workforce who will keep the island's kitchens and lodgings running smoothly through autumn. While the first day of summer arrives on the third week of the month, the first tsunami of summer visitors usually waits another week or two, until the Fourth of July. Which simply means that cinema-lovers attending the annual **Nantucket Film Festival** (508/325-6274, www.nantucketfilmfestival.org), an intimate and casual celebration of the art of screenwriting held over the third weekend of the month, have a chance of finding both lodging vacancies and restaurant reservations. For a precise schedule, give the festival number a call or visit their website.

JULY

July 4th on Nantucket is celebrated in traditional style: races and games in the late afternoon, a band concert in the early evening, and fireworks at dusk. Jetties Beach is the center of the fun; for details, call the Parks and Recreation Commission (508/228-7213).

AUGUST

If you like browsing through other folks' old furnishings, mark this month's first weekend in your calendar: Friday–Sunday, the Nantucket Historical Association (508/228-1894, www.nha.org) sponsors their **Annual August Antiques Show** at Nantucket High School.

Among the most highly anticipated events of the summer calendar is the annual **Boston Pops on Nantucket** benefit performance by the Boston Pops Esplanade Orchestra outdoors at Jetties Beach, usually the second Saturday of the month. Proceeds support the Nantucket Cottage Hospital, whose online gift shop starts selling tickets early in the spring (www.nantuckethospital.org, click on the Events link). General admission simply lets you pick a spot on the beach, so plan on bringing a beach chair or blanket.

On the third weekend of the month, Nantucketers turn out for the **Annual Sand Castle and Sculpture Day** (508/228-1700, www.nantucketchamber.org) at Jetties Beach on that Saturday, while sailors compete that Sunday in the East Coast's oldest wooden boat race, the **Opera House Cup Regatta** (508/325-7755, www.operahousecup.com), outside Nantucket Harbor. Join race-watchers at Brant Point, and admire the regatta cheerleading squad, a band of small sloops with bright-hued sails known as the Rainbow Fleet.

A few days before the end of the month the local Arts Council kicks off their **Arts Festival,** a week-long extravaganza comprising a prodigious display of resident creativity. Gallery exhibits in all media, live music in the streets, staged readings, and daily author kaffeeklatsches run right up through Labor Day. For details contact the Arts Council (508/325-8588, www.nantucketartscouncil.org).

OCTOBER

On the first Saturday of the month, the Nantucket Conservation Foundation (508/228-2884, www.nantucketconservation.com) holds its annual **Cranberry Festival** at the Milestone Cranberry Bog on Milestone Road. Watch harvesters suction up the acres of ripe berries, enjoy hayrides and other family diversions, and snack on cranberry-themed treats.

The Saturday after Columbus Day welcomes the annual **Chowder Contest** (508/228-1700, www.nantucketchamber.org) to the big tent set up for the occasion in the Grand Union parking lot at the foot of Main Street. A nominal fee lets you sample the savory wares of local restaurateurs vying for a year's worth of bragging rights. Top honors are determined by popular ballot, so don't hesitate to compare tasting notes with your fellow judges.

DECEMBER

During the first full weekend of the month, shoppers are lured out to Nantucket by its annual **Christmas Stroll,** sponsored by the Chamber of Commerce (508/228-1700, www .nantucketchamber.org). In conjunction with contests for best shop-window and residential-door display, the Whaling Museum exhibits trees decorated by the community. Don't miss the Town Crier welcoming Santa to the island (he gives his reindeer a rest and comes on a Coast Guard cutter).

Shopping

Locals joke that Nantucket is where billionaires hire millionaires to mow their lawns, so it should come as no surprise that cheap and funky shopping is in short supply. (In how many other places might you overhear someone complaining about stooping to rent a jet because the one they own is being serviced?) Nor will you find the usual national chains in downtown Nantucket, thanks to a ban enacted in 2006 after a Ralph Lauren Polo store opened up on Main Street. While plenty of windows discreetly announce sister locations in equally fashionable resort towns around the world, the parent companies must have fewer than 14 outlets. (Since the law wasn't retroactive, the Polo store remains.)

On the other hand, there's no shortage of shops filled with apparel and accessories for women with a single-digit dress size and a six-figure credit line. If you're seeking gold jewelry and couture clothing, you've definitely come to the right place.

There are also a handful of singular shops that sell inimitable goods particular to the island or region. One leading example is **Murray's Toggery Shop** (62 Main St., 508/228-0437 or 800/368-2134, www.nan tucketreds.com, 9 A.M.–5 P.M. daily mid-Apr.–Oct., 9 A.M.–7 P.M. daily July–Aug., 9 A.M.–5 P.M. Mon.–Sat. off season), whose very name captures a bygone age of local retailing. Murray's is best known as the fount of all Nantucket Reds, the brick-red cotton canvas clothing for both men and women that, upon fading to a pinkish tomato-bisque hue, has become emblematic of the island.

You'll find Nantucket hand-hooked rugs at **Claire Murray** (11 S. Water St., 508/228-1913, www.clairemurray.com, 10 A.M.–6 P.M. daily), in a variety of traditional and contemporary styles. This flagship store of the ever-expanding Murray empire also features Nantucket lightship baskets, plus a large selection of other items for the home, from bedding to dinnerware.

For home furnishings step into the showroom of **Stephen Swift–Furnituremaker** (47 Main St., 508/228-0255, www.stephenswift furnituremaker.com, 10 A.M.–5 P.M. Mon.–Sat.). Designed and built with real Yankee craftsmanship, the huntboards, desks, chairs, dressers, tables, and other beautiful handmade furniture you'll see are all available custom-made to your specifications.

Nantucket's long-standing maritime tradition of treating the world as its shopping basket finds a modern heir in **L'Ile de France** (8 India St., 508/228-3686, www.frenchgen eralstore.com, 10 A.M.–5 P.M. daily May–Christmas, hours vary Jan.–Apr.). Called "The French General Store" by the hands-on owners, Michel and Joyce Berret, it's stocked with items exclusively from Michel's native land. Drop in for such kitchen essentials as copper cookware by Lagorsse and Gérard Leclerc (flambée pans, quail pots, crêpe pans, and that perfect *un moule* for baking tarte tatin), olive-wood utensils, Opinel knives, and the indispensable *sabon huitre,* a wooden oyster shoe, which protects soft hands from sharp shucking blades. Or pick up a few round marble-topped, brass-edged, cast-iron pedestal tables, made by the last of France's original bistro-table companies.

DUMP DIVING AT THE MALL

When locals talk about going shopping at the mall, don't assume they intend to take the ferry to the mainland to hit the big box stores in Hyannis. It's just as likely they're heading to the "Madaket Mall" – or, as it is more formally known, the Madaket Landfill. That's right: One of the top "shopping" destinations for residents and second-home owners is the town dump.

The reason? Recycling. Until the 1990s Nantucket, like so many municipalities, simply burned its garbage or piled it in a big heap as far out of sight as possible. Obviously that approach had its limits on a small island with a seasonal population of a medium city. Incineration was environmentally unsound. The landfill, high enough to jokingly be called the "Ski Nantucket" mountain, couldn't expand. It also became a health hazard: Chemicals were leaching into the surrounding soils, threatening the local water supply. The state demanded the landfill be closed and that all solid waste be shipped to the mainland.

Faced with the prospect of skyrocketing garbage disposal costs, the town aggressively sought to reduce waste at the source. Everything that can possibly be recycled is removed from the refuse that islanders cart to the dump. Not only traditional materials like paper, metal, plastic, and glass are sorted out, but also tires, white goods, mattresses, and construction debris. Yard waste and organic garbage is fed to giant state-of-the-art "digesters" that produce topsoil-grade compost for local landscaping. And any appliance, book, CD, hardware, furniture, clothing, or building material that might possibly have a second life in someone else's possession is sent to the "Take It or Leave It" building.

Seagulls used to swarm the landfill back in the days before it was capped. Now islanders flock to the landfill to sift through the Take It or Leave It offerings. There are occasional instances of valuable antiques being found among the jetsam, and one local architect even built and furnished an entire house from scavenged material. But most of the leavings are prosaic: outgrown clothing, the dross of someone's music collection, furniture in need of refurbishing. Because of the huge number of visitors who leave things behind, though, there are genuinely plenty of items that have seen little use – many books, in particular, are often like new. Madaket regulars thus consider spring and fall, when rental property managers redecorate or clean house, to be the best times to hang out at the "mall," but summer Sundays are equally popular for the leftovers from weekly yard sales.

Since everyone who lives here has to go to the landfill anyway to drop stuff off, it's easy to spend a little extra time dump diving. It can also be a very lively social scene – as you'll see if you go, poking through each other's trash is an irresistible conversation-starter. As for the overall program, it is one of the most successful waste-management projects in the U.S. – over 80 percent of what would have been tossed in the landfill is now diverted to recycling or repossession. The old landfill is now even being excavated to keep up with the demand for construction fill.

Located off Madaket Road just east of Long Pond, the "mall" is open seven days a week, 7 A.M.-3 P.M. Monday-Friday and 8 A.M.-noon Saturday-Sunday, even in January.

Of course there's so much more: artisanal soaps from Marseilles, collectible figurines, striped cotton sailor's jerseys, wicker baskets by a master artisan of the French National School of Basketry (*c'est vrai*, there is such a place), hollow spruce-branch *bouffadous* (blow through them to kindle fires), crystal champagne flutes, hand-painted pottery from Brittany, and *bien sur*, Limoges porcelain. Staying on the island a while? Consider placing an order for a two-kilo loaf of fresh bread from Lionel Poilâne, FedEx'ed overnight once a week. And to dip the bread in, don't miss the extra-virgin organic olive oil from a fourth-generation Provençal farm.

A block away and a world apart from this

corner of France is David Place's **Manor House Antiques** (31 ½ Centre St., 508/228-4335, 10 A.M.–11 P.M. daily May–Nov., 10 A.M.–5:30 P.M. Dec.–Apr.), filled to bursting with all manner of estate-sale goods. Downtown Nantucket used to have a handful of such knickknack dealers, but such retail variations on the old American yard sale are now as rare as genuine whale ivory. One of the last of this dying breed, David cheerfully caters to every pocketbook and a wide range of tastes with a bountiful and ever-changing inventory of the old, the odd, the obsolete, and the truly antique, all just waiting to be appreciated anew.

Antiques are also frequently featured at the regular **Rafael Osona Auctions** (508/228-3942, www.nantucketauctions.com) held in the American Legion Hall at 21 Washington St., 9:30 A.M. Wednesday the last week in May and each week from late June–mid-September, plus once more each month October–December. Whether or not you join in the bidding it's well worth a visit to glimpse whatever museum-quality sampling of memorabilia, paintings, and crafts associated with Nantucket are currently on offer, usually along with exquisite furnishings consigned to sale by the changing fancies or fortunes of the island's more affluent residents.

Plenty of shopping opportunities are also found along the waterfront, with Straight Wharf holding the edge on cute little boutiques and Old South Wharf taking the lead in sculpture and painting galleries. Of course the wharves are also home to **Nantucket Ship Chandlery** (23 Old South Wharf, 508/228-2300, 8:30 A.M.–5:30 P.M. Mon.–Sat. and 10 A.M.–2 P.M. Sun. mid-June–early Sept., 9 A.M.–5 P.M. Mon.–Sat. and 10 A.M.–2 P.M. Sun. mid-Sept.–early June except closed Sun. Columbus Day–late May and closed entirely Jan.–Mar.), catering to all your yacht-fitting hardware needs. Landlubbers will appreciate the Chandlery for its wide selection of outdoor apparel, sunglasses, and beach bags.

BOOKSTORES

Beach-blanket or fireside reading material abounds at both **Nantucket Bookworks** (25 Broad St., 508/228-4000, www.nantucketbookworks.com, 9:30 A.M.–10:30 P.M. daily), next to The Brotherhood of Thieves, and **Mitchell's Book Corner** (54 Main St., 508/228-1080, www.mitchellsbookcorner.com, 9:30 A.M.–10 P.M. Mon.–Sat. and 10 A.M.–10 P.M. Sun. late May–early Sept., 9:30 A.M.–5 P.M. Mon.–Sat. and 11 A.M.–4 P.M. Sun. mid-Sept.–mid-Apr., 9:30 A.M.–6 P.M. Mon.–Sat. and 11 A.M.–5 P.M. Sun. mid-Apr.–late May) on downtown's cobblestoned main square diagonally across from the Pacific National Bank. True to form for independent bookstores, the staff of both shops are knowledgeable about everything they carry and as helpful as you could want. Mitchell's has a particularly impressive quantity of titles related to all things Nantucket. The Bookworks, as a member of Book Sense, the national association of independent booksellers, honors gift certificates from that organization. Both stores are happy to ship books worldwide.

Additional selections of local-interest books can be found at the Whaling Museum and the Maria Mitchell Association gift shops.

NANTUCKET

Recreation

While outdoor fun on Nantucket is almost invariably synonymous with going to the beach, there are plenty of good reasons to explore dry land, too. The first is obvious: While everyone else is at the beach, hikers and birders will often have conservation property trails to themselves. But you don't have to be a contrarian to enjoy spring wildflowers blooming in a grassy plain, the tall summer stalks of blue vervain adding strokes of violet to a wetland meadow, or the turning autumn leaves of a tupelo grove. Besides the pleasures of nature afforded to walkers and beachgoers, no Nantucket vacation is complete without getting on a bike or in a boat.

MIDDLE MOORS

Though much of Nantucket's interior has historically been described as "moors," any resemblance to Scotland's peat-based landscape is purely superficial. While some acidic peat-soiled bogs do exist here, Nantucket's moors are mostly combinations of grassy sandplains and dry shrubby heathlands—two very distinct (and increasingly rare) plant communities here intermingled nearly to the point of interchangeability.

The Middle Moors, a great expanse of undeveloped land between Polpis and Milestone Roads east of town, is a good example of this grass and heath mixture—and also illustrates the probable fate of the island's heathlands, which are being overrun by native scrub oak. This sort of plant succession is entirely natural and would eventually return the island interior to the wooded state it was in when Europeans arrived. But prior to colonial settlement, the heaths flourished close to shore—where salt air put trees at a disadvantage—and in forest openings created by fire. Homeowners covetous of ocean views cleared much of that away, and fires are now suppressed to prevent property damage, so the heaths and their dependent ecosystem of insects, birds, and small mammals are headed toward extinction.

Altar Rock, a glacial erratic embedded in the overgrown ridge (Saul's Hills) defining the moor's northern edge, affords the best panorama over the huckleberry, false heather, and intruding scrub oak barrens. Though a mere 100 feet above sea level, this viewpoint and the four other hills in the ridge that share the same elevation are among the highest points on the island. Only Sankaty Bluff (at a skyscraping 109 feet), Folger Hill (at 108), and part of the $28 million Rees Jones golf course to the east are higher. Altar Rock also offers one of a declining number of island vistas whose foreground isn't speckled with vacation homes. The most direct route to the rock is via the signposted sand track off Polpis Road, exactly opposite the Quaise Road turnoff; head toward the radio antenna.

To identify other trails through the moors, pick up an all-island *General Information and Properties Map* from the **Nantucket Conservation Foundation** (118 Cliff Rd., 508/228-2884, www.nantucketconservation .com, Mon.–Fri. only). Thirty miles of sandy roads accommodate mountain bikers—although to reduce erosion, bikers are requested to stay off trails blocked by posts or obviously narrow and suited only for walkers. Like all NCF holdings, the Middle Moors are distinguished from private land by the organization's gull/waves/hills logo, affixed to maroon posts at the boundaries.

CRANBERRY BOGS

Cranberries are as native to Nantucket as the thick morning fogs, but only since the mid-1800s have they been cultivated. To keep the island's remaining cranberry bogs from disappearing beneath more cedar-sided saltbox summer homes for the rich and famous, they were purchased and donated to the Nantucket Conservation Foundation. Through the NCF, **Windswept Cranberry Bog,** off Polpis Road opposite the Wauwinet turnoff, and **Milestone Road Cranberry Bog,** about five miles east of town along the 'Sconset bike path, remain open to active cultivation, with hundreds more acres of marsh, ponds, and forest open to the public. The mix of floristic communities makes for good bird-watching throughout the warmer months, and budding naturalists will find plenty of blossoms lending their colors to the landscape, from subtle little crowberry blooms to the more showy, pink, crane-like cranberry flowers. A trail map specifically for the Windswept property is available at the NCF office on Cliff Road.

When wholesale prices make the harvesting economically feasible, come mid-October the fruits of these acres are reaped with mechanical "water reels" that plow through submerged bogs beating the cranberry vines, creating great crimson oceans of floating berries in their wake. The crop gets vacuumed up for shipment off-island, where the berries are turned into the jellies and sauces you may be buying for Thanksgiving. (Wet-harvested berries are never sold raw because the water starts breaking down their natural waxy coating, eliminating any chance of a viable retail shelf-life.) As you'd expect, local bakeries and restaurants often demonstrate the versatility of these tart treats in all manner of sweet and savory dishes during the late fall—although not necessarily with native-grown berries.

◖ COSKATA-COATUE WILDLIFE REFUGE

One of The Trustees of Reservations' many fine properties, Coskata-Coatue (pronounced ko-SKATE-ah ko-TWO; 508/228-0006, www .thetrustees.org), encompasses Nantucket's longest barrier beach, largest salt marsh, a cedar forest, and—at the far north end of that beach—Great Point's lighthouse. Tidepools hold plenty of shellfish such as scallops, clams, and mussels, while wild roses, the elusive beach plum, and even cactus grow amid the dunes. Hundreds of terns from a summer nesting colony wheel and dive over the surf, northern harriers ride thermals rising from the sun-heated sand, and the occasional shearwater, a pelagic visitor more commonly found far out at sea,

can be spotted resting on shore. Fiddler crabs scurry away from your approach, oystercatchers stalk the surf line for buried mole crabs, and beneath the sweep of the lighthouse beacon cocky young seals sun themselves on the beach between bouts of play in the strong fickle currents of the offshore rip.

To protect the fragile dunes from wind erosion, you're strongly discouraged from climbing them. And swimming isn't recommended, due to dangerous riptides. With over 10 miles of shoreline on three bodies of water—the Atlantic, Nantucket Sound, and the enclosed harbor—this is the place to take long meditative walks on the beach. Depending on how the stripers and bluefish are running, you may find a lot of serious surfcasters out at Great Point contemplating how to tempt a fish to swallow a hook.

From May through October, the Trustees offer 2.5-hour narrated excursions out to the lighthouse via a comfortably air-conditioned SUV (9:30 A.M. and 1:30 P.M. daily, $40 adults, $15 kids 12 and under, discounts for Trustees members). Your driver is a naturalist who has lived on the island year-round for over two decades. She provides well-informed commentary and binoculars, too. On Tuesdays in July and August there's an additional sunset trip, and if you have a group of six (or are prepared to buy six seats) you can arrange a custom excursion.

Tours depart promptly from the gatehouse in the Wauwinet Inn parking lot at the end of Wauwinet Road, the access point for the property (call 508/228-6799 for reservations, which are required). The tours typically sell out ahead of time, so booking in advance (a week or more for weekends and sunset trips) is definitely advisable. Although insect repellent is customarily recommended for any visit to the refuge due to the prevalence of biting greenhead horse flies, the only time you'll be outside the tour vehicle is at the lighthouse, where stiff ocean breezes keep the insects firmly at bay.

When not restricted for beach-nesting plovers and terns, four-wheel-drive vehicles with the proper permits may use designated roads out to the lighthouse, too. Permits ($125 a year for private off-island vehicles, $60 for Trustees family-level members), information, and maps are all available late May–mid-October from the gatehouse.

THE SANFORD FARM

On Madaket Road, about two miles west of the waterfront on the Madaket shuttle route, are a small parking area and trailhead for the former Sanford Farm, now one of several contiguous parcels of public conservation land stretching nearly three miles to the South Shore's Cisco Beach. Several miles of trails traverse a varied set of habitats bounded on one side by Hummock Pond, whose waters fill a narrow glacial outwash valley. Swamps and sloughs where you might see turtles napping in the sun, old fields surrendering to bayberry and wild grape, grassland meadows known as the "Ram Pasture," woodlands browsed by white-tailed deer, and plenty of wild blueberries are among the treats for walkers and cyclists (others are described on the 26 interpretive markers spread along the six-mile loop to the ocean). If you can't spare a few hours to go the whole way, at least go as far as the barn—about 30 minutes' walk from the Madaket Road gate—for great views to the ocean.

BEACHES

Over 20 named beaches dot the island's shore, from remote windswept ones shared only with gulls to a handful that are fully catered with food concessions, bath houses, and lifeguards. In general, beaches facing south or east receive the big breakers, strong currents, and fine sand, while those facing Nantucket Sound to the north are warmer and more calm (though also more pebbly).

Sometimes sustained windy conditions will propel flotillas of the stinging jelly-like Portuguese man o' war into local waters from its normal habitat in the Gulf Stream a dozen miles to the south. Lifeguards post warnings at the entrances to the major public beaches when this occurs, and the local media quickly issue advisories, too, since touching the creatures,

even after they have washed up on shore, can be painful enough to require medical attention. North shore and inner harbor beaches are less prone to closure due to man o' wars than southern and eastern ones.

While the vast majority of Nantucket's 80-plus miles of shoreline have historically been open to public use, most beach frontage is actually under private ownership. Leaving no trash behind on any beach and being courteous to adjacent homeowners is thus not just good manners but also greatly appreciated by all the future beachgoers who would suffer if "no trespassing" signs were erected at every private property line.

In Town

Kid-friendly **Children's Beach** wins the popularity contest for beach-going families seeking to avoid an all-day excursion out of town on account of its location a few blocks north of Steamboat Wharf, as well as all its extras: playground, snack vendor, restrooms, and showers. It's also a perfect spot to watch the ferries and other boats come and go.

Other harbor swimming spots include modest **Francis Street Beach**, out toward the end of Washington Street Extension, and **Brant Point**, by the lighthouse. The first is as placid as a pond, but the Point boasts a stiff current (swimmers beware). Neither one is staffed by lifeguards, and only Francis Street has a restroom.

North Shore

Generally calm conditions prevail at all the north shore favorites. With its windsurfing concession, beach volleyball, snack shack, adjacent public tennis courts, and shuttle bus service, **Jetties Beach** is *not* the place to seek splendid isolation, but it's also deservedly popular precisely for its convenience (you can even walk to it from downtown), amenities, and just-right water conditions. It has seasonal lifeguards, restrooms, and changing rooms, too.

A short distance west, past the private stretches of shore belonging to the Galley Beach Restaurant and Cliffside Beach Club, is

Steps Beach, accessible from a long wooden staircase at the end of Lincoln Avenue. There is no lifeguard or bathroom here, but the water is relatively warm, the surf is light, and the views are worth millions—just ask the owners of the big mansions above.

At the end of the 3.5-mile bike path along Madaket and Eel Point Roads is half-mile long **Dionis Beach** which can also be reached by a combination of the NRTA's Madaket route to the Eel Point Road stop and walking the final mile and a half. It's well protected from shore breezes by high dunes, and is large enough so anyone unburdened by kids and coolers will likely find some elbow room. Like Jetties, it features seasonal lifeguards and a bath house with changing facilities and restrooms.

Farther west along Eel Point Road is **40th Pole Beach,** owned by the Nantucket Land Bank and named for the number of telephone poles between Madaket Road and its parking lot. Although it shares the generally warm and calm conditions of Dionis, unfortunately it is also exceedingly popular with the I-can't-live-without-my-SUV-on-the-beach crowd.

South Shore

The island's main magnet for the young, blonde, and bronze (and everyone else who feigns indifference to holes in the ozone layer) is **Surfside,** at the end of the eponymous road and bike path. Restrooms, showers, and food are all available in season, as is shuttle bus service from downtown. Surfside is huge, but it still fills up, especially with SUVs belonging to people unable (or unwilling) to carry a beach umbrella more than five feet.

Walk east a mile, and you can join the lighter ranks of surfing enthusiasts who favor the big breaks at **Nobadeer Beach,** virtually under the end of the airport runway. Here, too, the Expeditions and Navigators sometimes seem to outnumber actual people, and the high school vibe is loud and strong. If "beach" isn't synonymous with "parking lot" in your dictionary, then walk west from Surfside. Just be aware that if you walk far enough you'll eventually arrive at the one part of Nantucket's shoreline

frequented by the clothing-optional crowd. (Strictly speaking nude sunbathing is illegal, but this is the one spot where it is overlooked—at least by authorities, if not by prurient guys with binoculars.)

Although it has neither lifeguards nor restrooms nor any other amenities, **Miacomet Beach,** at the end of West Miacomet Road, is a family favorite because behind the beach is Miacomet Pond, whose warmer, shallow, calm waters are ideal for small children. Meanwhile the ocean side drops off deeply underwater, creating strong surf close to shore.

At the end of Hummock Pond Road is **Cisco Beach,** a.k.a. End of the Road Beach, a favorite of surfers. To the west, past the foot of Hummock Pond, is a sparsely-frequented stretch of beach generally referred to as **Clark's Cove** after the body of water it divides from the ocean. This so-called cove, which once comprised the western third of a much larger Hummock Pond until shoreline shifts bisected the two, is surrounded by rural conservation land (including Sanford Farm, see *The Sanford Farm* entry), which adds to the sense of splendid isolation. Offshore rips can be quite strong in this vicinity, so know your strength as a swimmer—there are no lifeguards to come to your rescue here, and there may be no other swimmers in earshot, either.

The other beach with southern exposure is the vast sweeping expanse of **Madaket Beach,** as far west as the island's shuttle buses and bike paths go. Besides invigorating waves that leave you feeling like a sock in the spin cycle, Madaket is the best place on Nantucket for lovely ocean sunsets. And, unlike Cisco, it also has restrooms.

East Shore

In summer, there are shuttle buses to 'Sconset from Nantucket Town (on Washington Street at the corner of Main); from the bus stop at the Main Street Rotary it's just a short stroll down to **'Sconset Beach.** Known for its rough breakers, the most swimmable portion lies between the village and the Coast Guard's LORAN navigational radio masts to the south. For sustenance after arriving in the village, consider a box lunch from **Claudette's,** whose shady patio faces the Rotary across from the bus stop, or fetch take-out fare from the small **'Sconset Market** next to the post office, since there are no food concessions at the beach. There aren't any toilets at the beach, either, but public restrooms are located off Pump Square (site of the old village pump) just north of the market.

One of the island's least well-known swimming spots is **Quidnet Beach,** north of Sankaty Light on shorefront property owned by the Massachusetts Audubon Society. While the open ocean is on one side of the dunes, on the other is Sesachacha (se-SACK-atcha) Pond, a favorite of kayakers. To get to this overlooked spot follow Quidnet Road nearly to its end, then turn right on Sesachacha Road to the parking area near *its* end.

WATER SPORTS
Surfing
While New England doesn't stand in the company of traditional surfing meccas like Hawaii and Australia, Nantucket ranks near the top of all the eligible spots in the Northeast for the consistency of its surfing conditions. The wind-driven shore breakers along the south side of the island usually range from gentle rollers for beginners to waist-high swell for more practiced surfers, depending on the location. During late summer and early fall, hurricanes in the Caribbean and mid-Atlantic region can produce big "double overhead" waves for days on end—and Nantucket's south-facing beaches are the first part of New England to feel their energy.

Surfers who have left the board back home can rent one from either the **Nantucket Island Surf School** at Cisco Beach (508/560-1020, www.nantucketsurfing.com), or give a call to **Nantucket sUrfari** (508/228-1235, www.nantucketsurfari.com) for a complete door-to-beach, gear-included, guided surfing experience. Both outfits also conduct surf lessons for new students of stoke. When you're ready to take the plunge and equip yourself

for the surfing life head downtown to **Force 5 Watersports** (6 Union St., 508/228-0700) for all your gear needs, from boards to wetsuits, sunglasses to Crocs. And since everyone knows surfing is such hard work, reward your efforts with a visit to their Candy Room, filled with the island's largest selection of packaged sweet treats.

Throughout the summer, windsurfers have only one place to keep in mind: Jetties Beach. That's where **Nantucket Community Sailing** staffs its seasonal concession (508/228-5358, mid-June–Labor Day) for sailboard lessons and rentals, youth windsurfing clinics, adaptive windsurfing lessons for disabled athletes, and other sail- and paddling-related activities.

Paddling
With its long protected harbor lined with interesting estuaries on one side and beautiful secluded beaches on the other, plus a handful of very large ponds with easily accessible put-ins, Nantucket offers lots of options to kayakers.

Kayaks may be rented from friendly **Sea Nantucket** at the Francis Street Beach (508/228-7499, Memorial Day–early or mid-Oct., $15 per hour–$60 per day, slightly more for double kayaks). Their non-rollable singles and doubles are ideal for beginners, who have the entire protected length of Nantucket Harbor to play around in—from Coatue's gull rookeries east to Wauwinet. The company also handles deliveries, if you want to row around inland waters like long, narrow Hummock Pond, west of town, or large Sesachacha Pond, on the eastern shore by Quidnet Beach.

For self-propelled boating with a twist, try pedal-powered kayaks from **ACKKayak** (15 Commercial St., 508/332-3394, June–mid-Oct., $60 half day, $80 full day, slightly more for double kayaks). Resembling a recumbent bicycle in both the speed gained from minimal effort and the way in which the pedaler sits, these unique kayaks belong in an entirely different orbit than typical ungainly pedal boats in which the rider perches on a bench well above the water. Like all its fellow outfitters, ACKKayak is happy to rendezvous

Nantucket Harbor

wherever you want to go, and also has a 27-foot skiff that staff can use to transport both you and your kayak east to the Head of the Harbor, giving you a big head start on exploring Coskata's shore.

Sailing

If you're making yourself at home on the island for the whole summer, **Nantucket Community Sailing** (508/228-6600, www.nantucket sailing.com) can help you work on that tan *and* learn how to sail. For a $150 membership and $215 course fee, you get 10 hours of instruction over five days; pass the qualifying exam at the end and you'll earn sailing privileges with NCS boats for the remainder of the season. If you already know how to sail, you can rent boats for day sailing at **Nantucket Harbor Sail** (Commercial Wharf, 508/228-0424).

Indoor Swimming

Year-round, if inclement weather or ice-cold water keep you away from the shore, you can still swim laps at the **Nantucket Community Pool** (508/228-7262, ext. 1353, $8 day-use fee) at the intersection of Atlantic and Sparks Avenues, next to the high school (reachable on the NRTA South Loop shuttle). The Olympic-sized, heated, indoor facility offers a varied schedule of adult, senior, and youth lap swims, water aerobics classes, open family swims, and other organized programs. Bring your own towel and a lock for your belongings.

ORGANIZED TOURS
Walking and Driving Tours

A good way to get a broad overview of Nantucket is by taking one of the small van tours available in season. Both **Gail's Tours** (508/257-6557) and **Sabra's Tours** (508/574-0382) offer informative all-island tours lasting around 90 minutes for $20–25 per person. Both pick up from any in-town guesthouse or inn (or from the ferries, if you let them know when you'll be arriving). Both operate year-round, with up to three tours daily in season. Obviously they let their phones ring through to an answering service while conducting tours, so the best time to reach them in season is before 9 A.M. or after 5 P.M.; usually calling a day

NANTUCKET

ISLAND ANGLING

It should come as no surprise that the islands constitute an angler's heaven. Whether fly-fishing for "bones" (bonito); trolling deep waters for mackerel, tuna, and swordfish; or jigging for flounder and pollack near coastal rocks, there's plenty of variety to keep beginners and experts occupied. Sometimes the warm Gulf Stream even brings southern exotics like mahimahi into local waters. But most prized by local fish fanciers are two species favored by surfcasters – striped bass and bluefish.

Stripers are nocturnal feeders who school up in local waters starting around mid-May. Blues tend to start their runs past the islands in mid-to-late June. Blues are like oceanic attack animals, making slash-and-run moves on anything in their paths – from flesh to fishing tackle (if you get bitten, you won't suffer as much as the bait – but you'll definitely feel it). Hence the nickname "the Nantucket alligator." Schools of blues are easily detected by the tremendous commotion of other fish leaping out of the water to escape their high-speed pack attacks.

Both species have felt the impact of over-fishing and pollution – stripers in particular were nearly wiped out in the region a decade ago – so strict regulations have been set on the size and quantity you can take home. Consult local tackle shops for current restrictions on keepers.

On Nantucket, anglers can choose among a half dozen sportfishing boats ready and waiting down on Straight Wharf, such as the **Just Do It Too** (508/228-7448, www.justdoittoo.com), which offers up to four scheduled daily departures in season, and the **Althea K** (508/228-3471, www.altheaksportfishing.com). If you're staying out on the west end of the island, ring up **Capt. Tom's Charters** (508/228-4225, www.capttom.com) or Capt. Bill Toelstedt's **Nantucket Outfitters** (917/584-5270, www.ackoutfitters.com), both of which depart from Walter Barrett Pier, the public landing at the end of F Street in Madaket. Or stop by **Cross Rip Outfitters** downtown at 24 Easy Street (508/228-4900, www.crossrip.com) to arrange for an on-shore surfcasting or fly-fishing expedition, including all equipment and transportation.

in advance is sufficient for finding a space, although if you have one of their specific departure times in mind you would be well advised to book at least a few days ahead. Sabra also offers an hour-long off-road tour ($30) from That Crooked House, the Madaket summer home of the late Fred Rogers (of *Mister Rogers* fame), to the Head of Harbor in Wauwinet—which is why her van is marked with "Nantucket pinstripes" from wild brush raking through the dust on the sides.

If you'd rather experience local history at a pedestrian's pace, both the Nantucket Historical Association and the Nantucket Preservation Trust offer seasonal **walking tours** of the town historic district. The tours of town guided by NHA interpretive staff originate at the Whaling Museum (11:15 A.M. and 2:15 P.M. Mon.–Sat. and 2:15 P.M. in summer, $10), while the NPT tours commence

from in front of their office at 2 Union Street (9:30 A.M. Wed. and Thurs. June–Sept., $10, or $35 including a copy of their coffee-table book about the area covered by the walk). The NPT also sponsors a popular annual tour of private kitchens in the historic district to demonstrate that preservation is perfectly compatible with modern living. Reserve tickets for this **Summer Kitchens House Tour** (the third Thursday in July, $40) by calling their office (508/228-1387, www.nantucketpreservation.org).

Sailing Tours

Some folks would say the best way to get the lay of the land is from offshore, where Nantucket's true nature as a fragile outpost amid the waves is all the more manifest. Whether or not you need such a fancy excuse to get out on the water, several sailing boats offer cruises in local waters. For a reasonably priced outing aboard a classic traditional wooden boat, try the **Endeavor,** a gaff-rigged Friendship sloop that makes trips of up to 90 minutes around the harbor and Nantucket Sound. Drop by their slip at Straight Wharf to check the latest list of departure times (508/228-5585, daily May–Oct., $15–35 depending on length and type of trip, www.endeavorsailing.com). The *Endeavor* also offers "pirate adventures" for kids, cruises accompanied by a traditional fiddler or singer of sea shanties, and private charters.

The same friendly folks commissioned the reproduction of a classic mid-1800's Beetle whaleboat, the *Wanderer,* now used by the **Nantucket Whaleboat Adventure Rowing Club** (508/228-2505, www.eganmaritime .org) for weekly rowing sessions in the harbor. Anyone can join—emphasis is on participation and teamwork, not individual achievement. For reservations or information about either, give them a call (508/228-5585) or visit the office on Straight Wharf.

Cruises

The tiny islet of Muskeget (mus-KEE-git), a half-dozen miles off Nantucket's western tip, is home to a year-round colony of gray seals. The only way to observe these fat fellows—they're mostly bachelors—is by boat. If you don't have your own, then join one of the two fun-lovin' guys who do: Capt. Blair Perkins's **Shearwater Excursions** (508/228-7037, www.explore nantucket.com, year-round, $90), or Capt. Mark "Schark" Scharwenka's **Nantucket Adventures** (508/228-6365, www.nan tucketadventures.com, mid-April–mid-Oct., $72–90). Both depart from the Town Pier at 34 Washington Street, just past Brant Point Marine, a few blocks east of Straight Wharf. Making reservations a week or two in advance of your on-island arrival is highly recommended, and all but essential in July and August, since visitors who have lined up their summer rentals start booking their excursions as early as March and April.

You might also consider a Nantucket Adventures private seal-watching charter, which includes extra time for making a landing on a remote West End beach. Capt. Schark's boat can run right up to the sand for an off-the-bow landing, so all your picnic goods can stay dry.

Shearwater offers various other excursions, too, from a cruise around Nantucket Harbor while snacking on ice cream (90 minutes, $50) to privately scheduled cocktail cruises (three hours, $1500 for up to 30 people) and whale-watching trips (six hours, mid-June–mid-Oct., $140). Although the Stellwagen Bank portion of Massachusetts Bay, north of Cape Cod, is the most well-known local whale habitat—in part because it's the destination of nearly all other Massachusetts whale-watching tours—whales can be spotted wherever there are enough fishy snacks to satisfy their outsized appetites. Nantucket's Great South Channel is one such place—its depth, currents, and water temperatures make for the kind of shallow, fertile feeding ground perfectly tailored to lunching leviathans and, consequently, curious humans. Veterans of Massachusetts Bay whale-watching may be interested to know there are some species here off Nantucket—pilot whales, for example—almost never seen on trips from mainland ports.

NANTUCKET

Accommodations

Scores of Nantucket's 18th- and 19th-century houses have been converted to inns, many of which epitomize the traditional, frilly stereotype of the Olde New England B&B, brimming with wide wood flooring, tchotchke-laden mantelpieces, lacy curtains, stenciled walls, and period antiques. But affordable accommodations are an oxymoron here. Snoozing in canopy beds under handmade quilts in this living museum of Colonial and Early American decorative art doesn't come cheap, especially June–September, when three-night minimums prevail and even rooms with shared baths (euphemistically dubbed "semi-private") can run more than $150. A handful of simple guesthouses offer some relief, but most real savings don't arrive until the warm weather is gone.

You'll find many more staff-run inns than archetypal owner-operated B&Bs. This means, of course, you can end up paying luxury-hotel rates for places presided over by inexperienced, summer-only staff. You should also anticipate having to make basic compromises—an inn with refrigerators in every room, top-quality mattresses, and down-filled pillows that prolong your dreams may have no place to put your clothes other than on the floor. Conversely, a property offering walk-in closets and private baths may have pillows resembling Styrofoam blocks and walls so thin that you'll be forced to listen to the favorite TV show of not only your immediate neighbors, but the guests down the hall, too. (As a rule, B&Bs fashioned out of 19th-century homes have thin walls and creaky floors; book ones with TVs in every room at your peril.)

Of course, there are exceptions, and not just in price—places where impeccable taste, authenticity, consummate professionalism, or sincere attention to your comfort justify every dollar charged. I've tried to highlight those standouts on these pages, but for additional aid in booking a room or renting a cottage, consider a reservation service such as **Nantucket Accommodations** (508/228-9559, www.nantucketaccommodation.com).

The Nantucket Visitor Services Bureau downtown (25 Federal St., 508/228-0925) keeps a list of last-minute availability, or more precisely, availability within the next one to three days, and are happy to furnish you with the relevant contact numbers (if you call) or to even place the phone call themselves and then hand you the receiver (if you show up in person at the Bureau's office). However, the Bureau's desk staff scrupulously avoids identifying prices on their list, so in practical terms be prepared to encounter serious sticker shock as you cold-call the available options trying to find one that fits your vacation budget.

In general, the difference between expensive and very expensive or luxury is in the details: mirrors over the sink (try shaving with a mirror two feet from the faucet to appreciate how important this is), nightlights and hair dryers, umbrellas or beach towels for guest use. Free WiFi, on the other hand, is nearly universally available, even in the least expensive lodgings.

When choosing, weigh in-town convenience against out-of-town serenity. Mopeds buzzing by your downtown window at 7:30 A.M. may not be the wake-up call you want on your vacation, and over-loud voices of late-night drinkers may not be the evening serenade you anticipated. Of course, if you're the one doing the carousing or getting up early to hit the beach, such considerations hardly matter.

BED-AND-BREAKFASTS AND INNS

As on the Vineyard, bed-and-breakfast homes and inns almost all serve continental breakfasts, so if you want more than cereal, muffins, and fruit without leaving the premises, you'll have to stay at one of the dozen luxury-priced, full-scale hotels with restaurants, or at the exceptional Union Street Inn (value-conscious travelers will want to take advantage of the off-season drop-in rates at such upscale places).

If you want to awaken to a view of boats swaying gently at their moorings, don't get your hopes up too high—valuable waterfront views are more prevalent among weekly cottage rentals than small inns, but if price is no object make a beeline for **The Cottages** at the Boat Basin on Old South Wharf. Finally, if you're after a romantic off-season getaway curled up in front of a crackling fire, keep in mind that because of the liability insurance for historic wooden buildings, most places restrict guests to using compressed firelogs rather than kindling real, roaring wood fires. A notable exception is the **Union Street Inn.**

Under $50

The only budget option on the island is **Hostelling International Nantucket** (31 Western Ave., 508/228-0433 or 888/901-2084, www.usahostels.org, late May–late Sept., $32–35 HI members, nonmembers add $3) out at the end of the Surfside bike path. Common rooms, dining rooms, and kitchen facilities occupy a handsome 1873 former life-saving station with Victorian gingerbread trim; guests have a choice of separate, single-sex dorms or a large, 13-bed co-ed room. Despite the perpetually full house, the staff's good humor more than makes up for nights in a room full of snorers. They have only 49 beds, so reservations are essential most of the season. International guests who aren't yet HI members can buy a "Welcome Card" for $18, while U.S. citizens can purchase the $28 American Youth Hostel membership outright upon arrival.

The nearest markets are back on the edge of town, so pick up groceries before arriving.

$50-100

Between Memorial Day and Columbus Day? You'll only find accommodations in this price range if you're traveling solo, and are prepared to sleep in a tiny single bed in a tiny unventilated room with a shared bathroom somewhere on the premises. Otherwise, only travelers in

the depths of the off season (Dec.–mid-April) can find a double room at this price point. The Massachusetts Office of Travel and Tourism website (www.massvacation.com) is a good starting point for finding such winter specials.

$100-150

In high season the pickings in this price range are exceedingly slim. (And be prepared: none have private baths.)

One of the few places available in this category in summer is **The Nesbitt Inn** (21 Broad St., 508/228-0156, mid-Apr.–early Dec., $125–140). The oldest purpose-built inn on the island, this 1872 Victorian encourages society rather than seclusion, with a hospitality born of repeat guests who greet one another like family. You're more likely to find people chatting in the common room or the front porch than checking their email over the inn's WiFi. There are no private baths for any of the standard rooms—which is why this remains one of the island's most affordable inns—but at least the rooms have their own sinks.

If you've been Googling around for low rates you've probably come upon **The Periwinkle Guest House** (7 and 9 N. Water St., 508/228-9267 or 800/837-2921, www.theperiwinkle .com, year-round) in the quiet blocks behind the Whaling Museum. It actually comprises a pair of adjacent properties, the second of which, The Scallop Inn, has no private baths or A/C, and thus stands out for its high-season affordability ($140–165 d June–Sept.). The Internet can't convey just how small and thin-walled its least expensive rooms are, though—or how miniscule the shared bathroom is. There's no denying that the location is excellent, and the price is nearly impossible to beat. But are you willing to risk your relationship to test whether your traveling companion is truly as content with Emersonian simplicity as you are?

In winter, many properties that are open year-round fall into this range. Inns that have shoulder-season pricing—usually through mid-June (Memorial Day weekend excepted) and after either mid-September or mid-October—also tend to have offerings in this category.

NANTUCKET

The Hawthorn House, The Pineapple Inn, and **The Cobblestone Inn,** all downtown or close to it, are excellent choices for the shoulder seasons, with rates well within this price range.

$150-250

One of the better values in town is the ◖ Hawthorn House (2 Chestnut St., 508/228-1468, www.hawthornhouse.com, year-round). Doubles, all with private bath, run $170–255 mid-June–mid-September (there's also a two-room suite for $275); the low end of that range represents selected rooms outside of July and August. In the shoulder season before Memorial Day and after Labor Day, rates drop up to $75. A $9 coupon is given to each guest for breakfast at either of a couple of nearby local eateries—enough to get you a hot entree, not just muffins and juice. The premises are enlivened by an extensive collection of fine art and unique crafts by the owner and his family, including his wife's beautiful needlepoint pillows, his own art glass lamps, and his dad's hooked rugs. The wide-ranging aesthetic brightens the 1849 house at least as much as the sunlight that so many of the rooms offer. The absence of phones in the individual rooms mirrors the tranquility of this little downtown block, so near to shops yet off the main path of traffic. In sum, this is an attractive and comfortable oasis.

Right across the street is the **The Chestnut House** (3 Chestnut St., 508/228-0049, www.chestnuthouse.com, year-round). Four of its five rooms are actually two-room suites, superior in price and size to many other offerings in the area ($250 in season). The fifth room is a king double ($210). All are half price during the off-season. Owners Jeannette and Jerry Carl are both artists, so her paintings, ceramics, and baskets and his hooked rugs are found throughout the premises, complementing the Arts and Crafts fixtures and furnishings. If the cozy library doesn't erase the disappointment of waking up to thundershowers (or snow—they're open year-round), the decanter of sherry in each room surely will. Guests are given a $9 coupon toward breakfast at either of a pair of popular downtown eateries—and

if that sounds familiar, it's because Mitch, the owner of the Hawthorn House, is the Carls' son, and borrowed their idea. For such a central location, Chestnut Street is remarkably quiet, and the property's garden only adds to the serenity.

Two short blocks north of Broad Street is **The Cobblestone Inn** (5 Ash St., 508/228-1987, year-round) with just four rooms, all with private baths ($175–195 d), including a full top-floor two-room suite with harbor views that's ideal for families ($250). The oldest portion of the house is from 1725, but the guest rooms benefit from a thorough rehab that retained the simple character of the original structure, with its hardwood floors and low ceilings, while enabling the owner to add central air, an amenity that is exceedingly rare on the island. Beach towels and, if inclement weather strikes, rain umbrellas are provided, and a continental breakfast of fruit and baked goods is included.

Lower Centre Street is thrice blessed: It's quietly separate from—yet quite close to—downtown boutiques and restaurants, it's home to the beautiful First Congregational Church, and its inns offer eclectic room configurations spanning a wide price range. One prime example is **Centre Street Inn** (78 Centre St., 508/228-0199 or 800/298-0199, www.centrestreetinn.com, April–early Dec.). Behind the cheerful yellow clapboard sit more than a dozen rooms: spacious ones with queen beds, private baths, and fireplaces ($195–275 d); odd-shaped garrets under the gables on the third floor that share a pair of baths ($155–175); even a tiny single. Before mid-June or after mid-September prices generally drop $80 or more. Though built in the mid-1700s and decorated to evoke a sense of the past—wicker, canopied, or antique brass beds, pine mantles, tasteful stenciling, floral or gingham fabrics—this former merchant's home is no museum. Hospitality comes first, and the owners take great care to make guests feel right at home.

One block south of Main Street is **The Ships Inn** (13 Fair St., 508/228-0040, www.shipsinnnantucket.com, mid-May–late Oct.), occupying a mansion built in 1831 by one of Nantucket's more prominent whaling captains, Obed Starbuck, credited with the discovery of several small islands in the Pacific, including one that still bears the name of his cousin and fellow whaler Valentine Starbuck. Operated as an inn since 1913, it is filled with a dozen rooms that capture the essence of a traditional historic village inn. No two are alike, although most have at least a queen bed and private bath, including one room with a classic lion's claw-footed tub ($195–275 d, peak prices July–mid-Sept.). Solo travelers will find this inn has a pair of the most comfortable single rooms available in town, sharing a good-sized and well-maintained bathroom ($100–135). Besides the customary amenities that typify this price range—in-room mini refrigerators, hair dryers, ironing boards, beach towels, WiFi, continental breakfast—there are a few extras, such as umbrellas for both the beach and bad weather, beach coolers, a guest pantry stocked with refreshments, and a complimentary 5 p.m. cocktail reception in the unpretentious colonial-themed Dory Bar beside the low-key, fine-dining restaurant in the basement.

$250-350

On a quiet block just minutes' walk north of downtown sits **The Carlisle House Inn** (26 N. Water St., 508/228-0720, www.carlislehouse .com, year-round). Built in 1765, this large inn has a relaxed summer-by-the-sea ambience imparted by the friendly staff and the used books in every room, perfect for taking to the beach. Guests favor the pleasant garden as the breakfast room, weather permitting. Hallway carpeting helps deaden traffic from the 13 rooms and suites in the main house; all have TVs, some have DVD players. Four rooms come with huge fireplaces, and all come with mini-refrigerators and the inn's signature sateen-clad terrycloth robes. Double rooms with private baths are $225–295 from mid-June to early October, and $160–245 in the shoulder season before mid-June or after mid-October. The pair of single rooms that share a bath are $95–125 in

high season, $65 in low (there's a double that shares the bath, too, for $155 in summer).

In between downtown and the NHA's Hadwen House stands the **76 Main Street Inn** (508/228-2533 or 800/876-6858, www.76main.com, mid-April–mid-Oct.), occupying a large captain's mansion built 1876–1883. The Victorian style of the first floor—with its original inlaid wood floor and double-width vestibule doors—is carried through to the reproduction furnishings in both the main house and six-room patio annex. While first-floor rooms are best suited to morning people who won't be awakened by the foot traffic to and from the kitchen and front entryway, upper floors are quiet and solidly constructed after having been rehabbed down to the joists and wiring. Rates for double rooms are $285–310 mid-June–mid-Sept., $185–225 in the shoulder season, including continental breakfast. A number of rooms have multiple beds, making this one of the few inns to genuinely welcome families, as opposed to merely tolerating them. Puzzles and games are available, for instance, and breakfasts include plenty of sugar-laden Kellogg's cereals. The sheer size of the premises makes it possible for couples in search of a romantic getaway to coexist with Monopoly-playing kids without friction, though. Additional amenities include central air-conditioning for unobtrusive summer comfort (and bathroom heat lamps for chilly spring and fall days), secluded backyard patio with arbor, and a separate bathroom for guests who have checked out but spend the remainder of the day on the island before leaving.

Half a block west of Centre Street is **The Pineapple Inn** (10 Hussey St., 508/228-9992, www.pineappleinn.com, April–Oct.). The dozen rooms are decorated with all the classicism associated with an upscale New England inn: Oriental carpets over hardwood floors, fishnet lace canopies on the four-poster beds, contemporary English country fabrics, wingback chairs, TVs concealed within armoires, and marble private baths. Eleven of the rooms are $230–375 for a double in high season; the smallest is $215. Arguably the most attractive reason to stay here, however, is that it belongs to the Summer House collection of inns, which entitles high-season guests to take advantage of free daily jitney service to their flagship property in 'Sconset to enjoy either beach or pool, with shade umbrellas, chairs, and towels included.

$350-500

Occupying a large gray-shingled home a block off Main Street is 【 **The Union Street Inn** (7 Union Street, 508/228-9222 or 800/225-5116, www.unioninn.com, April–Oct.). Attractively restored and furnished with antiques as befits its colonial heritage, the inn is professionally managed with a thoroughly cosmopolitan dedication to comfort. The crisp white duvets, tasteful fabrics, and restrained wallpaper designs create an air of understated elegance that surely would earn approval from the Quaker captain who built the place circa 1770. (He might also appreciate that the owners have respected the builders' lack of leveling tools: no doorframe is square at the corners, and no marble will roll across the floor in a straight line.) Half the 12 rooms include working wood-burning fireplaces, and all have fully modern private baths. It's the *only* B&B-style property on the island to provide an honest-to-goodness made-to-order hot breakfast with the bed. It even can be served *in* bed, if you fancy. After Memorial Day doubles run $285–475, but start out at $150–350 for the first six weeks or so of their season (a suite is also available for $255–550). The inn's refreshingly hyperbole-free website deserves special mention for clearly showing the size, shape, and character of every room, too.

If the iPod's designers ever chose to decorate a boutique hotel, the result probably would be similar to 【 **The Veranda House** (3 Step Ln., 877/228-0695 or 508/228-0695, www.theverandahouse.com, May–mid-Dec.). The muted contemporary elegance of the monochromatic decor—snow-white comforters, linen-gray floor coverings on bare hardwood, ebony furnishings, black-and-white toile—is accented with bold splashes of color, flat-screen

DVD-playing TVs, and rainfall showers. The three-story building, greatly expanded over the centuries from its original incarnation as a 17th-century farmhouse, stands head and shoulders above its neighbors, giving its namesake triple tier of wraparound porches unparalleled views over town and harbor. But this place isn't just about good looks and a great lookout. The owners pride themselves on their consummate professional service, in particular their ability to assist you plan, book, or procure just about anything on the island. The four rooms under $300 are small enough to avoid; better to spring for the rooms $369–469 d, or leap into the next price category with a splurge on the spacious top-floor quarters ($569–589 d). Gourmet breakfast and homebaked treats for afternoon tea are of course included, and beach gear is available.

If "guest house" conjures up images of simple accommodations in homey surroundings, the boutique inn found behind the trim white clapboard of 【 **The Nantucket Whaler Guest House** (8 N. Water St., 888/808-6597 or 508/228-6597, www.nantucketwhaler.com, April–mid-Dec.) will certainly make you think again. Don't let the structure's age fool you, either: The stylish interiors of this 1850 residence harmoniously blend the traditional with the contemporary. Think early American and English country furnishings—wooden sleigh, pencil-post, and metal-frame trundle beds, well-upholstered armchairs—on one hand, and riverstone-floor rainfall showers, Aveda personal care products, and flat-screen TVs with iPod-compatible DVD players on the other. Most of the 10 rooms are large one- or two-bedroom suites with fully equipped efficiency kitchens and their own decks or patios; even the two smallest studios offer more room than many other quarters at any price in town. In short, if you want to be surrounded by sophisticated, comfortable, modern luxury, look no farther ($200–400 d, two-bedroom suites up to $695, breakfast *not* included).

The Vanessa Noel Hotel (corner of Chestnut and Centre St., 508/228-5300, www.vanessanoel.com, year-round), was Nantucket's

SLEEP IN AMERICA'S LAST LIGHTSHIP

Without a doubt the most out-of-the-ordinary lodging choice on the island is the **Nantucket Lightship WLV-612** (617/821-6771, www.nantucketlightship.com) a 128-foot ship with distinctive twin masts topped by bulbous light beacons and the name "NANTUCKET" painted in giant white letters along its bright red hull. Usually seen tied up at the Nantucket Boat Basin, the private marina on Commercial Wharf, this rare vessel has been completely retrofitted inside with 4,000 square feet of luxurious living space, including a kitchen equipped for gourmet entertaining, a recreation room, library, and five private staterooms, which together are comfortably able to accommodate up to 12 total guests.

Lightships were designed as stationary navigational aids for locations unsuited to lighthouses. Until they were replaced by lighted navigational buoys and "Texas towers" – deepwater platforms adapted from offshore drilling rigs – over 170 vessels served in the American lightship fleet between 1820 and the 1980s. Only 13 of those ships still exist, three of which served at some point in their careers on Nantucket's South Shoals.

The South Shoals was the most remote of all American lightship stations, over 50 miles from land. It was also quite hazardous, subject to fierce storms that could cripple a vessel and powerful waves that could pound a steel hull to pieces if the ship were to run aground. Even the maritime traffic the lightships tried to pro-tect from harm could pose a danger. Such was the case on the South Shoals in 1935 when a sister cruise liner to the H.M.S. *Titanic* accidentally sank the lightship stationed there after ramming it in the midst of dense fog. Seven of the 11 crewmen were lost.

Built in 1950, WLV-612 replaced the largest and oldest Nantucket lightship, LV-112, now a designated National Historic Landmark owned by the National Lighthouse Museum. WLV-612 has the unusual distinction of being the last lightship to have served on each of its four stations, two on the Pacific coast and two in the Atlantic. Along with its relief vessel, WLV-613 (also now privately owned), this became the last operational lightship in America when it was posted to the South Shoals in 1975.

In 1983, when the shoals were finally marked by a 40-foot buoy, WLV-612 began a checkered retirement before ending up at auction on eBay. The buyers, an environmental lawyer and his wife who fell in love with the colorful ol' tub, spent two years painstakingly turning it into the elegant and tastefully appointed accommodations now available for your enjoyment. Available by the week June–September, you can choose to remain moored at the marina, just steps from town, or at anchor in the harbor off Coatue, with a motorized 26-foot whaleboat tender to shuttle you to shore when desired. Charter rates of $35,000 per week include the services of a chef and the option a special catered event for up to 144 people.

NANTUCKET

first boutique accommodation—literally, since it occupies floors above the shop selling this New York designer's exclusive feminine footwear. It's a bastion of adult comfort (no kids allowed), more contemporary Manhattan than ye olde New England, and it swaddles guests in imported this and luxury that, from fine linens and flat-screen TVs to the minibar stocked with designer water. But many rooms are *tiny*—if you brought more than a clutch purse you'll have no place to put anything, no space to sit or stand, in some cases not even enough leeway to fully open the door. If you're look-ing for a memorable place on which to splurge ($340–480 d high season), the preceding options are better.

$500 and Up

While other properties put the word "beachside" in their names despite being blocks from the water, **The Cliffside Beach Club** genuinely lives up to its moniker (46 Jefferson Ave., 508/228-0618, www.cliffsidebeach.com, May–Nov. 1). Bright and airy, with cathedral ceilings and casual yet classy wood-accented decor, the club's waterfront rooms (some fashioned out of the early 20th-century bathhouses in which patrons traded their formal street attire for bathing costumes) all have views of Nantucket Sound and access to the beach. High season rates for these doubles (mid-June–Sept. 1) are $450–710, and $875–1,745 for condo-sized suites, cottage, and a three-bedroom apartment.

When the late humorist Art Buchwald wrote, tongue in cheek, "I had simple tastes and didn't want anything ostentatious, no matter what it cost me," he might have been referring to **The Summer House** in 'Sconset (17 Ocean Ave., 508/257-4577, www.thesummer house.com, April–Dec.). Comprising a collection of 16 small, plain, wood-beamed tourist cabins refurbished with a white-on-white minimalism accented by hand stenciling, modern tile bathrooms, and flat-panel TVs, this property proposes that perhaps the greatest luxury is none at all ($575–995). This of course will not be to everyone's taste. Given what the same nightly tariff will buy in the way of sensory-overloading glitz in Las Vegas or Waikiki, it may seem faintly ridiculous that so much less can cost so much more. But if you feel that over-the-top bling is fast becoming America's lowest common denominator, then you will probably recognize the bygone simplicity of 'Sconset and the Summer House as priceless rarities. Or you can simply reckon that you're paying a premium for location, exclusivity, privacy, and service: steps from a vast beach, also a pool if you prefer, far from the in-town crowds of summer, more twinkling stars for company at night than you'll see almost anywhere else in America, a manager/concierge who hides her Germanic efficiency behind an affable southern drawl, and good dining on the premises.

If you came to Nantucket aboard a private yacht and snagged a slip at one of the wharves, congratulations for having the best location for enjoying the tranquility of the harbor and the excitement of supping and drinking in town, just steps away. For everyone else who wants to share in the same experience without investing in a floating mobile home, there is **The Cottages** at the Boat Basin (1 Old South Wharf, 866/838-9253 or 508/325-1499, www .thecottagesnantucket.com, May–Nov. 1). These shipshape little studio, one-, two-, and three-bedroom units, all with kitchens and most with decks, are perched right over the water on the same wharves at which yachts are berthed. The net result is like being on a boat but with more headroom and no rocking when the tide turns. In a word, unique ($450–1,000).

Steeply discounted Sunday–Thursday rates for the weeks before Memorial Day and after Columbus Day are usually posted to The Cottages' website in the spring; early birds who can take advantage of these special offers can land a room at a fraction of the high-season rate.

HOTELS

The following are the Nantucket equivalent of standard mainland motels and hotels, albeit wrapped in locally appropriate shingle or brick. Instead of idiosyncratic rooms nestled in every corner of an 18th- or 19th-century mansion, these places have rooms with private entrances, TVs and telephones (most with data ports for laptop modems), private baths, and sometimes two double beds. Many have outdoor swimming pools, and some have full-service restaurants. All those listed here offer a complimentary continental breakfast in high season. The quality of in-room and on-premise amenities varies with price, of course, although the relationship isn't always as direct as you would hope.

Prices at the following places peak almost in tandem with the calendar summer—that is, late June–mid-September, with slight differences by a week or so at most.

$250-350

Nantucket Inn and Conference Center (1 Miller's Way at Macy's Lane opposite the airport terminal, 508/228-6900 or 800/321-8484, www.nantucketinn.net) is the closest thing to a modern hotel in ambience, amenities, and decor. It has a pool, restaurant (full breakfast included), hourly downtown shuttle, and courtesy pickups for Steamship Authority passengers available in season; open April–October and Friday–Monday during first weekend of December. Rates are $265–360 (off-season rates drop about $100, and kids under 18 stay free in parents' room at any time).

Jared Coffin House (29 Broad St., 508/228-2400 or 800/248-2405, www.jared coffinhouse.com, summer rates $150–450 d, off-season rates as low as $125) is a relative steal for its center-of-town location, historic decor, and restaurant. Open year-round.

$350-500

The Beachside at Nantucket (30 N. Beach St., 508/228-2241 or 800/322-4433, www .thebeachside.com, $325–420 d), a 90-room 1960s-era motel renovated in 2000, is a five-minute walk to Jetties Beach. Open mid-April–early December.

$500 and Up

The White Elephant (50 Easton St., 800/475-2637 or 508/228-2500, www.whiteelephant hotel.com, $550–1,700) is a classic deluxe seaside hotel beside the harbor boat basin, with patios and porches under striped awnings, pool, fitness room, library, croquet, jitney service to beaches, shuttle to ferry, upscale cosmopolitan restaurant, and lounge entertainment. Open May–October.

The Wauwinet (120 Wauwinet Rd., 508/228-0145 or 800/426-8718, www.wau winet.com, $600–1,700 d) is a grand Great Gatsby–era seaside inn offering sophisticated casual relaxation amid antique-filled luxury (under the same ownership as the White Elephant). There's a concierge, video library (order a title and it's delivered with hot popcorn), tennis, croquet, bicycles, water sports, jitney service to town, two private beaches on Nantucket Bay and the open ocean, and a restaurant with the island's top wine cellar. Open April–early December. The Wauwinet regularly woos travel magazine editors (no, not me) with freebies, and coincidentally gets rave reviews all over the place.

Food

True to its nature as a high-end resort island, Nantucket has many small, upscale restaurants serving fine food and drink. Fortunately, in the past few years the overall quality of dining around town has caught up to the prices. While you'll still pay extra for just about everything because the island exists within an inflated economic bubble, it is increasingly possible to be rewarded with true culinary excellence. Nevertheless if paying $150 for dinner for two—before wine or tip—isn't in your daily budget, stick to the pizza-and-beer joints. Or, do what many of the locals do: Order takeout from Cape Cod, to be picked up at the airport when the half-hourly flights from Hyannis come in.

BREAKFAST AND BRUNCH

Fortunately, eating well in the morning on Nantucket doesn't have to break the bank. That's especially true if you step on over to **C Black-Eyed Susan's** (10 India St. at Center, 508/325-0308, www.black-eyed susans.com, 7 A.M.–1 P.M. daily mid-May–Oct., varied schedule April–mid-May and Nov.–early Dec., cash only). The food is creative, fresh, and filling, and the ambience is closer to that of a college town café than a fussy old Nantucket institution. No reservations are accepted and lines form on weekends, so arrive early to put your name on the list, and they'll assign you a time to come back and eat up.

Another local sit-down favorite is **Arno's at 41 Main Street** (508/228-7001, www.arnos .net, breakfast, lunch, and dinner daily April–Dec.), especially if you're a late riser—breakfast is served daily until 2 P.M. If great cinnamon buns sound better, head over to the

Fog Island Café (7 S. Water St., 508/228-1818, www.fogisland.com, 7 A.M.–9 P.M. Mon.–Fri., 7 A.M.–1 P.M. Sun. mid-May–Oct., call for schedule April–mid-May), which also serves reasonably priced omelets, fruit pancakes, cheddar-laced veggie home fries, and other fine egg dishes and griddle fare.

If you're staying on the fringes of town, you needn't go all the way into the center for good chow: **Something Natural** (50 Cliff Rd. north of the Oldest House, 508/228-0504, www.somethingnatural.com, 8 A.M.–6:30 P.M. daily late April–mid-Oct.), **Nantucket Bake Shop** (79 Orange St. several blocks south of Main, 508/228-2797, 6:30 A.M.–5 P.M. Mon.–Sat. April–Thanksgiving), and the **Nantucket Bagel Company** (5 West Creek Rd. near the Milestone Rotary, 508/228-6461, 5:30 A.M.–3:30 P.M. daily July–mid-Sept., 5:30 A.M.–2:30 P.M. daily otherwise) are all worthwhile stops for takeout coffee and breakfast bakery goods.

When longtime residents speak of "real" restaurants—as opposed to all those tourist joints—it's usually the 【 **Downyflake** (18 Sparks Ave., 508/228-4533, 6 A.M.–2 P.M. Mon.–Sat. and 6 A.M.–noon Sun., closed for four weeks in Feb. and/or Mar., cash only), across from the Stop & Shop plaza, that they have firmly in mind. It offers diner food with a Nantucket twist: chowder and cod-fish cakes are on the menu alongside burgers, dogs, BLTs, and tuna salad. All at genuine diner prices—consequently, it's hugely popular. And it's super casual, just as you'd expect from a place with a giant doughnut out front. Jeans-clad waitresses banter with the regulars, patrons at the Formica-top counter read papers or watch the cable TV slung on the back wall, and kids in high chairs eat cereal with their hands. Those doughnuts are legendary, and the light, fluffy omelets are worth the 20-minute walk from in-town lodgings.

CASUAL DINING

If you'd prefer to hoist a few cold ones over a burger plate or fish-and-chips, rather than decide between smoked tomato broth and truffle butter sauce, check out **The Rose and Crown** (23 S. Water Street, 508/228-2595, www.theroseandcrown.com, 11:30 A.M.–1 A.M. daily Apr.–Dec.). After a square meal at a great price, hang out at the lively bar with scads of young seasonal workers.

Instead of a TV in the background, **The Brotherhood of Thieves** (23 Broad Street, 508/228-2551, www.brotherhoodofthieves.com, 11:30 A.M.–12 A.M. Mon.–Sat. March–Jan., 12 P.M.–10 .M. Sun., closed Feb.–mid-Mar.) accompanies its pub grub with regular live folk music. Named after a riot-inciting 1842 accusation leveled against island clergy by abolitionist Stephen Foster, this 19th-century whalers'-bar-turned-bohemian-hangout is a true local institution. The burgers, sandwiches, and seafood are eclipsed by an extensive bar menu of cordials, spiked coffees, cognacs, single malt Scotches, and other fine spirits.

Finally, since most of the pizza passed off on tourists down by the ferry piers is a waste of your time and money (you're much better off waiting until you get back to Hyannis), impatient pizza lovers would do well to bike out to **Pi Pizzeria** (11 West Creek Rd. near the Milestone Rotary, 508/228-1130, www.pipizzeria.com, 11:30 A.M.–2:30 P.M. and 5:30–9 P.M. Wed.–Mon. April–Sept., Wed.–Sun. Oct.–Mar.). The classic thin-crusted Neapolitan flavor combinations are made with organic flour and fresh ingredients and baked in a wood-burning brick oven. The prices are also just like on the mainland.

Not every restaurant in town induces sticker shock. A prime example is the casual 【 **Cambridge Street Victuals** (12 Cambridge St., 508/228-7109, www.cambridgestreetnantucket.com, 5–10 P.M. daily April–Dec., $10–25), basically a big, friendly, boisterous bar with kick-ass food. The menu trawls the spicy cuisines of the world for bright, fiery flavors. That means Caribbean jerk chicken, Moroccan-spiced tagine, lamb schwarma, and pad Thai, among others. As the home to the island's only in-house meat smoker, it is also a great place to feed your cravings for pulled pork and other barbecued meats. Given the portions, grazing on salads and appetizers is a perfectly appropriate way to save room for the excellent sour cream–style key lime pie, or just another round of Nantucket's own Cisco microbrews. Those kinetic candy-colored liquid-acrylic paintings in the bar area are the handiwork of local artist and clothing designer Hannah Stone, more of whose work may be seen at www.gohannahstone.com.

More good value for your dining dollar may be found at **⟨ Black-Eyed Susan's** (10 India St. at Center, 508/325-0308, www .black-eyedsusans.com, 6–10 P.M. Mon.–Sat. mid-May–Oct., varied schedule April–mid-May and Nov.–early Dec., $22–28, cash only). Like the breakfasts, their dinners reflect the chef-owners' appreciation for fresh veggies and ethnic spices—it's world music for the mouth. Seafood lovers and vegetarians who care about taste more than candlelight and starched linen will be enchanted. Susan's also boasts a commendable policy of offering plenty of dishes in generous but money-saving half portions.

Thanks to Nantucket's high-priced dining, sushi is actually one of the less expensive meals to be had. Just ask the local cops who grab their grub at **Sushi by Yoshi** (2 E. Chestnut St., 508/228-1801, www .sushibyyoshi.com, 11:30 A.M.–2:30 P.M. and 4:30 P.M.–close daily Apr.–Oct., $9–37), a handkerchief-sized spot opposite the police station. *Maki* rolls prepared by the Tokyo-born and -trained chef and his crew are the mainstay, but Yoshi also offers inexpensive noodle dishes, cooked salmon and veggies over rice, shrimp tempura, and chicken teriyaki, among other items. Given its size, there's a brisk business in takeout orders—helpfully there are benches on the sidewalk opposite as well as a block away facing the harbor—but there are a few indoor tables and petite sushi bar, too (BYOB).

The nearby **Centre Street Bistro** (29 Centre St., 508/228-8470, www.nantuck etbistro.com, 8 A.M.–1 P.M. Sat.–Sun., 11:30 A.M.–2 P.M. Mon. and Wed.–Fri., and 6–10 P.M. Wed.–Mon. mid-June–early Sept., 8 A.M.–1 P.M. Sun., 11:30 A.M.–2 P.M. Wed.–Sat., and 6 P.M.–close Wed.–Sun. mid-Sept.–early June, $19–28) is yet another of the most reasonable in-town eateries, with generous risotto, pasta, and fresh seafood dishes, a pleasant little sidewalk patio for al fresco dining in summer, and an extensive wine list. They're also open for lunch weekdays and brunch on weekends.

FINE DINING

Reservations are typically recommended in peak season for nearly all the fine-dining restaurants in town. If you prefer to put your trust in serendipity just be prepared for the likelihood of a long wait, although waiting for your table at the bar is a good introduction to a major part of Nantucket society. Or consider dining early: Since most reservations will be for 7 P.M. or later, parties of two who promise hostesses not to linger for hours over a meal usually have no difficulty being seated promptly at the very start of the evening dinner service.

Casual elegance and good eating can both be found at **Cioppino's** (20 Broad St., 508/228-4622, www.cioppinos.com, 5:30 P.M.–10 P.M. daily May–mid-Oct., $16.50–28), but without making you feel you have to whisper or wear a black tie. Personable, attentive service and conversation-friendly small rooms in a beautiful old house—or breezy tables on the patio—are a perfect match for the flavorful Mediterranean-influenced dishes and real San Francisco–style cioppino (seafood stew). Sunday–Thursday, the prix fixe two-course early-bird specials ($28.50) are also a great way to save money without resorting to sandwiches or pizza.

Adorned in shades of white and gray, **⟨ Water Street** (12 S. Water St., 508/228-7040, www.waterstreetnantucket.com, 6 P.M.–9:30 P.M. Mon.–Sat. mid-April–late May and early Sept.–Dec., 6–10 P.M. daily Memorial Day–Labor Day, $26–44) is not just one of the most chic of the island's eateries in its appearance—it also one of the best, period. While portions may be modest, the sensational tastes are anything but. Elements combine on the plate for incredible effect, undoubtedly helped by the kitchen's efforts to use as much organic produce and local, sustainably-harvested products as possible. Even the wine list has organic and biodynamic selections. The menu would not be out of place in an Italian *ristorante,* with the first of its three savory courses highlighting *crudo* dishes such as raw oysters, fish ceviche, or lamb tartare, a second course of soup, salad, or handmade pasta, and finally the main entree of fresh seafood, meat, or poultry. The ethereally light and soft gnocchi, made daily, are good enough to require a double take just to be certain that it's Nantucket outside the window and not Siena. If you're looking for food that will make you swoon, this is the place.

Open year-round is the **Boarding House** (12 Federal St., 508/228-9622, www.board inghouse-pearl.com, 5:30 P.M.–close daily and 10 A.M.–2 P.M. Sat.–Sun. late May–early Oct., hours vary Apr.–mid-May and mid-Oct.–mid-Dec., $24–39). The bar and bistro scene here is a cornerstone of island gay social life, and the relaxed dining room is at the forefront of contemporary but classic cuisine with light but intensely flavored stocks and sauces, perfectly prepared fresh vegetables, and presentations as wonderful to view as to eat. Up the street, **21 Federal** (508/228-2121, www.21federal .com, 5:30 P.M.–9 P.M. daily mid-May–mid-Oct., and Thanksgiving–early Dec., $28–37) is one of the better local practitioners of New American regional cooking, emphasizing seafood and New England fare.

Regional cooking is also the star at **(C American Seasons** (80 Centre St., www .americanseasons.com, 508/228-7111, 6 P.M.–close daily June–Aug., 6 P.M.–close Thurs.–Tues. Sept.–early Oct., hours vary Apr.–May and mid-Oct.–early Dec., $26–34), set in a modest home among the graceful old inns at the foot of the First Congregational Church a few blocks north of Broad Street. Looking at the menu of dishes drawn from the traditions of different parts

of the country, you'd be forgiven for feeling a tad skeptical. How can anyone pull off such varied fare? Cast aside your doubts. If you care about good food—sushi-grade fish, pick-of-the-market produce, and exceptional house breads—you've come to the right spot. The award-winning wine list doesn't forget to include good affordable choices for patrons lacking trust funds, and the desserts are not only visually delightful, but scrumptious as well. The dining room tables, each representing a different board game, were painted by local artist Joanna Kane; Kevin Paulson did the murals on the walls.

Tucked up on the second floor of a house facing the harbor, **(C Òran Mór** (2 S. Beach St., www.oranmorbistro.com, 508/228-8655, 6–9 P.M. Tues.–Sat. late April–early Dec., 6 P.M.–close daily mid-May–early Oct., $32–39) is a delightful example of a contemporary American bistro. At first the menu reads like a slightly exotic garden and pantry tour, with various wild mushrooms, pickled vegetables, unusual chutneys, Asian spices, and uncommon grains and legumes. But while the top-grade ingredients may be unfamiliar, these are dishes that you do in fact know—grilled steak, roasted fowl, sautéed fish. You just get to rediscover them in deceptively simple yet novel new guises, the recognizable flavors coming together in unexpected, and utterly captivating, combinations. It's the sort of place where the initial thought of, "why didn't I think of that?" is quickly followed by, "who would have ever thought of that?"

Sitting virtually in the harbor, **(C Straight Wharf Restaurant** (6 Harbor Square, 508/228-4499, www.straightwharfres taurant.com, 11:30 A.M.–2 P.M. and 5:30–10 P.M. daily June–early Sept., 5:30–10 P.M. Tues.–Sun. mid-Sept.–mid-Oct., $25–40) has been a fixture of Nantucket dining for about as long as anyone can remember, but has new energy thanks to the young chef-couple who recently took it over. The old warhorse was reborn in 2006 as one of the state's top dining spots after securing the talents of Amanda Lydon and Gabriel Frasca, a pair of critically acclaimed Boston chefs. Under barn-like beams draped in midnight blue cloth sprinkled with stars, enjoy classic seaside fare—chowder, clam bake, grilled chicken and fish, ice cream floats—served with unparalleled gourmet flair. The seafood positively sings with freshness, fruit and produce is as passionately ripe as summer itself, and the desserts are dreamy. In a word, wow.

OUTSIDE THE HISTORIC DISTRICT

Off the day-trippers' beaten path is a reliable local favorite: **The SeaGrille** (45 Sparks Ave. by the Milestone Rotary, 508/325-5700, www.theseagrille.com, 11:30 A.M.–2:30 P.M. and 5:30 P.M.–9 P.M. daily year-round, $9.95–24.95), about a 20-minute walk from Main Street. It's a family-friendly surf-and-turf place specializing, as the name suggests, more in the surf, but the pasta and veal dishes are handled as well as the offerings of lobster, fillets, chowders, and steamers.

Out by the airport (or on the way to 'Sconset) is one of the island's most affordable dining options: **El Rincon Salvadoreño** (17 Old South Rd., 508/332-4749, 7 A.M.–10 P.M. daily, $6.50–14), hidden almost entirely from view behind tall hedges. True to its name, the menu at this casual eatery offers a piece of El Salvador, including such *comidas típicas guanacas* as pupusas, pastelles, and tamales. There are also Mexican selections—burritos, quesadillas, fajitas—and hearty platters of pork and beef, all authentic enough to make you cry, *¡Vamanos a Nantucket!*

'SCONSET

Nearly hidden from the street by ivy-draped trellises, **The Chanticleer** (9 New Ln., 508/257-4499, www.thechanticleer.net, noon–2 P.M. Tues.–Sun. mid-June–Aug.,

6–10 P.M. daily, mid-June–early Oct., schedule varies May–mid-June, $29–39) has long been a Nantucket icon. It has changed owners more than once since it first started serving meals in 1909, and it just keeps getting better and better. In keeping with the latest trends in Parisian dining, the brasserie menu updates traditional French cuisine with a modern awareness of the health and worldly tastes of today's well-traveled food lover. That means fragrant, savory broths, aiolis, rémoulades, and ragouts are favored over artery-seizing cream sauces, and great care is given to sourcing ingredients at the peak of their natural season. The tables under the rose-draped arbor in the flower-filled garden are rightly ranked among the most romantic on the island.

Al fresco dining doesn't get much more casual than **The Beachside Bistro** (17 Ocean Ave., 508/257-4542, www.thesummerhouse.com, 11:30 A.M.–3 P.M. and 6–10 P.M. daily late June–mid-Oct., $33–39), right on the sandy margin below the Summer House cottage resort. Its location beside the resort's outdoor pool, within the sight and sound of the Atlantic surf, means patrons are more likely to be in T-shirts and flip-flops than dinner jackets and designer dresses. Since this is Nantucket, though, casual doesn't mean cheap in any sense of the word: Burgers are made from Wagyu beef, salads are composed from the freshest local mixed greens, fish is all sushi-grade, and the lobster roll bun is actually brioche. Large umbrellas over the tables provide shade when the sun's up, and the ever-attentive well-tanned staff will fire up space heaters and break out blankets if the air turns too cool. Whether the food lives up to the prices is highly debatable, but the setting is truly delightful. At the very least, let the bartenders mix you one of their rejuvenating elixirs in the golden glow of late afternoon and watch all earthly cares ebb away with the tide.

NANTUCKET

Information and Services

ATMs

Automated teller machines with 24-hour access are found at 20 Federal Street opposite the Visitor Services building; at the Nantucket Bank offices (one is at 2 Orange Street just around the corner from Main and the others are out near the Milestone Rotary at 104 Pleasant Street and 1 Amelia Drive); on the left side of the Pacific Club building at the foot of Main; and in the Steamship Authority terminal (except when the night watchman is out doing his 15-minute rounds). During regular business hours, additional ATMs are found in the Pacific National Bank on the main square, at both the Grand Union and Stop & Shop supermarkets, and at the airport.

MEDIA AND INFORMATION

To immerse yourself in local news, pick up one of the two island weeklies, either Wednesday's *Nantucket Independent* (online edition at www .nantucketindependent.com), or Thursday's *The Inquirer and Mirror* (known to some as the "Inky Mirror," www.ack.net), founded in 1821 and now owned by a subsidiary of the News Corporation.

Are you one of those public radio listeners who suffers withdrawal if you go a week without *Car Talk, Fresh Air,* or the *BBC World News?* No worries, you should have no trouble tuning in to your favorite NPR shows broadcast over the local transmitter for **WNAN-FM 91.1,** part of the Cape and Islands radio network affiliated with WGBH in Boston, even from the terribly cheap little bedside radio

alarm clocks found in many local accommodations. (Oh, and Click and Clack come on at 10 A.M. Saturday, and noon Sunday.)

Like the Vineyard, Nantucket is also home to **Plum TV** (Channel 22), the upscale local access cable station that's part of a network familiar to anyone who has spent time channel-surfing in resort communities around the country.

The downtown **Visitor Services and Information Bureau** (25 Federal St., 508/228-0925) should top your itinerary if you're looking for brochures. Many of the same brochures and lodging listings are also available at the **Nantucket Chamber of Commerce** (48 Main St., 2nd floor, 508/228-1700, www.nantuck etchamber.org), whose very polished *Official Guide* makes an attractive free keepsake (or you can call ahead and order a copy for $7 postage and handling within the U.S.) and also helps in scoping out accommodations.

PUBLIC RESTROOMS

Bathrooms are found behind the Visitor Services and Information Bureau, around on the East Chestnut Street side of the building; on Straight Wharf by the Hy-Line ferry dock; and in the airport terminal. During the summer season, facilities are also opened up at Children's, Dionis, Jetties, and Surfside Beaches.

MEDICAL EMERGENCIES

The island's only year-round, round-the-clock, full-service health-care provider is **Nantucket Cottage Hospital** (57 Prospect St., just west of the Old Mill, 508/228-1200).

Getting There and Around

PUBLIC TRANSIT

Between the third Saturday in May and the end of Columbus Day weekend in October, the **Nantucket Regional Transit Authority** (508/228-7025, www.shuttlenantucket.com) revs up regular public bus service around town and to 'Sconset. From June through early or mid-September (depending on the route) service increases in frequency and additional routes are added to the airport, beaches, and the western end of the island.

Buses out to Madaket depart hourly from Broad Street in front of the Peter Foulger Museum (every half hour between the end of June and Labor Day weekend), while all other inland routes depart from Salem Street at the corner of Washington, around the back of the Main Street building with the famous compass rose painted on the side.

Those other routes include three different 'Sconset shuttles; Miacomet and Mid-Island Loop shoppers' shuttles, which run every 15–30 minutes to various peripheral commercial and residential areas; and an airport shuttle running every 20 minutes 8 A.M.–6 P.M. daily. Find route maps almost everywhere tourist brochures are displayed. Shuttle stops are marked with gray poles with red and maroon stripes. Except for the airport route, all shuttles operate until 11 P.M. or even later, depending on the route.

Fares are $1 in town and $2 for long-distance destinations. If you intend to hop on and off a half-dozen times a day over a long weekend, purchase a one-, three-, or seven-day pass ($7–20) from any bus driver. Thirty-day, full-season, senior, commuter, and student passes ($40–80) are also available from the NRTA office (3 E. Chestnut St., directly behind the Visitor Services building) during weekday

summer sunset as seen from Nantucket

business hours. Tired or out-of-shape cyclists will be happy to know all the NRTA buses are equipped with bike carriers.

Warm weather also prompts the NRTA to commence its **beach shuttles** to Jetties and Surfside Beaches from in front of the Peter Foulger Museum and Salem Street stops, respectively. These are weather-dependent: Rain storms keeps them grounded, and a cold spell may delay their start times. Ideally, however, shuttles run daily, every 30–40 minutes, 10 A.M.–5:30 P.M., mid-June–Labor Day.

A complete Rider's Guide is available for download from the NRTA website.

BIKE RENTALS

By far the best way to avoid the frustration of summertime traffic is to avoid contributing to it. Bicycles are justly popular, given the relatively short distances you're likely to be traveling; from the steamship piers, every beach is within a nine-mile radius, and most lodgings are within just a mile or two. Level terrain and five paved bike paths radiating in all directions from town are added incentives. Mind the stiff winds, though—they speed dehydration, and a thirsty cyclist is soon a very exhausted cyclist (you'll find fountains on two of the bike paths, but a personal water supply is always a good idea). Rentals are available right off the boat: **Young's Bicycle Shop** (on Steamboat Wharf, 508/228-1151, www.youngsbicycleshop .com) and **Nantucket Bike Shop** (on both Steamboat and Straight Wharves, 508/228-1999 or 800/770-3088, www.nantucketbike shop.com). Ever-friendly and helpful, Young's is open from March to December, while the Nantucket Bike Shop is open mid-April to mid-October. Both offer a standard 24-hour day rate or, for day-trippers, "shop day" rate (i.e., bring it back before the shop closes). Rentals by the week, month, or season are also available; the longer the rental, the greater the discount off the daily rate. A couple of blocks from Steamboat Wharf is **Cook's Cycle** (6 S. Beach St., 508/228-3644), a small, friendly shop next to (and affiliated with) Affordable

Rentals car rentals. If you're staying out near the airport, you may find it most convenient to rent from **Island Bike Co.** (25 Old South Rd., 508/228-4070 or 877/228-4070, www .islandbike.com). Another option if you're not downtown is to call **Easy Riders Bicycle Rentals** (508/325-2722, www.easyriders bikerentals.com) for island-wide delivery of top-notch bikes at very competitive prices, particularly for a week or longer (delivery is free with multi-day rentals).

No matter where you rent, anticipate shelling out $25–30 a day for either a hybrid fat-tire touring bike or all-terrain mountain bike. Full-seat and front-post suspension systems and ergonomic or gel seats have also become standard at island rental shops, so don't let the sight of all those bumpy cobblestones deter you from trying a little pedaling. Helmets and locks are tossed in for free—local law requires all riders age 16 or under to wear a helmet. Everyone also carries kids' bikes, child seats for adult bikes, baby trailers, jogging strollers, trail-a-bike attachments, and of course tandem bicycles. (Island Bike also rents in-line skates, if you can find a surface smooth enough to use them.) Most also offer free road service if you get a flat, and Young's offers discounts for Hostelling International members.

TAXIS

Taxi rates are based primarily on a flat-rate system based on specific point-to-point routes: $6 for a single passenger traveling anywhere within town, for instance, or $11 from downtown to the airport, two fare zones away. Each additional passenger costs another $1. Mileage fees are charged only for cross-island trips that exceed the established base rates. After 1 A.M. surcharges are added (up to an extra $5 3–6 A.M.). Drivers are also allowed to charge for more than two pieces of baggage, bikes, pets, and driving on dirt roads, if they want.

If you need to be fetched from outside of town, it wouldn't be uncommon to find yourself waiting an hour, so schedule pickups as far in advance as practical. You'll find cab stands at the airport and both ferry piers; a list of over

30 taxi operators—including those that take bikes—is available from Visitor Services.

CAR AND MOPED RENTALS

If you arrive by ferry, you'll find all the downtown bike shops also offer car or scooter rentals, or both. **Young's Bicycle Shop** (on Steamboat Wharf, 508/228-1151, www.youngsbicycle shop.com) offers cars, Jeeps, and SUVs from March through December, and generally tries to beat everyone else's prices by at least a dollar or two. **Nantucket Bike Shop** (on both Steamboat and Straight Wharves, 508/228-1999 or 800/770-3088, www.nantucket bikeshop.com) offers single- and double-seat scooters. And **Affordable Rentals** (6 South Beach St., 877/235-3500 or 508/228-3501, www.affordablerentalsofnantucket.com) offers cars, Jeeps, convertibles, *and* mopeds, April–October.

If you arrive by plane, or simply are staying out by the airport, the rest of the island's rental agencies are found in the airport terminal or on Macy's Lane between the airport and adjacent Nantucket Inn. These include **Hertz** (508/228-9421 or 800/654-3131, www.hertz.com), **Nantucket Island Rent-A-Car** (508/228-9989 or 800/508-9972, www.nantucketislandrentacar.com), and **Windmill Auto Rental** (508/228-1227 or 800/228-1227, www.nantucketautorental.com).

All of the companies mentioned here offer to pick you up almost anywhere on the island for no charge. Summer rates hover from around $100 a day for a compact car to $250 a day for a 4-by-4 sport utility vehicle; off-season, everybody halves their prices. Toys such as Jeeps are generally off-limits to anyone under 30.

BEACH DRIVING

Four-wheeling on any beach requires a permit between May and October, either from the local police at the special permit window on East Chestnut Street behind their South Water Street headquarters (508/228-1212, $100 for off-island vehicles), or, for driving within the Coskata-Coatue Wildlife Refuge, from The Trustees of Reservations ($125 per year; discounts for Trustees family-level members). Trustees permits are available from the Wauwinet Gatehouse at the Refuge entrance (508/228-0006, late May–Oct. 15). Even with all the proper permissions, beach driving may be heavily restricted or even completely denied in some areas through mid-August, when endangered shore birds finally leave their nests.

Most rental vehicles capable of driving in sand come with one or both of the necessary beach permits, but be sure to ask if that's why you're renting in the first place.

NANTUCKET

BACKGROUND

The Land

The land beneath Massachusetts has suffered a lot of abuse over the last billion years, having been thoroughly folded, spindled, and mutilated by the forces of plate tectonics. Throughout the Paleozoic Era, 350–570 million years ago, continental plates carrying the bulk of the present North and South American, European, and African landmasses alternately split apart and rammed together, finally fusing into the supercontinent known as Pangaea. At the beginning of the Mesozoic Era, some 225 million years ago, the tectonic convection that once smooshed Massachusetts into Scotland and Morocco shifted gears, opening up a rift in Pangaea that eventually became the Atlantic Ocean. Ever since then Massachusetts has remained on the trailing edge of this big planetary demolition derby. As the Atlantic widened, mountains were born in Nevada and California; New England simply eroded.

In recent geological time—the last couple of million years—a score of ice ages have come and gone, abetting the erosion process by grinding away the peaks of the old Paleozoic mountain ranges. But the glaciers were only borrowers, not thieves. When they retreated north, they left behind everything they'd taken from these central uplands and then some. Cape Cod's long limb of glacial drift and the offshore islands of Nantucket

© KATHRYN OSGOOD

and Martha's Vineyard are partially such remnants, fashioned 14,000–21,000 years ago by the great Laurentide ice sheet of the Wisconsin glacial stage.

Compared to the billion-year-old landscape of most of Massachusetts, Cape Cod is thus a veritable newborn. It also has a relatively short life expectancy for a landmass—the Atlantic Ocean may erase the Cape from New England's rocky coast within another 5,000 years. That's based on an extrapolation of today's rate of loss, but rising sea levels caused by global warming could cut that figure dramatically. In fact, rising seas currently claim nearly three times as much acreage every year as surf erosion, and predictions are that storm tides will produce increasing flooding in such low-lying areas as downtown Provincetown.

As for the erosion, if it happened any faster it would be like watching Alaskan glaciers calving icebergs; the 14-mile stretch of cliffs and barrier beaches along the Cape's outer shore already recede an average of several feet a year. For a graphic illustration of how dynamic these shorelines really are, check out the short film presented at the Cape Cod National Seashore's Province Lands visitors center, or the Cape Cod Museum of Natural History's before-and-after photos of Chatham's storm-punctured outer bar.

MORAINES

The advancing and retreating glacial lobes of the last ice age are responsible for giving the region its current topography. Three discreet lobes from this continental ice sheet covered Cape Cod and what's now the surrounding continental shelf; Nantucket, Martha's Vineyard, and the Elizabeth Islands around Buzzards Bay are evidence of these lobes' farthest advance. Like a carpet wrinkled by sliding heavy furniture across it, sedimentary layers up to 100 million years old in the glacier's path were folded into ridges, or moraines, that now form the backbone of these islands.

The rocky spine of unsorted stone and sediment along upper and middle Cape is another such end moraine, bulldozed into its present

location during a brief southward push in the thick ice sheet's 15,000-year meltdown. Known to geologists as the Sandwich moraine, the ridge is now topped by the Mid-Cape Highway, U.S. 6, and in selected conservation areas its uneven slopes provide the region's most challenging mountain biking. South of the moraine, the landscape is characterized by outwash plains formed after the glacier resumed melting, releasing everything from fine-grained clay to gravel and larger boulders.

OUTWASH PLAINS

When the two-mile-thick glacier finally began to melt faster than the icebox up north could replenish it, the runoff spread outwash plains of glacial drift—all the rocks, sand, and soil scraped up and ferried southward in the great ice sheet—like skirts around the hips of these terminal moraines. (Think of a 1,000-foot-thick ice sponge that's been wiped across all of New England, sopping up a sample of every bedrock surface it crosses. When that ice melts, it's just as if you gave that sponge a squeeze.) Some of the material deposited has been matched to unique bedrock formations, such as the Brighton volcanics—igneous rocks dating back to the ancient heyday of a Boston-area volcano. These are good indicators of the path of the original glacial advance, southeast from Canada.

Probably the best way to experience these glacial features is by bicycle; you can actually feel them in your leg muscles. On Martha's Vineyard, for example, most of the paved bike paths inscribe the great level outwash plain filling the island interior, but ride out of the port of Vineyard Haven and you can't miss the slope of the plain's eastern edge, collapsed after the retreat of the glacial ice like a row of books that has lost its bookend.

Outwash deposits give Nantucket, too, a low, flat profile. But there's actually a big difference between the island's oldest plain, spread evenly in front of where the glacier's leading edge used to be (a clear shot on a bike from Nantucket Town east to Siasconset), and the dips and curves of the younger plain on the western end of the island, along the bike path to Madaket. This more varied terrain was formed as the receding Laurentide glacier shed enormous chunks of ice and then buried them in glacial drift too heavy to be borne out to the coastline (then some 70–80 miles south) by meltwater streams.

As these big ice cubes melted, the surface of this newly formed plain was left with kettles—holes or pockets of subsidence, sometimes many acres in size. When deep enough to reach the water table, these depressions form distinctive, nearly circular ponds. Gull Pond in Wellfleet, Cliff Pond in Nickerson State Park, Nantucket's Head of Hummock Pond, and Uncle Seth's Pond on Martha's Vineyard are all prime examples.

RISING WATERS

As the ice age ended, rising oceans swollen from melting ice inundated the conifer- and tundra-covered continental shelf around the Cape and Islands, submerging habitat once roamed by mastodons and mammoths, according to dental records dredged up offshore. By about 6,000 years ago, the ocean had filled Nantucket Sound and Cape Cod Bay and begun biting away at the Islands' moraines, creating prominent marine scarps at Nantucket's Sankaty Head and the Vineyard's Aquinnah Cliffs. The geologic record revealed at these sites is hardly as accessible as in the walls of the Grand Canyon, though—at Sankaty Head, the Laurentide glacial deposits are tossed with sands a good 100,000 years older, while Aquinnah interleaves folds of Tertiary and Cretaceous strata 5–75 million years old.

Although the rate at which the oceans are rising has slowed considerably over the last few thousand years, the water is still creeping upward (and may in fact accelerate if predictions about human-induced global warming prove accurate). The shorelines of Nantucket and Martha's Vineyard already lose an annual average of about 30 feet to the tides and winter storms; by some estimates, tiny Nantucket will be a mere shoal under the waves within the next 700–800 years.

Land loss isn't even or gradual, by the way: some shores may be stable for years, then lose a hundred yards in a single storm season. In the meantime, the Islands are migrating slowly toward Cape Cod, as northbound currents relocate a portion of the material eroded from beaches and shore cliffs. This "longshore drift" is most visible in the lengthening of the finger-like sandbars at Nantucket's Great Point and the Vineyard's Cape Poge.

CLIMATE

Weather on both Cape Cod and the Islands is governed by the ocean. Slow to heat up, and equally slow to cool down, the surrounding saltwater acts as a vast heat sump that keeps local temperatures from hitting the extremes recorded around the rest of the state—much the same way that the air in your home dilutes the effect of either your freezer or oven when the door is held open. The briny reservoir is itself warmed by the 50-mile-wide Gulf Stream current, which comes pouring up the eastern seaboard from the Caribbean and brushes within a few dozen miles of the Islands' southern shores en route to northern Europe. Despite the Islands' being surrounded by water, humidity is kept at bay by the sea breezes that both residents and innkeepers rely upon to make even August heat waves quite tolerable—which is why many island lodgings offer no air-conditioning.

Remember that since the wind in this region is always cooler coming off the ocean, this means that if you go out sportfishing on a broiling, 90°F August afternoon, you'll probably regret it if you don't dress for 68°F. In winter, when the prevailing wind shifts around to the northeast, a simple waterfront walk can become downright painful.

Spring, a quiet season of daffodils and days that call for a sweater, comes earlier and lasts longer on the Islands than on the Cape, with average temperatures in the upper 40s and low 50s. **Summers** are ideal, with the average high for July and August pegged at only about 80°F on the Cape and Martha's Vineyard, and in the mid-70s on Nantucket, although increasingly stifling traffic conditions will make drivers feel anything but cool and relaxed.

Early **fall** is valued not for its foliage but for

Quissett Harbor in Woods Hole, Cape Cod

its tranquility, as the hectic hordes of summer visitors return to school and jobs. Discerning or contrarian folks, who don't mind that restaurants may be short-staffed or that some public shuttles no longer run, will find their stay rewarded with warm weather (in the 60s and low 70s), slightly fewer rain days than in the rest of the year, and water temperatures nearly unchanged from balmy August.

After October, cool nights become downright chilly, and short days usher in brisk lashings of **winter.** December boasts the lowest lows—down to 0°F. While January features a brief warm spell, it and February are overall the coldest months, with temperatures dipping down to the 20s through early March. Though usually spared the heavy snowfalls that routinely blanket roadways from Boston to Western Massachusetts, the Cape and Islands receive rough compensation from ferocious northeasters ("nor'easters" in the parlance of folksy meteorologists) and their accompanying storm surges. These huge waves—amplified by winter's high tides and the storm's own low-pressure center, can turn beachfront homes into beached rafts, punch holes in barrier beaches, take mammoth bites out of shoreline dunes and cliffs, and otherwise demonstrate the impermanence of oceanfront real estate. Needless to say, even the 400-ton island ferries tend to batten down in their snug Cape Cod harbors when these North Atlantic Valkyries come calling.

Newspapers from Boston to the Cape print daily forecasts year-round. Although there is no recorded weather information specifically available for the Islands, the Mid-Cape forecast from the website of **WQRC-FM** (www.wqrc.com) at least apprises you of the general weather in the vicinity. Just bear in mind that temperature and humidity on the Islands are typically lower than at this Hyannis radio station. Online, both www.intellicast.com and www.accuweather.com summarize weather conditions based on local meteorological stations and offer extended forecasts, too.

Stormy Weather

Hurricanes occasionally hitch rides up the Gulf Stream between July and October, the fast-moving columns of rising air sustained

COURTESY OF THE CAPE COD CHAMBER OF COMMERCE

by the current's warm waters, but the cold-air phenomenon known as the "Bermuda High" keeps most of these Caribbean inter-lopers from ever making it this far north. The downside of this neighboring high-pressure cold is that it can keep summer thunder-storms stalled over the Islands for a few days at a time, too. Otherwise, storm fronts blow quickly out to sea, so while precipitation is evenly spread across the calendar (with most months averaging 10–12 days of rain or light snow), it's unusual to have more than a couple of days in a row spoiled by wet weather.

Given the risk from northeast storms, any circumnavigating sailor crazy enough to win-ter over in this region rather than farther south should haul his or her boat into dry storage—unless it's a weather-tight Great Lakes trawler with enough bow and stern anchors to keep it from becoming a waterborne bulldozer in a gale. But for temporary refuge from passing summer depressions, Hadley Harbor (at the northern end of the Elizabeth Islands, facing Woods Hole) and Vineyard Haven Harbor are as well protected a pair of hurricane holes as you could ask for in these parts.

Beach Tips

Since clouds, fog, and lower temperatures are more prevalent where the cool sea breezes come ashore, bathers may wish to keep in mind that the prevailing winds in summer are southwesterly, which means that the pro-tected beaches on the lee side of the Islands—e.g., the north shores—are apt to be sunnier and warmer than those on the windward side. Sometimes the differences are quite sharp: Passengers disembarking from the ferry in Vineyard Haven can be squinting in the sun and reaching for their shades at the same time that frustrated beachgoers on the other side of the island are wondering who brought the pea-soup fog.

When the wind swings around to the northwest in summer it brings sultry, sticky weather from the mainland, and in winter it delivers blasts of Canadian-chilled air—"Alberta clippers." Swimmers should note, too, that no matter what the provenance of the offshore Gulf Stream, local waters are warm compared to the Gulf of Maine, not to Miami Beach. While Cape Cod Bay, Nantucket Sound, and Vineyard Sound are diminutive enough to heat up a good 10–20°F more than the open ocean in summer, swimming in this latitude of the Atlantic is otherwise guaranteed to cool you off, often quite briskly. The goosebumps raised by waves in the mid-60°F range lapping on each island's southern shores, for example, can be the perfect antidote if you (or your children) have overheated.

Flora and Fauna

FLORA

Thanks to the temperate, ocean-warmed climate, growing conditions on the Cape and Islands differ from those elsewhere in Southern New England. Plants more common to Chesapeake Bay, for instance, flourish here at the northern limit of their range. Examples include Maryland meadow beauty, Eastern sil-very aster, St. Andrew's Cross, and post oaks, which in these latitudes grow only knee-high to their stout Dixie cousins. Even more unusual are Arctic species, such as broom crowberry and caribou moss that advanced ahead of the ice age glaciers and then adapted sufficiently to survive after the big thaw. The moss will be fa-miliar to architecture students and model rail-roaders; when dried, its tiny treelike branches often serve as Lilliputian shrubbery.

Along the Coasts

Great grassy meadows once flourished along Southern New England's sandy margins, but coastal development has all but eradicated this globally rare ecological community. Most of

© KATHRYN OSGOOD

Plenty of plants and grasses thrive in the temperate ocean climate of Martha's Vineyard.

the planet's remaining acreage of this sand-plain grassland is found on the Islands—an estimated 90 percent on Nantucket alone. Sandplain grasslands are geological twins of the sandplain pine barrens found between Rhode Island and Cape Cod, but they visually and botanically resemble Midwestern prairies. Asters, wild indigo, goat's rue, and bluestem grass are typical of these oft-overlooked meadows; so is Nantucket shadbush, a feathery-white May bloomer common to both islands but a rarity anywhere else.

Sandplain grasslands are rich in other rare or endangered wildflowers such as bird's foot violet, sand-plain flax, New England blazing star, and bushy rockrose—and insects such as the tiger beetle, American burying beetle, and moths so uncommon that they are known only by their Latin names. The terrain is also vital habitat for northern harriers (marsh hawks), short-eared owls, and grasshopper sparrows—ground nesters made rare on the mainland by territory lost to housing subdivisions and eggs lost to raccoons, skunks, and other mammals.

(Consider yourself particularly lucky to catch sight of the owls; only a couple dozen breeding pairs remain in all of New England.)

Human activity hasn't been exclusively detrimental to the grasslands, by the way. At Katama Airfield—a historic 1929 grass-strip "airpark" on Martha's Vineyard, once visited by Charles Lindbergh—the sandplain grasses have been unwittingly perpetuated by the mowing and burning used to keep runways clear of invasive shrubs and seedlings; now conservationists on both islands practice controlled burns to try to aid the survival of this diminishing landscape.

Heaths are another distinctive feature of the regional landscape, primarily on Nantucket and parts of the Outer Cape. A shrub-dominated plant community, it's disappearing across the region, like the sandplains, due to forest succession and habitat loss.

In the Forest
The ancient oak, cedar, and beech trees whose huge proportions amazed the earliest English

explorers to these shores were long ago felled by settlers' axes. Their successors have largely been fast-colonizing species able to thrive in depleted soils and desiccating salt air, which "burns" most deciduous trees' fragile leaves where they are unprotected by topography or other trees.

The most abundant survivors are the salt- and fire-resistant pitch pine (native to the Cape and Vineyard, introduced on Nantucket), well adapted to the task of securing sandy ground laid bare by overgrazing and firewood gathering, and the even more salt-tolerant scrub oak, which seeds rapidly and germinates in even the poorest soil.

With its superior growing conditions, the Vineyard has reacquired some of the diversity described by 17th-century English settlers. Both islands have also acquired a whole host of introduced species: ornamentals such as cockspur thorn, Russian olive, and purple loosestrife; seafaring souvenirs or old-country natives including Japanese black pine, Scots pine, and English oak; and others, such as the red pine, planted for their economic value in reclaiming damaged land and providing a source of new timber.

FAUNA

This region routinely ranks among the nation's top bird-watching destinations, thanks to active local bird-watchers; a closely packed array of diverse habitats, from shore and marsh to woodlands and meadows; and its location on a migratory flyway used by more than 300 species of songbirds and shorebirds. Plenty of terns, cormorants, gulls, herons, osprey, and other seafood eaters are resident in both summer and winter, as are cardinals, woodpeckers, mourning doves, and some finches.

Spring and fall see the largest number of migrants pass through, from Canada geese and gannets to song sparrows and warblers. Some—particularly shorebirds like the plover and sandpiper—come all the way from Mexico specifically to spend the season munching fly larvae on the Islands' beaches.

Winter brings large flocks of sea ducks down

bird tracks on the beach

© KATHRYN OSGOOD

from Canada: scoters, scaup, mergansers, goldeneye, bufflehead, and thousands of mollusk-loving eiders (North America's largest duck). Some years, when their winter food supply in northern New England gets skimpy, even snowy owls from the Arctic put in an appearance on local shores.

The increase in off-road-vehicle use in the last 20 years has made piping plovers and least terns the most endangered beach nesters, although protection programs on the Cape and Islands have caused their numbers to rebound. Curiously, the very success of the beach-driving restrictions has brought pressure to relax them. Adopting the kind of weird logic that would suggest seat belts and airbags are no longer necessary now that they've saved so many lives, periodically proponents of off-road recreation try to open up beaches to plover-squashing Jeeps and dune buggies again.

White-tailed deer are the largest animals in the region. You may catch them at dusk browsing in fields, munching tulip buds in the backyard of your B&B, or risking a dash through your high

THE QUARTER-BILLION-DOLLAR CRAB

Ever since the early 1970s, a simple 15-minute chemical test has been the regulatory standard for identifying whether drugs and medical devices are contaminated by endotoxins, a common bacteria of the type that produces toxic shock syndrome, typhoid, and spinal meningitis. The key ingredient in this test, which requires nothing fancier than a test tube and the ability to see the color blue, is Limulus amoebocyte lysate (LAL). This compound is found in just one place on earth: the blood of the horseshoe crab, a veritable living fossil whose 500-million-year-old Paleozoic family (*Limulidae*) is considered more closely related to spiders than to true crustaceans.

Before the LAL test was discovered by marine biologists working in Woods Hole, detecting bacterial contamination in drugs required injecting live rabbits with samples from each batch produced and then waiting to see if the rabbits developed fever. By making the *in vivo* rabbit test obsolete, LAL revolutionized drug manufacturing. Science writer William Sargent, author of *Crab Wars: A Tale of Horseshoe Crabs, Bioterrorism, and Human Health,* estimates that millions of lives have since been saved by LAL.

Rapid growth in pharmaceuticals and biotechnology has in turn made the LAL industry worth several hundred million dollars. The safety of vaccines, intravenous devices, and surgical instruments everywhere, from the nation's top hospitals to rural Third World clinics, now depends on an undiminished supply of horseshoe crab blood. You would think, then, that the horseshoe crab is an extremely valuable commodity, protected with the same diligence that is reserved for strategic stocks of minerals or oil. Alas, not so.

With proper handling, crabs bled for LAL can be returned to the ocean alive, but hundreds of thousands of crabs continue to be harvested as bait for the politically astute mid-Atlantic conch and eel fisheries, whose economic value is less than one percent of the LAL industry's. Habitat loss on coastlines and pollution from shoreline development also puts pressure on crab populations, which have been steadily declining all along the East Coast. Even some of the major LAL producers have shortsightedly resisted efforts at regulating horseshoe crab collection.

Cape waters, which include sanctuaries in both the Monomoy National Wildlife Refuge and the Cape Cod National Seashore to protect crab spawning grounds, supply about a quarter of the horseshoe crabs used by the biomedical industry. On the other hand, Massachusetts also used to have the second-highest harvest quota among the 12 Atlantic states that regulate horseshoe crabs. But in 2008, the commonwealth cut that allowance in half after stocks in some Cape estuaries were depleted by bait collectors driven north by stricter limits in the mid-Atlantic states, where population declines have been the most dramatic.

Since it takes about a decade for the crabs to reach reproductive maturity, many more years must pass before it will be known whether conservation efforts are succeeding. Hopefully greater awareness of its vital importance to humanity will keep us from carelessly wiping out a critter that has been crawling along the continent's shores since before the first dinosaur.

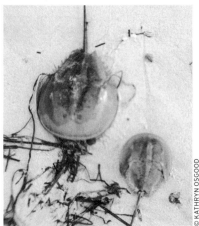

vacated horseshoe crab shells

© KATHRYN OSGOOD

beams on some back road far from town. Harbor seals also frequent some coastal areas, and signs of elusive river otter and muskrat can be found at certain ponds, even on the Vineyard.

ISLAND DIFFERENCES

Although 5,000 years of separation from the mainland have given rise to some endemism on the Islands—there's a species of vole on Nantucket's Muskeget Island, for example, that is found nowhere else—there are more noticeable differences in what's missing. Mammals such as the red fox and the wily coyote, who has even trotted across the Cape Cod Canal bridges and swum to the Elizabeth archipelago, haven't yet figured out the ferry schedules to Nantucket or the Vineyard. Nantucket doesn't even have raccoons or skunks. There are no poisonous snakes on the Islands, either—the shy little red-bellied *Storeria occipitomaculata*

you may chance to see are dangerous only to slugs and worms.

Anyone interested in plant and animal identification will be disappointed to find that most regional nature guides treat the Islands almost as an afterthought to the more heavily visited Cape Cod. Island-specific field guides for trailside flora and fauna are so rarely stocked by Massachusetts bookstores—even on the Cape—that your best bet is to simply do your book-buying after you arrive on the Islands. The independent retail bookstores in Nantucket, Edgartown, and Vineyard Haven are particularly worth visiting, although for the widest range of natural history titles you would do well to check out Nantucket's Maria Mitchell Association gift shop; for the Vineyard, stop by the store at the Massachusetts Audubon Society's Felix Neck Wildlife Sanctuary.

History

NATIVE AMERICANS

At the time of first contact with 16th-century Europeans, Southern New England's indigenous Native Americans are estimated to have numbered in the thousands in the region now within Massachusetts's borders. At least 100 villages have been identified as having belonged to bands of some half-dozen tribes: the Massachusett, Wampanoag, Nipmuck, Pawtucket, Pocumtuck, and Mahican. Each tribe comprised many bands, some more loosely allied than others. All shared the language of the Eastern Algonquian, the linguistic group encompassing most of the tribes on the East Coast between the Carolinas and the Iroquois Confederation. Although effectively a dead language (the last native speaker died in the early 1900s, and, in 1995, a Wampanoag Indian who had spent some 21 years working to revive it passed away, too), several Algonquian nouns have made their way into English, including "skunk," "chipmunk," and "powwow."

The Europeans brought with them, among other things, several diseases against which the natives had no resistance. These afflictions, particularly smallpox, proved disastrous for New England's Indians. An epidemic in the years just prior to the arrival of the Pilgrims at Plymouth virtually depopulated the entire Boston basin (Squanto, famous for serving as both a friend to and interpreter for the Pilgrims, was kidnapped from his village on Plymouth Bay in 1614, and by the time he returned from his adventures in Spain and England, the Patuxet band to which he belonged had been utterly wiped out by disease). A second major epidemic swept the New England tribes again after the Puritan migration in the 1630s, and smaller scourges took place periodically well into the 1700s. But despite the depredations of disease, loss of tribal identity through acculturation, and two devastating wars with the English, the Native Americans did not entirely vanish. Indeed, they're still here: Several bands of the Wampanoag and Nipmuck tribes reside in Massachusetts, and two—one each from Cape Cod and Martha's Vineyard—have even obtained federal recognition.

EARLY EXPLORERS

After the Pilgrims had desecrated a few Native American burial mounds in their explorations of their landing spot on Cape Cod, they decided that it was "odious unto [the Native Americans] to ransack their sepulchres." But one mound was uncommonly large, which made them curious enough to dig into it. What they found was a double grave, containing a child and blond-haired man—who had been buried with belongings including a knife, "a saylers canvas Casacke, and a payre of cloth breeches." The following spring, a solitary Indian strolled into the settlement at Plymouth and greeted the surprised Europeans in clear English. Plainly, the Pilgrims were not the first Europeans to have visited these shores.

Royal Ambitions

The English claim to North America is based on John Cabot's 1497–1498 voyage along the Atlantic coast, in search of the fabled Northwest Passage to Asia. It's unlikely that Cabot, a.k.a. Giovanni Chabotte (Giovanni the Coaster), an Italian navigator sailing under the patronage of England's King Henry VII, ever actually laid eyes on New England. But given the prevailing climate of political and economic rivalry with other European powers, his voyage was a convenient pretext for giving the first royal sanction to a New England colony in 1578. The lucky fellow who obtained Queen Elizabeth's permission to try housekeeping on the Maine coast was Sir Humphrey Gilbert, author of an influential treatise that used classical Greek cosmography to prove the Northwest Passage's existence. In addition to searching for the passage, Gilbert intended to use his New World manorial estate (he was a lord, after all) as a base for attacking Spanish treasure galleons in the West Indies. Unfortunately for captain and crew, Gilbert's ship sank on its first voyage to claim his prize.

THE NORSEMEN COMETH... OR NOT

Amateur historians and local mythmakers have been beguiled for generations by the idea that Vikings were the Bay State's first European visitors, arriving sometime around A.D. 1000. The most basic justification for these conclusions relies on a conflation of the Norse and English languages: the Vikings' mentions of "Vinland" within the sagas of their voyages, the argument goes, must refer to what is now Martha's Vineyard (or any other wild-grapevine-covered beach between Maine and New Jersey, depending on where the person advancing this argument is from). But despite gaining a measure of credibility from various less-than-scholarly museum displays and tour guides in the region, there is no real evidence to distinguish such claims from pure theory.

For a start, linguistic research suggests the Old Norse word *Vÿnlâd* may refer to grasslands, not grapevines. Moreover, although almost 50 years have passed since archaeological traces of a Norse settlement were discovered at L'Anse aux Meadows in Newfoundland, there's never been incontrovertible proof of any settlement farther south. This isn't to say that Vikings didn't venture up the Charles River, through Vineyard Sound, or around Narragansett Bay, but lines from Norse sagas describing days longer than those in Iceland and wood resembling oak aren't enough to support the assertions of most modern theorists.

Far East or Bust

In the decades between Cabot and Gilbert, the English devoted themselves more to trying to find a way around the new landmass to their west—that Asia obsession again—and to fishing offshore, than to exploring the land itself. The realm of the Great Khan was also the goal of the first European who can reliably be said to have laid eyes on Massachusetts, Giovanni da Verrazzano, the Italian navigator sailing on behalf of the French crown. He passed by Cape Cod in 1524 on his way from Narragansett Bay to the Gulf of Maine.

Estévan Gomez, a Portuguese mariner who moved to Spain and won the patronage of that nation's sovereign, sailed along the same shores in the opposite direction in 1525. Two years later, an Englishman, John Rut, cruised by en route from Labrador to the West Indies. Before the end of the century at least a handful of other explorers, sailing on behalf of various European maritime powers, at least observed Cape Cod as they sailed between Newfoundland and Florida searching for passage to the Sea of Cathay.

With the possible exception of Rut, who vaguely alludes to going ashore someplace along his journey, and various anonymous fishermen, who traded trinkets with local Indians while curing their catch on the coast, none of the others saw any reason to set foot on Massachusetts soil, or to meet any of its indigenous people.

This is not to say that Europeans were disinterested in the Americas. The codfish-rich waters off the New England coast became well known to whole fleets of Portuguese, Basque, and Bristol fishermen by the early 1500s. And England's competitors actively pursued resources elsewhere on the continent. Thus, by the end of the 16th century, Spain's lucrative South and Central American conquests had already spun off permanent settlements in both present-day New Mexico (San Juan Pueblo, founded 1598) and Florida (St. Augustine, founded 1565). France, meanwhile, had established a steady fur trade in the Gulf of St. Lawrence by the 1580s, and attempted permanent settlement in Canada as early as 1542.

Most of the English, on the other hand, still dreamed of a northern route to the Spice Islands. With the exception of Sir Gilbert and his half-brother, Sir Walter Raleigh (who tried twice to establish a foothold for his sovereign on North Carolina's Outer Banks in the 1580s), England at the end of the Elizabethan age was at risk of being left out of the New World by trying so hard to get around it.

England Plants the Flag

The start of the 17th century brought significant changes in Old World attitudes toward "Norumbega," as New England was then known (possibly derived from Indian usage—nobody knows for sure—Norumbega made its debut as a place-name in 1529). Highly embellished maps and journals published during the prior century's rush of exploration fanned the notion that Norumbega was a fruit-filled Garden of Eden whose capital city rivaled London.

A temporary lull in wars among the major European powers enabled the French, English, and Dutch to stake overlapping claims to this tantalizing new destination, and dispatch expeditions to back them up. It hardly mattered that exploratory voyages by England's George Weymouth in 1605, Samuel de Champlain for France in 1603–1609, and the Netherlands' Henry Hudson in 1609 (among others) dispelled the more outrageous Norumbegan myths. By making much ado about what they did find—from the best fishing they'd ever seen to soil more fertile than any overworked farm back home—they contributed to the momentum for imperial expansion.

English territorial ambitions finally made their first mark on the New World during the reign of King James I, who succeeded Queen Elizabeth upon her death in 1603. Two pro-colonial cartels backed by wealthy financiers and aristocrats were each awarded land grants and patents—royal permissions—in 1606. With their new king's blessing, these companies invested in settlements from the Kennebec River in Maine to the James River in Virginia.

The initial results were decidedly mixed. While the London Company, a.k.a. the First Virginia Company, did well with its Jamestown colony, most of the Plymouth Company's efforts fell far short of their founders' aspirations.

For Money and Country

Ships laden with cod, sassafras, and beaver pelts were what motivated the deep-pocketed speculators—along with continued dreams of finding that elusive northwest shortcut to the riches of the Orient—but domestic problems in England made colonization as important as profit-making. Exploding population, crop failures, and the societal shift from self-sufficient villages to a market society created a large migrant pool of tenant farmers and landless artisans willing to emigrate to wherever they might be able to eke out a living. Thousands had already gone to Europe in the decade before the *Mayflower* set sail. Any risks in the New World—violent clashes with Indians, for a start—were conveniently dismissed by colonial promoters.

English nationalism also fueled the promotional rhetoric. Although the French, too, had more failures than successes—only Québec, founded in 1608, lasted more than a single winter—their attempts at settling the Maine coast posed a great financial and theological threat to Protestant England. Even the Dutch were getting into the act, setting up year-round shop on Long Island in 1617 after several years of seasonal trading voyages to the mouth of the Hudson. Given the urgent need to build bulwarks against the expansion of these economic rivals, it's hardly surprising that English writers gave positive spin to their descriptions of what lay in store for would-be colonists.

PILGRIMS AND PURITANS

Captain John Smith, now remembered primarily as the founder of Virginia's successful Jamestown, was one author of glowing reports on New England's bountiful resources. It was Smith, in fact, who gave New England its name, partly in an attempt to stimulate financial support at home for his voyages. Among the audience for his public relations campaign was a small group of "separatists," disaffected Protestants repeatedly harassed by King James's campaign against religious nonconformity. James picked up where the reign of "Bloody Mary" left off, jailing and terrorizing the Church of England's critics after a half-century of Elizabethan compromise.

The separatists, by choosing to contest the whole purpose of the Anglican hierarchy, took a seditious step further than their fellow dissidents, the Puritans, who merely sought to "purify" the Church of England of its pagan-based rituals—such as Christmas and Easter—and other allegedly Catholic pomp. King James rightly detected that separatist reformers, hostile not only to the "Roman rites" of Catholicism but to the very existence of English bishops, would someday reject his authority, too. Scorned by king and most countrymen, scores of separatists—or "Saints," as they called themselves—fled to Holland, where all manner of religious practices were tolerated.

The principal separatist congregation grew discontent with Dutch life after a decade of self-imposed exile in Amsterdam and Leyden. Their unhappiness stemmed partly from unshakable poverty—most of the group had never been more than simple working-class villagers and journeymen, even in England. But the group's members were also concerned that Holland's permissive society would corrupt their impressionable young children. In short, Dutch freedom of religion became almost as odious as England's lack of it.

The Saints Come Marching In

Once they resolved to establish their own private theocracy someplace in the New World, where they half-believed that they might be united with the Lost Tribe of Israel, a quick process of elimination brought the Leyden Separatists to consider New England, which was conveniently out of reach of any Anglican authorities. Captain Smith, still trying to find customers for his "planting" schemes, offered to guide them to their proposed new colony, but the separatists declined, frugally preferring to simply buy his book and sea chart and try their luck on their own. Financial backing came from a middle-class group of London venture capitalists known to history as the Merchant Adventurers.

Fear, hardship, dissent, and family responsibilities whittled the final number of emigrating Saints down to 41, less than one-sixth of the full Leyden congregation. To meet the needs of establishing a colony, the Merchant

A FEW MYTHS ABOUT THE PILGRIMS

Myths about the Pilgrims and the Puritans run rampant, and cottage industries have sprung up to both stoke and debunk them. For example, compare the following to what you learned in high school.

Myth: The Pilgrims were bound for Virginia and made landfall at Cape Cod only because they were lost.

Facts: The Pilgrims had originally been given a grant to settle in northern Virginia, but the royal grant for "Virginia" initially comprised everything between the Jamestown settlement and the 41st parallel (around present-day New York City). William Bradford, the Pilgrims' most thorough annalist and sometime governor, recorded that their destination was the mouth of the Hudson, but there's plenty of evidence that the Pilgrim leaders never intended to subject themselves to the Old Dominion authorities in Jamestown, and merely took a patent from them as a precaution in the event that their other plans failed to materialize.

Before they left England, it was known that Sir Ferdinando Gorges, an ambitious colonialist who already had a string of failures to his credit – from Massachusetts to Maine – had requested a new royal patent for his "Council for New England." In fact, royal transfer of the northern territories from the First Virginia Company to Gorges became official just days before the Pilgrims landed. As soon as the newly empowered Council had word of the *Mayflower*'s success, the charter the Pilgrims probably hoped to have all along was dispatched without any negotiation, granting the autonomy the Pilgrims desired.

The historical record is sketchy, but it's hard to believe that the Pilgrim leaders had no dealings with Gorges prior to their departure. Bradford even had a copy of a firsthand report from one of Gorges's agents, Thomas Dermer, assessing the colonizing potential of different parts of Cape Cod Bay, including Plymouth.

Myth: The Mayflower Compact is one of the cornerstones of American democracy.

Facts: There is some merit to this statement, in light of the fact that until the 20th century, American "democracy" legally abridged the rights of anyone other than white males. The Mayflower Compact was never signed by most of the indentured servants, or by any of the women. But it really wasn't conceived in a generous democratic spirit – mutiny was afoot, and the compact was the tool used to quash it. The Pilgrims felt threatened by at least one of the Strangers. This was probably Stephen Hopkins, a survivor of the Bermuda shipwreck that befell another Virginia-bound company in 1609. Hopkins had encouraged fellow wreckmates to reject their governor's authority on the grounds that his jurisdiction was limited to their original destination, not the site of their accident. Although those efforts were nearly fatal – Hopkins only escaped execution by begging for mercy on behalf of his family – he may have voiced the same seditious logic 11 years later at Cape Cod.

The compact thus kept the group from being splintered by what Bradford called "mutterings of dissent." That it should be remembered now for codifying the principle of majority rule is deeply ironic. Throughout the Plymouth colony's existence, some 80 percent of the population was neither permitted to vote nor hold office – so it would seem that the notion of "majority rule" may not have represented to the Pilgrims what we may like to think it did.

Myth: The Pilgrims landed in a howling wilderness with nothing but their wits and industriousness to save them.

Facts: The *Mayflower* contingent chose for their settlement the site of an abandoned Indian village – one not at all unknown to Bradford and others. Champlain had thoroughly charted it 15 years earlier, when it and the surrounding bay was still occupied by some 2,000 Patuxet Indians (before they were wiped out by a European epidemic). Thomas Dermer, whose letter Bradford carried, had been to the village site just five months before the Pilgrims arrived. "I would that the first plantation might here be seated," Dermer wrote his sponsor (although he did go on to warn that the local Indians were hostile to the English, whom they accused of murder). The *Mayflower* pilot had also been to the place before. And its name appeared on Captain Smith's six-year-old chart of the New England coastline, which the Pilgrims used to guide them to Cape Cod.

The village site included fields cleared for cultivation, overgrown only two or three years. Paths through the woods were well maintained by regional Indian bands engaging in constant social and trading activities. Thanks to the Indian's forest-management practice of setting small fires in order to improve game hunting, much of the forest understory was so clear that all the settlers remarked on how easy it was to ride through the woods.

One hardship they *did* encounter was the weather (their arrival was ill-timed with the start of winter). Probably the greatest obstacle they faced, however, was their own lack of skills appropriate to building a coastal colony. As villagers and artisans, none of the settlers was very proficient at fishing or farming, for example. And they were so incurious about their new surroundings that it took some three months to venture even as far as two miles from their settlement (and then only because one young Pilgrim, having climbed a tree, thought he saw an inland sea, which turned out to be a large pond).

Myth: After difficult beginnings, the Pilgrims celebrated their first harvest with a big Thanksgiving feast, including turkey and all the trimmings.

Facts: Pilgrim theology permitted but three holidays: Sabbath, Fast Day, and Thanksgiving. These last two weren't necessarily regular events tied to a specific day, as the Sabbath was. Instead, church leaders would declare a day of penance or thanks if and when they thought it necessary. In the fall of 1621, the Pilgrims did indeed hold a three-day feast, but they didn't feel they'd acquired enough of God's bounty to declare a proper Thanksgiving until two years later.

Thanksgiving proclamations continued to be random events. The warring American colonies joined in the first common Thanksgiving in 1777 to celebrate victory over the British at the Battle of Saratoga. (Two years later, George Washington's proclamation of a national Thanksgiving was ignored as premature.) Various state governors continued the practice up through 1827, when Boston *Ladies' Magazine* editor Sarah Josepha Hale took up the cudgel, inaugurating an editorial campaign on behalf of an annual national Thanksgiving. President Lincoln finally made it a holiday after Gettysburg, in 1863.

As for the practice of including turkey in the meal, that most likely derived from the English custom of a turkey *Christmas* dinner, established some 35 years before the Pilgrims departed for the New World. The meal the Pilgrims ate that first fall comprised more venison than wildfowl. While there were wild turkeys in New England, the Pilgrims preferred domesticated European breeds, which are, in fact, the progenitors of the turkeys we eat most commonly today.

Adventurers hastily rounded up an equal number of new recruits, dubbed "Strangers" by their self-sanctified shipmates. Both groups also brought along indentured servants, manual laborers who would work for seven years in return for room and board.

Finally, after three years of preparation, weeks of last-minute delays, and two aborted departures, the tiny *Mayflower,* with 102 passengers and an unknown number of crew, leaving behind its leaky companion, the *Speedwell,* made its solo crossing of the stormy Atlantic in late 1620. Nearly 10 weeks later, landfall was made at present-day Provincetown, on the tip of Cape Cod. Over a month after that, having failed to locate a suitable source of freshwater, the emigrants moved across Cape Cod Bay and established their "plantation" at Plymouth.

Half of these settlers died during their first winter in the new land. But eventually, with infusions of new blood from home and life-saving agricultural lessons from their new Native American neighbors, these separatists, "Strangers," and their servants (all lumped together under the rubric of "Pilgrim" only after 1840) did well enough to both completely repay their investors and attract a slew of new homesteaders to burgeoning outposts from Boston Harbor to Cape Cod.

Puritans Pull a Fast One

Eight years after the arrival of the Pilgrims, a small group of Puritan "lord brethren" arrived in present-day Salem, on the northern shore of Massachusetts Bay, and seized control of an English fishing community, a remnant of a failed settlement farther up the coast. Within two years, these zealous brethren's simple land grant was converted into a royally chartered trading organization called the Massachusetts Bay Company. This set the stage for John Winthrop, an influential autocrat, to come a-calling in the *Arbella* and a fleet of over a dozen other ships. This huge flock, dissatisfied with their first landfall and seeking something better, moved twice before settling on the hilly peninsula they named Boston.

Like the Pilgrims, the Puritans eluded direct English control by design. Winthrop, a well-trained lawyer, recognized an omission in the text of his company's charter. While stockholder meetings to direct the company had to be held where the charter was kept, nothing required the charter to be kept in England. This loophole made it possible to simply pocket the document and bring it along to America—putting the whole wide Atlantic between the colony and oversight by parliament and the Crown.

Unlike the hereditary or proprietary (i.e., feudal) royal charters given to Maryland's plantation owners or the Duke of York, the Massachusetts Bay political framework of "freemen" (stockholders) assembling in a General Court established the basis for representative government by a company of equals. This may sound democratic, but only shareholders could vote, and out of 1,000 emigrants, exactly *four* were first enfranchised in the Great & General Court. Only mutinous threats forced revision of the court's composition, creating a bicameral chamber—one part elected by all freemen, the

other appointed by Bay Company officers—and expanding voter eligibility to other men of property.

Back home, dissent against the Anglican bishops and economic stagnation from farm shortages proved so widespread that within a generation, 20,000 English—predominantly from East Anglia—joined the Great Migration to the Bay Colony.

Intolerance

Despite legal documents that seemed to institute a measure of democratic rule, the early Puritan colony, under Governor Winthrop, was as harsh a theocracy as that of Iran under the Ayatollah Khomeini. Religious and social dissenters faced serious censure, cruel punishment, or even death for disagreeing with or denying the will of church leaders. Since Puritans equated change with sin, the status quo justified the most abominable abridgments of what we now call civil and human rights.

The Pilgrims in the adjacent "Old Colony" were no better. You could get part of your ear sliced off if you were caught eavesdropping. Doze off during the many hours of sermonizing on the Sabbath, and your tongue might be impaled on a sharp stick. Notwithstanding such cruelty—and the liberal application of both banishment and the death penalty—the authorities of both colonies left records rich in reports of drinking, incest, adultery, homosexuality, bestiality, and plain old crooked business dealings.

These early English settlers were often a disputatious lot and frequently dragged each other into court. Despite an apparent love of legalisms and litigation, actual justice was in short supply—particularly with regard to relations with various indigenous peoples. After enduring epidemics and the consequent destruction of tribal alliances, native populations around Massachusetts had managed to stabilize. But this increased the potential for cultural misunderstandings over all sorts of issues, especially as the English became hungry for more land. Tensions quickly escalated after the 1661 death of the Pokanoket (Wampanoag) chief

Massassoit, a steadfast Pilgrim ally, and after the subsequent death of his son and successor, Alexander, who died of an illness after being forcibly detained by the English on suspicions of conspiring against them.

Unfortunately for all concerned, the colonists' fears became self-fulfilling. Alexander's brother, Philip, known to his people as Metacom, strategized with various allies across Massachusetts to boot the Anglos back across the Atlantic.

King Philip's War

Philip came close, but not close enough. His rebellion began prematurely, in 1675—after the colonials had gotten wise to his intent—and without the vital cooperation of a couple of other tribes in Central and Western New England. So the "Red King" missed his mark, though not without inflicting serious setbacks on both Pilgrim and Puritan colonies: 50 of 90 existing towns were destroyed, many more were abandoned by fearful settlers, and the colonial militia was given a run for its money. Ultimately, however, victory over Metacom's coalition brought uncompromising and indiscriminate revenge and reprisals against Native Americans throughout the region.

The colonists paid a heavy toll in the war besides lost lives and abandoned towns. The cost of arming and operating its military force financially crippled them. Plymouth's share of the debt exceeded the value of all its real estate. A further consequence was that the troubles called into question the colonies' ability to conduct their affairs outside the purview of English authority, and ended the prized independence. Parliamentary demands for security after the war reinstituted imperial dominion. Thus, in 1684, the Restoration Monarch, Charles II, officially dissolved the Puritan charter. Seven years of political suspense followed, filled with jockeying by various scheming factions, the death of the Merry Monarch, the brief reign of his brother James II, and England's Glorious Revolution. Finally, in 1691, a new charter was issued by England's imported co-regents, William and Mary. With that, at long last, Massachusetts became a true royal province.

INDEPENDENCE

During the century following the Crown's imposition of control over its wayward colony, the bond between the English colonists and their king deteriorated as ineluctably as had the earlier generation's relations with the Native Americans. Some scholars point out the influence of mercantile interests, which effectively used propaganda to sway the colonists in what was actually a struggle to practice unfettered capitalism. Others suggest that this is a simplistic view, especially in light of evidence that antipathy toward England's bullying tactics cut across social and economic classes. Even subsistence farmers, who made up the vast majority of the colonial population, became radicalized by the unfolding tug-of-war between the Crown and the colonial middle class. But the notion of the aggrieved American yeoman putting aside his plow to fight a parasitic monarchy in defense of some inalienable rights—an indelible part of the nation's founding self-image—is an oversimplification, too. As subsequent events clearly demonstrated, farmers were equipped and encouraged to serve as soldiers only so long as it was in the interests of the colony's moneyed men.

Push Comes to Shove

Revolution finally erupted in Lexington and Concord on April 19, 1775, when a makeshift force of British regulars and their fellow German soldiers (hired by the shorthanded English from their Prussian allies) fired on local militia while searching for a stash of munitions. Colonial forces harassed the retreating infantry in a running battle all the way back to Boston. The British occupiers were forced out of the city after an eight-month siege by newly commissioned George Washington and his fledgling Continental Army. Thereupon the land war moved to New York and the mid-Atlantic states.

By the time independence was declared on July 4, 1776, Massachusetts had shifted from a central to a supporting role, furnishing the war effort with soldiers, sailors, and military stores. Although a large contingent of the British Navy was stationed throughout the war in next-door Newport, Rhode Island, its commanders preferred the comforts of their busy social lives ashore over armed action against the sparsely populated Cape and Islands.

Within this region, the major action of the war was a four-day raid on Martha's Vineyard in September 1778 by a fleet of 82 ships, led by British Major-General Grey. It resulted in a loss of some 10,000 sheep and 600 oxen, as well as the destruction of every cornfield and root crop within two miles of the British landing. During the harsh winter that followed, the populace nearly starved to death.

British landing parties also attempted to harass the town of Falmouth in 1779, but local militia repelled the effort. Other than more thefts of cattle from the Islands, where no attempt could seriously be mounted to oppose them, the British mostly confined themselves to maneuvering their fleet offshore. By the end of the war, fears of a major invasion by sea had never fully materialized.

GROWING UP ON SALT AND FISH

The 50-some years between the Revolutionary War and the Industrial Revolution witnessed steady population growth across the region, despite the depletion of terrestrial resources. The abundant forests that greeted the earliest "old comers" had been largely used up for construction materials and fuel during the colonial era, which had the corollary effect of hurting agriculture as unprotected topsoils were then free to be blown or washed away. As Henry David Thoreau observed on one 1850s visit, "All an inlander's notions of soil and fertility will be confounded by a visit to these parts, and he will not be able, for some time afterward, to distinguish soil from sand." Cape Codders and their island neighbors thus sought to make a living from the surrounding ocean, from which they harvested crops of salt, fish, and whales.

All across the Cape, windmills were erected

to pump seawater into evaporation vats to produce salt, which was then used for curing locally caught fish and tanning leather, or was shipped to urban markets. Until serious competition arose from both imported and domestic salt producers by the 1850s, hundreds of saltworks occupying mile upon mile of shoreline annually produced tens of thousands of bushels of table and industrial salt.

The transportation of salt and dried fish by packet vessels plying coastal trade routes from nearly a dozen regional harbors helped sustain other related industries such as boat building, shipfitting, and fish processing. Recognizing the navigational needs of this increased maritime traffic, the nation's young federal government paid for a dozen new lighthouses to be built around the region.

Lighthouses alone couldn't reduce the navigational hazards posed by dangerous shoals and constantly shifting sandbars in the waters surrounding the Cape and Islands. Thus throughout the early 19th century there were periodic outbreaks of "canal fever" as proponents of various shortcuts between Cape Cod Bay and other bodies of water pitched their proposals. Most projects were abandoned before barely turning a spade of dirt, although in 1804 a short swampy trench known as Jeremiah's Gutter, large enough for shallow-draft boats carrying salt, was successfully dug in Eastham between Cape Cod Bay and the Atlantic.

A TRUE MELTING POT

Throughout the 18th and early 19th centuries, the regional population was quite racially and culturally mixed. The local whale fishery, with its extended international voyages on which captains filled out their crews in overseas ports, brought back an assorted cast of men from the Azores, Cape Verde, South America, the Caribbean, Hawaii, and various South Pacific islands. These men established residences in local port towns, joining Native Americans and free blacks (Massachusetts abolished slavery in the 1780s) similarly drawn to maritime occupations.

The region also subscribed to an unusual degree of religious pluralism. Throughout the decades of Puritan control over the Massachusetts Bay colony, doctrinal free-thinkers who upset the Boston-based ecclesiastic authorities often relocated to the Cape and Islands, which were too sparsely populated and too distant to be tightly supervised. While Massachusetts towns were required by law to construct meeting-houses and hire ministers who then customarily served for life, clergymen on the Cape were routinely dismissed if they weren't pleasing to their parishioners. Quakers, Baptists, and Methodists who were deemed heretics to Puritan orthodoxy all found willing congregations in the region, fostering a tolerance for freedom of religious expression.

Such liberal-mindedness set the stage for embracing the evangelical Protestantism of the Second Great Awakening, which swept the nation from 1800 through the 1830s. Itinerant preachers had already been prosthelytizing in the region since immediately after the end of the Revolution, but starting in 1819 large Methodist tent revivals began to be held each summer from the outer Cape to Martha's Vineyard. In concert with the anti-war and anti-slavery teachings of local Quakers, the revival movement is widely recognized as having spawned a variety of social reform movements before the Civil War, from abolitionism to temperance. Locally it also helped usher in a trend that would eventually prove to be equally momentous: tourism.

TOURISTS TO THE RESCUE

Traveling to the Cape and Islands for purely recreational purposes dates back to the late 1600s, when the Elizabeth Islands, an archipelago off the western shore of Martha's Vineyard, were stocked by a wealthy Bostonian with deer and fowl in the tradition of the English private hunting estate. Hunting and fishing for sport remained nearly the sole draw for outsiders up through the early 1800s, although Nantucket's "bracing air" and "excellent water" were also being promoted as treatment for invalids as early as 1792.

vintage Cape Cod postcard

Regular visitors from outside the region became a much more widespread phenomenon with the establishment of regular ferry service in the first half of the 19th century. The ferries enabled people to attend the large revivalist camp meetings convened on the Vineyard throughout the mid-1800s.

During the same period the region suffered from major population loss, beginning with the 1849 Gold Rush. Thousands of local "Argonauts" were lured westward to try their luck in the California mineral lottery. The following decades also saw the collapse of local industries undercut by large-scale competitors from outside the region. The rise of tourism couldn't staunch the dramatic exodus precipitated by these events, but it took the sting out of the economic decline that accompanied them.

By the late Victorian era, speculators were thoroughly capitalizing on the fresh sea breezes and quaint seaside villages to market relaxation to urbanites from every teeming metropolis between New York and Boston. The exclusive little hunting lodges accessible by stagecoach at the beginning of the 1800s were by century's end superseded by grand resort hotels served by coastal steamers and regional rail lines.

In 1890 the region attracted national attention when President Grover Cleveland purchased a fishing lodge in Bourne between his first and second terms in the White House. The social cachet of summering on the Cape and Islands brought wealthy seasonal residents whose property taxes helped swell small town treasuries.

But the real boom in tourism came by car: The Depression-era public investment in improved roads started to pay off even before the end of the New Deal, putting much of the Cape within reach of "day-trippers" from off-Cape. On the eve of World War II, fully three-quarters of the region's towns were reliant on tourism for up to 75 percent of their income.

These days those numbers have changed somewhat as the region becomes home to a growing number of both long-distance commuters who work in the Greater Boston area and second-home owners who spend their weekends here. Besides contributing to increasing suburbanization, these trends have helped the Cape become the fastest-growing part of the state. But tourism continues to be the region's top economic engine, hands down. And its influence on lifestyles, people's livelihoods, and even the very landscape remains profound.

ESSENTIALS

Getting There

Massachusetts may seem to sit on the edge of any U.S. map, but it is thoroughly connected to the rest of the country and much of the world by air, rail, road, and water. What follows is a general outline of your transportation choices to get to the Bay State from wherever you live.

BY AIR
Off-Cape Gateways

The major point of entry into New England for commercial airline passengers is **Logan International Airport,** in Boston. With no single carrier dominating, there is a fair amount of competition. But don't assume that's true for all routes. Budget carrier Southwest Airlines flies into **T. F. Green Airport,** a relatively short distance due west of Cape Cod in neighboring Providence, Rhode Island, so selected fares within the markets they serve may be significantly cheaper than if you fly into Boston. Other regional airports—particularly Manchester, New Hampshire, about an hour north of Boston—may also offer enough outright savings to offset the greater distance and cost of ground transportation. The bottom line is this: When using your favorite online flight search engine be sure to include other nearby airports in your search before settling on arriving at Logan.

© KATHRYN OSGOOD

AIRLINE CONTACT INFORMATION

DOMESTIC

*Airlines with direct service to the Cape or islands are marked with an asterisk. Of the ones so marked, only Cape Air and USAirways Express offer year-round service.

AirTran, 678/254-7999 or 800/247-8726, www.airtran.com

Alaska Airlines, 800/252-7522, www.alaskaair.com

American Airlines/American Eagle, 800/433-7300, www.aa.com

***Cape Air,** 508/771-6944 or 800/352-0714, www.flycapeair.com

Continental Airlines, 800/525-0280, www.continental.com

***Delta Air Lines/Delta Connection** (and **Delta Shuttle** from New York's LaGuardia Airport), 800/221-1212, www.delta.com

***JetBlue Airways,** 800/538-2583, www.jetblue.com

Midwest Airlines, 800/452-2022, www.midwestairlines.com

Northwest Airlines, 800/225-2525, www.nwa.com

Southwest Airlines, 800/435-9792, www.southwest.com

Spirit Airlines, 800/772-7117, www.spiritair.com

United/United Express, 800/241-6522, www.ual.com

***US Airways/US Airways Express** (and **US Airways Shuttle** from New York's LaGuardia Airport), 800/428-4322, www.usairways.com

INTERNATIONAL

Aer Lingus, 800/474-7424, www.aerlingus.ie

Air Canada/Air Canada Jazz, 888/247-2262, www.aircanada.com

Air France, 800/237-2747, www.airfrance.com

Alitalia, 800/223-5730, www.alitaliausa.com

British Airways, 800/247-9297, www.british-airways.com

Cayman Airways, 800/422-9626, www.caymanairways.com

Finnair, 800/950-5000, www.finnair.com

Iberia, 800/772-4642, www.iberia.com

Icelandair, 800/223-5500, www.icelandair.com

KLM, 800/374-7747, www.klm.com

Lufthansa, 800/645-3880, www.lufthansa.com

SATA, 800/762-9995, www.sata.pt

Swiss, 877/359-7947, www.swiss.com

TACV, 866/359-8228, www.caboverde.com

Virgin Atlantic Airways, 800/862-8621, www.virginatlantic.com

BETWEEN THE CAPE AND ISLANDS

All of the following depart from Barnstable Municipal Airport (HYA). Only Cape Air flies to Martha's Vineyard (MVY); the rest fly to Nantucket (ACK).

Cape Air, 800/352-0714, www.flycapeair.com

Island Airlines, 800/248-7779, www.islandair.net

Nantucket Airlines, 800/635-8787, www.nantucketairlines.com

Nantucket Shuttle, 866/588-2251, nantucketshuttle.net

US Airways Express, 800/272-5488, www.usairways.com (seasonal)

OTHER REGIONAL AIRPORTS

The following two airports are listed in order of proximity to Cape Cod. The first has direct daily bus service to Cape Cod and the ferry terminals for Martha's Vineyard and Nantucket; the second has services daily to Boston's South Station bus terminal.

T. F. GREEN AIRPORT (PVD),
Warwick, Rhode Island,
www.pvdairport.com
Airlines: All the major domestic carriers, a handful of regional commuter lines, Air Canada, and SATA International. Direct daily nonstop service from Atlanta, Baltimore, Charlotte, Chicago, Cincinnati, Cleveland, Detroit, Fort Lauderdale, Las Vegas, Minneapolis, Nashville, Newark, New York, Orlando, Philadelphia, Tampa, Toronto, and Washington DC.
Car rentals: Alamo, Avis, Budget, Dollar, Enterprise, Hertz, National, Thrifty, and U-Save. Low base rates are offset by high taxes: 23 percent.
Transit to Cape Cod (83 miles to Hyannis; 80 miles to Woods Hole): Peter Pan Bus Lines (888/751-8800, www.peterpanbus.com) makes a handful of daily runs to Hyannis from downtown Providence (2 hours 20 minutes-2 hours 40 minutes not counting the required airport-downtown Providence transfer via local public bus), with connecting service in Bourne to Falmouth and Woods Hole ferry (2 hours 35 minutes-almost 4 hours depending on connection layover). It's $56 round-trip to either Woods Hole or Hyannis.
Transit to the Vineyard: 15 minutes' shuttle ride from the airport (Airport Taxi & Limousine Service, 401/737-2868 extension 2, www.airporttaxiri.com, $15/pp) is the embarkation point for the year-round Vineyard Fast Ferry to Oak Bluffs (www.vineyardfastferry.com).

MANCHESTER-BOSTON REGIONAL AIRPORT (MHT),
Manchester, New Hampshire,
www.flymanchester.com
Airlines: Seven major United States and Canadian carriers and four regional or commuter airlines, with daily nonstop service from Atlanta, Baltimore, Charlotte, Chicago, Cincinnati, Cleveland, Detroit, Fort Lauderdale, Las Vegas, Minneapolis, New York, Orlando, Philadelphia, Phoenix, Tampa, Toronto, and Washington, DC.
Car rentals: Alamo, Avis, Budget, Dollar, Enterprise, Hertz, National, and Thrifty. Base rates used for advertising purposes are low, but combined taxes and fees are high: 18 percent plus $4.25 per day.
Transit to Boston (60 miles): Until recently, the airport operated a *free* van service, the Manchester Shuttle. Alas, there really is no such thing as a free ride. The shuttle service was recently replaced by a private operator, Flightline (603/893-8254 or 800/245-2525, www.flightlineinc.com), which departs for Boston within 30 minutes of every flight, making the trip to Sullivan station on the Orange Line subway in 75 minutes ($19 pp, reservations required). From Sullivan, South Station is a $2, 20-minute subway ride away. The shuttle service also offers door-to-door rides to many locations in New Hampshire and Eastern Massachusetts for a charge of $50-90 for up to three people, depending on distance. Additional riders pay additional fare of $10 per person.

Neither should you overlook the potential savings offered by small, cut-rate, no-frills carriers you might not have heard of, and whose budget-friendly fares stay low because they don't pay for placement in any of the major travel comparison websites. These include AirTran, with cheap direct flights from Atlanta, Baltimore, Chicago, Milwaukee, Sarasota, Fort Myers, and Midwest Airlines, connecting from numerous cities west of the Great Lakes via its Milwaukee and Kansas City hubs.

At any hour of day or night you can obtain the latest fares and schedules of all the buses and boats that will be available to you after arriving at Logan—plus up-to-the-minute traffic reports on airport roadways—by calling the automated **Massport Ground Transportation Information Service** (800/235-6426).

THE AIR CHARTER OPTION

If you've ever wished you could call on an airplane like a taxi (and skip the trip to the big metropolitan airport), if your transcontinental arrival comes in too late to meet the last scheduled commuter flight, or if you've just heard a report that the traffic jam down to the Vineyard ferry landing is five hours and growing, maybe you should consider chartering a plane. Sound pricey? If you're traveling with another couple or a group, chartering a plane to the Vineyard or Nantucket from Long Island, Philadelphia, Washington, or New Bedford might actually be cheaper than flying the scheduled big-name alternative. Even when nothing can beat the price of that 21-day advance Internet fare with the hour-long layover in Boston, the sheer convenience of a direct flight that leaves right when and where you want may make up for the difference.

Charters charge by the hour, and the meter's running from the minute the plane leaves its home field to the minute it returns. Obviously, the most cost-effective method is to use an outfit whose home base is the beginning or end point of your trip.

Several charter companies routinely make summer roundtrips by turboprop to the islands from the Boston and New York metropolitan areas. Passage aboard these fixed-schedule "shared charters" is sold on a per-seat basis just like typical airfares, and is competitively priced against the major scheduled airlines. Examples include **Linear Air** (914/761-7776 or 800/759-2929, www.linearair.com), serving Nantucket from Bedford, Massachusetts, and White Plains, New York; and **Tradewind Aviation** (800/376-7922, www.tradewindaviation.com) serving Nantucket and Martha's Vineyard from White Plains.

Among the charter operators whose service will make you feel like a CEO, two are based on Nantucket: **Ocean Wings Air Charter** (508/325-5548 or 800/253-5039, www.flyoceanwings.com), with several planes for 7-8 passengers, and **Nantucket Express** (508/364-4277 or 888/626-8825, www.ack-express.com), with a single twin-engine Cessna for 6-7 passengers.

Flying Direct to the Cape and Islands

The leading year-round airline to the Cape is **Cape Air** (508/771-6944 or 800/352-0714, www.flycapeair.com), whose fleet of nine-passenger Cessnas flies to Barnstable Municipal Airport in Hyannis (the middle of the Cape), Provincetown Airport at the very tip, and both islands. A regional code-sharing partner of JetBlue Airways, Cape Air offers discounted one-day round-trips on nearly all its routes and joint fares with nearly all major foreign and domestic airlines flying into Boston and Providence, its principal gateways to the region, as well as year-round direct flights from New York City (LaGuardia)

The only other regular carrier offering year-round nonstops to the region is **Colgan Air/US Airways Express** (800/428-4322, www.usairways.com), serving Barnstable Municipal Airport from New York City (LaGuardia) and Nantucket Memorial

Airport with regional jets from New York City (LaGuardia) and Boston.

In summer, service to Hyannis and Nantucket expands to include **JetBlue** from New York (JFK and LaGuardia). Meanwhile US Airways Express adds direct flights from Philadelphia and Washington DC to both Nantucket and Martha's Vineyard. Some small air charter services also offer regular summer flights.

Thrifty international passengers from countries with ridiculously cheap direct flights to New York City may be tempted to think that the relatively short distance between New York and Cape Cod can be bridged more cheaply by ground than by air. Think again. For someone originating travel from New York, the answer would generally be yes (Internet-only airline specials or student fares are potentially an exception), but anyone flying to America from overseas can ordinarily get that last domestic leg from their U.S. port of entry to their final destination at a steep discount if it's booked as a continuation of your over-the-water flight. Unless you want to make a Manhattan stopover that's otherwise strictly forbidden, the ground connection will *not* be a painless alternative to paying that extra airfare.

Airport Car Rental

You'll have your pick of a handful of car rental agencies and taxis at Barnstable Municipal and both island airports. (There are taxis at the Provincetown Airport, all of which charge the same flat fee to town, but no car rentals.) All terminals except Provincetown's are also on the route of public transportation, although on Nantucket the airport shuttle only operates from late June through early September, and in Hyannis the local bus service only swings by the terminal at the request of departing passengers, not arriving ones.

BY RAIL

While there's no direct rail service to Cape Cod, it's possible to connect from **Amtrak** (800/872-7245, www.amtrak.com) to year-round Cape-bound bus service in either Boston or Providence, Rhode Island. Providence is accessible from the south by Amtrak's coastal line through Rhode Island, Connecticut, and New York City—a line served by Acela Express, which runs North America's fastest trains. From the west, Boston may be reached via Amtrak through Albany, Buffalo, and Chicago. From the north, there's a short Amtrak line to Boston from Portland, Maine and southern New Hampshire.

The Amtrak station in Providence is walking distance to the intercity bus platforms in downtown Kennedy Plaza. In Boston, trains from the south and west arrive at the intermodal South Station Transportation Center, from which all buses to the Cape depart. Trains from northern New England arrive a mile and half away at North Station, a short taxi or subway ride from South Station (switch at Park Street from the Green/Orange Line to the Red Line).

In summer, Amtrak riders bound for Martha's Vineyard have the added option of connecting to the **RI-Vineyard Fast Ferry** from North Kingstown, Rhode Island, whose dock is only 15 miles from the Kingston, Rhode Island, Amtrak station. A list of taxi services that can connect the two is available at www.vineyardfastferry.com.

Island-bound train riders coming from the New York metro area would be well advised to use **Catch-A-Train** (800/457-3549, www. catch-a-train.com), a service that saves you the logistical headache of studying all the train, bus, and ferry schedules to coordinate getting from New York to the Vineyard or Nantucket. Just identify the most desirable travel option purely by schedule and price, and Catch-A-Train will handle bundling the necessary tickets and transfers.

BY BUS

The most affordable year-round alternative to driving to the region is to take a bus. No matter where you're coming from in the U.S. or Canada, you can reach Cape Cod and the Islands using a major interstate bus company, such as Greyhound or a member of the Trailways network, in conjunction with the two regional companies that cover the final New England leg of the journey.

Don't assume buses to the island ferry terminals coordinate their schedules with the boats; long layovers are more the rule than the exception, and some buses from both Boston and New York arrive in time to miss the last ferries of the day entirely. Even when bus arrival times *do* appear to be perfectly synchronized with boat departures, don't bet on it: Traffic conditions routinely make buses just late enough to foil attempt at avoiding a layover. Therefore it is never worth purchasing passenger ferry tickets in advance online if you are arriving by bus, despite the recommendations that the ferry companies make about doing so for their high-speed services. (Don't worry, they never sell out.)

To the Upper Cape and the Vineyard

Direct bus service to the Steamship Authority dock at Woods Hole, the year-round gateway to Martha's Vineyard, is provided by **Peter Pan Bus Lines** (888/751-8800, www.

peterpanbus.com) from New York City, Albany, and Boston (both Logan Airport and the South Station bus and train terminal). The Manhattan route runs via coastal Connecticut, while the inland route from Albany runs through western Massachusetts. These two New York routes converge in Providence, Rhode Island, and make stops in Southeastern Massachusetts (Fall River and New Bedford) before arriving on the Cape. All routes make stops in Bourne and Falmouth en route to Woods Hole.

To the Mid-Cape and Nantucket

Peter Pan also provides service from New York via Providence, Fall River, and New Bedford to Hyannis, the year-round gateway to Nantucket. To reach Hyannis from Logan Airport or Boston's South Station, however, you must take one of the dozen daily buses of the **Plymouth & Brockton Street Railway** (508/746-0378, www.p-b.com). The Hyannis Transportation Center at which all buses arrive is about a 15-minute walk from either the Hy-Line or Steamship ferry docks. A free Steamship Authority shuttle van swings by the transportation center as it makes its rounds between satellite parking lots and the South Street ferry terminal, but frankly walking is often just as quick.

To the Outer Cape and Provincetown

After stopping at the Hyannis Transportation Center, 1–3 daily selected P&B buses from Boston continue to Provincetown and five towns in between—at least a four-hour trip from the big city all the way to the outermost tip of the Cape. Given the possible connections in Hyannis to Peter Pan buses from Providence and points west, with optimum scheduling a trip from Manhattan's Port Authority to P'town would take about eight hours and cost just under $65. An intrepid rider from Toronto could make it in about 20 hours.

BY FERRY

Ferries are the year-round lifeline for the Islands, transporting passengers, vehicles, and cargo from the Cape to both Martha's Vineyard and Nantucket several times daily, every day of the year. Of course the greatest variety of service blossoms in high season between May and October. That's when additional passenger-only service ply the waters between New York, Rhode Island, and southeastern Massachusetts and the Vineyard; between the Vineyard and Nantucket; between secondary ports along the Cape's south shore and both islands; and between Boston and Provincetown at the tip of the outer Cape.

To the Vineyard

Year-round, Vineyard-bound travelers have three choices: the **Steamship Authority** at Woods Hole (508/477-8600, www.steamshipauthority.com, year-round, 45 minutes), **Patriot Party Boats** at Falmouth (25 minutes), and **New England Fast Ferry** at New Bedford's downtown State Pier (60 minutes). The Steamship Authority has the greatest number of daily sailings—over a dozen even in the dead of winter—while the others each have at least a couple from which to choose, although the New Bedford boat doesn't run on weekends in winter.

Only the Steamship Authority vessels take vehicles; the others are passenger-only. The New Bedford ferry is a large high-speed catamaran; Patriot Boats operates a small traditional monohull. All take bikes and pets.

If you find yourself stranded after missing the last scheduled ferry, Patriot Boats also offers 24-hour water taxi service. Since the Vineyard depends on Patriot for the daily newspapers from the off-island world, as well as some express parcel delivery services, you can also count on them to continue operating during the kinds of stormy conditions that force the large ferries to cancel trips. Call 508/548-2626 for more information.

Between spring and autumn, several other companies weigh anchor with their own passenger-only services, departing from Falmouth, Hyannis, Rhode Island, and Long Island, New

VINEYARD FERRIES

All fares are one-way unless noted. Vehicle rates do not include driver, passengers, or surcharges if 17 feet or longer. Only the Falmouth–Edgartown ferry requires passenger reservations; for the rest, just show up before they lift the gangway. Tickets for children aged 5–12 are generally half the regular adult price (discount on high-speed services is about 30 percent), younger kids are generally free. (Senior discounts are only offered by the Steamship Authority, but only for local Cape and Island residents.) Note that parking rates are per calendar day, so a simple overnight on the Islands will cost you two days' worth of parking. Steamship Authority parking lots accept credit cards.

© JEFF PERK

FROM WOODS HOLE (UPPER CAPE)

Steamship Authority, 508/477-8600 for schedule and advance auto reservations, 508/477-SHIP (508/477-7447) for same-day reservations, 508/693-9130 for on-island advance auto reservations, 508/693-0367 for on-island same-day standby conditions; www.islandferry.com

- **To Vineyard Haven:** passengers $7.50, bikes $3, cars $67.50 April-October, $42.50 off-season; dockside and four satellite parking lots $10-12 mid-May-mid-October, $8 otherwise; daily service year-round

- **To Oak Bluffs:** passengers $7.50, bikes $3, cars $67.50 April-October, $42.50 off-season; dockside and four satellite parking lots $10-12 mid-May-mid-October, $8 otherwise; daily service late May to mid-October

FROM FALMOUTH (UPPER CAPE)

Patriot Party Boats, 508/548-2626 or 800/734-0088; www.patriotpartyboats.com

- **To Oak Bluffs:** passengers $9, bikes free, no cars; parking $15; daily year-round except Federal holidays

Island Queen, 508/548-4800; www.island queen.com; cash and travelers checks only

- **To Oak Bluffs:** passengers $8.50 ($16 round-trip), bikes $3, no cars; parking $15; daily service late May–early October

Falmouth Ferry Service, 508/548-9400; www.falmouthferry.com

- **To Edgartown:** passengers $25 ($50 round-trip), bikes $5 ($10 round-trip), no cars; parking $25; Friday–Sunday service starting in late May and ending in mid-October, daily service mid-June–early September

FROM HYANNIS (MID-CAPE)

Hy-Line Cruises, 800/492-8082 for schedule, guaranteed tickets, and parking info; 508/693-0112 on-island; www.hyline cruises.com

- **To Oak Bluffs:** Standard service: passengers $21.50, bikes $12, no cars; parking $17; daily service mid-May to mid-October; High-speed service: passengers $36 ($67 round-trip), bikes $12, no cars; parking $17 mid-May to mid-September, $10 otherwise; daily service April–November

FROM NEW BEDFORD (OFF-CAPE)

New England Fast Ferry, 866/MV-FERRY; www.mvexpressferry.com

- **To Oak Bluffs:** passengers $40, bikes $6, no cars; parking $10; daily service mid-May-mid-October

(continued on next page)

VINEYARD FERRIES (continued)

- **To Vineyard Haven:** passengers $40 bikes $6, no cars; parking $10; daily service mid-Apr.-Nov., weekdays only in winter

- **Montauk Harbor-Vineyard Haven:** passengers $75 ($120 round-trip), bikes $10, no cars; parking $10; one round-trip in August

FROM NORTH KINGSTOWN, RHODE ISLAND
Vineyard Fast Ferry, 401/295-4040; www.vineyardfastferry.com

- **Quonset Point-Oak Bluffs:** passengers $52 ($75 round-trip), bikes $6, no cars; parking $10; daily service late May-early October

FROM LONG ISLAND, NEW YORK
Viking Fleet, 631/668-5700; www.vikingfleet.com

INTER-ISLAND
Hy-Line Cruises, 508/778-2600 or 800/492-8082 for schedule, 508/228-3949 on Nantucket, 508/693-0112 on the Vineyard; www.hylinecruises.com

- **Nantucket-Oak Bluffs:** passengers $30.50, bikes $12, no cars; daily service mid-June-mid-September

---

York. Most competitive with the Steamship Authority's Vineyard run in both price and speed is the **Island Queen,** from Falmouth's Pier 45, on the east side of the harbor on Falmouth Heights Road, to Oak Bluffs (40 minutes). If you would rather be strolling around Edgartown within the hour, head over to Pier 37, on the west side of the harbor at 278 Scranton Avenue next to Falmouth Marine, and catch one of the daily departures of the **Falmouth Ferry Service** (508/548-9400, www.falmouthferry.com, late May-mid-Oct., 60 minutes). They also have ample—and expensive—parking.

From the Mid-Cape, **Hy-Line Cruises** (508/778-2600, www.hy-linecruises.com, May-Oct.) operates a fast cat between Hyannis and Oak Bluffs (55 minutes), and supplements it in summer with a more leisurely and less expensive traditional ferry, albeit just once a day (90 minutes).

From Rhode Island, the high-speed, 400-passenger **Vineyard Fast Ferry** departs to Oak Bluffs from south of Providence at Quonset Point in North Kingstown, just minutes from I-95, up to four times daily (90 minutes). For anyone coming up I-95 from Connecticut or New York, this means you can be sauntering around the Vineyard in about the same time it would otherwise take to get to any of the Cape ferry terminals and park your car.

Last but not least, New York–based **Viking Fleet** runs a passenger-only boat to the Vineyard from Montauk, Long Island, a six-hour journey each way. Although it only makes *one trip all summer*—on a Sunday through Tuesday in August—it certainly opens up possibilities for a land-sea grand circle tour of Long Island Sound and southern New England.

To Nantucket

The sole year-round gateway for Nantucket is Hyannis, where travelers may select from either the Steamship Authority's poky car ferry or Hy-Line Cruises' deluxe, passenger-only, high-speed catamaran. Weather permitting, the Authority has at least three daily slow ferry crossings in winter (twice that in summer) from its South Street docks on Hyannis Harbor to Nantucket's Steamboat Wharf (140 minutes). Hy-Line's fast cat, the *Grey Lady,* makes at least five round-trips between Ocean Street in Hyannis and Straight Wharf, year-round (60 minutes).

From mid-April through the end of

NANTUCKET FERRIES

All fares are one-way unless noted. Vehicle rates do not include driver, passengers, or surcharges if the vehicle is 17 feet or longer. Only high-speed ferries (and Hy-Line's first-class lounge on their standard service) accept passenger reservations; for all other boats, just show up prior to departure. Tickets for children age 5–12 are generally half the regular adult price (discount on high-speed services is about 30 percent), younger kids are generally free. (Senior discounts aboard Steamship Authority vessels are only available to local Cape and Island residents.) Pets are not allowed on the high-speed boats. With one exception noted below, parking rates are per calendar day, so a simple overnight on the Islands will cost you two days' worth of parking. Steamship Authority parking lots accept credit cards.

FROM HYANNIS (MID-CAPE)

Steamship Authority, 508/477-8600 for schedule and auto reservations; 508/228-0262 on-island (information only); www.steamshipauthority.com

- **Standard service:** passengers $16.50, bikes $6, cars $190 April–October, $130 off-season; parking $15 mid-May–mid-September, $5 January–March, and $10 all other times (Brooks Road lot by airport is $10 both shoulder and high seasons); daily service year-round

- **High-speed service,** 508/495-FAST (508/495-3278) for reservations: passengers $32.50, bikes $6, no cars;

parking rates as above; daily service mid-April–December

Hy-Line Cruises, 800/492-8082 for schedule, guaranteed tickets, and parking info, 508/228-3949 on-island; www.hylinecruises.com

- **Standard service:** passengers $21.50, bikes $12, no cars; parking $15; daily service mid-May to mid-October

- **High-speed service:** passengers $41 ($75 round-trip), bikes $12, no cars; parking $17 mid-May to mid-September, $5 early December–late April, $10 all other times; daily service year-round

FROM HARWICH PORT (OUTER CAPE)

Freedom Cruise Line, 508/432-8999; www.nantucketislandferry.com

- **From Saquetucket Harbor:** passengers $39 ($64 round-trip), bikes $12, no cars; parking $15 per night (free for same-day return); daily service late May–early October

INTER-ISLAND

Hy-Line Cruises, 508/778-2600 or 800/492-8082 for schedule, 508/228-3949 on Nantucket, 508/693-0112 on the Vineyard; www.hylinecruises.com

- **Oak Bluffs–Nantucket:** passengers $30.50, bikes $12, no cars; daily service mid-June–mid-September

December, the Steamship supplements their car ferry with daily trips aboard the swift catamaran *Iyanough*, departing from the same dock (60 minutes). In summer Hy-Line Cruises does just the reverse and supplements its zephyr-like catamaran with a slower traditional boat from Hyannis to Nantucket (110 minutes).

If you want to avoid the crush of traffic around the Hyannis docks, consider Harwich Port's **Freedom Cruise Line,** with three daily round-trips to Nantucket in summer and one a day in both spring and fall, from Saquatucket Harbor on Rte. 28 (80 minutes).

To Provincetown
Crossing Cape Cod Bay off season requires a friend in the fishing fleet, but come summer several passenger ferries make the 90-minute

dash between Boston and the South Shore to Provincetown, at the tip of the Outer Cape.

Bay State Cruise Company (617/457-1428 or 508/487-9284, www.provincetownfastferry. com) offers the *Provincetown III,* a high-speed catamaran that makes the three-hour round-trip three times daily from mid-May until mid-Oct. It disembarks from the Commonwealth Pier in South Boston, beside the World Trade Center, across the street from that building's eponymous Silver Line bus rapid transit station. (The Silver Line puts the ferry within minutes of both Amtrak service at South Station and Logan Airport.) Tickets are $48 one-way, $77 round-trip.

Boston Harbor Cruises (617/227-4321, www.bostonharborcruises.com) also makes the Boston–P'town run with their flagship, the 600-passenger high-speed catamaran *Salacia.* It casts off from downtown Boston's Long Wharf, next to the New England Aquarium, every morning daily from early May through early October. For Memorial Day weekend and then mid-June through early September, additional afternoon and weekend evening departures are added to the schedule, with the last boat back to Boston scheduled late enough to allow a leisurely P'town dinner and dessert.

Tickets for both Bay State and BHC catamarans are $46 one-way or $71 round-trip (discounts for seniors and children), and may be purchased in advance on their respective websites. Bikes are an extra $5 each way. For those travelling from Northern New England, Boston Harbor Cruises has a Gloucester to Provincetown ferry service from the North of Boston fishing port. Departing once daily, trips are $45 one-way, $80 round-trip.

South of Boston, historic Plymouth is the departure point for **Capt. John Boats** (508/747-2400 or 800/242-2469, www.captjohn.com). With a 90-minute crossing and five full hours in Provincetown, this, too, offers day-trippers more time on land than on water. Service begins on weekends in mid-June, then daily late June through Labor Day in September. Catch the boat from the State Pier opposite the *Mayflower II*—and be back on Plymouth Rock by 6 P.M. Fares are $22 one-way, $37 for round-trip (discounts for seniors and children), and $5 round-trip for bicycles.

Whichever boat you choose, call to confirm departures if the weather is unsettled—occasionally, trips are canceled due to rough seas.

Taking a Car to the Islands

Though all the slow Steamship Authority vessels carry vehicles, car owners—particularly those bound for Nantucket—are strongly urged to leave them behind on the Cape. If you actually enjoy spending your vacation in what by summer often resembles the roll-off line of a Detroit assembly plant, by all means fork over that $135–155 to the Vineyard or $380–430 to Nantucket (summer round-trip price based on vehicle size, over and above the cost for driver and passengers) and you, too, will be able to savor life in a quaint seaside parking lot. On the other hand, for less money and hardly any less convenience, you can hire taxis as necessary on Nantucket, or choose between a couple weeks' worth of shuttle bus tickets, several days of bike rentals, and a couple of cross-island cab rides on the Vineyard. Sure, a car-less vacation in America is almost worthy of *Ripley's Believe It Or Not!,* but unless you're traveling in winter, staying at a rural Vineyard B&B, or carting around toddlers, there's little excuse for adding to the congestion of the Islands' roadways.

If, after all this, you still can't be parted from your car, then at least do yourself the favor of planning ahead. Auto reservations are mandatory for Vineyard-bound traffic the Thursday–Tuesday of Memorial Day weekend, every weekend (Fri.–Mon.) during the summer high season (late June–early Sept.), and the whole week before and after July 4. They're accepted up to a half-hour before sailing, but keep in mind that some popular weekends have been known to sell out months in advance.

The Steamship Authority starts accepting summer car reservations via mail or their website, www.islandferry.com, on the second Friday of January, and by phone two weeks later. Though not mandatory, car reservations for the spring season (i.e., through mid-May) are accepted after New Year's.

Prices are based on vehicle length, so if you are planning on taking a rental car but don't have the actual vehicle in hand when making reservations (you need to give a license plate number to complete the reservation process), the agents may initially charge you for the maximum car length (i.e., the SUV rate). When you show up at the dock to pick up your ticket, make sure the rate accurately reflects the size of the car you actually have. Reservations also incur a fee if canceled, so making multiple speculative bookings is inadvisable.

Whenever reservations are not required, show up and try your luck in the daily standby lines. Call 508/548-3788 to inquire about the length of the wait for the Woods Hole boats, call 508/771-4000 for standby conditions in Hyannis, or go to their website and follow the link from www.islandferry.com to Operation/Parking Info. Since neither port has unlimited space, there are caps on the number of vehicles that can wait on standby; preference is given to anyone staying on-island more than five days. Up-to-the-minute service bulletins—plus the latest schedule and fare information—are also available from Boston-based **SMARTraveler,** a free traffic monitoring service (call 617/374-1234, then press 72-star).

As a further disincentive to car owners with inflexible schedules, be warned that if the ferry for which you hold a reservation is canceled due to bad weather, you'll be stuck on standby with the exact same status as someone driving up without reservations. Depending on how many vehicles get bumped, how heavily booked the boats are when they start moving again, and whether you're willing to sit in parking lots for hours on end, even after routine service resumes you can easily get stranded on-island for a couple of *days.* When it happened to me, I just chalked it up to research, but will your boss be as understanding?

Leaving Your Car Behind

Island-bound passengers sensibly leaving their cars behind should allow some extra time. For example, Woods Hole is so small that in high season, ferry parking is usually available only in one of the five satellite lots in Falmouth and Cataumet, a few miles away. (Electronic signs posted along Rte. 28 coming from the Bourne Bridge will direct you to whatever lot has space available.) Free bike-rack–equipped passenger vans shuttle from these outer lots to the docks daily, and a van specifically for bicycles and baby carriages is provided Friday–Sunday in the late spring pre-season and daily through the summer. Cyclists may enjoy a beautiful four-mile ride along the paved **Shining Sea Path** from Falmouth direct to the ferry landing.

If you spend the night in Hyannis before or after catching one of the ferries there, be sure to inquire from your motel or innkeeper about reduced-rate parking—it can cost appreciably less than the ferry company lots. And if you arrived at either Hyannis or Woods Hole by bus—and intend to return the same way—don't forget that the ferries and buses are not fully synchronized; be careful not to end up marooned for the night after getting off the boat.

Ferry Tips

Friday and Sunday in summer see the most sailings from Cape and Island ports, with evening or nighttime departures (as late as 10:45 P.M. for the Steamship Authority) added to regular weekday schedules. The reason for the extra boats, of course, is the extra demand; be prepared to face larger crowds, shorter tempers, and less parking if you choose to travel on these days. Phone reservations are not accepted for passengers on the so-called traditional boats (with the exception of certain early and late sailings on the Falmouth Ferry), but they are for all the high-speed services, although tickets purchased in advance don't always guarantee seating. All sailings are, of course, dependent upon the weather—if in doubt, call ahead.

BY YACHT

If you're coming on your own boat, you'll find nearly every Cape harbor has at least a couple of anchorages or berths for visitors. Marinas and yacht yards able to accommodate at least a few dozen cruisers are found at Cataumet, on Buzzards Bay; Falmouth, Osterville, and Hyannis, on the south shore; and Provincetown.

The Islands are among the world's yachting centers, so book a mooring in advance. For an extended anchorage, consult the local town harbormasters, who generally deal in season-long leases; transients, meanwhile, are better off calling the private mooring rental companies. The cost of an overnight mooring to sober up from shore leave before braving the infamous rips and shoals of Nantucket Sound ranges from a low of $30 per night in Vineyard Haven Harbor to $60–100 per night at Nantucket.

In Nantucket, the Town Pier's **harbormaster** (508/228-7261) can either help you directly or refer you to an appropriate private marina. On the Vineyard, you can choose between anchorages in each of the bustling down-island towns or a more sedate berth amid the small up-island fishing fleet at Menemsha. The numbers for their respective harbormasters are Vineyard Haven (508/696-4200), Oak Bluffs (508/693-4355), Edgartown (508/627-4746), and Menemsha (508/645-2846). Transients visiting the Elizabeth Islands should call Cuttyhunk's harbormaster (508/990-7578) for advance information on public moorings.

Since all fuel sold on the Islands has to be shipped in, budget-conscious cruisers will want to top off their tanks at a mainland marina if at all possible. Launch services, haul-out, dry storage, and all manner of repairs are available on both islands, but don't count on public showers or dockside pump-out facilities at all moorings. Not that there aren't compensations: On summer mornings, the Vineyard Haven Launch Company (508/693-7030), for example, makes the rounds of that harbor's mooring field with bagels, muffins, juices, the *Boston Globe*, and other essentials.

No cruiser should venture into local waters without a proper reference book near the chart table. In addition to the don't-sail-from-home-without-it *Eldridge Tide and Pilot Book*, (sold at marine stores from Maine to Florida), the traditional companion for sailors heading to Massachusetts is the latest edition of *Cruising Guide to the New England Coast*, by Roger F. Duncan, Paul W. Fenn, W. Wallace Fenn, and John P. Ware (New York: W.W. Norton). An equally valuable work, more specific to the Islands, is Lynda and Patrick Childress's *Cruising Guide to Narragansett Bay and the South Coast of Massachusetts* (Camden, ME: International Marine). Despite its obvious appeal to powerboaters and amateurs, die-hard yachties shouldn't overlook *Embassy Cruising Guide: New England Coast*, either, from Maptech (www.maptech.com). With its NOAA coastal charts, GPS waypoints, extensive anchorage descriptions, and marine service summaries for every harbor in the state, the latest spiral-bound edition puts GoogleMaps to shame.

Getting Around

BY AIR

Island visitors looking for alternatives to the ferries between the Cape and Martha's Vineyard or Nantucket—or fans of the kind of flying where you can watch the wheels leave the ground, or even look over the pilot's shoulder—have a choice of Cape Air (508/771-6944 or 800/352-0714, www.capeair.com), **Nantucket Airlines** (508/228-6234 or 800/635-8787, www.nantucketairlines.com), **Nantucket Shuttle** **Airlines** (508/771-2711, www.nantucketshuttle.net), or tiny **Island Airlines** (508/228-7575 or 800/248-7779 www.islandair.net). The last three fly exclusively between Hyannis and Nantucket, about a 15-minute hop. Between them these companies operate a veritable airborne conveyor belt: Nantucket Airlines and Island Airlines each offer between 20 and 30 daily flights between Barnstable Municipal and Nantucket Memorial Airports year-round, while their young competitor, Nantucket Shuttle Airlines, offers about a dozen. It's no wonder that Nantucket racks up more takeoffs and landings than many of the nation's major metropolitan airports. If you're going to make this run frequently, you should ask about books of ten unrestricted one-way coupons, offered by all three companies for a slight discount over the advance-purchase round-trip fare.

BY CAR

On most interstates and some state highways within Massachusetts, the speed limit is 65 mph, but along the Mid-Cape Highway—U.S. 6—it's 55 mph or less. You'll soon see—from traffic in most areas—that these are more polite suggestions than true limits. Still, don't push it—when the selective dragnet finally picks you, the tickets will make you wince (for speeding violations along the two-lane portion of U.S. 6 between Dennis and Orleans, fines are doubled). Also, don't forget to buckle up; it's the law. And don't even *think* of drinking and driving—driving while intoxicated entails automatic license suspension, among many more serious risks.

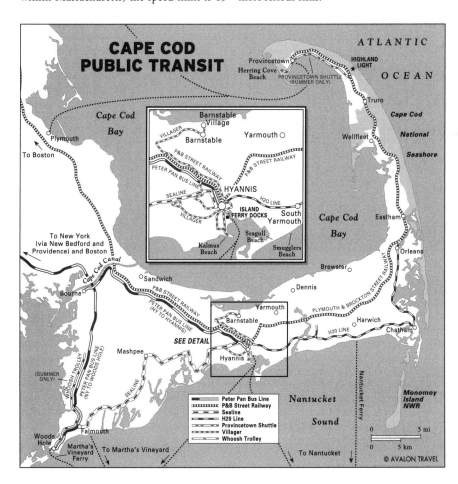

Speeding tickets may be paid by phone with a call to the Registry of Motor Vehicles' Customer Phone Information Center (617/351-4500); have the citation number and a valid credit card handy. You can also pay online at www.mass.gov/rmv. Treating tickets as souvenirs—not to be taken seriously once you're safely back home or across the border—is inadvisable, since Massachusetts shares outstanding ticket data with many states and several Canadian provinces.

BY PUBLIC TRANSIT

If you don't have a car, don't worry. The region is well served by public buses and tourist park-and-ride trolleys. Many operate year-round (Nantucket excepted), although of course the greatest quantity of service to the widest number of destinations is offered in summer.

With just a little patience and a few dollar bills, it's possible to reach almost every town on the Cape with **The Cape Cod Regional Transit Authority** (800/352-7155, www.capecodtransit.org) and its collection of year-round bus lines and summer trolleys—in combination with the all-season Plymouth & Brockton (8 Industrial Park Rd., Plymouth, 508/746-0378, www.p-b.com) and Peter Pan (888/751-8800, www.peterpanbus.com) buses. (The most notable missing link is Sandwich. When it comes to bus travel, you can't get there from here.)

The Plymouth & Brockton provides local service from the Mid-Cape (Hyannis) to Provincetown via U.S. 6, with stops at all the Outer Cape communities from Orleans north, while Peter Pan makes local stops in towns along the Buzzards Bay side of the Upper Cape, from the Cape Cod Canal down to Woods Hole. Every south shore and backside town between Woods Hole and Orleans is served by a combination of the **Hyannis-Falmouth/Woods Hole Sealine** and **Hyannis-Orleans H2O** bus routes, which operate daily from late June through early September and Monday–Saturday otherwise, plus **the Shuttle** between

North Truro and Provincetown, which runs seven days a week right through mid-October. Though Hyannis is the hub of the system, connections in Orleans make it feasible to do a circle trip around most of the Mid-to-Outer Cape area.

Fares on the Hyannis-area routes and both summer shuttles are $2 per ride or $6 for an all-day pass. While the shuttles run well past sundown—past midnight in some cases—year-round buses favor daylight hours. Pick up a complete system timetable at the Hyannis Transportation Center, town information booths, or almost anywhere you see racks of tourist brochures, or visit the website (www.capecodtransit.org). You can also call the CCRTA directly (508/385-8326 or 800/352-7155) and press the appropriate buttons to get prerecorded schedules.

Cyclists should note that all the CCRTA vehicles are equipped with bike racks—unlike the Peter Pan and P&B buses, which only take bikes as last-priority baggage (i.e., if there's room and so long as no risk is posed to other luggage). All buses and shuttles are also wheelchair accessible.

Getting around each of the Islands is thoroughly detailed within the relevant chapters themselves.

BY BICYCLE

On the islands of Martha's Vineyard and Nantucket, short distances, relatively flat terrain, an established network of bike paths and the high cost and scheduling hassles of ferrying a car from the mainland all combine to make bicycles a thoroughly appropriate transportation alternative. Rental shops are found in all the gateway towns within minutes' walking distance of arriving ferries. Public buses on both islands are also equipped with bike carriers on the front, making it doubly easy to get yourself back to whence you started if either fair weather or willpower abandons you.

Recreation

Summer recreation here is synonymous with at least some time in or on the water. Luckily, the Cape and both islands are well equipped to offer aquatic fun–seekers a busy time aboard a wide variety of human-, wind-, wave-, and engine-powered inventions. Underwater sports are another matter—the marine life of the temperate zones is too monochromatic to interest most casual snorkelers, and only one outfitter currently offers a dive boat to any of the worthwhile shipwrecks in the vicinity. Hard-core dive rats may be able to get a fix by making friends with local boat owners knowledgeable about the local waters (there are dive shops on the Cape and both islands), but most recreational scuba and snorkel divers should probably leave the fins and masks at home and use the luggage space for something else, like sunscreen.

Don't want to get wet? Dry land offers plenty of diversions, almost none of which will cause vertigo. Bird-watching is a major activity—the region is smack-dab on the migratory route of numerous North American bird species, but you don't have to know or care that the nearby songster is a rufous-sided towhee to enjoy the backcountry walks through local conservation lands. Bike riding is another favorite activity for visitors, especially on Martha's Vineyard and Nantucket, both of which have extensive paved bike paths for safe and comfortable family cycling.

As for sports, golf is Cape Cod's secular religion—it's one of the most golf-course-saturated regions of the U.S., with dozens of clubs welcoming the public to their courses. Public tennis courts are also widely available.

PARKS

Easily one of the most influential events in the last century of Cape Cod's history occurred in 1961, when President Kennedy signed into law the legislation that created the **Cape Cod National Seashore.** That pen stroke protected a huge 40-mile chunk of the Outer Cape from future development, including al-most all of Provincetown, most of Wellfleet and Truro, and portions of three other towns. The Seashore is unequivocally one of the region's crown jewels, not only in terms of things to do and see there, but also in terms of what *can't* be done and seen: You can't shop at malls built on paved-over salt marshes or exhaust your allowance in video arcades overlooking the ocean, and, unlike on much of the Cape's south shore, rich people can't buy up all the best beachfront real estate in which to build ostentatious mansions fringed with security fencing and No Trespassing signs. Under the terms of the park's creation, private property holders were grandfathered in, but property improvements are limited to maintenance, not expansion. As a result, the Seashore preserves not just natural habitat and endangered ecosystems, but also a view of Cape residential life circa 1959—possibly an instructive contrast to what has evolved elsewhere in the region over the intervening decades.

The other major federal presence is that of the U.S. Fish and Wildlife Service, custodian to the 2,750-acre **Monomoy National Wildlife Refuge** off the coast of Chatham, and the **Mashpee National Wildlife Refuge** on the south shore of the Upper Cape, whose current 2,000-plus acres may eventually triple in size if proponents and refuge partners succeed in their conservation goals. Like the unique **Waquoit Bay National Estaurine Research Reserve** located nearby, all these refuges are accessible to one degree or another for passive recreation, and are of course outstanding places to experience firsthand Cape Cod's reputation as a bird-watcher's delight.

The **Department of Conservation and Recreation (DCR)** is the keeper of the state's public lands. It has only a modest presence in the region, most notably with the 25-mile **Cape Cod Rail Trail, Nickerson State Park** in Brewster, and **Manuel Correllus State Forest,** on Martha's Vineyard. All state parks and forests—particularly those with fishing

COURTESY OF THE CAPE COD CHAMBER OF COMMERCE

Nickerson State Park in Brewster

and camping—are reasonably well signposted from adjacent major roadways.

PRIVATE LANDS FOR PUBLIC USE

Complementing the national and state holdings are a number of sanctuaries and conservation properties owned by private organizations, most notably **The Trustees of Reservations**—perhaps the oldest land protection organization in the world. Founded in 1891 (with a charter that became the model for England's National Trust), the Trustees' mission is to acquire for public enjoyment lands of "uncommon beauty and more than usual refreshing power, just as the Public Library holds books and the Art Museum pictures." By any measure, their nearly 100 Massachusetts preserves are among the state's finest open lands. Among this remarkable collection of properties are wildlife refuges on Cape Cod, Martha's Vineyard, and Nantucket, outstanding island beaches, and historic lighthouses. A few of these regional properties charge admission for

nonmembers in high season, so if you want a good discount on beach parking and various ancillary services—including summer canoe rentals and natural history tours—consider becoming a member. Join online at www.thetrustees.org, or call the membership office at 978/921-1944. The website also offers information about individual reservations, including directions and upcoming events.

The other major conservator of nature here is the **Massachusetts Audubon Society,** whose sanctuaries showcase the diversity of the region's habitats, from Wellfleet Bay's saltwater marsh, on Outer Cape Cod, to the heaths of Nantucket. Several of the Audubon sanctuaries offer programs throughout much of the year, from canoe trips and after-hours stargazing to butterfly watching, reptile talks, and nature walks. The frequency of the offerings increases with warm weather and demand. Advanced reservations are usually required; for current calendars, call the individual properties or check out the society's website (www.massaudubon.org). All Audubon sanctuaries charge a nominal admission to nonmembers, so here, too, you may find membership quickly pays for itself, especially if you go on a binge at any of their gift shops—members get discounts on cash purchases. (Members of the national Audubon Society have no privileges with Mass Audubon. The two are wholly separate entities.) Become a member online at www.massaudubon.org, or call 800/AUDUBON (800/283-8266).

CYCLING

When it comes to building bike paths or enhancing existing roadways and bridges to more safely accommodate cyclists, Massachusetts trails nearly the entire nation. Tens of millions of dollars in both federal appropriations and state-authorized bonds are available, and towns across the Commonwealth have a long list of popular proposals in need of funding. Yet for some inexplicable reason, the Massachusetts Highway Department seems determined to keep bike-related projects from ever seeing the light of day—even going so far as taking control of millions of federal dollars that legally may go directly to local planning agencies, and then leaving three-quarters of it unspent. Despite such an unfortunate circumstance, the Cape and Island region leads the state in designated bikeways and converted railroad beds, including the state's premier rail-to-trail conversion, the 25-mile Cape Cod Rail Trail. Moreover, scores of back roads are simply perfect for exploration by cyclists.

No need to lug your own bike along, either; inexpensive rentals are found throughout the region, and are almost ubiquitous on both Martha's Vineyard and Nantucket. A searchable database of bike shops can be found online at www.capecodbikeguide.com, along with detailed descriptions of both paved bike paths and off-road trails. Jane Griffiths' *Short Bike Rides on Cape Cod, Nantucket & the Vineyard,* one of many fine guides published by Globe Pequot Press, is a recommended addition to your pack. You'll find it in any cycling shop, bookstore, or recreational outfitter around the region, or from online book retailers.

A mountain bike or a slick-tired hybrid comes in handy for negotiating sandy back roads—and Nantucket's cobblestones—but, given all the miles of well-paved roads and bike paths, there's little reason to rent fat tires if you have your own skinny-tire touring cycle at hand. Serious mountain bikers won't find this terrain all that challenging; with a few exceptions, off-road island cyclists face more deep sand than steep grades. The fragility of the open land also means that the damage done by even one or two bikes lasts an entire season (or longer), so heed restrictions where they exist, and please be sure to use established trails wherever you go.

BEACHES

Free, public, warm-weather swimming is a rarity in Massachusetts. In summer (June through early September), most bodies of water—either fresh or salt—are restricted to local residents and summer renters or saddled with stiff parking fees. Thankfully, pedestrians and cyclists are usually exempt from parking fees or resident-sticker requirements, but not always; selected resident-only beaches check the status of everyone who attempts to enter during daylight hours all summer (caveats are included where necessary in these pages). About the only place where public beaches are free and unrestricted is offshore, on Martha's Vineyard and Nantucket. Needless to say, while beaches on both are free, the boats to reach them are not.

Scores of beautiful beaches line Cape shores, and from the end of June through Labor Day, in early September, hardly a single one has free parking. In most instances, you pay a daily fee to a gatekeeper to gain entrance, but some beaches reserve parking exclusively for residents, or for guests who purchase special weekly stickers or season passes at the appropriate town hall (bring vehicle registration and proof of local property rental or motel or B&B stay). Since applicable fees are collected only until 5 P.M. but most beach parking is kept open in summer until at least sunset (and as late as midnight in some towns), there's a nice window of opportunity for those who care more about catching a quick swim or a good sunset than a day of tanning. Individual town

MASSACHUSETTS BEACH ACCESS: NO TRESPASSING

In nearly every coastal state in the U.S., you have the legal right to walk along the beach. This simple right is wholly independent of who you are, where you live, or what you own. Four states have placed *all* tidal land in "public trust" (a legal arrangement dating back to the Roman Empire), thus preventing any private property ownership below the high-tide line. Seventeen other states let owners of waterfront property build wharves and otherwise exercise "franchise rights" in the *inter*tidal zone – the area between high and low tides – only so long as beach users aren't impeded from passing over or under whatever is built. Only Massachusetts and Maine (which was part of Massachusetts until 1821) allow private ownership of the coast to extend all the way down to the mean low-water line. With over 70 percent of the Massachusetts coast in private hands, it should therefore come as no surprise that you'll often encounter No Trespassing signs at both ends of nearly all public beaches.

This sad state of affairs is a relic of a 1647 colonial ordinance enacted to promote maritime industry. However, that same 1647 law enshrines three exceptions to these exclusive property rights. The public, it says, has the right to use the intertidal zone for "free fishing and fowling"; also, the public may not be prevented from freely passing by "boats or other vessels...to other men's houses or lands." In general, this means that you can walk across otherwise private beaches (always below the high-tide mark, usually indicated by a wrack line of organic debris) only if you're engaged in surf-casting or bagging blackbirds with a blunderbuss (simply carrying a fishing rod doesn't count). Massachusetts courts *have*

upheld certain modern activities as natural derivatives of one or another of the allowable uses – sport hunting and windsurfing, for example – but many coastal towns have their own restrictions concerning both guns and sailboards, so don't get your hopes up. On the other hand, courts have been unequivocal about most other beach pastimes. The law in no way allows you to set down a towel or a chair, stop for a picnic or sunbathe, or practice beachcombing or bird-watching.

Back in the 1970s, an attempt was made to amend the colonial statute to include walking as one of the legal uses of privately owned beaches, but it took 17 years to finally arrive at wording that wouldn't violate the Massachusetts Constitution. When finally passed, in 1991, the law simply said that since it would be a good idea to give the public access to the state's entire coast, the state's Department of Conservation and Recreation has a mandate to acquire the necessary rights for trespass on the intertidal zone. In other words, the state authorized one of its agencies to dicker with landowners to let the unwashed masses take a walk by the water. Given that shoreline property tends to belong to the wealthier and more influential of the state's citizens, the execution of this mandate is an extremely contentious issue.

The bottom line is this: Posted restrictions should be taken seriously. Ignoring them doesn't just put you at risk of arrest but also jeopardizes the entire effort to persuade beach owners that people won't abuse the right to trespass, if that right is ever granted. Someday, the amendments found on a few signs – Walkers Welcome – may become more widespread. In the meantime, if you want unfettered beachcombing, go to Virginia.

information kiosks (all prominently placed at strategic highway junctions or right downtown) can provide a fairly thorough list of local beaches, but the ones most welcoming of non-residents are also well-signed from major roads, such as Rte. 28 and Rte. 6A.

The heaviest (and coldest) surf is from the Atlantic Ocean piling up along the backside beaches of the Cape Cod National Seashore. Summer's prevailing southwesterly winds can fatten up the waves on the south shore, too, but in general the Nantucket and Vineyard

Old Silver Beach in Falmouth, Cape Cod

Sound beaches (and Buzzards Bay) are either more sheltered, shallower, or otherwise kinder and gentler than those on the Outer Cape. By virtue of the great tidal flats extending far from shore, bayside beaches are most serene in summer and relatively tepid. Offshore, the Bay is actually colder than the surrounding Atlantic Ocean, because the northern Labrador current, coming down along the coast of Maine, gets embayed by the Cape's hook, while the Atlantic is warmed by the Gulf Stream 100 miles to the southeast.

Before undertaking certain shore hikes (at the Namskaket Sea Path in Nickerson State Park, for example, or Great Island in Wellfleet), digging clams, windsurfing, or ocean kayaking, it would be wise to check for the high and low tides. Consult the tide tables printed in any of the local Cape daily papers, or pick up a handy free chart from the outdoor enthusiast's year-round friend, the Goose Hummock Shop, located at the Town Cove in Orleans on Rte. 6A, and at Rte. 28 and Main Street in Hyannis.

SAILING

The Cape is a sailor's joy—steady winds mean great sailing throughout the warmer months. There are plenty of opportunities to rent boats, since nearly every village and town along the coast has a marina, and many host various charter services during the summer season.

For the true do-it-yourselfer looking for something longer than a few turns about the local harbor, the only bare-boat outfit in the region is on the Buzzards Bay shore, in the Bourne village of Pocasset. **Argonaut Ocean Services, Inc.** (508/563-2851, http://argonautinc.com) has a Cal sloop, Irwin ketch, and trawler-style yacht, all in the 38–41 foot range, available for experienced sailors.

GOLF

If you ever needed proof that Cape Codders saunter to the beat of a much more relaxed drummer than most of the rest of us, you need only know that the Cape has scores of golf courses—one of the highest number per capita in the nation, right up there with Florida and Myrtle Beach. With almost twice as much real estate given over to golf than to agriculture, golf courses are indeed *everywhere*, from championship layouts designed by the most famous names in the business to the scenic rough heathland links of the Outer Cape, where you can go back to the game's Scottish roots at one of the nation's oldest golf courses still in operation. Most are open year-round, and in typical years when lingering snowfalls are a rarity, there are die-hard players squeezing a few rounds of practice into even the chilliest midwinter afternoons.

A good place to start planning your tour of the region's fairways is with a visit to **www. golfcapecod.com,** a commercial website with links to many of the 30-some public courses in the region. The **Cape Cod Chamber of Commerce** (888/332-2732 or 508/362-3225, www.capecodchamber.org) also has information about hotels in the area that specialize in golf vacation packages.

Accommodations and Food

Familiar interstate hotel names are a distinct rarity in the region, with only a handful of chain affiliates on the Cape, two on Martha's Vineyard, and none whatsoever on Nantucket. What you *will* find are hundreds of character-rich small hotels, inns, B&Bs, and B&B inns (that blurry category of establishments which dress a motel's economies of scale in B&B frills and ruffles). Predictably, discounts of any kind (including those for AARP or AAA members, or for corporate travelers) are almost as rare as those chains, but, as always, it never hurts to ask.

Accommodation prices are generally on the high side, comparable to being in a big city (i.e., well north of $100 nightly for most of the year). But the region isn't completely devoid of cheap places to sleep. There are several Hostelling International–affiliated hostels, including one on each island, plus a variety of campgrounds, including some that offer cabins. Only Nantucket takes a dim view of sleeping under the stars; the fine for camping there is a hefty $200.

Whether romantic or rustic, a number of Martha's Vineyard and Nantucket bed-and-breakfasts still eschew air-conditioning, offering fans instead. First-time visitors—Southerners in particular—are skeptical about booking a room without air-conditioning, but island nights really are bearable—especially near the water—except during the muggy dog days of August. Just leave those flannel pajamas at home. And consider the upside of screen windows (the Islands' most popular cooling system)—if you've slept in air-conditioned houses all your life, you've probably never had the pleasure of being awakened by songbirds perched outside your open window singing a gentle morning reveille.

LODGING OPTIONS

Not all the superlatives applicable to Massachusetts are favorable. The state ranks among the nation's top 10 most expensive in terms of dining and lodging costs, according to AAA's annual survey of American vacation costs. Boston can take a good chunk of the blame for this ranking, but the abundance of deluxe prices on the Vineyard and Nantucket surely contribute to skewing the average, too. Private baths, generous breakfasts, large rooms, fireplaces, and proximity to water are all extras. Any one of them, as a rule, will add about 25 percent to the rate for your basic four walls and a mattress—and a combination of several can quickly spike the price from $100 to $280. In this book, exceptions—mostly among B&Bs rather than motels—are noted where they exist. It should go without saying that places with reputations for good value have darned low vacancy rates, so, you need to plan ahead a little if you want to try to save a little.

Wheelchair travelers and anyone unable to negotiate stairs should never assume—ever—that anything in Massachusetts called a motel or inn (even in major resort areas) is in compliance with Americans with Disabilities Act guidelines for accessibility. Major national chains all have fully accessible rooms, but the situation is very different in smaller places—especially historic homes converted to quaint inns. It's easy to find out who does comply, though: Order a copy of the *Massachusetts Getaway Guide* from the Massachusetts Office of Travel & Tourism (800/227-6277 or 617/973-8500, www.mass vacation.com). Its accommodations listings identify accessibility.

Camping

When it comes to state-owned campgrounds, Massachusetts is hard to beat. For $15 or less, the state offers some of the cheapest moonlit sleeping spots in the nation. There are four state-owned campgrounds in this region, all on Cape Cod. (Two are nice, but the other pair are clunkers.)

The campgrounds on Cape Cod tend to be open from mid-April to Columbus Day, although self-contained vehicles (RVs with septic and gray-water holding tanks) may use a couple of the Cape's campgrounds on weekends (Thurs.–Sat.) any time of year.

With a credit card, you can make reservations for most sites in the state campgrounds up to six months in advance with ReserveAmerica (877/422-6762, www.reserveamerica.com) for an additional $9.25 service fee per campsite reservation. Their website is highly recommended—you can pick out specific campsites from easy-to-use interactive campground maps, obtain site-specific descriptions (double-wide driveway? shaded site? access for the disabled?), and see what amenities each campground features.

More family-oriented camping is also available at some 20 private campgrounds in the region, which are often equipped with recreation and game rooms, playgrounds, convenience stores, RV hookups, and laundry facilities.

Download a free, annually-updated Cape and Islands regional directory (a full statewide version is also available) from www.camp-mass.com, the website of the Massachusetts Association of Campground Owners.

Hostels

Hostels are just about the only budget accommodations on Cape Cod or the Islands that don't require sleeping outdoors. They are not just for kids: Budget-conscious travelers of all ages and backgrounds may be found enjoying the stereotypical dorm-room bunk beds of the region's hostels. There are five in the region, four of which are branches of Hostelling International, which means they offer discounts to HI members from around the world. The fifth in is an independent backpackers' hostel in Provincetown.

Membership in HI can be purchased at any affiliated hostel in the world. Currently the annual fee in the United States for anyone age 18–54 is $28, free if under 18, or $18 if 55 or older. For a complete guide to affiliates in eastern Massachusetts, visit www.usahostels.org.

Bed-and-Breakfasts

There's plenty of charm in local B&Bs, but there are also several factors to keep in mind. For example, expect to encounter minimum-stay requirements in high season, or single-night surcharges, especially at very small owner-run properties (these may also pass along the fee they get docked for accepting your credit card, if they take plastic at all). If using a booking service, expect a reservation fee. Deposits are usually required by both services and individual properties, and you should take those cancellation policies seriously—they aren't just for show. As a courtesy to the many small B&B owners who have already logged a 10-hour workday by the time five o'clock rolls around, pay close attention to their check-in policies. Owner-operated B&Bs should never be confused with 24-hour hotels, and the fastest way to totally stress out your host—or even forfeit your room and its deposit if you haven't shown up when you were supposed to—is to neglect arranging for a late check-in, if needed. Finally, when comparing prices, keep in mind that places with three rooms or fewer are not required to charge tax, so you save some of what you'd pay at larger establishments.

You won't find many places truly overlooking the waves on Massachusetts's coast, because those places get washed away in storms. If you're looking for a room with windows speckled by salt spray, look to places on the firm granite ledges of the coast north of Boston. Oodles of places on Cape Cod and the Islands are, however, within eye- and earshot of water. A few places also have "private beaches"—but on the Islands this usually means something about the size of a sandbox, and on the Cape they're usually attached to large Daytona Beach–style motels catering to large families.

Purists who want to be sure they're getting both bed *and* breakfast must be sure to ask—nothing in this niche of the hospitality industry can be taken for granted anymore. If it's important to you, inquire closely, too, about what is really meant by such terms as "hearty" or "gourmet continental"; personally, I think a continental breakfast is still skimpy even if I have the whole box of shredded wheat and basket of mix-and-bake muffins to myself. Not all the onus for skipping full breakfasts rests with innkeepers, however—some communities, particularly on Martha's Vineyard and Nantucket, erect steep regulatory obstacles to prevent B&Bs from competing with local restaurants. (At least, that's the innkeepers' side of the story. Local health inspectors have a differing view.)

Travelers with diabetes or other special needs will find most traditional owner-operated B&Bs willing to handle special breakfast requests if you give them clear guidance. For anyone looking for a kosher bed-and-breakfast, the nearest one is the Sharon Woods Inn (781/784-9401), in the Boston suburb of Sharon, at least a 70-minute commute from even the nearest point on Cape Cod.

The increasingly common self-styled "B&B inn," which pretends to represent the best of both worlds, may prove less tractable to menu

the Tuesday Room at the Belfry Inne in Sandwich, Cape Cod

COURTESY OF THE CAPE COD CHAMBER OF COMMERCE

modifications—especially those run by seasonal staff who don't quite have the hang of the concept of "customer satisfaction."

Nothing substitutes for planning ahead when it comes to landing a room where and when you want it, but don't give up on last-minute luck—there's always a cancellation someplace, and with patience and a bit of phone work, you may just find it.

Motels and Hotels

Although many of the major chains are represented on Cape Cod, you'll find independently-owned accommodations far outnumber them throughout the region. Don't use appearance as a gauge of price. Some of those pocket-sized New Deal–era bungalows and dreary-looking little motel courts straight out of *Key Largo* are anything but cheap (the high prices keep the riffraff away). Some of these places have had the same owners and the same regular customers for over a generation. While single-sex couples and anyone young enough to think nose rings are cool may detect a different type of coolness upon check-in, don't take it personally—the ice will thaw and downright gracious hospitality blossom forth if you judiciously refrain from trashing your room, playing hip-hop at top volume in the wee hours, or otherwise enacting the owners' worst nightmares.

Splurges

Cape Cod and the Islands have more than their share of sumptuous B&B inns and full-scale resorts, ready to swaddle you in service and comfort. Provincetown dominates the category, but within these pages also look to Nantucket and Martha's Vineyard for other leading examples.

FOOD AND DRINK

Fortunately for visiting food mavens, Massachusetts cookery over the past couple of decades has embraced salutary influences—of, among others, former resident Julia Child—raising awareness for good food throughout the state and firmly putting to rest comparisons to the infamous cuisine of New England's namesake across the Atlantic. Century-old ties to Manhattan's social and artistic elite also ensures that restaurateurs in Wellfleet, Provincetown, and the Islands must routinely satisfy palates accustomed to New York's finest dining.

Admittedly, mediocre meals are by no means an endangered species (Cape Cod swims in them), and plenty of the national fast-food chains or their local imitators are only as far away as the next strip mall on Route 28. But if you aren't indifferent to what you eat, you won't have to look far to find stellar food, whether in trendy, chef-owned bistros that draw customers from clear across town lines (the true measure of success among parochial Bay Staters), homey neighborhood holes-in-the-wall where natural-born cooks hold court, or, at its most elemental, in the roadside stalls of the region's few remaining farms.

The rampant resort pricing endemic to the Cape and Islands makes for a fine line between mediocrity and robbery—such as a gourmet café charging $9 for yesterday's stale dessert, or a B&B inn shamelessly serving a supermarket-doughnut and coffee as continental breakfast to guests paying $225 a night. Every attempt is made in these pages to highlight establishments offering good value, but neither this nor any other guide can predict the rapid shifts in quality from one year to the next—the result of extremely high turnover in staff and even ownership, particularly among restaurants.

From Land and Sea

Massachusetts is no California or Tuscany, but the movement epitomized by California cuisine, with its firm emphasis on super-fresh regionally grown ingredients, is one that's strongly evident among the better restaurants around the region. Enjoying meals prepared from the cornucopia of Massachusetts farms usually (but not always) carries a premium price, since small-scale and organic farmers with short growing seasons can't hope to compete in price with America's agribusiness giants. When it comes to taste, of course, there's no competition whatsoever. As every backyard gardener knows, nothing picked when immature and artificially ripened while in storage or during transcontinental shipping can compare to the flavor of fresh, picked-when-ready local produce. If getting a taste of New England is important to you, come during the summer or fall and visit local farm stands. Or leave room on your credit card for a small splurge at the kind of restaurant that respectfully pays homage on every plate to those of our neighbors who have chosen to keep farming and dairy farming alive.

Most out-of-state visitors to Massachusetts come looking for seafood. It's one expectation that's easily met, from humble clam shacks and family-friendly chowder houses to the sushi bars and upscale restaurants highlighting exotic or underutilized fish species. Luscious quahog clams, fresh oysters, mussels, scallops, lobster, monkfish, halibut, bluefish, striped bass, shad, yellowtail flounder, bluefin tuna, and, yes, even cod are all worth the tariff on local menus. (Scrod, it should be noted, isn't actually a species of fish—it's a catchall term at the Boston fish auction for baby cod, haddock, and any other flaky white-flesh fish under 2.5 pounds in weight.)

Do not, however, fall into the common trap of assuming that waterfront restaurants are the best places to dine on the bounty of the sea—some of the finest seafood meals to be had in the state are hours from any coastline. Given that Massachusetts is a net importer of seafood (overfishing has caused offshore fisheries to collapse, rendering numerous species commercially extinct), you may also be disappointed to learn that even here in seaside towns with local fishing fleets, there are restaurants whose scallops are more likely flash-frozen and then shipped from Asia or Iceland than they are fresh out of the water off Martha's Vineyard. Even worse, a restaurant's delicious-sounding special salmon is probably raised on the same aquaculture farm up in Maine that express ships its product to Atlanta and Chicago. But don't worry—plenty of places cited in these chapters do serve tonight something caught this morning by that picturesque boat at the end of the working pier.

In this age of overnight cargo, don't let my caveats obscure the more relevant fact that Massachusetts draws on such a deep tradition of seafood preparation that you could give many of its chefs a frozen fish stick and they'd still make something so wonderful and tasty of it that you'd never know or care what it looked like or where it came from before ending up on your fork.

Specialties of the House

Like Memphis ribs, Cincinnati chili, or the ollalaberry pies of the Pacific Northwest, Cape Cod has its own set of recipes and restaurant specialties that, while not necessarily unique to the state or the region, are definitely idiomatic. Lobster rolls, for example. A basic commodity at beachfront concession stands and other indigenous fast-food stalls, these resemble tuna salad served on a hot dog bun, except that lobster meat is used in place of the tuna. Clam chowder is equally ubiquitous, and though it's never, ever made with tomatoes (that's Manhattan's recipe), diligent chowderheads will find almost no two

versions alike. Chain restaurants that come in from outside the region often mistakenly assume that New England clam chowder should have the texture of wallpaper paste, but don't be fooled—proper "chowda" never requires a spackling knife. Cod cakes have been getting a boost from creative chefs who dress them with garlicky aiolis, peppery Asian spices, or other multicultural exotica—but at their most traditional, these deep-fried patties of minced white fish are served for breakfast.

Though the national franchising of Subway sandwich shops has diluted regional differences in food terminology, sub sandwiches in this region are often still called "grinders," as they are in New Hampshire and Rhode Island (it's a "hero" to New Yorkers, a "hoagie" to Philadelphians).

Indian pudding (a cornmeal and molasses concoction) and Grape-Nut custard aren't as common as they used to be, but you'll still find them on diner menus here more often than elsewhere in the country. Saltwater taffy and homemade fudge are summertime standards throughout the region, and super-premium ice cream, though found nationwide, achieves perfection at summer ice cream shops around the Cape. If you want a milk shake from any of these places, order a "frappe" (rhymes with trap) or you'll get nothing more than milk flavored with syrup.

Finally, chocolate lovers will be gratified to learn that Massachusetts has a serious addiction to sinfully rich chocolate desserts. Even local ice cream parlors typically have a core selection of six or ten variations on dark chocolate, white chocolate, chocolate mousse, chocolate fudge, chocolate chips, or some combination of chocolate and coffee.

International Cuisine

As is the case throughout much of the United States, Italy and China are the most common contributors to the region's ethnic dining, although the influences of both are in general rather heavily Americanized. The Portuguese who dominate the fishing industry—particularly in Provincetown, where many Portuguese historically settled—have made the Cape one of the best places in New England for a taste of their robust seafood stews, kale soup, and spicy sausages known as chouriço (pronounced shur-REES, *not* chor-REET-zo; that's the Spanish version).

In more recent years the most pronounced influence on local dining has been the seasonal influx of immigrant service-industry labor from the Caribbean and Brazil. Jerk seasonings show up on a number of otherwise staid American surf-and-turf menus, and Brazilian-style *churrascarias* (steakhouses featuring all-you-can-eat rotisserie-grilled meats) have appeared in Hyannis and on Martha's Vineyard.

Drinking

If you seek a taste of *terroir,* there are four wineries in the region, two on Cape Cod, one on Nantucket,and one on Martha's Vineyard, all of which offer tours and tastings at least during summer. Aficionados of craft beer should keep an eye out for the logos of the Vineyard's Offshore Ale Co., Nantucket's Cisco Brewers, and Hyannis's Cape Cod Beer in liquor stores and at selected restaurants throughout the region. Nantucket is also home to the state's only distillery, whose Triple 8 brand spirits (particularly the vodka) are available from Provincetown to Pocasset and on both islands.

Minimum legal drinking age in the state is 21. Valid identification (passport or international driver's license along with your home country license) is required to purchase alcoholic beverages in stores or bars. Many clubs won't admit anyone under the legal drinking age. At these places, you'll be asked for photo ID at the door. Nightclubs that advertise "18-plus" shows provide fluorescent wristbands to patrons who can prove they're 21 or over, without which the club bartenders will refuse to serve you alcohol.

Happy hours are illegal in Massachusetts, and bars close at 2 A.M. or earlier. Taking your libation to go? Hard alcohol, beer, and wine are sold in package liquor ("packy") stores, except in "dry" towns (several of which are concentrated on Martha's Vineyard). Supermarkets can't sell liquor, and only a few are permitted to sell beer and wine, thanks to the outsized political clout of the state's beverage distributors, who don't want their profit margins squeezed by big chain retailers demanding volume discounts.

Take note that many areas have open-container laws, meaning you can't walk down the street with an open beer or bottle of whiskey in hand, though if you keep a low profile at your outdoor picnic, it shouldn't be an issue.

Health and Safety

No part of Massachusetts is so remote that it isn't within range of emergency services, so when an ambulance, firefighters, or police are required, dial 911 to be instantly connected with an emergency dispatcher. In most communities around the state the dispatcher's computer will track your number and address, enabling authorities to locate you should the call be cut off.

PRESCRIPTIONS

If you use any sort of prescription medication, be sure to bring the medicine (not the prescription) when you come to the state.

Massachusetts pharmacists are prohibited from refilling any prescription from out of state.

TICKS

Before you go striding off through marsh reeds or bushwhacking through the woods in spring, summer, or fall, remember that this region is the home to both the bloodsucking wood or dog tick and the more notorious deer tick, *Ixodes dammini,* which, as its Latin name suggests, is a little damn thing—no bigger than the period at the end of this sentence. Though indigenous throughout the state, these ticks are most common on Cape Cod and the Islands.

To avoid getting bitten by a tick, wear a hat and light-colored clothes with long sleeves and legs that may be tucked into socks. Commercial tick repellent is also advisable. Avoid favorite tick habitats such as tall grasses and the edges of woods and meadows. If you do find a tick on yourself, there's still no reason to panic, but early removal dramatically improves chances for avoiding illness (it usually takes a day or two for any infectious agents to be transmitted to the host). The deer tick's larval stage, which it reaches in July and August, is when it is believed to be most capable of passing on bacteria or parasites, but it is infectious throughout its life.

Above all, use the proper removal technique (described by Dirk Schroeder in *Staying Healthy in Asia, Africa, and Latin America*): If it isn't visibly walking and can't be lightly brushed away, use tweezers to grasp the tick's head parts as close to your skin as possible and apply slow steady traction. (Don't squeeze—you don't want its saliva in your skin.) Don't attempt to get ticks out of your skin by burning them or coating them with anything like nail polish or petroleum jelly. If you remove a tick before it has been attached for more than 24 hours, you greatly reduce your risk of infection. After you've removed the tick, wash the bite with soap and clean water, and watch for signs of infection over the following days.

Tick-Borne Diseases

Precautions against tick bites are advisable because of the diseases they can transmit to their hosts. Dog ticks carry Rocky Mountain spotted fever, while deer ticks have been identified as carriers of Lyme disease, human babesiosis, and human granulocytic ehrlichiosis (HGE). None of these maladies is serious if treated early and properly, since all are caused by either bacteria or microscopic parasites susceptible to antibiotics.

Lyme disease may produce a distinctive concentric-ringed rash—like a tiny bull's-eye—around the point of infection and such flu-like symptoms as fever, chills, aches, fatigue, and headaches. These first-stage indicators may not appear for up to a couple weeks after a bite. As the disease progresses, it affects muscles, joints, the heart, and the nervous system, ultimately attacking the brain and producing Alzheimer-like conditions. Babesiosis is a parasite that attacks the red blood cells much like malaria, with similar symptoms and results: fever, chills, swollen liver and spleen, and dangerously depressed red blood cell count. HGE is the latest addition to the deer tick's arsenal, a potential immune system suppressant with flu-like symptoms.

POISON IVY

Poison ivy is native to the entire region. Growing as either a plant or vine, it's often found amid beach grass, where it exacts its itchy revenge on those who ignore dune-climbing restrictions. It's recognizable by its three shiny leaves on woody or hairy stems, sometimes accompanied by clusters of small, off-white berries. In fall, the leaves turn red.

PERSONAL SAFETY

Most casual travelers to Cape Cod and the Islands will never have to worry about making headlines as victims of violent crime. It's unlikely you'll witness the alcohol and drug abuse and domestic violence for which the region is known in law enforcement circles, unless you settle down in the community. On the other hand, petty theft is certainly a fact of life during the high season, so don't let the casual resort atmosphere lull you into leaving valuables conspicuously unattended in unlocked vehicles, at the beach, or overnight on the porch of your summer rental.

Information and Services

SMOKING LAWS

Massachusetts has completely banned smoking in civic buildings, theaters and cinemas, malls, and aboard public transit (including all the island ferries), plus wherever food and drink is served. That's right: There's no smoking allowed in any restaurant or bar anywhere on Cape Cod, the Vineyard, and Nantucket.

MONEY AND BANKING
Foreign Exchange

If you're traveling from abroad, you'll find that while credit cards are almost universally accepted, there are still certain kinds of transactions for which only cash will do. Parking and snack concessions at public beaches, for example, don't take plastic, and most of the region's public buses also require payment in currency or coin.

If you choose to bring travelers checks, make sure they are denominated in dollars. True to the vendors' claims, almost everyone but taxi drivers will treat them like cash.

If you're spending any time in Boston at the start of your visit to the region, you can take care of your exchange needs there. Keep in mind that despite competition among the city's banks and brokers, there's enough range in rates and fees to make shopping around worth a few local phone calls. If Boston isn't in your travel plans, learn to recognize the Citizens Bank logo—it's the state's only bank chain with branches outside Boston that can handle on-the-spot foreign exchange of major international currencies. You'll find that only the most luxurious resorts offer immediate foreign exchange—and, even with competition within walking distance, you will pay dearly for the privilege of trading pesos and pounds for portraits of dead American presidents.

Be aware that different brands of travelers checks are not treated equally if they're in the denominations of your own national currency. Foreign-denominated checks are cashed for free only by local affiliates of the issuer—and only American Express has a large number of such offices outside of greater Boston.

ATMs

Destination chapters note specific ATM locations where necessary (e.g., if obscure), and any unusual absences of the machines. Otherwise, you may assume some sort of ATM will be self-evident in the vicinity of listed attractions and restaurants. Most belong to the Cirrus, Plus, and NYCE banking networks. Most also charge you up to a couple of bucks to use them. ATMs are required to carry notices about their fees, or to alert you before you complete your transaction, so at least you needn't worry about being charged unknowingly.

Sales Tax

The statewide sales tax on all goods, except groceries and clothing, is 5 percent, while lodging tax is 9.7 percent. Bed-and-breakfasts with three or fewer rooms are tax-free.

MAPS

Massachusetts is like one of those suspicious foreign nations in which accurate cartographic information is kept under lock and key—the better to foil the treasonous plots of enemies of the state. For getting to and from major destinations via numbered state and federal highways, the free map available at MassPike information booths is sufficient. For more detailed coverage of local roads, most existing maps are flawed, although most of the inaccuracies won't impede the casual visitor.

If you're a stickler for accuracy, consider forearming yourself with the series of combination bicycle and road maps from **Rubel BikeMaps** (http://bikemaps.com). One map covers both Cape Cod and the Islands, another focuses solely on Martha's Vineyard and Nantucket. Look for them in Massachusetts at well-stocked bookstores and most bike shops, have your local bookstore order them through

MapLink, or order them online from the eMapStore link at http://bikemaps.com.

COMMUNICATIONS
Mail
The U.S. Postal Service is not hard to find or use. Seasonal workers or transient boaters will find poste restante mail-holding services available from post offices in most communities.

Internet Access
Internet cafés came and went on Cape Cod and the Islands, since free wireless Internet access is available in nearly all the region's accommodations and many of its coffeeshops. Towns throughout the Cape and Islands are also installing community-wide public WiFi networks; much of the region is now covered. Signal strength, however, is quite fickle, which is why gaggles of summer visitors may often be seen seated on the steps, sidewalks, and benches near public libraries and other unsecured WiFi hotspots, hunched over their laptops.

If you are not carrying a laptop or PDA, your best bet for public Internet terminals is a public library. You may find yourself subject to user limits and possible preferential treatment for local cardholders, but it's a free means of logging on if you're in need of a technology fix.

Telecommunications
Phone numbers in the Cape Cod and the Islands are preceded by one of two possible area codes: 508 or 774. Therefore any phone call originating from within the region, regardless of whether it is local or long distance, must be dialed with 1 + (area code).

Public pay phones are not all alike. Of the dwindling number still available to cell phone–free travelers, many belong to third-party service providers, and rates for making collect or direct-dial calling-card calls on these phones are far from competitive. If a pay phone doesn't carry a brand name you recognize, use an access code to reach your own trusted long-distance carrier or you'll likely be billed for the equivalent of a conference call to Mars. Alternatively, you can purchase prepaid phone cards in varying denominations at every post office and most convenience stores in the region.

For local and national directory information, dial 411. To report an emergency or to summon police, fire fighters, or emergency medical assistance, dial 911.

Some convenience stores are often able to handle outgoing faxes, although if you want the most experienced and reliable fax capabilities, look for a copy shop or ask at the staff of your inn or motel.

Ten-Digit Dialing
Because every community in Eastern Massachusetts shares two active area codes, all phone calls, whether local or not, must be dialed with 1 + (area code) first, as if they were long distance.

Since the second overlay area code for Cape Cod, Martha's Vineyard, Nantucket, and Cuttyhunk (774) has not yet frequently shown up in daily use, you may safely assume that 508 should be dialed in front of any seven-digit phone number given to you by a Cape or Island native, or observed on local signage.

Business Hours
Hours vary depending on the type of business. Generally speaking, banks are open 9 A.M.–5 P.M. Monday–Friday, although some major consumer banks also open select locations for a half-day Saturday. Other public and private businesses keep the general hours of 9 A.M.–5 P.M. daily, though hours do vary. Many retail stores are open extended hours, especially throughout the high season. Many convenience stores, some "super" supermarkets, and a few gas stations stay open around the clock. When in doubt, call ahead and confirm hours of operation.

Holidays
Major public holidays in the U.S. shut down the whole country (Christmas Day, New Year's Day, July 4th, and Thanksgiving, the fourth Thursday in November). Others only affect private businesses, banks, government offices, mail and package delivery services, and

schools. Retail stores, on the other hand, typically stay open, often with special holiday sales and extended hours. These legal holidays, usually observed on a Monday or Friday to create a three-day weekend, include the following: New Year's Day (January 1); Rev. Martin Luther King Jr.'s birthday (third Monday in January); Presidents' Day (third Monday in February); Memorial Day (last Monday in May); Labor Day (first Monday in September); Columbus Day (second Monday of October); and Veterans' Day (November 11).

Time Zones

Cape Cod and the Islands function on eastern standard time, five hours behind Greenwich Mean Time. The sprawling continental U.S. contains four time zones. For a specific breakdown of time zone borders in the rest of the country, consult the map in the local phone books, which contain combination area code/time zone maps toward the front. All states, with the exception of Hawaii, Arizona, and large parts of Indiana, convert to daylight saving time from midnight on the second Sunday in March to midnight on the first Sunday in November. Daylight saving time advances or reverses the clock one hour across U.S. time zones.

Weather

For current Cape-wide weather conditions, call the WQRC-FM forecast phone at 508/771-5522.

RESOURCES

Suggested Reading

RECREATION

Evans, Lisa Gollin. *Paddling Coastal Massachusetts: From the North Shore to Cape Cod.* Boston: Appalachian Mountain Club Books, 2000. Sea-kayaking, a favorite Bay State pastime, is made even more accessible with this detailed guide to over 45 trips among the state's tidal estuaries, offshore islands, and other attractive coastal waters. Has all the necessary contact information for outfitters and guides, too, in case you aren't already a kayak owner.

Mullen, Edwin, and Jane Griffith. *Short Bike Rides: Cape Cod, Nantucket, & the Vineyard.* Guilford, CT: Globe Pequot Press, 1999 (7th edition). With this book in hand, riding around the state's most popular region for recreational cycling couldn't be easier.

Weintraub, David. *Walking the Cape and Islands.* Birmingham, AL: Menasha Ridge Press, 2006. This book features descriptions of over 70 walks and hikes, all accompanied by a trail map, directions, lists of flora and fauna, and a wealth of practical details, ranging from overall sun exposure to the estimated number of calories you'll burn completing each one.

NATURE

O'Brien, Greg, ed. *A Guide to Nature on Cape Cod and the Islands.* Marstons Mills, MA: Parnassus Imprints, 1995. Excellent set of essays on Cape and Island geology; marsh ecology; bird, plant, and sea life; and weather—all followed by useful question-and-answer sections.

Oldale, Robert N. *Cape Cod and the Islands: The Geologic Story.* Marstons Mills, MA: Parnassus Imprints, 1992. The definitive text on regional geology.

Trull, Peter. *A Guide to the Common Birds of Cape Cod.* Brewster, MA: Cape Cod Museum of Natural History, 1991. More than 120 of the region's most common species are handily identified in this slender book, illustrated in black and white.

HISTORY

Primary Documents

Bradford, William. *Of Plymouth Plantation: 1620–1647.* Edited by Samuel Eliot Morison. New York: Alfred A.Knopf, 1952. The leader and sometime governor of the Pilgrim settlement in Plymouth tells the story in his own inimitable style (helpfully edited, annotated, and indexed by one of the foremost scholars of colonial and maritime history). Unless you have a special interest in Bradford's orthography, no other edition can compare—which is why this one has never gone out of print.

Burrage, Henry S., ed. *Early English and French Voyages, Chiefly from Hakluyt: 1534–1608.* New York: Barnes & Noble, 1959, c. 1906. There were two 16th-century Richard Hakluyts—cousins some 20 years apart in age. Each supported English colonial ventures in the New World, the elder as a lawyer-investor, the younger as a geographer-publicist. Burrage draws on the younger Hakluyt's 1589 *Principall Navigations, Voiages, and Discoveries of the English Nation,* a multivolume work compiled from interviews and first-person accounts. Precolonial Massachusetts and its inhabitants are described by several of the explorers featured.

Champlain, Samuel de. *The Works of Samuel de Champlain.* Edited by H. P. Biggar. Toronto: Champlain Society, 1922–1936. Six-volume work includes the observant French captain's detailed log of his anchorages along the Massachusetts coast during his 1605–1608 voyage, with descriptions and the harbor chart for the Indian village at Patuxet (which became the site of the Pilgrims' Plimoth Plantation).

Smith, John. *Travels and Works of Captain John Smith.* Edited by Edward Arber. Birmingham, England: English Scholar's Library, 1884. The writings of the man who named New England, and whose map, used by the *Mayflower* Pilgrims, already contained the name of their settlement—Plimoth—thanks to the arbitrary choice of 10-year-old heir-apparent Prince Charles, with whom Smith wished to gain favor.

St. John de Crèvecoeur, J. Hector. *Letters from Nantucket and Martha's Vineyard.* Bedford, MA: Applewood Books, 1986. This text features selections from this 18th-century French immigrant's well-observed correspondence about his life as an American farmer in both New York and Massachusetts. This one is a classic.

Wroth, Lawrence C., ed. *The Voyages of Giovanni da Verrazzano: 1524–1528.* New Haven, CT: Yale University Press, 1970. Includes the Florentine navigator's descriptions of the Massachusetts coast, particularly Martha's Vineyard and Cape Cod (before either island or the commonwealth had those names), written during his attempt to find a sea lane to the Far East.

Native Americans and Indian-Colonial Interaction

Cronon, William. *Changes in the Land: Indians, Colonists and the Ecology of New England.* New York: Hill and Wang, 1983. Articulate and meticulously researched. The curious reader will easily amass a vast additional reading list on its interdisciplinary content—colonial history, Indian history, ecology, anthropology—from the exceptional bibliographic essay that ends this highly recommended, prize-winning book.

Jennings, Francis. *The Invasion of America: Indians, Colonialism, and the Cant of Conquest.* New York: W. W. Norton, 1975. One of the major so-called revisionist histories, scrutinizing the motives of the Pilgrim/Puritan migration to these shores. Was war a deliberate strategy to abet land-grabbing (itself a policy stemming from a strict interpretation of Scripture)? Read the evidence in this impressive work.

Other Historical Works

Allport, Susan. *Sermons in Stone: The Stone Walls of New England and New York.* New York: W. W. Norton, 1990. An exceptional miscellany full of history, geology, and local lore, including an interesting chapter about Martha's Vineyard. Demonstrates how much about the historical landscape one can learn from careful observation of a few piled stones.

Barbo, Theresa Mitchell, John Galluzzo, and W. Russell Webster. *The Pendleton Disaster off Cape Cod: The Greatest Small Boat Rescue in Coast Guard History.* Charleston, SC: The History Press, 2007. An account of the nearly suicidal, but ultimately successful, 1952 rescue of the crew of a large tanker that foundered off the Cape in a fierce winter nor'easter.

Brown, Dona. *Inventing New England: Regional Tourism in the Nineteenth Century.* Washington,

D.C.: Smithsonian Institute Press, 1995. An excellent treatise on the artifices of "colonial" townscapes and quaint fishing villages designed purely to appeal to urban dwellers who wanted to see "real, natural New England."

Conway, Jack. *Head Above Water: Building the Cape Cod Canal.* Frederick, MD: PublishAmerica, 2005. A recounting of how the region's most economically vital waterway was built by New York financier August Belmont, Jr., who financed it primarily with his own money.

Karttunen, Frances Ruley. *The Other Islanders: People Who Pulled Nantucket's Oars.* New Bedford, MA: Spinner Publications, 2005. An eloquent exploration of Nantucket's diverse heritage, thoroughly researched and beautifully illustrated. A marvelous keepsake.

Kittredge, Henry Crocker. *Cape Cod: Its People and Their History.* Marstons Mills, MA: Parnassus Imprints, 1995. A classic account originally penned in 1930, nicely written, with a 1968 post-epilogue by the distinguished nature writer John Hay.

Morison, Samuel Eliot. *The Maritime History of Massachusetts: 1783–1860.* Boston: Northeastern University Press, 1979. Another Morison classic, written with a clear love of the sea and sailing.

Nickerson, Joseph A., Jr. and Geraldine D. Nickerson. *Chatham Sea Captains in the Age of Sail.* Charleston, SC: The History Press, 2008. A chronicle of 25 seafaring men from the town at the Cape's elbow and their adventures from the 18th through the early 20th centuries.

O'Connell, James C. *Becoming Cape Cod: Creating a Seaside Resort.* Durham, NH: University of New Hampshire Press, 2002. This history of Cape tourism over 150 years is a blend of comprehensive social documentary and ecological wake-up call, generously illustrated with antique and vintage postcards from the author's private collection.

Philbrick, Nathaniel. *Away Off Shore: Nantucket Island and Its People, 1602–1890.* Nantucket, MA: Mill Hill Press, 1994. In this richly anecdotal and factually grounded work, episodes in the lives of several dozen islanders become the lens through which three centuries of island history is refracted.

Railton, Arthur R. *The History of Martha's Vineyard: How We Got to Where We Are.* Beverly, MA: Commonwealth Editions, 2006. A journalistic narrative, broad in scope yet fleshed out with plenty of local detail, written by the highly-regarded former editor of the Martha's Vineyard Historical Society's quarterly journal.

Schneider, Paul. *The Enduring Shore: A History of Cape Cod, Martha's Vineyard, and Nantucket.* New York: Owl Books, 2001. Skillfully weaves a broad historical narrative from the author's experiences exploring the region by kayak and afoot. An absorbing contemporary heir to the intellectually wide-ranging, wryly discursive, and personally ruminative style of Thoreau. Highly recommended.

MISCELLANEOUS

Beston, Henry. *The Outermost House.* New York: Holt Paperbacks, 2003. Originally published in 1928, this is a classic account of a year spent on the dunes of Outer Cape Cod.

Clark, Admont G. *Lighthouses of Cape Cod, Martha's Vineyard, Nantucket: Their History and Lore.* Hyannis, MA: Parnassus Imprints, 1992. Everything you ever wanted to know about the 28 lighthouses in this part of Massachusetts. Available only in hardcover.

George, Diana Hume, and Malcolm A. Nelson. *Epitaph and Icon: A Field Guide to the Old Burying Grounds of Cape Cod, Martha's Vineyard, and Nantucket.* Marstons Mills, MA: Parnassus Imprints, 1983. The title says it all.

Kurlansky, Mark. *Cod: A Biography of the Fish That Changed the World*. New York: Walker & Co., 1997. A highly readable exploration of one of the former economic mainstays of the region.

Miller, John, Tim Smith, and Alice Hoffman, eds. *Cape Cod Stories: Tales from the Cape, Nantucket & Martha's Vineyard*. San Francisco: Chronicle Books, 2002. Essays and excerpts from longer works by a wide-ranging cast of authors who have set foot in the region and then written about it, including Edgar Allan Poe, Helen Keller, John Updike, Kurt Vonnegut, Herman Melville, and many more.

Ruhlman, Michael. *Wooden Boats: In Pursuit of the Perfect Craft at an American Boatyard*. New York: Penguin Books, 2001. An eloquent, detailed profile of the construction of two wooden boats, and of the builders, Ross Gannon and Nat Benjamin of Martha's Vineyard.

Thoreau, Henry David. *Cape Cod*. New York: Penguin Books, 1987 (first published 1865). Thoreau, the travel writer hiking the Outer Cape, is as engaging and piquantly observant as Thoreau the pondside philosopher.

Whynott, Douglas. *Giant Bluefin*. New York: Farrar Strauss Giroux, 1995. A look at the lives of Cape Cod bluefin anglers, in the tradition of Tracy Kidder and John McPhee.

Williams, Wendy, and Robert Whitcomb. *Cape Wind: Money, Celebrity, Class, Politics, and the Battle for Our Energy Future on Nantucket Sound*. New York: PublicAffairs, 2007. A trenchant dissection of the hard-fought battle over the proposal to build the nation's first offshore wind farm near the summer homes of some of America's wealthiest and most politically powerful families.

PUBLISHERS

Special mention must be given to the following small firms for their dedication to producing titles on local subjects that are good enough to deserve a much wider audience:

Cape Cod Historical Publications (P.O. Box 281, Yarmouthport, MA 02675, 508/362-4761) specializes in works with a specific thematic focus, such as histories of local industries—railroads or glassmaking—and major events.

Parnassus Imprints (105 Cammett Rd., Marstons Mills, MA 02648, 508/790-1175, fax 508/790-1176) specializes in books about Cape Cod and maritime subjects. They're also the exclusive distributor for **Mill Hill Press,** a good source for Nantucket-related titles.

Internet Resources

Cape Cod Bike Guide
www.capecodbikeguide.com

Detailed descriptions of all the region's paved bike paths and off-road mountain bike trails, with an accompanying database of bike shops and links to other cycling-related resources.

Cape Cod Online
www.capecodonline.com

Owned and run by *The Cape Cod Times,* this is the place to find the area's latest news, beach information, and community happenings, plus shopping, events, and real estate listings.

Cape Cod Pathways
www.capecodcommission.org/pathways

A project of the Cape Cod Commission, supporting the development of a Cape-wide network of walking trails from the Canal to P'town.

Cape Cod Regional Transit Authority
www.thebreeze.info

Features information and a route-finder for the CCRTA's own fixed-route transit services—the Breeze—as well as links to regional bus lines, ferries, and airlines that provide service to the Cape and Islands. Also has real-time local traffic reports, weather, roadway construction updates, and webcam links for the two Cape Cod Canal highway bridges.

Commonwealth of Massachusetts
www.mass.gov

The state's offical website, with links to town URLs and "community profiles," which contain a wealth of local statistical census, economic, and demographic data.

Electronic Atlas of the
Cape Cod Environment
www.whrc.org

(Click on atlas link under "Education.") A project of the Woods Hole Research Center, an environmental think tank, this is an online compendium of information about all the different ecosystems and habitats on the Cape. Descriptions, photos, historical statistics on development and population growth—highly recommended.

The Fish Database
www.fishbase.org

After eating, catching, seeing, reading about, or hearing of a particular fish on the Cape and Islands that you'd like to know more about, this is where you will want to turn. Over 30,000 species (and counting), with over 45,000 identification photos, plus a multilingual search engine for common names in English, Arabic, Russian, Greek, Chinese, and other languages.

Maptech Historical USGS Maps
http://historical.maptech.com

Online library of U.S. Geological Survey top-

ographical maps from 1894–1950s, scanned at actual size, covering coastal states from Maine to the mid-Atlantic. Follow links to Massachusetts for a glimpse at the Cape and Islands in their pre-development days.

Massachusetts Department of
Environmental Management
www.mass.gov/dem

The homepage of the guardian of all state parks, forests, and reservations: hours, fees, camping seasons, phone numbers, and more.

Massachusetts Maritime Academy
www.maritime.edu

The maritime academy is located at the western end of the Cape Cod Canal, and home to the control center for all canal shipping. The MMA's homepage features links to their two live canal webcams.

National Weather Service
http://iwin.nws.noaa.gov/iwin/ma/
ma.html

One-stop weather site for the whole state: Click for current forecasts, marine reports, aviation reports, and up-to-the-minute conditions at any of the NWS data collection stations in Massachusetts.

Virtual Cape Cod
www.virtualcapecod.com/chambers

This particular page is a list of links to the home page of every Chamber of Commerce on Cape Cod and the Islands, most of which feature event calendars, member directories with links where available, current weather, and photos.

Index

List of Maps

www.moon.com

DESTINATIONS | ACTIVITIES | BLOGS | MAPS | BOOKS

MOON.COM is all new, and ready to help plan your next trip! Filled with fresh trip ideas and strategies, author interviews, informative blogs, a detailed map library, and descriptions of all the Moon guidebooks, Moon.com is all you need to get out and explore the world—or even places in your own backyard. As always, when you travel with Moon, expect an experience that is uncommon and truly unique.

MAP SYMBOLS

░░░░	Expressway	🄲	Highlight	✘	Airfield	⚲	Golf Course
░░░░	Primary Road	○	City/Town	✈	Airport	🄿	Parking Area
░░░░	Secondary Road	◉	State Capital	▲	Mountain	▰	Archaeological Site
░░░░	Unpaved Road	⊛	National Capital	✦	Unique Natural Feature	♟	Church
-------	Trail	★	Point of Interest			🄶	Gas Station
··········	Ferry	•	Accommodation		Waterfall		Glacier
▬▬▬	Railroad	▼	Restaurant/Bar	▲	Park		Mangrove
░░░░	Pedestrian Walkway	▪	Other Location	🄣	Trailhead		Reef
▥▥▥	Stairs	⋀	Campground	⚐	Skiing Area		Swamp

CONVERSION TABLES

$°C = (°F - 32) / 1.8$
$°F = (°C \times 1.8) + 32$
1 inch = 2.54 centimeters (cm)
1 foot = 0.304 meters (m)
1 yard = 0.914 meters
1 mile = 1.6093 kilometers (km)
1 km = 0.6214 miles
1 fathom = 1.8288 m
1 chain = 20.1168 m
1 furlong = 201.168 m
1 acre = 0.4047 hectares
1 sq km = 100 hectares
1 sq mile = 2.59 square km
1 ounce = 28.35 grams
1 pound = 0.4536 kilograms
1 short ton = 0.90718 metric ton
1 short ton = 2,000 pounds
1 long ton = 1.016 metric tons
1 long ton = 2,240 pounds
1 metric ton = 1,000 kilograms
1 quart = 0.94635 liters
1 US gallon = 3.7854 liters
1 Imperial gallon = 4.5459 liters
1 nautical mile = 1.852 km

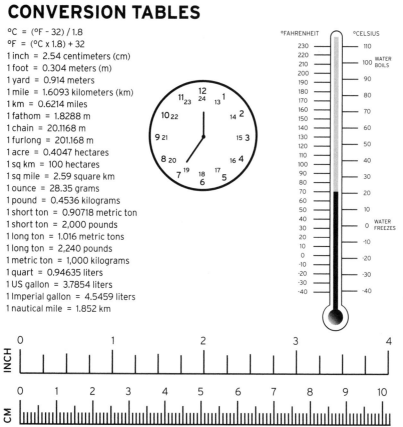

MOON CAPE COD, MARTHA'S VINEYARD & NANTUCKET

Avalon Travel
a member of the Perseus Books Group
1700 Fourth Street
Berkeley, CA 94710, USA
www.moon.com

Updaters: Michael Blanding and Alexandra Hall
Editor: Elizabeth Hollis Hansen
Series Manager: Kathryn Ettinger
Copy Editor: Maura Brown
Graphics and Production Coordinator:
    Domini Dragoone
Cover Designer: Domini Dragoone
Map Editor: Kevin Anglin, Mike Morgenfeld
Cartographers: Chris Markiewicz, Jon Niemazyk,
    Jon Tweena
Indexer: Valerie Sellers Blanton

ISBN-13: 978-1-56691-829-9
ISSN: 1545-6528

Printing History
1st Edition – 2004
2nd Edition – June 2009
5 4 3 2 1

Front cover photo: Boardwalk in Sandwich, Cape Cod, © Omniphoto. Title page photo: Gay Head Cliffs, © Kathryn Osgood.

Front color section photos: pages 4 (top), 5 (left and center), 6, 7 (top right and bottom right), 8, 10, and 16 © Jeff Perk; pages 4 (left), 5 (bottom), 7 (bottom left), 12, and 15 © Kathryn Osgood; page 4 (center) Courtesy of Mansion House Inn; page 4 (right) Courtesy of Mass Audubon's Felix Neck Wildlife Sanctuary; page 5 (right) © 123rf.com/Ian MacLellan; page 7 (top left), and 11 Courtesy of the Cape Cod Chamber of Commerce; pg 14 © Peter Vanderwarker.

Printed in United States by RR Donnelley

KEEPING CURRENT

If you have a favorite gem you'd like to see included in the next edition, or see anything that needs updating, clarification, or correction, please drop us a line. Send your comments via email to feedback@moon.com, or use the address above.